The Joy of X

An Overview of the X Window System

1993

The Joy of X

An Overview of the X Window System

Niall Mansfield

ADDISON-WESLEY PUBLISHING COMPANY

WOKINGHAM, ENGLAND • READING, MASSACHUSETTS • MENLO PARK, CALIFORNIA • NEW YORK
DON MILLS, ONTARIO • AMSTERDAM • BONN • SYDNEY • SINGAPORE
TOKYO • MADRID • SAN JUAN • MILAN • PARIS • MEXICO CITY • SEOUL • TAIPEI

Cover designed by Designers & Partners, Oxford
and printed by The Riverside Printing Co. (Reading) Ltd.
Camera-ready copy prepared by the author.
Printed and bound in Great Britain by The University Press, Cambridge.

First printed 1992.   Reprinted 1993 and 1994.

British Library Cataloguing-in-Publication Data
A catalogue record for this book is available from the British Library.

Library of Congress Cataloging-in-Publication Data is available

ISBN 0-201-56512-9

Preface

The X Window System (**X**) has, over the last few years, become increasingly important, and it is now accepted as *the* windowing system for workstations, minicomputers, mainframes and supercomputers. It has become the standard means of providing graphical facilities on these classes of computers, and is even available on PCs, running instead of, or in conjunction with, Microsoft Windows. And just as Microsoft Windows has revolutionized the PC, **X** is doing the same for its users, for two reasons. First and most visibly, **X** allows standard graphical user interfaces to be provided on all the computers used by an organization, no matter which underlying hardware or operating system is used. Second, **X** allows applications running on one computer to be used by people working on other computers elsewhere on the network; the applications are 'network transparent', and all applications can be made available to all the users, independent of what type of computing platform they have. This is true Open Systems in action — it gives users and system managers the freedom to choose the best software and the best hardware for their needs, with the confidence that it will integrate simply and reliably into their overall computing environment.

X began in 1984 at the Massachusetts Institute of Technology (MIT) as a joint project between the Laboratory for Computer Science and Project Athena, with much of the early work sponsored by DEC and IBM. By 1986 **X** was becoming significant in commercial computing; and the system as we know it, **X** Version 11 (X11), was released in 1987. Since then **X** has been considerably enhanced, largely under the management of the MIT **X** Consortium, which defines the standards for the system and has ensured that current X11 implementations remain compatible with earlier releases.

About This Book

A lot of information about **X** is available, but much of it is unpublished or difficult to find. We wanted to pull together material from different sources, and provide a book which gives a complete view of the system so that you can understand the important features and issues, and see how the various aspects of the system fit into the overall picture. We hope this book will act as a springboard, and give you what you need to develop your particular interest in **X**, whether as programmer, user or system manager.

Our aim was to write a *small* book about **X**, to make it more accessible, and to counter the view that some **X** books are sold by weight rather than the volume! As a result, we have sometimes had to omit some low-level detail, in the interest of making the book more readable. Even so, where it is essential for an understanding of the system, we include some fairly complex material.

Who Should Read This Book

You don't need any special knowledge to read this book — it is suitable for anyone who is interested in **X** and has some experience of computers. You will find the book particularly useful if:

- You have heard about **X** and want to find out more about it — for instance, what is special about it, and how it compares with other window systems.

- You are a **system manager**, and need to understand the architecture of **X** and the techniques and tools you will need to use when you are running an **X** system.

- You are an **IT director** or **manager**, deciding whether your organization should 'go the **X** route'; and you need to know what the implications of such a strategy are, and what developments are likely in the future.

- You are confused by the 'GUI' wars between OPEN LOOK and Motif, and want to see what these things really are, and the issues involved in choosing between them.

- Your are involved in **technical support**, and need a good understanding of how **X** works, and what your customers are likely to be doing with **X** and why.

- You are a **programmer**, and want to get an overview of the system before exploring **X** programming in depth.

- Your are involved in **sales** or **marketing**, and need to understand how **X** can help your customers, where it can be applied, and how some implementations have competitive advantages over others.

Structure of the Book, and How to Use It

The book is divided into three Parts:

1. **X** *in a Nutshell.* This is a quick 'management overview' of the system, its architecture, and how using it can benefit your organization.

2. *How* **X** *Works, in Detail, and How the User Sees It* explains the operation of the system, and describes the **X** server, client application programs and how they are built, 'look and feel' issues, toolkits and window managers.

There may be more detail here than you need; if so, just dip into the sections you need once you have read Part 1.

3. *Using the System, System Administration, Performance, and Programming* covers what you need to start using an **X** system, how it is administered, managed and customized, what the performance considerations are, and how you write **X** programs. (For more details about hands-on use of the system, see the companion volume, *The X Window System: A User's Guide*, Addison-Wesley 1991, ISBN 0-201-51341-2.)

The book consists of 'Modules', each of which consists of two pages. The left-hand page of the two starts with a summary of what the module is about, followed by the main text of the module. The right-hand page usually contains diagrams, tables or screen-shots. To make it easier for you to skip straight to the sections that interest you, we have tried as far as possible to make each module a unit in itself. Because of this, there is some duplication in places, though you will often find that different perspectives are offered in different sections. For example, in Chapter 3 we describe how the server uses fonts to draw text, whereas in Chapter 11 we cover fonts from the system management point of view. Some modules are marked

(If technical details aren't so relevant to you, you can skip over this module.)

You can bypass these on your first reading of the book, or skip them completely if you are not particularly interested in complex technical issues.

Software Used

The book deals with the standard MIT software (which is broadly representative of many vendors' offerings) and other widely available commercial software such as OPEN LOOK (we used Sun's OpenWindows, Version 2) and Motif (we used Version 1.1). We also used the Motif version of the FrameMaker document preparation system, and the Motif version of IST's XDesigner user-interface management system. In some sections we have described software which is not yet widely used, but which illustrates some particular point, or which is an indication of what may be become commonly available in the future.

We prepared and wrote the book on a Sun SPARCstation running SunOS 4.1.2, and the standard MIT Release 5 of **X** Version 11. The text was edited with GNU emacs from the Free Software Foundation, and typeset with LaTeX using style-files prepared by Paul Davis at the University of Washington. The index was processed using the LaTeX Makeindex system, and the screen-shots were processed with the pbmplus Extended Portable Bitmap Toolkit. We used make and imake for configuration management and SCCS for source-code control of the text.

Acknowledgements

Many people have been very helpful. Paul Davis kindly spent much of his spare time developing the LaTeX style-files required for the book's special format, and also helped with some LaTeX problems. Steve Jamieson of NCD supplied information about server configuration files. Tony Morris of AWM Computer Consultants, and the White Company, Cambridge, provided facilities for scanning images. From the European X User Group, Bob McGonigle and Peter Whitehead helped with the printing of early drafts, and Bevis King and John Harvey provided much useful documentation. Selwyn Castleden of TOP-LOG and Frame Technology very generously helped with the production of illustrations. The (anonymous) reviewers of early drafts of the manuscript made many helpful and constructive suggestions about content and presentation. We are also grateful to *Sun Technology* magazine, for permission to include the illustration in Module 7.1.

Others have been just as helpful, although more indirectly. First we must include all those people on the xpert mailing-list who reply to queries for clarification and assistance, and the authors of the **X** software itself, such as David Rosenthal of Sun who published the 'Hello, World' programs, included in Chapter 5, as one of the first tutorials on **X**. Then there are the authors of articles and books which over the years have given much background information and offered different perspectives on aspects of **X**, and the many people I have had discussions with, and whose tutorial sessions I attended. In particular I recall Jim Gettys' ideas on customization, Doug Young's approach to constructing **X** applications, and Larry Maki's characterization of benchmarks.

Finally, I owe a great debt to Oliver Jones for his wonderfully generous encouragement and help when I thought this book would never be finished. This constructive and cooperative atmosphere is what makes working in the field of computer software so satisfying and rewarding, and indeed contributes to the joy of **X**.

Niall Mansfield
User Interface Technologies
PO Box 145
Cambridge CB4 1GQ, England

e-mail: N.Mansfield@uit.co.uk

Contents

Preface   v

PART 1   X in a Nutshell

1   A Brief Overview of the X System   3

  1.1   **X** is a client/server window system   4
  1.2   The user interface is not built into the base **X** system   8
  1.3   The unique features that make **X** so useful   16
  1.4   How **X** compares with other systems   18

2   The Benefits X Gives You   21

  2.1   **X** gives you all the usual benefits of a window system   22
  2.2   **X** integrates applications on different hardware and operating systems   .   26
  2.3   Benefits of a standard GUI throughout your organization   38
  2.4   **X** allows distributed computing, or centralized, or both   40
  2.5   **X** fundamentally changes software and hardware decisions   42
  2.6   The financial benefits of using **X**   44
  2.7   How **X** can help different categories of people   48

PART 2   How X Works, in Detail, and How the User Sees It

3   The Server — the Display Control Software   53

  3.1   The role of the server   54
  3.2   Implementations of the **X** server   58
  3.3   How the server handles output to the screen   64
  3.4   The server contains the only display hardware dependence in the system   70
  3.5   Handling text and fonts   72
  3.6   Handling colour   78
  3.7   Pictures and images — bitmaps, cursors and pixmaps   88
  3.8   Extras you may want or need: server extensions   94

4   Communication between the Server and Clients **99**

4.1   Clients send high-level 'requests' to the server 100
4.2   The server uses 'events' to communicate input and status changes to the
        client 104
4.3   Intercepting input and requests for special handling 112
4.4   **X** can work over many different network types, as well as locally 116
4.5   What load does **X** impose on the network? 118
4.6   **X** Version and Release numbers, and compatibility issues 120

5   Clients — the Application Programs **125**

5.1   An overview of the client and its role 126
5.2   What **X** clients consist of, and how they are built 128
5.3   Internationalizing and localizing applications — Xi18n 138
5.4   Examples of **X** application programs 144

6   'Look and Feel' Part 1 — Toolkits for Application Programs **149**

6.1   'Look and feel' means how the user sees the system 150
6.2   **X** allows many different look and feels 154
6.3   Motif and OPEN LOOK — the standard look and feels 156
6.4   How look and feel is implemented: toolkits 158

7   The Standard X Toolkit — Intrinsics and Widgets **163**

7.1   The standard **X** Toolkit, 'Xt' 164
7.2   Widgets and widget sets are building blocks 168
7.3   The 'Intrinsics' lets you manipulate widgets 176
7.4   Event handling and 'callbacks' 180
7.5   Some implementations of Motif and OPEN LOOK use Xt 186
7.6   Other **X** toolkits 190

8   'Look and Feel' Part 2 — Window Managers **193**

8.1   What you need a 'window manager' for 194
8.2   Using the window manager 198
8.3   The window manager's look and feel 200
8.4   How a window manager works 204

9   Using Many Applications Together — 'Inter-Client Communications' **209**

9.1   Why applications need to communicate with each other 210
9.2   'Properties' — the basic mechanism for inter-client communications . . 212
9.3   Advanced communications mechanisms 216
9.4   The Selections Service — a high-level communications mechanism . . . 220
9.5   ICCCM — the rulebook for inter-client communications 226
9.6   Desktop managers 228

PART 3   Using the System, System Administration, Performance, and Programming

10 Using the X System   233

10.1 What you need to get started 234
10.2 How you use the network facilities 238
10.3 Using character-based applications — terminal emulators 242
10.4 Integrating **X** with other systems 250
10.5 Where to get the software 252

11 System Administration   255

11.1 Starting up the system 256
11.2 Customizing server settings 264
11.3 Administering fonts 266
11.4 Security 268
11.5 A summary of **X** system administration 278

12 Customizing Applications   281

12.1 Customizing applications 282
12.2 The Resources mechanism for customizing applications 284
12.3 How the Toolkit uses resources 290
12.4 Translation tables resources and keyboard mapping 292
12.5 Tools for customizing resources 296

13 Performance Factors   299

13.1 Server performance 300
13.2 Network performance 304
13.3 Client performance 308
13.4 Benchmarks and tests 312

14 Writing X Programs   317

14.1 Programming the system, and development tools 318
14.2 User interface management systems and other development tools 326
14.3 Migrating old applications to **X** — enhanced terminal emulators . . . 328
14.4 Porting from other window systems, and multiple-platform applications . 332
14.5 User interface design, and programming 334

15 Epilogue   337

15.1 The MIT **X** Consortium 338
15.2 The **X** standards 340
15.3 Sources of further information and assistance 342

Index   345

Throughout this book we refer to Motif as a convenient shorthand for OSF/Motif.

1

X in a Nutshell

*This first Part of the book gives you an overview of what the **X** Window System is, and how it works. This is deliberately not very detailed; it is only an introduction to get you started and to give you a feel for where you are going. There are pointers to other modules of the book where the various features are covered in more detail, so if you are really interested in some topic, you can go straight to it. However, it is probably best to skim through at least Chapter 1 to begin with, before exploring further.*

*This Part also contains a full description of the benefits **X** can give you, explaining how the system's technical features can help you solve real-life problems for your organization or in your particular job.*

*When you have finished Part 1, if you are interested in the practical points of how you get to use **X**, you can jump straight to Part 3 (Using the System), but if you want to explore the deeper concepts of **X** and want to understand more of its internal operations, just continue on to Part 2 (How **X** Works, in Detail).*

Chapter

1

A Brief Overview of the X System

1.1   X is a client/server window system

     1.1.1   X can work locally or across a network

1.2   The user interface is not built into the base X system

     1.2.1   Standard graphical user interfaces

     1.2.2   The Motif and OPEN LOOK graphical user interfaces

     1.2.3   The user interface has two separate parts

1.3   The unique features that make X so useful

1.4   How X compares with other systems

Introduction

This chapter gives you a very brief outline of what X is, its component parts, and what is special about it. We have included in this chapter just enough information for you to understand the benefits X can give you (which we cover in the next chapter) and to give you a framework of understanding for you to build on, when we look at the system's operation in detail in Part 2 of the book.

1.1   X is a client/server window system

X lets you run many simultaneous applications on your display, each with one or more windows of its own. The display is controlled by software called the **X** 'server'. Applications cannot interact with the display directly. Instead they send requests across a communications channel to the server to perform actions for them — they are **X** 'clients'.

Like other window systems, **X** lets you have many applications displaying on your screen simultaneously. Each application has its own window, and all the windows can be active simultaneously: you can be typing in one window while another application is outputting to a different window. That is how **X** is similar to other systems; now let's see where it differs from them.

The **X** system consists of three main parts:

1. The **server** — the software that controls the user's display, including the screen, keyboard and mouse.

2. The **clients** — the application programs, which are completely separate from the server.

3. A communications link, which connects the clients and the server. This link can take many forms, as we see below.

The separation of client from server is fundamental in **X**, and it is what gives **X** most of its unique benefits.

The server controls the display

As shown in Figure A, the server controls the display hardware. It, or the underlying operating system, contains device drivers for the keyboard, mouse, and screen; the server contains the only hardware dependencies in the system. The server accepts **requests** which are sent across the communications link from client (application) programs to create windows on the screen, to change the size or location of windows, and to draw text or graphics in these windows. It also sends **events** back to clients, telling them about input from the keyboard or mouse, or indicating that certain changes in the status of windows have happened.

A server can handle multiple simultaneous connections from clients, that is, you can have several applications each with its own window on the screen, all active at once. The terms **display** and **server** are often used interchangeably. (You can also think of the server as a **seat**, to use a common workstation term.)

The client is the application program

The client program contains the code to perform the function the user requires — send electronic mail, handle the payroll, maintain a database or whatever — as well as the code needed to support **X** and to provide a graphical user interface. Figure B compares the **X** server/client operation with the more familiar file-server/diskless client case, and you can see why the **X** terminology is correct. (It's confusing only because in so many other cases the 'server' is the remote component; if you think about what is happening and what each element of the system is doing, the terminology becomes clear).

A client can work with *any* display, as long as there is a suitable communications link between them. You don't have to recompile or relink the client when you want to use it with a new display, so clients you write now will work with the next generation of servers produced in the future. For example, new super-fast servers may be developed to take advantage of advances in semiconductor technology and networking.

A client can connect to multiple displays, for example a teacher can run a single application which displays to servers on each of her students' desks.

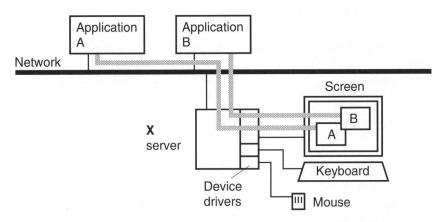

Figure A. The server controls the display and is separate from the clients.

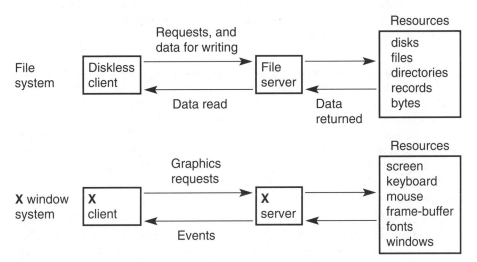

Figure B. Analogy of file server and X server.

1.1 X is a client/server window system

1.1.1 X can work locally or across a network

The client and server are completely separated and only require a communications link between them to function. This link can be a local area or wide area network, so applications can execute on one machine but display to another somewhere else on the network.

As shown in Figure A, the communications link is the third major component of the system. (The first two components are the server and the client.) *All* communication between client and server goes across this link, and the only requirement for the system to work correctly is that this link exists. It follows that it doesn't much matter what type of link it is.

There are two main situations of interest:

1. **Client and server are executing on the same CPU.** (A typical example of this is where a workstation is being used to run **X**.) Here the communications link can be any available form of inter-process communication; for example, shared memory, streams, named pipes, UNIX sockets, etc. (Figure B).

2. **Client and server are on different CPUs.** Here the link is across a network (Figure C). **X** can run over almost any type of network — it is **network independent**. On the physical level, Ethernet, token ring, X.25 and serial lines have been used. At the protocol level, **X** can run over TCP/IP, DECnet and OSI (see Module 4.4 for details).

   The two machines don't have to have the same architecture (same CPU type) or operating system, because the requests and events that are transmitted between server and client are device independent. They are expressed in terms of high-level 'objects' rather than as device-dependent commands or sets of pixels to be drawn. (For example, a line is specified by its start and end points, and its width.)

So, you can run your application on the same machine as your server (which you are sitting at), or you can run the application somewhere else on your network. In other words, you can run the client **locally** or **remotely**. This is true of any **X** application, and this feature of **X** is called **network transparency** — that is, the program can work across a network, and it sees no difference. When you use the application on your display you have the illusion that it is running on your machine — the network is transparent to the user as well as to the system (Figure D). Note that the program isn't just outputting to the screen on your display: it is taking its input from your keyboard and mouse, so you can detect no difference whatever in its operation.

Later on we'll see how useful this can be, particularly where an application *must* run on a particular machine, but it isn't feasible to give everyone a machine of this type. For example, large company-wide database systems require big computers with a lot of disk storage and a lot of CPU power. By using **X**, all users can execute the database application on the large machine, but interact with it and display the output on their own workstations on their desks (Figure E).

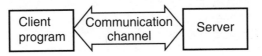

Figure A.   The communications link is the third component of the system.

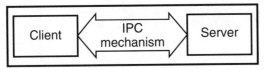

Figure B.   Client and server executing on the same machine.

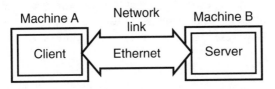

Figure C.   Client and server executing on different machines.

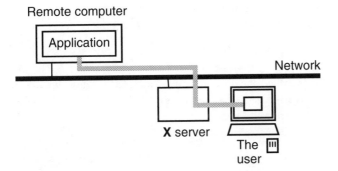

Figure D.   Remote execution is transparent to the user.

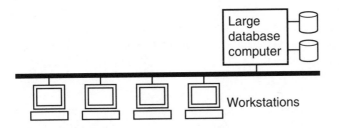

Figure E.   Remote execution lets users share a special machine.

1.2   The user interface is not built into the base X system

Scrollbars, menus, push-buttons and all the other elements of the graphical user interface of an **X** application are part of that application and not of the server. Because these components are not in the server, **X**'s whole user interface is alterable, so **X** can support many different interfaces.

Unlike almost every other window system, **X** does not provide a standard user interface. The user interface components that we take for granted in most systems — the scrollbars, pull-down and pop-up menus, buttons, etc. — are not provided by the base **X** system at all. In other words, they are not part of the server; therefore they must be provided by the client. **X** and other window systems are compared schematically in Figures A and B.

This design may seem strange, but it was a deliberate decision made by the **X** developers. Their aim was to produce a system that would be as widely useful as possible without restricting how people would use it: they wanted **X** to provide 'mechanism, not policy'. So, they provided everything needed to build whatever style of user interface anybody wanted, but they left it to others to use these tools to design and build the actual interfaces. There were many reasons for this feature of **X**:

- The user interface is what people use to interact with the computer. To design it correctly you have to study the *people* as well as the computer. The **X** developers modestly realized that good user interface design is the job of psychologists and human factors specialists, not of computer scientists.

- When **X** began, user interface technology hadn't matured enough. There was no interface that was obviously the best. (And many people say there still isn't.)

- User interfaces are an emotional and controversial area. If **X** had chosen one particular interface, many companies and people who favoured other styles would have refused to support and use **X**. So it was 'politically' expedient not to define a standard.

- Interface design is a major area for research and development. By not defining a standard interface, **X** can be used for exploring new interfaces and styles of interaction.

- One of the design principles for **X** was that anything that didn't absolutely *have to* be in the server was left to the clients. Omitting the user interface details from the server made it smaller, simpler and more robust, as well as making it easier to change or fix the user interface code during development. (It also reduced the time needed to develop the server!)

In the next three modules we see how a standard interface can be made available across all machines and operating systems, and how the interface is actually provided.

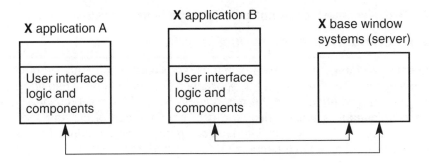

Figure A.   The user interface code is in the X client.

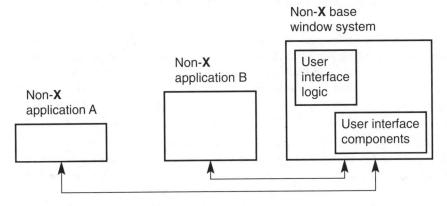

Figure B.   The user interface is an integral part of other window systems.

1.2   The user interface is not built into the base X system

1.2.1   Standard graphical user interfaces

The user interface components — buttons, scrollbars, etc. — are programmed into the application. Originally each application programmer designed and coded their own user interface and the components in it. Then, subroutine libraries were developed to simplify writing the user interface part of programs. Finally, toolkits of standard, consistent, interface components were produced and widely distributed, and some have become de facto standards.

In the early days of **X**, each programmer, or each group of programmers working on a project, developed their own user interfaces. They each developed their own pushbuttons and scrollbars and wrote their own systems for handling menus. Apart from being time consuming, this meant that if you were using several **X** programs from different suppliers, each of them had its own style of interface, and they all worked differently.

Initially the user interface part of each program was written using just the low-level features provided by the basic **X** system, in the Xlib library of standard **X** functions or subroutines. For example, if you wanted a menu, you had to create a window for the menu background, then windows for each menu pane, write code to display the appropriate text in the panes, and detect when the user clicked on a menu item, and process it. Thus the structure of an **X** program was as shown in Figure A.

As the system matured, people developed **toolkits** — subroutine libraries or sets of predefined functions which the application programmer can use — to provide well-defined consistent interfaces. These subroutine libraries or toolkits are built into the application when it is compiled (Figure B). The toolkit lets the applications programmer build up the user interface of the program being written from ready-made modules. Many of the **X** toolkits are object-oriented, and the ready-made modules are user interface objects, which you can think of as building blocks. The applications programmer takes these prefabricated building blocks and assembles them into the structure she wants, giving a program with the standard look and feel of the toolkit used, without having to worry about the internals of each object.

More recently, MIT itself and companies like AT&T, Digital, Hewlett-Packard, and Sun have developed toolkits, and considerable resources have been invested in marketing some of them. These interfaces have been very widely adopted, so that now they are de facto standards and are available across a wide range of platforms. Application programmers no longer have to worry about writing their own user interface systems. The style of the user interface is decided by the designer of the toolkit, and all interfaces built with the same toolkit will have the same graphical user interface (GUI) or **look and feel**: what the interface looks like (the 'look') and how you operate it (the 'feel') are similar in all applications.

The dominant user interface look and feels are currently Motif and OPEN LOOK, which are illustrated in the next module. (There are lots of other look and feels too, but they haven't caught on.)

Providing the same user interface on different platforms

Making the same toolkit available on different machine types is easily done, by writing it in a portable and widely available language such as 'C' (which is what **X** itself has been implemented in on most systems). Remember that the user interface has nothing to do with the server — it's all within the application. So, to port a toolkit to different machines you have to ensure that the toolkit running on, say, a VMS VAX sends the same set of requests to the server as the toolkit running on a Cray supercomputer, for example, or a Hewlett-Packard mini. A request is just a group of bytes ordered in the specific format required by **X** so, at a practical level, all that an implementation of the toolkit has to do is package the request appropriately and pass it to the particular network software underlying **X** on that machine. After that, the toolkit can forget about it, because the lower layers of the system software look after transporting the request to the server. (For more detail see Chapter 6, especially Module 6.4.)

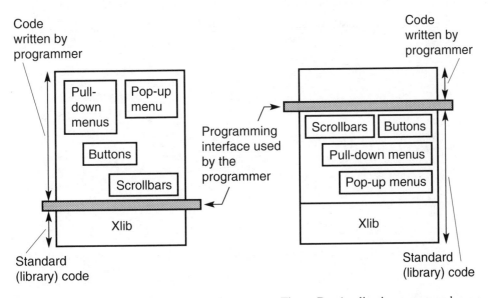

Figure A.   Structure of early X programs.

Figure B.   Application programs have user interface subroutine libraries (toolkits) built-in.

1.2 The user interface is not built into the base X system

1.2.2   The Motif and OPEN LOOK graphical user interfaces

Two commercial GUIs are predominant. These are Motif from the Open Software Foundation, and OPEN LOOK from UNIX System Laboratories. They both provide broadly similar facilities but differ in appearance and how they operate.

The Motif GUI was developed by the Open Software Foundation (OSF) which is a non-profit consortium of manufacturers including DEC, Hewlett-Packard, IBM, and others. The look and feel of Motif is similar to that of Presentation Manager and Microsoft Windows. An example Motif screen is shown in Figure A.

The OPEN LOOK GUI was developed primarily by Sun Microsystems and AT&T, and is now owned by UNIX System Laboratories (USL). OPEN LOOK's look and feel is based on the pioneering user interface work carried out by Xerox in the early 1980s. A sample OPEN LOOK screen (using Sun's OpenWindows) is shown in Figure B.

We cover these standard interfaces in depth in Module 6.3.

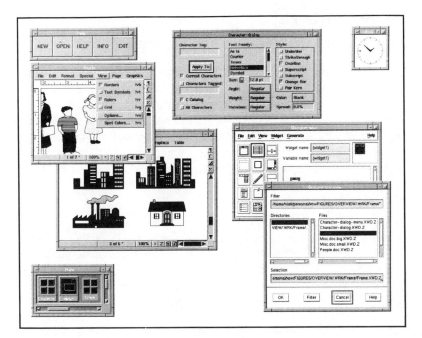

Figure A.   The Motif look and feel.

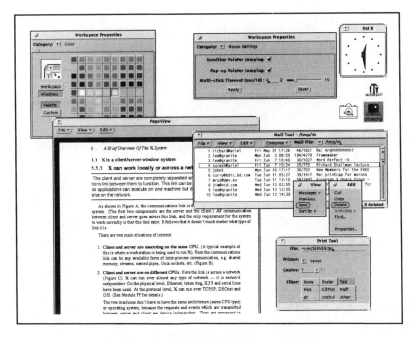

Figure B.   The OPEN LOOK look and feel.

1.2   The user interface is not built into the base X system

1.2.3   The user interface has two separate parts

The overall interface presented to the user consists of the look and feel built into each application, plus the controls necessary to manage the application windows themselves — position them on the screen, resize them, and so on. This second aspect of the user interface is not built into the application or the server, but is provided by a separate client program called a 'window manager'.

There are two separate components of the overall system which control the user interface as seen by the user:

1. The subroutine libraries or toolkit mentioned in the previous modules, which determine the interface *within* a particular program built with those libraries. In general this part of the interface cannot be altered without altering the source code of the program and recompiling; so effectively, when you buy software (without source code) from a vendor, its user interface is fixed.

   This part of the interface is called the **application interface**.

   Because the user interface is compiled into the particular program and doesn't affect any other applications, it follows that different applications can have different user interfaces even though they are running on the same display (that is, on the same server). In other words, each application can have its own distinct application interface.

2. A separate client program called a **window manager**, which controls how you manage your screen desktop — how you move windows, make them bigger or smaller, stack them, get rid of them, etc. Because this is a separate program and not built into the server (Figure A), you can change it and therefore the user interface provided by it. In general, any window manager should work with any set of applications, so you can easily switch from one window manager to another without having to change any other part of your system. You *don't* need to recompile or alter your application programs; in fact, you cab even switch window managers in mid-session while other applications are still running.

   This part of the user interface is called the **management interface**.

   Because the window manager controls all the application windows on your display, the management interface for all applications is the same. You can use a different window manager and so get a different management interface; therefore while you can choose your management interface, at any one time all the applications on your display share that single management interface.

This separation of the user interface into two parts, and the fact that none of the interface is built into the server, are major differences between **X** and other window systems. The management interface is probably the most visible aspect of any window system and the part most utilized by users. In fact, one of the main attractions of Motif is that its window manager interface is very like Presentation Manager and Microsoft Windows, so a Windows user can use a Motif system with little or no retraining. Figure B shows a screen containing only those elements that are provided by a Motif window manager, and from this you can see that many of a screen's recognizable features are due to the window manager. Thus, being able to change the management interface just by starting a different window manager is a very important feature of **X**.

We discuss all these interface issues in much greater detail in Chapter 6 (Look and Feel — Toolkits) and Chapter 8 (Look and Feel — Window Managers).

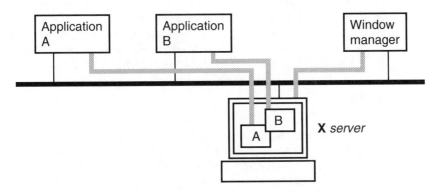

Figure A.   Window management is handled by a separate client program.

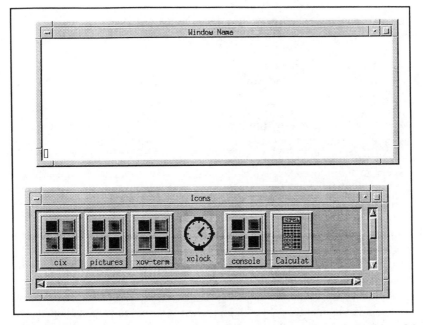

Figure B.   The elements of an application's window and the screen provided by a Motif window manager.

1.3   The unique features that make X so useful

The combination of **X**'s ability to work locally or across a network ('network transparency'), its device independence, and flexibility of user interface enable **X** to solve many problems in delivering computing into organizations, and have made **X** very popular. Widespread adoption of **X** has been easy because **X** was initially implemented with the emphasis on portability, and the source code is freely available.

When the **X** developers at MIT began their work they defined a set of requirements for the system so it would meet the needs of its target users. Even at that time, MIT had a very mixed ('heterogeneous') computing environment, with many different types of machines from various manufacturers. The design goals of **X**, and the architecture that was produced to meet them and the benefits that result, stem largely from the constraints such a heterogeneous environment imposed on the system. Some of the resulting features are:

1. **Network transparency**. Applications running on one machine can use the display on another. In practice this allows you to use programs running on other machines, but have them display on your screen and take input from your keyboard and mouse just as though they were running on your machine (see Figure A). In turn this lets you distribute applications around your network, as we'll see in Module 2.2.1.

   You don't have to be a network expert to write an **X** application program: network transparency is easy to use — the system makes it available 'for free'.

2. **X is network independent.** It doesn't depend on features specific to one network protocol, so it can work over many different types of networks (see Module 4.4).

3. **Device independence of applications**. You don't need to recompile or even relink your application for it to work with a new display, in the same way that if you buy a new serial-line character-based terminal you don't expect to have to change your application. For example, if you replace an existing Digital VT100 terminal with a VT220, your program should continue to run unaltered. For more detail, see Module 3.4.

4. **Minimal device dependence of server**. The server was developed as portably as possible, so that **X** could be implemented on as wide a variety of hardware displays as possible. For example, **X** runs on small PCs with limited memory, small workstations with simple frame-buffers, and high-performance workstations with complex graphics co-processors and lots of real and virtual memory. In addition, when it is run on workstations the **X** server is usually not embedded in the operating system, but is just another user-level program. This makes it easier to debug (if the server crashes,

you don't have to wait for the whole machine to re-boot) and therefore to implement.

5. **Extensions to the system are possible.** For any system to be useful for a long time, it must be able to develop organically. But this is dangerous if it is not controlled: non-standard features will creep in, and the goals of device independence and perhaps network transparency will be violated.

   At the outset, the **X** developers realized that new demands would be put on the system (for example, **X** handled only two-dimensional graphics, but it was obvious that 3-D graphics would soon be required). So, an **extensions mechanism** was built into **X**, to allow new functionality to be added cleanly, and without affecting the continued correct operation of existing systems (see Module 3.8).

6. **X is 'policy-free'.** As we discussed in the previous modules, the user interface is not pre-defined, so the system can handle many different interfaces. This is especially useful if you want **X** to imitate (or emulate) the interface available on some other system.

7. **X is non-proprietary.** Many vendors got involved early on. Sample implementations of server and applications have always been available from MIT, free, and with virtually no commercial restrictions on their re-use. This let hardware and software developers get started on **X** very quickly. **X** went through a major re-design around 1987: this process was largely public, so a huge number of people from many different organizations were able to, and did, participate. This resulted first of all in a good design, and second, in widespread acceptability of **X**.

   In the next chapter we see how these features of **X** result in real-life benefits, letting you build flexible and powerful networks of interoperating machines (both new and old) with the minimum of restrictions.

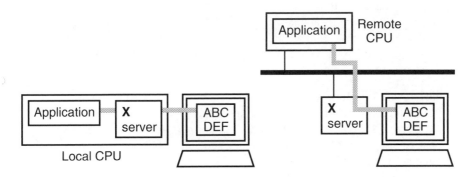

Figure A.   Local and remote applications look just the same to the user.

1.4   How X compares with other systems

Other network systems, such as telnet, allow character-based applications to execute remotely over the network. Other window systems, such as the Macintosh, provide a GUI and multiple windows, but don't support remote execution over the network. As the user interface is an integral part of these systems it cannot be altered: only **X** can offer its unique combination of flexibility and function.

Each one of the features that makes **X** so powerful is available on some other system, but individually they do not give the flexibility needed to provide all the computing facilities an organization needs. It is the *combination* of the features that gives what is required. Let's look at some of the other systems available, and see how they compare with **X**.

telnet is part of the TCP/IP networking system, and is designed for character-based terminals. It lets you log-in from your own machine on to another machine somewhere else on your network, and then run programs on that remote machine just as though your terminal were connected to that machine. (Similar facilities are the rlogin remote login program, and the VMS SET HOST command.)

So, telnet does offer remote execution, but only one session at a time (it doesn't give you multiple simultaneous applications unless you run several copies, in some type of windowing system, for example) and it is limited to character applications (you can't run a graphics program on the remote machine and have telnet display the full graphical user interface of that program on your terminal).

SQL database client systems, often run on PCs, let you interact with a large database system running elsewhere on your network. They usually provide a good graphical interface, and download some of the work of presenting the database information to your PC.

Again, you are getting some remote execution facility — the database is running elsewhere — and an improved GUI. These systems are not general purpose, but are highly restrictive: they only handle interaction with a database, and if you want to run any other programs you need some other system.

Microsoft Windows for DOS gives you a true windowing system on a PC, with a consistent GUI, and multiple applications which can be more or less active simultaneously. Like **X**, it is not part of the operating system, but is a separate and optional piece of software which you run on top of the operating system.

It differs from **X** in two important ways:

1. The user interface is fixed and built into the system, so you cannot change it. For example, if you wanted to emulate the Macintosh

interface you just can't do it with MS-Windows.

2. You can only run local applications, which means that you can only use applications written for DOS PCs. You cannot compile a program for VAX VMS, say, with the Windows GUI built into it, and run it on the VAX displaying to your PC.

The network usability of Windows can be improved by using it in conjunction with a good PC TCP/IP system which will let you run multiple telnet sessions within Windows, but you still don't get network-transparent graphics programs.

The Apple Macintosh, like Microsoft Windows, gives you a consistent GUI, and with the latest releases allows multiple applications to be active simultaneously. Again, the GUI is completely determined: if you don't like the Macintosh interface, don't use a Macintosh.

It differs from Microsoft Windows in that it is built into the kernel or heart of the operating system — you can't run a Macintosh without its window system.

Sun Workstations have offered three different window systems:

1. **SunView** was Sun's own native window system, and its characteristics are just like the Macintosh's — it is built into the operating system, it allows only local applications, and you can't change the interface.

2. **NeWS** (Network extensible Window System) is a client/server system like **X**, offering the same advantages. It is based on Adobe's PostScript language (developed for powerful laser printers and typesetters) and so offers very good facilities for DTP and text handling.

   However, NeWS is proprietary to Sun, and is used by almost nobody else.

3. **OpenWindows** is Sun's latest system, and is a mixture of NeWS and **X**. Any standard **X** program should work with OpenWindows, but the reverse is not true: many OpenWindows programs use the Sun-specific PostScript facilities and therefore won't work with standard **X** servers.

Other workstations. Hewlett-Packard's and Digital's systems now offer **X** as the standard window system (Digital's DECwindows is **X**).

Summary

This chapter has given you an overview of **X** and what is special about it. You've seen that the system consists of three main components:

1. The server, controlling the display hardware.

2. The client, which is the application program.

3. The communications link or network they communicate over.

This architecture lets you run an application locally (on the same machine as your server) or remotely (on some other machine). The user interface is not part of the server but consists of two parts:

1. The application interface which is built into each application when it is compiled, usually by means of a toolkit. Different applications can have different application interfaces. The application interface can usually be altered only by changing the program source code to use a different toolkit and then recompiling it.

2. The management interface which is provided by the window manager program, and which can be changed just by running a different window manager.

Thus **X** can support different interfaces. Finally, we compared **X** with other systems, and looked at its unique features. In the next chapter we consider the benefits these features can give you.

Chapter

2   The Benefits X Gives You

2.1   **X** gives you all the usual benefits of a window system
      2.1.1 **X** allows multiple applications and overlapping windows

2.2   **X** integrates applications on different hardware and
      operating systems
      2.2.1 Integrating an organization's computing on a local
             network
      2.2.2 Integrating head office, branches, and isolated sites
      2.2.3 Using non-windowed applications with **X**
      2.2.4 Using applications for other window systems with **X**
      2.2.5 X-terminals: cheap substitutes for workstations?

2.3   Benefits of a standard GUI throughout your organization

2.4   **X** allows distributed computing, or centralized, or both

2.5   **X** fundamentally changes software and hardware decisions

2.6   The financial benefits of using **X**
      2.6.1 Savings from freedom of choice

2.7   How **X** can help different categories of people

Introduction

This chapter looks at how **X**'s unique features can help your organization. The freedom to run applications remotely or locally lets you integrate all your computing facilities into a consistent whole, enhanced by a uniform graphical user interface. The result is a greater choice of both user and system management applications, better facilities for your users, and financial benefits overall.

2.1   X gives you all the usual benefits of a window system

Like most window systems, **X** allows you to write programs that present information graphically and which you interact with by directly manipulating graphical controls instead of typing commands from a keyboard. This 'graphical user interface' to applications helps make people more productive, by making systems easier to learn and to use.

X is primarily a window system. And like other window systems, many of its benefits come from being able to display information graphically — in the form of graphs or pictures, perhaps with colour, and different fonts — and being able to interact with the information directly using a mouse. (By contrast, character-based (ASCII or EBCDIC) terminals are usually limited to single-font displays, and you can only interact with them using a keyboard.)

- Quantitative information displayed graphically is often much easier to understand than a large set of numbers ('a picture is worth a thousand words').

- Other information is often much more quickly assimilated when shown as a picture rather than in words, and can be understood by people of different nationalities without having to be translated.

- The controls for the program can be shown explicitly, as visible 'objects' such as scrollbars or push-buttons, whose function is obvious to the user. You interact with these controls by **direct manipulation**. You handle the data and invoke functions in the program by simulated physical actions (pressing knobs or buttons, or grabbing and moving sliders) rather than by abstract verbal reference (by typing in English words, or computer-language commands).

  In a well-designed application, these controls model real-world objects, so they provide an immediate hint about what function they perform, and each is suited to or specially designed for its particular task. Separate controls can be provided for each parameter or thing to be controlled, making it even easier to use the program. (Compare driving a car which has a separate control for each function, with figuring out how to adjust a digital watch which has only two buttons; the same two buttons have to be used to invoke all the different functions the watch provides.) Making a program easier to use makes it more popular with its users, so their productivity and job satisfaction are likely to be improved.

- Programs that use such a Graphical User Interface (GUI) are usually easier to learn, because it is more obvious how to use them. Using the menus, scrollbars, and other components of a GUI reduces the amount of information you have to remember to be able to use the application — these components on the screen are visual reminders. But menus and **dialogs** (separate pop-up windows which let you enter all the information relating to a particular aspect of the program, such as selecting and configuring the printer you want to use) also hide details while still making it obvious how to access them when necessary. Novices aren't confused, and the workspace isn't cluttered with unnecessary information. This principle of designing user interfaces is called progressive disclosure. (This is often applied in designing consumer equipment too; for example, the more complex controls on many televisions and video cassette recorders are often hidden behind an easily opened flap which is clearly visible on the front of the appliance.)

Using this approach can result in a program that you can use without any specific instruction, and which doesn't need a manual. The **X** clock (Figure A) needs no instructions at all. A more complex example, a calculator program written for **X**, and providing a GUI, is shown in Figure B. A child or a computer novice can use this program easily, because they can apply their knowledge of the real world to their task on the computer. By contrast, even experienced programmers have difficulty using the standard UNIX calculator dc (Figure C): it gives no clue about how to use it, it doesn't print a prompt, and worse, it uses 'reverse Polish' arithmetic notation (so instead of typing '3 + 4 + 5 =' to add and print three numbers, you enter '3 4 5 + + p').

Figure A. The X clock is easy to use – its interface is natural.

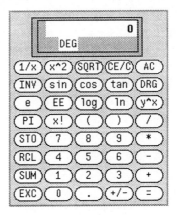

Figure B. An X calculator with a GUI.

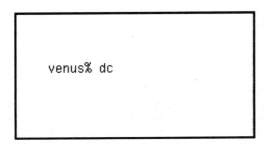

Figure C. The UNIX 'desk calculator'.

2.1   X gives you all the usual benefits of a window system

2.1.1   X allows multiple applications and overlapping windows

X lets you run multiple applications simultaneously on the same screen, each with one or more windows of its own. Each application runs independently, but you can cut and paste information from one window to another.

X lets you have multiple applications on your screen, each with its own window or windows (Figure A). These windows can be arranged side by side, or overlapped and stacked, just like papers on your desk. You can group programs near each other on the screen to suit the task you are doing, move them around, and put them away when you don't need them. You are effectively simulating a physical desktop. In the early days, many people saw this as **X**'s main benefit![1]

Your different applications can all be active simultaneously: you don't have to stop one to start another.[2] So, while you are watching the output of some long task appear in one window, you can be editing a mail message in another window, and writing a report with a DTP system in a third. This alone greatly improves the productivity of the system. But being able to **cut and paste** information, that is, copy it from one window into another, makes multiple windows even more useful. For example, if you need information from your database for your report, you just go to another window, perform your database inquiry, and cut and paste the information back into your DTP window.

In computer terms, window systems often use more resources (memory, CPU, disk space) than non-windowed systems. You are trading computer power against improving the effectiveness and productivity of the people using the computers. Computing costs are decreasing rapidly, and people costs are increasing, so this trade-off is constantly becoming more economic.

---

[1] To convince non-users, purchasing managers say, of how important this feature can be, suggest they try handling all their paperwork looking through a cut-out window in a piece of cardboard, allowing a view of only 80 x 24 characters.

[2] We deliberately use the long-winded phrase 'X allows multiple simultaneous active applications' instead of saying 'X is a multitasking environment'. Running the multiple tasks, locally or remotely, is not done by **X** — that is the job of the operating systems used, and it is the operating system that is multitasking or not. The **X** server is a single task which allows many windows to be active simultaneously, whether they belong to one application or to many.

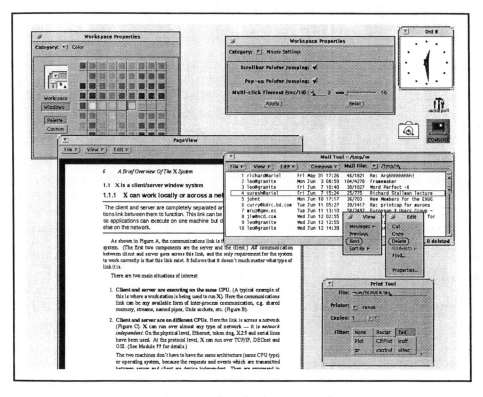

Figure A.   A sample X screen with many applications.

2.2   X integrates applications on different hardware and operating systems

---

X's network transparency lets users access applications running on different CPU types and different operating systems, just as though they were running on the user's own local machine. The user gets a rich and flexible environment, as all applications can be delivered to all users. This is the greatest single benefit of **X**.

Most large or medium-sized computer installations, and even a lot of small ones, are heterogeneous — they include different types of hardware, and usually many different operating systems too. For example, engineering companies have UNIX workstations for CAD work, PCs and/or Macintoshes for office automation tasks such as word-processing and mail, VMS systems for the company-wide database, and perhaps an IBM mainframe for the financial systems. In an environment like this, if you have to provide a new application, how do you make it available to everyone who needs it? What hardware do you run it on? Or if, for example, a vendor develops a network management system that runs on one type of hardware but needs to be accessed from many other workstations, how can it best be delivered?

X gives you an easy solution. Once you have set up your network so that all your users can use **X** (that is, their workstation or PC runs an **X** server), then *any* **X** application on *any* machine on your network can be accessed by *any* user.

As shown in Figure A, you are not restricted by the operating systems or type of machine the applications are running on, or the type of **X** server you have. Any application can be delivered to any user. (We'll deal with this in more detail in the next module.) Figure B lists some of the machines and operating systems for which **X** is available: you can see that the range is enormous, covering desktop PCs, through workstations, to supercomputers.

Running applications over the network is helpful in real life because there are always some applications which are available only on particular platforms (such as large database systems or financial packages) and now you can share them across all your users. It is also feasible to make use of applications that employ specialist or very expensive architectures and share them among many users. For example, some applications have to *execute* on supercomputers, but you can *interact* with them from your **X** display.

Integrating X with other widely used systems

Most people can't move completely to **X** immediately, because they have a large invest-ment in applications for other systems. They have to continue using existing programs, while using **X** for new applications, both those developed in-house as well as third-party ones.

Special **X** servers are available for many machines (for example, DOS PCs with or without Microsoft Windows, Macintoshes, Sun and NeXT workstations) which let you use **X** in conjunction with the native window system (Module 2.2.4). Most **X** systems also include a **terminal emulator** facility which lets you run ordinary character-based applications in an **X** window just as though it were a normal character terminal. Coexisting with other systems is covered in Module 2.2.3, and in Chapter 10. We also look at special hardware for **X** in the form of X-terminals, and see what benefits they give, in Modules 2.2.5 and 3.2.1.

In the next four modules we show how you can use **X** to integrate your organization's computing — at a single site, at multiple sites connected with a wide area network — and to merge in applications for **X**, for other window systems, and for character-based terminals.

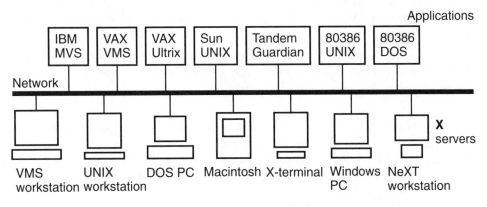

Figure A.   Sharing X applications on different hardware and operating systems.

AT&T UNIX System V Rel. 4 V2, AT&T WGS6386	Mach 2.5 Version 1.40, on OMRON Luna 68k
Acorn Archimides	Microsoft Windows NT
Amdahl	Motorola R32V2/R3V6.2 and R40V1
Apollo SR10.3 (BSD4.3 only)	NEWS-OS 4.1, on Sony NWS-1850
Apple Macintosh MacOS and A/UX	NEWS-OS 5.0U, on Sony NWS-3710
Atari	NeXT
Commodore Amiga	RISCOS 4.50
ConvexOS V9.0	Sequent
Cray UNICOS 5.1	SunOS 4.1.1, on Sun 3, Sparc 1, and Sparc 2
Data General DG/UX 4.32	Tandem Guardian
Hewlett Packard HP-UX 7.0, on HP9000/s300	UNIOS-B 4.3BSD UNIX: 2.00
IBM AIX 1.2.1, on PS/2	UTek 4.0
IBM AIX 2.2 and AOS 4.3, on RT	Ultrix-32 4.2, VAX and RISC
IBM AIX 3.1.5, on RS/6000	UNIX System V/386 Release 3.2, on ESIX, SCO, and ISC
IBM mainframes, MVS	UNIX System V/386 Release 4.0, on DELL
IBM PC with DOS or Microsoft Windows	VAX 4.3bsd
INTERACTIVE UNIX Version 2.2.1	VAX VMS
IRIX 4.0	X terminals from many, many, vendors
Mach 2.5 Version 1.13, on OMRON Luna 88k	

Figure B.   Partial list of platforms supporting X.

2.2   X integrates applications on different hardware and operating systems

2.2.1   Integrating an organization's computing on a local network

By using both local and remote applications on a LAN you can make applications available to all your users in a way that hides network details and simplifies the growth of your system.

The key to integrating your applications is being able to run a program on a machine somewhere else on your network, but having it use the display you are sitting at, as shown in Figure A. (Module 10.2.1 describes the commands you use to do this, if you are interested.)

You can have several remote applications connecting to your **X** display as shown in Figure B, and you can have both local and remote applications (Figure C.)

The advantages of this are:

- As a user you can access *any* of the **X** applications available on any of the machines on your network. For example, even if your **X** server is running on a DOS PC, you can run your database system on a VAX with the VMS operating system, and your accounts package on an IBM mainframe.

- If the system is set up properly — so that applications can be started just by making a selection on a menu, say — then you need not be aware that the applications are running over the network, or that your machine is even connected to a network!

X can completely hide the architecture of your network. When you have just started using a new application (an **X** spreadsheet, say), for reasons of licence costs you might make it available on only one machine on the network. Then, the command invoked by the menu item for the spreadsheet would be something like:

```
on remote machine XYZ run SPREADSHEET, displaying to
here
```

Later on, when the spreadsheet gains acceptance in your organization and is heavily used, you might choose to make a copy available on every machine. Then, just by changing the command invoked by the menu to be:

```
run SPREADSHEET here, also displaying to here
```

users are switched to the new system. They see no difference — press the menu button, and up comes the spreadsheet — even though what's happening behind the scenes is very different.

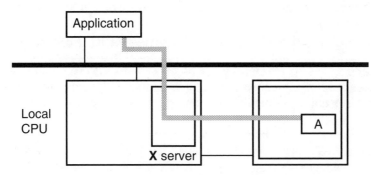

Figure A.   Application runs remotely but uses your display.

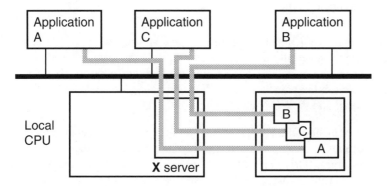

Figure B.   Several remote applications using your display.

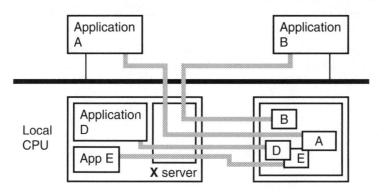

Figure C.   Local and remote applications together.

2.2 X integrates applications on different hardware and operating systems

2.2.2 Integrating head office, branches, and isolated sites

With **X**, and by using different types of network for different tasks, it is now practicable for an organization to link all its branches together — even one- or two-person outstations — providing a consistent set of applications to all its users everywhere.

Up to now our examples have all concerned local area networks (LANs) — those covering one building or a single site. But **X** can work over wide area networks (WANs) too, and this can be very useful for organizations with offices in several different locations.

Figure A shows three branch offices connected to a head office. All applications for Branch **A** run on machines back at head office. Branch **B** also uses the head office applications remotely, but it has its own workgroup computers running applications specific to the branch. The advantages are:

- Small branches (Branch **A**) need not have any technical staff to run their computers, since all the applications and all the data are back in head office (which presumably has DP and networking support staff). The only equipment in the branch is the machines running the stable and unchanging **X** servers, and the WAN communications link.

- Larger branches (Branch **B**), where workgroup or departmental computers, applications and data can be adequately supported, have their own computing resources. They can still use head office resources too, but even when there are problems with the WAN link they can continue to work on their own, although perhaps at a degraded level.

Branch **C** is a small, isolated site where just a single terminal is required. As with Branch **A**, the only computer needed is something to run the **X** server, plus a communications link to head office. This link can be provided over dial-up telephone lines or perhaps over ISDN if that is available, using SLIP (serial line Internet Protocol), or PPP (point-to-point protocol).

In all these examples, suitably fast communications links are needed if performance is not to be a problem (see Modules 4.5 and 13.2).

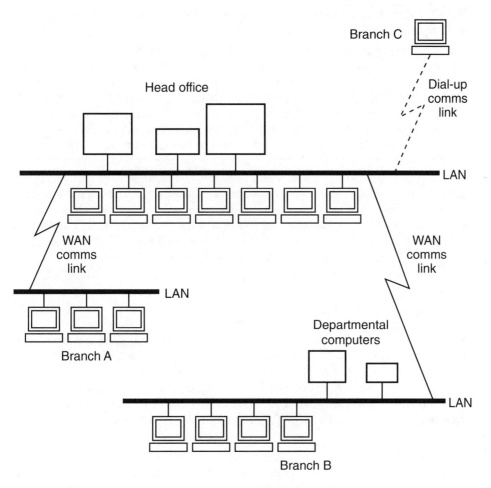

Figure A.   Remote branches using applications running at head office.

2.2   X integrates applications on different hardware and operating systems

2.2.3   Using non-windowed applications with X

You can run ordinary character-based applications in an **X** window using a special **X** client called a 'terminal emulator'. Other special clients emulate popular non-windowed systems, for example the IBM PC, so you can use their applications via your **X** system. Using these tools to run your old applications lets you migrate to **X** and to new applications with the minimum disruption to your organization.

If you already have a large investment (of money, or training, or organizational procedures) in applications, it isn't sensible to abandon everything you've got and start from scratch again with **X**. You want to continue using your existing software, while using **X** for any new applications that you purchase or develop in-house — it is 'your window onto the future'. We'll look at how you can use **X** in conjunction with applications for character-based terminals in this module, and in the next module we see how you can use **X** with other window systems.

Character-based applications

Most programs for workstations, micros, and medium-to-large sized computers were not written for any window system; they just output and read characters to and from the terminal, typically as ASCII. For example, commands to list the contents of directories, to print files (lpr on UNIX or PRINT on VMS), to compile programs (cc, f77, or FORTRAN), or edit text (vi, emacs, EDT, or TPU) all expect to be working with a character terminal such as a VT220, or a Wyse (or even a Teletype!).

On their own these programs can't work with **X** displays: they don't know how to issue requests to the server to write text to the screen, or handle events to get input from the keyboard. To overcome this problem, most **X** implementations provide a **terminal emulator**. This is an **X** client program which 'pretends' to the old application that it is a real terminal, but translates character output to **X** text-drawing requests, and translates **X** keyboard-input events into the equivalent input characters, as shown schematically in Figure A. The emulator doesn't have to run on the same computer as the 'old' application — they can be connected via the network as shown in Figure B.

We deal with terminal emulators (and software emulators for other systems) in more detail in Module 10.3. For now, it is enough to see that they let you use all your existing character-based applications without alteration on **X** systems, and you can run several simultaneously, each in its own **X** window.

Emulators for IBM PCs

There is a great deal of good software available for DOS PCs which people need to integrate with the rest of their organization's software environment. To avoid having a PC for some tasks and an **X**-based workstation for the rest, PC emulators have been developed which let you run a DOS application on your non-DOS, non-Intel platform, for example on your VAX or Sun workstation. The application uses your workstation's keyboard, and the PC 'screen' is shown in an **X** window on your workstation display. These systems emulate the CPU and graphics controller of the PC and don't require any PC hardware at all.

In the next module we look at systems that provide similar functionality but in a very different way — by running an **X** server within a DOS Windows environment on a hardware PC.

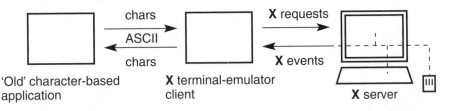

Figure A.   Terminal emulator translates character I/O to X events/requests.

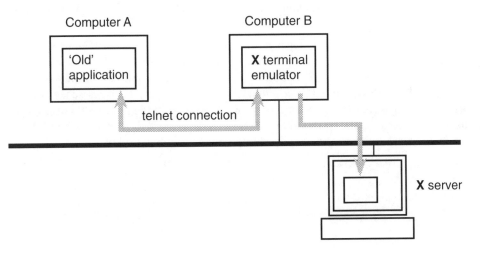

Figure B.   The terminal emulator program and the old application can run on separate computers.

2.2   X integrates applications on different hardware and operating systems

2.2.4   Using applications for other window systems with X

You can use applications for other window systems by means of special-purpose X servers running on top of the other system. This lets you migrate gradually from the other window system to **X**, or to continue indefinitely using applications for both systems.

If you are already running another window system, such as Microsoft Windows, Macintosh or SunView (or Atari or Amiga or NeXT), you can get special **X** servers that run on top of the original system, allowing you simultaneous access to both, as shown in Figure A. If you already have a (networked) PC, adding an **X** server to it can be a very cheap way to get **X** capability, especially if you need colour. (There are also PC **X** servers which run on native DOS and don't require Microsoft Windows, although for any of these systems your PC must of course have a network interface card and network software such as TCP/IP.)

Typically these servers allow you to cut and paste graphics and text between the two window systems; this can provide an almost seamless environment where the user doesn't really know which application is **X** and which is using the other window system. Figure B shows a network with many different types of **X** servers, illustrating the possibilities.

Very recently a different type of software has come on the market which allows you to run the other-window-system program on its native machine (for example, a Macintosh or a Microsoft Windows PC) but 'hijack' its input and display functions, so that these are performed on a remote **X** station![3] Figure C shows schematically a Macintosh application being used from an X-terminal. Using such systems, all your users can access applications written for these systems via **X**, instead of each user having a PC or Macintosh of their own in addition to their normal display.

Module 10.4 covers coexistence with applications from other systems in more detail.

---

[3]We use the term **X station** to mean any PC or workstation running an **X** server, or any special-purpose **X** display such as the X-terminals described in the next module.

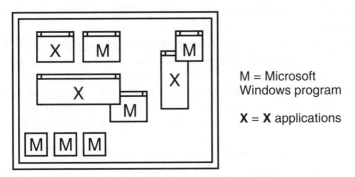

M = Microsoft
Windows program

X = **X** applications

Figure A. X server running 'on top of' Microsoft windows

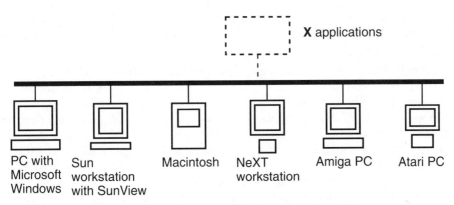

X applications

PC with   Sun   Macintosh   NeXT   Amiga PC   Atari PC
Microsoft workstation   workstation
Windows   with SunView

Figure B. Special X servers let you use X with many other window systems.

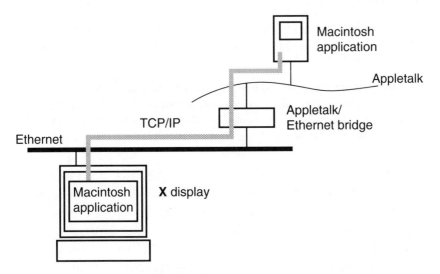

Macintosh
application

Appletalk

Appletalk/
Ethernet bridge

TCP/IP

Ethernet

Macintosh   **X** display
application

Figure C. Macintosh application connected to your X display.

2.2 X integrates applications on different hardware and operating systems

2.2.5   X-terminals: cheap substitutes for workstations?

X-terminals consist of the display hardware, an **X** server, and networking hardware and software manufactured as an integral unit. They give the user an environment that is just like a workstation, often offering simplified system administration, and sometimes at a lower cost. However, they may not be ideal for all applications.

Workstations are increasingly popular, for good reason: they give the user a better computing environment by allowing a windowed user interface and supporting multitasking — multiple simultaneous applications. But workstations have disadvantages. System administration is quite complex, as each workstation has its own configuration information and operating system that must be maintained. Workstations, especially when run diskless, can load the network heavily with both file traffic and program swapping or paging.

X-terminals — special hardware built just to run **X** — are intended to overcome these disadvantages, while still giving the user most of the benefits of the workstation, and often at a lower cost. An X-terminal is based on a simple and fast computer with an **X** server built in. The hardware includes a mouse, keyboard, graphics screen, and network interface; usually the server is stored in read-only memory, so a disk isn't needed. Because the **X** server is so completely and so cleanly separated from the applications, it is possible to isolate it in a package like this. Now *all* applications run remotely on other hosts, and what you've got is just a terminal! (But a terminal with a difference, because it runs **X**, and you can run lots of simultaneous applications from it.)

The advantages are:

- X-terminals give you the same interface as a workstation: you have a full **X** system, so you can run the same applications as before, though remotely over the network.

- System administration is   simplified. X-terminals are very like ordinary terminals: they don't have any operating system   to be maintained, so setting them up and moving them to another network is easy, and they are easier to restart after power failures as they don't have disks or filesystems to be recovered or rebuilt after failure.

- The X-terminal's hardware and software is simpler — no other applications are running on it, there's no big operating system, no disks, etc. — so it should more reliable than complex workstations.

- X-terminals can be cheaper than workstations, again because they are simpler and a lot of the complex hardware and software can be omitted. The entry price especially is lower, and is getting even less as X-terminals become commodities.

- Upgrading your overall system to get more power is cheaper. Your display elements (X-terminals) aren't altered: you only have to upgrade the application-running CPUs. If your network consists entirely of workstations, upgrading to a bigger CPU on the desktops often involves changing the display and keyboard as well, involving you in needless expense.

Performance of networks of X-terminals is satisfactory, and network loading isn't usually a problem (see Modules 4.5 and 13.2).

But remember, X-terminals are only terminals, so you still need central computers for your applications to run on — we're almost back to time-sharing! The classical argument in favour of this is: instead of giving N users one unit of CPU power each in the form of a workstation, provide a single CPU centrally with N units of power. Most of the time the majority of users don't use their full unit of power, so there is usually a lot of spare processing power available for anyone who has a transient requirement for more than a single unit. You can allocate CPU power in a precise way if you wish, by giving each workgroup its own host on which to run its applications.

Of course, for people working on their own, it doesn't make sense to buy one CPU for applications plus a separate X-terminal: a workstation is obviously the simplest solution.

For more about the implementation of X-terminals, see Module 3.2.1.

2.3   Benefits of a standard GUI throughout your organization

By using a consistent set of libraries (or 'toolkit') you can construct or buy applications, for all your different computers, which provide the same graphical user interface. Previously each vendor's computer had its own interface which was inconsistent with the others, making life difficult for users. Motif and OPEN LOOK are examples of widely available standardized user interfaces.

Before **X** was developed, one of the biggest problems for systems managers was getting computers from different manufacturers to interoperate with each other in a sensible, easy-to-use way. Initially there were networking problems; with the development of de facto practical standards like TCP/IP (and perhaps OSI in the future) these have been overcome.

But there was still a problem for the users of window systems: each vendor had their own system with its own unique (and often proprietary) interface. You could not run, say, a VMS windowed application onto your Apollo workstation — and even if it were possible, using it would be difficult because its style of interface would be completely different to all the other applications you were using. For example, the Macintosh interface, Presentation Manager/Microsoft Windows, and Sun's SunView are all completely different and incompatible.

X can now solve this problem by allowing the same interface to be provided on any and every **X** system.[4] (This is usually done by building a 'user interface toolkit' (Module 1.2.1) for each system that applications are to be written for, providing the same style of user interface on each platform, although here we are not really concerned with how a particular interface is implemented.) What is important to the end-user is the program's **look and feel**: the visual appearance of the components in the interface and how you operate them. In fact the same look and feel can be provided in different ways in different programs, and this is often the case in practice. For example, there are many different toolkits, written in different languages and not based on the same code at all, which provide standard user interfaces (Figure A). In other words, the interface seen by the user, and the programming interface used by the application developer (the API or application programming interface) are distinct and should not be confused.

Advantages of a single graphical user interface

Making the user interfaces consistent in all the programs you use has many benefits:

- New applications are *easier to learn*. Once you are familiar with a scrollbar in one program, you recognize it in all other programs as well, and can use it without further instruction (so your existing knowledge is leveraged).

- Well-designed applications are *easier to use*. Because menus, scrollbars, push-buttons, and so on, are always visible, instead of having to *remember*

---

[4]It's ironic that it is precisely because the **X** designers didn't provide a standard user interface that **X** is able to provide a universal user interface when desired!

what actions or options the program provides, the user just has to look at the screen and *see* what the program is offering. (There is a similar contrast between adjusting the time on a mechanical alarm clock which has separate, obvious, and labelled controls for its various functions, and setting an electronic watch which provides many, many functions, all of which have to be invoked by pressing only two buttons in apparently magic sequences that give different effects depending on which 'mode' the watch is in.)

This greater ease of use is particularly noticeable with programs used only occasionally, in which you never really get a chance to master all the commands and remember them fully.

- *Applications integrate seamlessly.* You may have on your screen at one time a mix of applications running on different VAXes, IBMs, and UNIX machines throughout the network, but they are all consistent visually and in the way they are used. That is, the way you use the scrollbar in the IBM applications is exactly the same as in the Hewlett-Packard ones. This is why scenarios such as those outlined in Module 2.2.1 are possible.

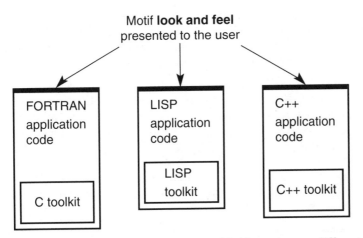

Figure A.   The same look and feel can be provided by many very different toolkits.

2.4   X allows distributed computing, or centralized, or both

You can decide whether to make an application available for users to run locally on their own workstations, or to provide it only for remote running on machines that are administered centrally by the DP/IT department. Centralized applications can give more secure administration and better control of the organization's data.

When running a network of distributed workstations you must ensure that data and applications on the workstations are backed up properly, and that applications and systems software are kept up-to-date and consistent across the whole network. By choosing the appropriate mixture of X-terminals (or PC **X** servers) connected to central hosts on the one hand, and workstations on the other, you can manage your software and data very precisely, giving them the appropriate level of control and security.

You can consider three different levels of 'ownership' for programs and data:

1. **Corporate**. The information belongs to the whole organization, so it needs to be administered centrally.

   All applications and data should be kept on central machines ('in the computer room'), with X-terminals or PC-based servers on the users' desks for access to the applications (Figure A). In this way, proper data security can be maintained, and only approved applications can be run.

   As the figure illustrates, even the remote offices use only X-terminals. System administration is kept very simple: no data or applications are stored at the remote site, so no technical support or operations staff are needed at the branch. 'Starting up' the system in the branch merely requires turning on the X-terminals.

2. **Departmental**. The information is specific to a department or workgroup. Applications run on machines within the department, again with X-terminals or PC **X** servers on the users' desktops.

   The example in Figure B shows three workgroups. Two are in the organization's head office, and one in a remote branch office connected via a wide area link. Even if this link fails, the users in the branch can continue working, using their departmental applications on the computers within the branch.

3. **Personal**. Individuals have their own programs and they look after their own data, which are stored on their own machines.

   The best way to implement this is to provide each user with their own workstation (Figure C). Users can load programs and data onto their machines as they require; if the machines are networked (even 'standalone' users occasionally need to swap information or electronic mail with other people), the users can continue to work even when the network fails, as all their resources are on their local machine.

Of course the three approaches can be combined. People often want to use the central facilities (such as the accounts system, or the company database) provided by the organization; they also need to use the special tools specific to their own department (such as a CAD system, or simulation package); and finally they have their own personal tools (for example, a name and address database, and their favourite, that is, non-standard, text editor, spreadsheet, etc.) As we mentioned before, if the system has been carefully set up, the users need not know which applications are running where — they may not realize that applications are running over the network, or even that there is a network at all!

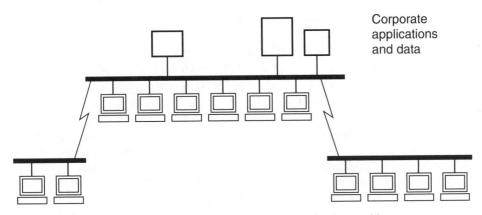

Figure A.   Centralized computing: X terminals and central hosts.

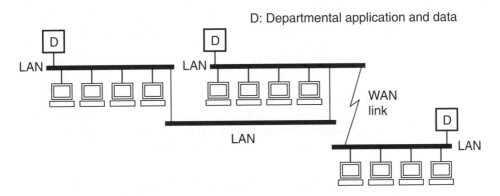

Figure B.   Departmental computing: hosts within workgroups.

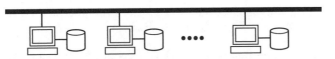

Figure C.   Distributed computing: local applications on workstations.

2.5 X fundamentally changes software and hardware decisions

Because you can deliver any application to your users, no matter what type of machine it's running on, your choice of hardware isn't so important any more. So now you decide 'which application is the best for our users', then you buy it (as well as the machine it runs best on, if you don't have one already!).

Computing is about helping people do their job better or more easily; it's about delivering applications to *users*. (In this context 'users' means anyone who needs a computer for their work — senior managers, secretaries, network managers, graphic artists, applications programmers, data-entry clerks, etc.) The more freedom you have in selecting applications, the more likely you are to give your users what they want and need. The emphasis should be on the *application*, and how good and how useful it is.

But because of technical limitations, until recently most organizations had to limit themselves to applications which ran on their 'official' choice of computer. There were many 'VMS shops' or 'IBM companies' using only software written for DEC's VMS, or for IBM's MVS operating systems, for their large applications. For desktop applications, many organizations standardized on either the PC or the Macintosh, and bought only PC or Macintosh applications. People made these decisions because there was no general method of providing all the necessary applications to their users on different platforms. And these decisions were sensible: there were major technological barriers to truly integrated multi-vendor networks. But there was a price: these organizations were locking themselves out of all the excellent software that was available for other systems, so their end-users were missing out on good tools which could have helped them.

X changes all this. Because any **X** application can display to any **X** station (X-terminal, PC **X** server, or workstation) you gain three major benefits when building your organization's system:

1. The choice of what hardware to put on the user's desktop is no longer critical. As long as it runs **X**, the user can access every application you provide. Your decision now reduces to questions that are relatively easily answered: about price and performance, whether the user needs colour, or a large screen, etc.

   Thus you might provide cheap monochrome PC **X** servers for data-entry clerks, and high-performance colour workstations for CAD designers. Both will be able to access your **X**-based electronic mail system, and both can use your **X**-based 'desktop' facilities such as diary-manager, calculator, etc. (Of course, if you are also using non-**X** applications this reduces your choice. For example, if users need access to a DOS word processor, giving them a PC with an **X** server is the easiest solution.)

2. When you are choosing **X** applications it doesn't really matter what hardware or operating system platform they run on; it's the quality of the appli-

cation that's important — how much it will benefit your organization and your users.

The factors influencing your decision about what hardware to use have changed completely. For example, even if you have only IBM mainframes currently, and Macintoshs on the users' desks, there is no technical reason why you shouldn't provide **X**-based DTP facilities running on central UNIX systems, and a new database on a VAX. Once you have found the application you want, you choose from the platforms that support it, considering factors such as hardware price and performance, software price, reputation of supplier, and whether you want to support extra operating systems with the extra training and maintenance costs that involves.

3. When developing a new application, you only have to write it once using **X**, for the platform of your choice. Then it's immediately available to everyone in your organization, unlike the old days when you had to port it to each of your platforms, and had to maintain these different versions for the lifetime of the application.

Thus, **X** is giving you true open systems.

A pleasant side-effect may be that your software licence costs are low. With a network of workstations, you usually have to license a separate copy of the application for each workstation. With **X**, you may be able to license a single copy for one central machine, and have several users running it simultaneously on that machine but displaying to their own **X** stations; some **X** software is licensed on this basis now. If the software is particularly expensive, it's often cost-effective to buy a single large machine dedicated to running that application for all the users on the network: the savings in multiple licence fees often more than offset the extra hardware cost.

However, increasingly, applications are being controlled with a **floating licence**; it doesn't matter which machine you actually execute the application on, but you are limited to a particular number of simultaneous users on the network. Floating licences remove this pleasant side-effect.

2.6   The financial benefits of using X

X preserves your investment in hardware, by letting you continue to use old hardware while still allowing you to migrate to new, X-based, applications. Your increased freedom of choice lets you benefit from the better price/performance ratios of hardware. You also gain from increased user productivity due to better interfaces.

Preserve investment

X can help you preserve your investment in existing hardware and software. You can continue to **use your existing software**, for both character-based terminals and other window systems, using the methods described in Modules 2.2.3 and 2.2.4 (and in more detail in Modules 10.3 and 10.4).

Elderly workstations, which may not have the power to run today's resource-intensive applications, can be used predominantly as X-terminals, but with some small applications running locally to minimise the load on central machines.

Old PCs, which again don't have the power required for even the new DOS applications, can also be used as X-terminals for non-intensive applications by means of PC **X** servers. **More powerful PCs** can be converted to use **X** as well as other PC applications. For many organizations this is particularly important, as they have hundreds or even thousands of PCs. Converting them to **X** is a cheap way of extending their useful life: the incremental cost is small, and you still have them available to run their own DOS applications when necessary. For the support staff this route provides easy and cheap migration; you are not removing anything — just adding to what is already there. (For system managers this can be a very attractive route, because it's often politically expedient not to throw out equipment recommended in the past, even if it is obsolete now.)

Take advantage of better price/performance

CPU power is becoming very cheap (if you buy the right CPUs!). For example, RISC workstations and workgroup computers, and 386- and 486-based PCs are very cost-effective ways of providing raw power. The challenge is to be able to make effective use of this cheap resource. **X** helps you do this, by letting you distribute your applications over the network on whatever CPUs you provide. You can choose between a huge central timesharing machine connected to **X** terminals, or have several central large RISC machines running different applications again connected to X-terminals, or cheap PCs as multitasking workstations on every desk running most of the individual user's computing load. With **X** you can take advantage of 'cheap MIPS' anywhere you decide to plug them into your network.

User productivity

The uniform user interface that **X** lets you provide across your whole computing environment also brings financial advantages. Your users learn new applications more quickly, which saves in time and training costs. They are likely to be happier with applications, and therefore to use them better. In particular, non computer-specialists will be much more comfortable using your organization's systems, so that introducing new applications, new procedures and tools across your organization may be feasible in a way that wasn't possible before.

At a high level in your organization, **senior management** may now be able to use the MIS systems directly rather than via an intermediary or by reading printed reports. This means that the senior people's expertise and knowledge can be applied more effectively to your organization's work. For example, if a manager uses printouts of a spreadsheet produced by someone else, the spreadsheet is only a static report, whereas if the manager uses the spreadsheet directly there is a two-way information flow. The spreadsheet becomes an interactive tool for examining the organization's business and dynamically exploring the information available, and the manager's knowledge and expertise is likely to be incorporated into the spreadsheet model where other people can make use of it too.

Other benefits — scalability and licensing

Because any **X** application running on a host computer can work with any **X** display, you take separate decisions about what hardware to run the applications on, and what to put on people's desktops. This lets you spend your hardware budget more effectively, because different users have different requirements in terms of performance and facilities, and you only buy what you really need to. We'll look at this in depth in the next module.

In the previous module we saw also that **X** can save you money on licence costs in some situations, by reducing the number of separate machines running the licensed application.

In the next module we look at how you benefit financially from being able to choose which hardware and software to provide in the various areas of your organization, and how **X** system upgrades can be very cost-efficient.

2.6   The financial benefits of using X

2.6.1   Savings from freedom of choice

The freedom of choice **X** gives you in buying applications and hardware can save you money by letting you apply funds where they are most needed. **X** gives more flexibility in upgrading your systems, too.

Users. Different users have different requirements in terms of performance and facilities. For example, in a very large organization a cross-section of needs might include:

- Data entry clerks: simple low performance monochrome screens.
- Secretaries: medium resolution screen for word processing, higher resolution and perhaps colour for DTP work and presentation graphics.
- Engineers: high-performance, high-resolution workstations for three-dimensional image processing and CAE or CAD design work.

Applications. Different types of applications also have a wide range of resource requirements:

- Large databases and other I/O bound applications: these need to run on central machines with large disks and fast I/O subsystems.
- Compute- and memory-intensive applications: these need large, fast machines or supercomputers.
- Real-time systems: for example, process control, network management, real-time financial displays. These often need special-purpose hardware, although their CPU-power requirements may not be great.
- Accounts systems: these need a balance of I/O and CPU power, typically provided on a mid-range machine.
- Office automation, electronic mail, and DTP: these often run on one or more small machines, serving specific groups of users.

From this you can see that the requirements for the desktop and the computer room are unrelated: Figure A shows a scenario with all permutations of machine performance requirements. What this means to you is that you buy only the hardware you really need, and you spend your money where it gives you the best value. Money you save on desktop units can be applied to buying large workhorse CPUs for your critical applications.

Improved upgradability

With **X** you get flexibility in the upgradability of your system. If an application is used by only a few people, run it on a small machine; if its use spreads later, you can upgrade that machine, and *only* that one, leaving everything else unchanged. (Apart from cost, this also minimizes the disruption to users, and the load on your support staff.) When you need more CPU power on your network, you can add it in arbitrary-sized pieces, by plugging in new central machines as needed. Contrast this with upgrading a network of distributed workstations: to give more power to everybody you have to upgrade each workstation, and often this will mean a complete replacement, swapping a perfectly good monitor and keyboard as well as the processing unit of the workstation. With **X** you will more often 'augment' rather than 'upgrade', as hardware manufacturers of small to medium machines rarely offer good value for true upgrades.

On the desktop too, you can upgrade incrementally. If one user's requirements grow, and they need faster graphics, etc., you need only upgrade that one machine, perhaps from a PC-based system to a workstation with special-purpose graphics hardware to provide the performance improvement needed.

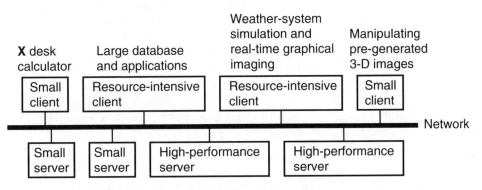

Figure A.   Different performance requirements for desktop and central computers.

2.7   How X can help different categories of people

X has been widely adopted because it solves real problems encountered every day in providing computer services. Almost everybody in your organization can benefit from it, from programmer to your director of IT.

In this module we pull together all the advantages of **X** that we have mentioned earlier, and see how they apply to different people within your organization, and in other parts of the computer industry.

The system manager has increased flexibility in buying software and hardware. Software can now be chosen on the basis of the benefit to the user without worrying too much about the difficulty of integration into the overall system. Hardware from different vendors, and even non-standard machine architectures (for example, special-purpose database engines or file servers) can be introduced relatively easily as long as they have an **X** interface.

Support staff have a smaller training and user-error correction load, as the applications have a consistent interface and are easier to use. Support of remote sites — your own or your customers' — is easier. If there is a suitable network connection you don't have to visit the site: instead, execute the application causing the problem remotely on the distant machine, displaying back to your own **X** station in your own office, so you can actually *see* what the problems are rather than having to debug verbally over the phone. This does not pose great security problems for most customers, because they are giving you neither the application nor the data it is using; they remain securely on the customer's premises.

(But we should also add that moving to highly distributed computing based on a network of **X** machines requires its own discipline, and will impose some extra load on technical support staff and the system manager, especially during the initial phases.)

Users have better-designed and easier-to-use interfaces, making their jobs less frustrating, and improving their productivity. Multiple applications on screen make many tasks possible now that were previously tedious or impossible.

Professional and management users can make more effective use of computers. Good applications are now more accessible, so instead of delegating tasks involving software tools to specialists, managers can do the work themselves, and they can interact with the systems and explore the information, which wasn't possible before.

IT director/CIO have the assurance that they have minimized their dependence on any one vendor, because of the freedom of choice for both central and desktop machines. The uniform user interface available across different vendors, and easier-to-use applications, make it possible to introduce new corporate systems and tools more quickly, more cheaply, and with less disruption of the staff.

Software developers, in-house and third-party, have a wider potential customer base. Commercial developers can now address much larger markets, instead of limiting themselves to sites that had standardized on their particular choice of platform. (For example, if your VAX VMS-based network management system is good enough, people in a traditionally Hewlett-Packard UNIX-based site can buy and use it if it is **X**-based). For small specialist developers, this larger market makes some projects economic which previously were not feasible.

Internal developers need to write an application only once for it to be available to everyone in your organization. In the old days, you had to provide a separate version for each machine-type you had — for instance, one for PCs, another for Macintoshes, yet others for VMS, UNIX, etc.

All developers benefit from lower development cost and time, as a lot of the programming and design work — for the GUI — has already been done. They can concentrate on the functionality of the system, rather than worrying about internal user interface details (in other words, what's inside the toolkit), and produce better applications.

With the emerging dominance of **X**, developers of large packages (for statistics, data analysis, graphics, and so on) can reasonably restrict their device support, making **X** their only standard for screen-based input and output. By having only one output format (instead of dozens — for DEC terminals, Tektronix terminals, etc.) they reduce their development load. They can also optimize the **X** implementation since they no longer need generalized code to handle all possible different output devices.

Hardware developers see increased demands for large-CPU machines to run the **X** applications. We have already mentioned that it is now good economics to use a lot of CPU power to make applications easier for the user, and the extra work involved in providing a GUI like **X** does use more resources.

Developers of new X-terminals and workstations supporting **X** have a large target market immediately. Before, they would have had to spend a lot of time and money developing a window system of their own design, and even more effort marketing it.

Sales and marketing have an attractive and powerful technology to sell, offering real benefits to the purchasers as well as the end users of the systems. Software and hardware products can be sold outside their traditional vendor-specific markets, because they are now so easily integrated. And finally, because the new **X** applications are much easier to use than their predecessors, a *user-led* demand is being created for the products — people are asking to buy!

Summary

This chapter has described the benefits you can get from **X**. It lets you integrate your applications on all your different platforms into a single cohesive computing environment for your users. This close integration is possible because **X** can provide the same user interface on any platform. You can manage programs and data centrally, or distribute them amongst the functional units of your organization. All this flexibility and freedom of choice can give you considerable financial benefits. Finally, we summarized the advantages people in different positions in an organization can derive from **X**.

This concludes the first Part of the book, '**X** in a Nutshell'. In the next Part we go back and look much more closely at how **X** works, examining each of its components in detail, and seeing how they interact with one another.

Part

2

How X Works, in Detail, and How the User Sees It

So far we have seen an outline of the architecture of **X**, *and the benefits that* **X** *can provide for your organization.*

In this second Part of the book we look at the internal mechanisms of the system in some detail — how to use the system is covered later, in Part 3. You need to understand some of the mechanisms so you can fully appreciate how the system is used, but if you are very keen to look at how the system is used, then jump ahead now, and come back to Part 2 later.

In Part 2 we are building on the quick overview of the system presented in Part 1, where you saw that **X** *consists of servers, clients, and communications between them. We are now going to look at the system components in much more depth and will cover:*

- *The server's role, and how it handles input, and output in particular.*

- *Communication between clients and server, including network factors and loadings, and how input is passed from server to client.*

- *Clients and how they are built up.*

- *Defining a 'look and feel', and how you use toolkits to provide a consistent user interface.*

- *Window management, and its contribution to the user interface.*

- *Mechanisms to support interworking of multiple applications.*

Chapter

The Server — the Display Control Software

3.1   The role of the server
    3.1.1 What the server does not include

3.2   Implementations of the **X** server
    3.2.1 Specific server implementations — X-terminals
    3.2.2 Extra features for X-terminals

3.3   How the server handles output to the screen
    3.3.1 Visibility of windows, and clipping
    3.3.2 Graphics requests — requests for output

3.4   The server contains the only display hardware dependence in the system

3.5   Handling text and fonts
    3.5.1 The **X** Font Server
    3.5.2 Graphics requests for text

3.6   Handling colour
    3.6.1 Device-independent colour specifications
    3.6.2 Calibrating hardware for device-independent colour
    3.6.3 Colour capabilities and colormaps
    3.6.4 Using many different colormaps together

3.7   Pictures and images — bitmaps, cursors and pixmaps
    3.7.1 Pixmaps — **X**'s most general picture format
    3.7.2 Cursors

3.8   Extras you may want or need: server extensions
    3.8.1 How extensions affect applications

Introduction

This chapter looks in detail at the facilities the server provides, how it is implemented, what it contains, and also what it does not contain but leaves to the clients to handle instead. Most of this chapter deals with output — drawing text and graphics. Input is covered in the next chapter; as we shall see, most of the input processing is handled not by the server itself but by the clients.

53

3.1   The role of the server

The **X** server receives requests from client applications and actions them, usually producing output on the display screen. It controls the display's input devices, and sends user input to client applications. It also manages internal resources such as fonts and cursors, manages colour tables, etc. The design goals of **X** have meant that the server contains as little as possible.

The server is the **base system**; everything else is in the client and can be relatively easily changed, but whatever is in the server is fixed. (Remember, the server is very analogous to a terminal: you can't change the server, just as you can't change the internal operation of a VT220 terminal after it has been manufactured.)

The main functions of the server (Figure A) are:

- **Processing output.** Requests arrive from many clients, and have to be actioned: by manipulating windows, drawing text and graphics, or sending information back to the client. This aspect of the server involves:

  - Creating, configuring and destroying windows.
  - Handling fonts and drawing text.
  - Drawing lines, arcs, areas, etc.
  - Drawing bitmapped (pictorial) images.

  Related to output, the server must **manage resources** at the request of clients. It has windows, fonts, cursors, off-screen images called **pixmaps**, colour lookup tables called **colormaps**, and tables called **graphics contexts** to control how graphics are drawn. These management and output functions are described in detail in the remainder of this chapter.

- **Processing input.** When you type on the keyboard or use the mouse the server has to detect this and send corresponding **X** events to the appropriate clients, to inform them of the input. However, as most of this work relating to input processing is handled by the client, we'll cover it in the next chapter.

- **Managing client-defined data** such as properties, which clients use to communicate with each other. Communication between clients is a topic in itself, covered in Chapter 9.

- **Handling network connections** to multiple simultaneous remote and local applications.

Of course, many of these functions require the server to handle the hardware it is running on, or at least interact with the operating system on the server's machine.

Server design considerations

As little as possible of the overall functionality of the system is contained in the server. The advantages of this approach are:

- The server remains small, allowing it to be implemented on a wide range of machines, not all of which will have large memory. It also makes it easier to implement the server in read-only memory (ROM), which is often necessary for X-terminals.

- The less there is in the server, the more stable and reliable it will be.

- Functionality in a client program is easier to change or enhance, whereas the server is difficult to change: it is complex system software, it has usually been supplied in binary form by a third-party vendor, and may even be in ROM. New user interfaces and sophisticated input handling can be provided within the application. For example, audio input, or special keyboard processing for physically disabled users can be handled by a client; these can then work with any standard server, whereas server-based implementations would be tied to a particular manufacturer's equipment. (See Modules 4.2.3 and 4.3.)

- The speed of any code in the server is fixed — it is determined by the CPU the server is running on. On the other hand, you can always speed up anything in a client by running it on a different, faster CPU.

The next module describes the functions you might expect the server to handle but which are in fact left to the client for the reasons above.

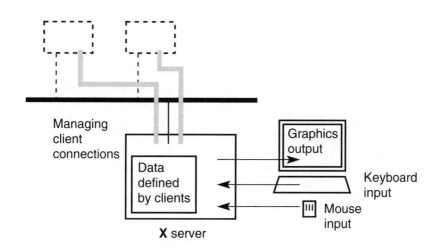

Figure A. The functions of the server.

3.1   The role of the server

3.1.1   What the server does not include

Many functions such as window management, the user interface, and interpreting keyboard input are not performed by the server but are left to the client. This makes it possible to implement the server on a wide range of machines, and makes the system much more flexible.

In **X** many system functions are left to the **X** client program, which in other window systems would usually be handled by the base window system:

- The **X** client has to redraw the contents of any of its windows which were covered up but which have become exposed again. Instead of remembering the contents of the obscured parts of the windows, the server just notices when they are re-exposed and sends a notifications to the client, effectively telling *it* to repaint the missing parts. It does this by sending an **expose event**, which specifies which area of the window has been freshly exposed (Figure A).

- There are no special facilities for resizing the image in an **X** window — zooming in or out, for example. This has to be done by the client, which recomputes at the new size whatever is to be drawn, and then sends requests to the server to clear the old image and draw the new one.

- All the application user interface code — for menus, scrollbars, pushbuttons, etc. — is in the client, so you can create any interface style you want by altering your own program, and without affecting the server. (Chapter 6 deals with the application user interface.)

- Window manager functions are performed by the separate window manager program, not by the server. As an example, when you are resizing a window by dragging the window border with the mouse, you get a 'rubber-band' outline to indicate the new window size; it is the window manager that is watching how the mouse moves and that is sending requests to the server to successively draw and erase the rectangles to give the rubber-band effect. All the server is doing is sending mouse-motion events to the window manager, and actioning any drawing requests it receives (Figure B). When the window size is finally determined, the window manager resizes the window (by sending the appropriate request to the server). The server sends an event to the application telling it that its window's size has changed, and only at this late stage does the application take any action — typically redrawing the window, and perhaps zooming the image to fit the new window size. (Chapter 8 covers window managers in detail.)

- Interpreting keyboard ('character') input. The server doesn't know whether the client wants key presses to be interpreted as ASCII characters, or EBCDIC, or as a representation of some non-English language; so it leaves this to the client. (We discuss this is depth in Module 4.2.2.)

- Interpreting mouse input. The server passes straight to the client information about where the mouse button-clicks, motion, etc., occur.

In the next module we go back and concentrate on the server and how it is implemented.

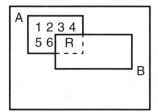 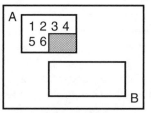

Lower window partially covered. When window B moves...

...rectangle R exposed. Server sends expose event to client A, specifing size and location of R

Then client A redraws rectangle R

Figure A.   The client redraws freshly-exposed areas of windows as they are uncovered.

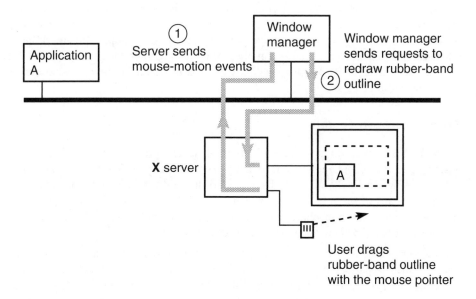

User drags rubber-band outline with the mouse pointer

Figure B.   The window manager client controls size and position of application windows in response to user actions.

3.2   Implementations of the X server

There are many different implementations of the **X** server for platforms ranging from standard multitasking workstations to simple PCs. Servers can contain extra system administration and usability features to make them easier to use and manage, as well as 'extensions' which provide graphics and other capabilities not offered by the basic **X** system.

The MIT **X** Consortium produces sample implementations of server and clients. Sample servers are provided for a wide range of systems. (By 'sample' we mean they are not 'reference implementations' — just because an MIT **X** program does something, it doesn't mean it is correct. The official standard is the document from MIT that defines the '**X** Protocol'; if a program disagrees with the Protocol, the program is wrong.)

All the machines supported by the MIT sample implementation are UNIX workstations, but that is only because MIT does not have the resources to port to non-UNIX systems. Hardware manufacturers and third-party vendors have developed servers for other workstations and operating systems, and other systems including X-terminals, DOS PCs and other personal computers such as Atari and Amiga. There are even plug-in cards containing server code, graphics controller and display memory, for a variety of systems.

Conceptually an **X** server is simple, and a schematic is shown in Figure A for the simplest case — a server running on a workstation. However, many implementations are more complex because of special requirements imposed by the target machine, or because of extra facilities added to the basic system. For example, Figure B shows schematically that an X-terminal is complicated by having to provide many of the basic facilities such as network handling which would be provided by the operating system in a workstation or PC.

Extra features in servers

While the **X** standards do not require it, almost all servers provide some convenient way of starting the first client application, so that you can initiate your **X** session. If the server didn't have this facility, you would have to start the application by entering commands on the keyboard of the remote host on which you'll be executing the application. So, effectively these startup mechanisms save you having to walk around your office to the remote machine. (System startup is described in Module 11.1.)

Another common extra is the facility of a **virtual screen** larger than your physical screen, which is particularly useful on PC **X** servers with low-resolution screens with relatively few pixels, for example, 600 x 480. The virtual screen may be much larger, say 1600 x 1000 pixels, and your physical window acts as a viewing port onto part of this larger area. This lets you start all the applications you need, but keep some of them off-screen out of the way, so that your limited screen space is kept uncluttered for the applications you are currently using. Some window managers provide a similar facility, illustrated in Module 8.1.1. (This facility is also sometimes called a **virtual desktop** or a **virtual root window**.)

Extensions to servers

When **X** was initially developed, its designers realized that certain functionality would have to be added to the system later, either because the technology had not yet matured enough, or because the functionality was not crucially important, or just because as any system develops people want it to do more and more. To handle add-ons like this cleanly, **X** has a well-defined mechanism for adding extended functionality to the server.

Specialised servers with extensions for live video windows, or PostScript or other special facilities are available. The extension mechanism is also used to incorporate new functionality into new releases of standard servers, for example the support for non-rectangular windows which was added in Release 4. By using extensions rather than adding in new functions directly, compatibility is maintained with earlier releases and consistent operation on servers from different vendors is possible. (See Module 3.8 for more detail.)

Now we look at X-terminals in detail, as they illustrate some important features of the **X** system as a whole.

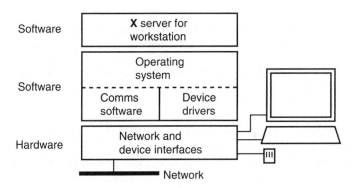

Figure A.   Schematic structure of an X server.

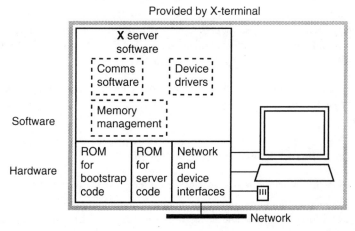

Figure B.   An X-terminal has to provide many non-X functions as well as the server code.

3.2 Implementations of the X server

3.2.1 Specific server implementations — X-terminals

Special-purpose X-terminals are becoming increasingly popular. An X-terminal is just a package consisting of an **X** server, the CPU and memory to run it on, mouse, keyboard, and network interface.

X-terminals illustrate some important features of **X**. In fact, a good way to understand **X** is to think of the server very much as a terminal. Most of the points mentioned below are also true for many of the **X** servers that run on PCs: these servers effectively transform the PC into an X-terminal. First we look at how X-terminals resemble ordinary terminals, and then at the important differences.

Similarity of X- and character-based terminals

Figure A illustrates many of the ways in which an X-terminal is like a character-based terminal:

- The terminal reads characters from the keyboard (or reads keyboard events in the case of **X**) and passes them 'over the wire' to the application.

- The application doesn't run in the terminal itself, but on a host at the other end of the wire.

- The application sends 'commands' (escape sequences) to the terminal, to affect the display, and the commands are fairly similar in the two cases. For example, the escape sequence to write characters 'ABC' at cursor position X,Y is similar to the **X** request to draw font characters 'ABC' at pixel coordinates X,Y. And the 'clear screen' sequence is analogous to the **X** 'delete window' request.

- X-terminals, just like other ones, 'are faster at night'. Because all the applications are running on central hosts which are shared among many users, you may have patches of poor performance during the day when many people are using the system heavily. But at night you probably have the machines to yourself, so they seem faster!

- Terminals don't have any disks or files that can be damaged by a sudden failure of the electricity supply. After a power failure, you just switch on again.

Differences between X- and character terminals

Of course, X-terminals have many advantages over ordinary terminals:

- You can run many simultaneous applications instead of having only one at a time on your screen.

- You can be connected to many hosts simultaneously instead of to just one.

- You can dynamically select the host you want for each **X** application, whereas character terminals have a hardwired connection to a single host (or to a terminal server, which is really just a special intermediate type of host).

- You have a full GUI instead of a simple character interface.

- You have the full functionality of the mouse.

One disadvantage of X-terminals is that they have a dynamic requirement for memory, which is not easily predictable: the more applications you run, and the more fonts and other resources you use, the more memory you need. Well-engineered X-terminals warn you if you are running out of memory, so you can avoid any serious effects. And, some recent X-terminals have virtual memory systems, paging memory over the network using NFS (the network file system), giving you practically limitless memory.

In the next module we look at how many X-terminals provide a lot of extra useful features.

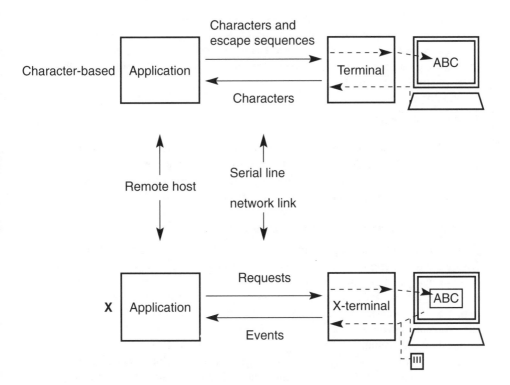

Figure A.   Similarity of X-and character-based terminals.

3.2   Implementations of the X server

3.2.2   Extra features for X-terminals

Many X-terminals provide a lot of extra functionality, both to make the terminals easier to use and administer, and to improve their performance.

Many innovations in **X** have been led by X-terminal manufacturers, not least because to survive commercially they must make their products as attractive as possible, and by adding features they have been able to differentiate X-terminals from competitive workstations, for example.

X-terminals provide many facilities that make it easy for the system manager to handle large numbers of X-terminals on a network:

- Facilities to start up a user session simply. (See xdm and XDMCP in Module 11.1 for much more detail.)

- Facilities for managing fonts for the network as a whole rather than on a per-machine basis. (See Module 3.5.1 for details of the **X** font server.)

- The option of storing the **X** server in ROM within the X-terminal (which makes getting the terminal up-and-running very easy) or of downloading the **X** server code from a file-server on the network (which makes it easy to upgrade the terminals' servers and ensure they are all using the same version or revision level).

Performance extras

Increasingly, X-terminals and PC **X** servers are allowing local clients. For terminals this is almost a contradiction in terms (if applications run inside it, it's not a terminal) but the clients provided are very restricted. The two most common options are a local window manager and a local telnet or local terminal emulator. These facilities simplify setup and reduce the amount of network traffic, which is especially useful when working over very slow network links such as serial lines.

The local window manager comes into its own where there is a high network latency, that is, the round-trip time from server to client and back again is long, which is often the case with satellite links or long-haul networks. If the window manager is tracking the mouse interactively, as when dragging a rubber-band outline, you get very bad response with high-latency connections; running a local window manager gets over this problem. However, for such networks you would probably be better off using a workstation and running as few applications as possible remotely. (For more about latency, see Modules 4.5 and 13.2.) The terminal manufacturers are also working (in conjunction with the MIT **X** Consortium) on standards to improve the performance of **X** over very slow networks (Module 13.2.1). As part of this, vendors are looking at running more applications locally in the terminal, to avoid the bottleneck of the slow network.

As these features develop and become more widespread, they are often adopted by other server vendors as well. This is especially true for PC **X** servers, because with these a PC is very little different from a true X-terminal.[1] In fact, most extras that are generally applicable are implemented on almost every commercial server in time, and many have been adopted as formal standards by the MIT **X** Consortium, or are included in their release so they become de facto standards.

---

[1] An interesting market prediction is that sales for **X** servers for PCs will overtake sales of purpose-built X-terminals in the next few years.

3.3   How the server handles output to the screen

X outputs graphics and text to windows on the screen. Windows are organized hierarchically in a tree structure.

Windows are the building blocks of **X**, and all output (drawing text and graphics) is performed in windows. In **X**, windows are cheap: they are not limited resources, so you can easily have hundreds of windows within an application. (Contrast this with other systems where each window in an application is equivalent to an open file: then you can only have a few tens of windows.)

Windows are arranged hierarchically in a tree structure, as shown in Figure A. The top of this tree is the **root window**, which covers the whole screen. Each application has its own window which is a **child** of the root window, and these are called **top-level** windows as they are at the top of the hierarchy. Application windows appear on top of the root window, and obscure the portions of the root window which are underneath. Within each application window there can be many **sub-windows**, each of which in turn can have its own sub-windows, and so on. Sub-windows are used to create separate objects or areas within the application. For example, a menu can be created out of one window for the menu background, with several child windows, one for each button on the menu, as shown in Figure B and Figure C. Or, in a simulation package you might use a separate sub-window for each component (valve, gauge, pipe, reactor vessel, etc.) in the model you are building.

You can change the size of windows, and their position relative to their parent. You can explicitly make a window invisible (remove it from the screen) by **unmapping** it, and bring it back later by re-**mapping**.

Windows are drawn on the display **screen**; **X** allows each display to have up to three screens (assuming the hardware can support this) as shown in Figure D. You still have only one keyboard and mouse; the three screens are controlled by the same server and it is the server, not the screen, that receives input. Multiple screens are very useful where large amounts of information must be displayed simultaneously, such as in mapping or geographical information systems, or in financial dealing rooms. They are also useful when debugging graphical systems; for instance, if you are developing your CAD package on one screen, it is helpful to be able to debug it from a different screen so that the debug windows themselves don't interfere with the application. Some **X** systems let you have multiple **virtual screens**: you switch between them by moving the mouse off the side of the screen, causing another virtual screen to be displayed on the physical monitor. (Note that the term 'virtual screen' here has a different meaning than in Module 3.2, where it meant a large virtual root window.)

In the next module we look in more detail at how the visibility of windows is controlled, and in the module after next at how the application requests output to the screen.

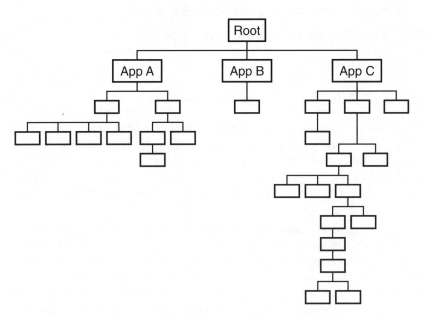

Figure A.   X windows are arranged in a tree hierarchy.

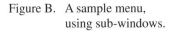

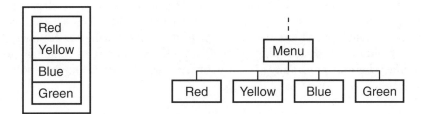

Figure B.   A sample menu,   Figure C.   The window tree for the sample menu.
using sub-windows.

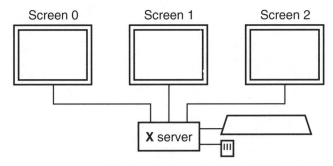

Figure D.   X allows three screens on a display.

3.3   How the server handles output to the screen

3.3.1   Visibility of windows, and clipping

The hierarchy of windows controls the visibility of windows. Child windows can be bigger than their parent, but those parts of them that are outside the parent's boundary are invisible — they are 'clipped'.

A child window is **clipped** by its parent: only the part of the child that is within the parent window is visible (Figure A). A child window can be bigger than its parent, but clipping implies that part of the child will be invisible. You can draw into windows even when they are invisible, or partly so (but what you 'drew' is effectively thrown away: if the invisible part is exposed again, the application will have to redraw that area).

This is a convenient feature in several ways. First, it lets the applications programmer create the window of a size best suited to the task at hand, to simplify the programming. For example, it is much easier to write 'ABCD' into an oversized window and let the window system itself clip off all of the 'D' and part of the 'C' as shown in Figure B, rather than having to calculate the size the string would be in the window, omit the 'D' and explicitly manipulate the image of a 'C' character and then draw the result. Secondly, being able to draw into a window without having to worry if it fully visible or not is essential if applications are to work with different styles of window management. When you are writing your program you have no idea what constraints a window manager will impose — for example, whether windows will be overlapping on the screen, or 'tiled' to lie side by side — so the more insulated you are from potential changes in visibility and size of your windows the better. Finally, the facilities of both types of virtual screens (Modules 3.2 and 3.3) rely on applications continuing to work when they are fully or partially off-screen (that is, outside their parent, the root window) and therefore fully or partially invisible.

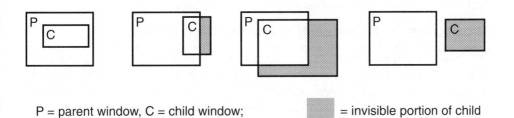

P = parent window, C = child window;  = invisible portion of child

Figure A. Child windows are clipped by their parent.

Figure B. Drawing into a clipped window.

3.3   How the server handles output to the screen

3.3.2   Graphics requests — requests for output

X outputs to the screen only in response to requests from clients. The requests specify what is to be drawn, or how windows are to be altered. Graphics requests are usually object-based; for example, a line is specified by its start and end points – not as a set of pixels to be drawn. You can draw graphics to off-screen images in memory ('pixmaps') as well as to windows.

(If technical details aren't so relevant to you, you can skip over this module.)

All **X** output is the result of requests from clients. There are many different types of request, covering all the operations required for manipulation of screens, windows, text, graphics, and input control. Requests are to **X** what system calls are to an operating system — the fundamental operations on which everything else is based. This module describes the types of requests **X** provides, and the context in which they work, and we point you to other modules dealing with the more important points in greater detail.

- **X** provides two-dimensional graphics. (3-D support is provided by PEX, the Phigs extension to **X**; see Module 3.8.)

- Operations provided include: drawing lines and polylines, arcs and polyarcs, points, filled rectangles, filled polygons and polyarcs, and copy-area functions. We won't cover these in any detail, because they are straightforward functions, and are typical of any graphics system.

- There are functions for manipulating fonts, and drawing and handling text (Module 3.5), and managing colour (Module 3.6).

- There are functions for drawing and manipulating bit-mapped images (Module 3.7).

- You draw into either a window, or an off-screen image called a **pixmap**. (**X** defines the term **drawable** to mean either a window or a pixmap.) You can transfer images between pixmaps and windows; this is often used to ensure satisfactory performance in handling expose events (see Module 3.7.1). You can also read back images from the screen into memory, where you can process them, for redrawing or any other processing you want.

- Drawing is a two-stage process:

    1. First you set up one or more tables which describe how you will want to draw. You specify how wide lines are to be, how multiple line segments are to be joined (rounded or angled joins), what colour you'll be drawing in, which font to use if you are drawing text, etc. These tables are called **graphics contexts** or **GCs**.

2. Then you issue the actual drawing request, specifying which graphics context is to be used for this particular operation, which drawable you are drawing into, and what you are drawing into it. As an example, details of a request to draw a line are shown in Figure A.

Doing things this way simplifies programming because a lot of work — specifying precise details of drawing — is done only once, when setting up the GC, rather than every time you draw. It also makes better use of the network: the large amount of information in the GC is sent to the server only once, when the GC is defined, and not in every single drawing request.

- **X** is a pixel-based system: all dimensions are in terms of pixels. Unlike systems such as PostScript, you cannot express dimensions in real-world units such as centimetres or inches (although some toolkits address this at the application level).

- The **X** coordinate system is rectangular and, again unlike PostScript, the server provides no facilities for scaling or transforming coordinates or dimensions.

opcode = PolySegment
length of this request
ID of window to draw in
graphics context to use
x,y – start point of segment 1
x,y – end point of segment 1
x,y – start point of segment 2
x,y – end point of segment 2

Figure A.   Detailed contents of a request to draw two line segments.

3.4 The server contains the only display hardware dependence in the system

Clients cannot access the display hardware directly — they can only send requests to the server, which in turn controls the hardware. So clients are independent of the type of hardware of the server, and the server's operating system.

One of the design goals of **X** was to make clients hardware independent. This is achieved by not giving them direct access to the display hardware, but insisting that they can only send requests to the server, which itself controls the display.

So, only the server knows what hardware is being used. For instance, if the server is running on a DOS PC, is the display EGA, or VGA, or some special graphics board? If the server is on a workstation, does it have a simple frame-buffer, or is there sophisticated graphics accelerator hardware as well? The server has to receive standard requests from clients and then translate them into the appropriate hardware commands (or deposit appropriate instructions in the hardware registers) to make the particular hardware do what was requested (Figure A).

The server has to know what hardware is present, and support it. As shown in Figure B, the server (or the operating system it is built on) contains device drivers for the display hardware, as well as the keyboard, mouse and any other input devices. Therefore, while the server has probably been designed to be as portable as possible with a modular internal structure, when it is finally implemented it is very hardware dependent, and of course will only run on the CPU-type it was compiled for.

Clients are mostly hardware independent

Clients are completely hardware independent in the sense that any client can operate with any server, no matter what the architecture or operating system the two of them have. But there are a few hardware features that clients have to take account of:

- Is the display colour or monochrome? If monochrome, then requests to draw text in a blue foreground on a yellow background may succeed, that is, not cause an **X** error, but the result may be white text on a white background, which isn't very readable.

- How big is the screen? If I develop my client on a workstation with a 1200 x 900 pixel screen, and assume that the client will always be operating on a screen at least this big, if you then try to use it on a PC with a 600 x 400 pixel display, you will have real difficulty.

- What is the screen resolution, how many dots per inch? If I write an application assuming a resolution similar to the PC I am using (40 d.p.i.) and base my font sizes on this, when you run the application on a high-resolution screen (120 d.p.i.), the text will be almost unreadable, because it will be only one third as high. This is because (as we'll see in the next module) fonts in **X** are handled in terms of pixels, and are resolution dependent; at 40 d.p.i. a 20-pixel character is $\frac{1}{2}$in high, but only $\frac{1}{6}$in at 120 d.p.i.

There are fairly easy solutions to these problems. By writing your application correctly you can make it very easy for the user to customize (access to the source code isn't required) so that they can specify colours, sizes, layouts, etc. which are suited to their configuration, as described in Module 12.1. It is also possible to specify fonts in a resolution-independent way, and to query the server for details of the display so that layouts can take account of the available screen space, etc.

Mouse support — how many buttons?

Mice have different numbers of buttons: the Macintosh has one button, most PC mice have two, and most workstation mice have three. The server has no problem — it handles up to five buttons — but what if the application requires you to press the third button, and you have only one?

Server developers have tried to get over this by simulating the extra buttons: pressing, say, both buttons simultaneously on a two-button mouse simulates pressing a middle button. This is a nasty solution, as the user interface of the application is distorted, making it hard to use. As above, the correct approach is to make the application customizable, so the *users* can choose how the functions normally invoked with the missing mouse buttons are to be invoked on their systems. (But until all applications are written correctly, the server developers have to continue with their inelegant simulations.)

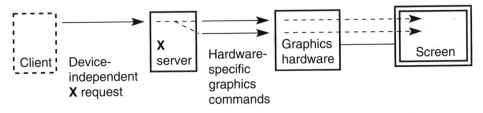

Figure A.   The server translates X requests into commands to the hardware.

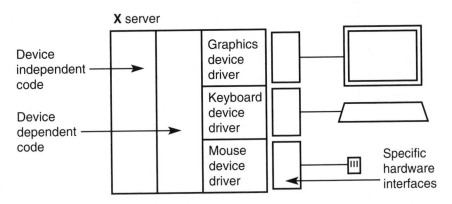

Figure B.   The server, alone, knows hardware is present.

3.5 Handling text and fonts

X supports multiple fonts and character sets simultaneously on the screen. Text can only be horizontal; fonts are stored as bitmaps, text cannot be rotated, but from Release 5 onwards it can be scaled.

X supports multiple fonts, and allows sophisticated use of English and non-English character sets. Characters in a font may be of fixed width (as you need for terminal emulators, and some spreadsheet applications) or of variable width (which you need for proper typesetting and DTP).

Server vendors usually provide a large set of fonts for use with their server (but there are no standard fonts, so you can't assume a particular font exists). Fonts are normally provided ready for use with your server. They may also be distributed in a portable, plain-text, format called **BDF (Bitmap Distribution Format)** which you then have to convert into the format your server needs using a font-compiler provided with your server. In Release 5, the format is **PCF (Portable Compiled Format)**: this stores the font information in an efficient internal form, but it is portable across all servers from Release 5 onwards. In Release 4 and earlier, the internal format was **SNF (Server Natural Format)**; in practice this often was portable across platforms, but the specification did allow it to be platform-specific, and BDF was the only guaranteed portable form.

X has a standard naming scheme for fonts, called **XLFD (X Logical Font Description)**. The XLFD name contains information about the type of font this is — the typeface, character size, whether bold or italic, etc. — so a lot of information about the font can be obtained just from the name, without having to load the whole font into the server first. We don't want to load unnecessary fonts, because they consume a lot of memory in the server. The server also accepts font specifications that contain 'wildcards', so when you are naming a font, you only have to give specific characteristics you are interested in, instead of having to name a font exactly. This lets you specify font names more or less generically, which makes you less dependent on specific fonts being available on every server (see Module 11.3).

Characters in a font are **encoded** as one or two bytes, that is characters in some **X** fonts are represented by 8 bits, and in other fonts by 16 bits. An 8-bit font can contain $2^8 = 256$ characters, which is adequate for English and European languages, and many sets of symbols. A 16-bit font can contain $2^{16} = 65536$ characters, and is required to accommodate the very large oriental character sets. The encoding of a character within a font just means its number or position in the font; for example the ASCII encoding of upper-case B is 66, that is, when a byte containing 66 is interpreted as an ASCII character, it is taken to mean B. Where possible **X** uses the encodings specified by ISO, the international standards body. In fact the final parts of the XLFD name specify the encoding. 'ISO8859-1' specifies 'ISO Latin alphabet number 1', which is more or less ASCII with extras covering some symbols and letters with diacritical marks (accents, etc.) for European ('Latin') languages. Other ISO8859 encodings cover Cyrillic, Hebrew, Greek and Arabic languages, and there are also standard encodings for the oriental languages.

Up to and including Release 4, **X** fonts were stored exclusively as bitmaps on the server (as 'files', usually in ROM on an X-terminal or on disk on a workstation), and in Release 5 most files are still in this form. There are several consequences of this:

- Even though characters are stored as bitmaps, they are actually in the server, so drawing characters does *not* involve transmitting bitmaps over the network.

- If you want the same font at a different size, you have to have a separate font file for it. This takes extra storage space, and also uses memory in the server when the font is loaded for use.

- Text must be horizontal. It can run from left-to-right or right-to-left, but it cannot be rotated. Even if you want text rotated 90° to label the axis of a graph, **X** gives you no help. (You have to pull the character bitmaps from the font into your applications, rotate the bitmap using graphics manipulation techniques, and then paint the rotated bitmap.) Most applications only need horizontal text, so these limitations are not as serious as they initially appear, and some of them are likely to be removed in future releases (see Module 15.1).

With Release 5, a mechanism has been provided for scaling fonts, in three ways:

1. A scaler for bitmap fonts has been included, which lets you use any bitmap font at any size. But it is a simple mechanism and the results can be slightly ugly unless you are increasing the size to an exact multiple of the original (Figure A).

2. The Bitstream Speedo system for scalable outline fonts has been incorporated. Instead of representing each character in the font as a bitmap, it is stored as a set of curves representing the shape of the character, which can be scaled to whatever size is necessary and then converted to a bitmap for drawing the character on the screen.

3. The user-contributed software release contains a PostScript Type 1 font scaler, plus some Type 1 scalable outline fonts.

In the next two modules we look at the **X** font server which allows fonts to be managed centrally, and at the requests used to draw text.

```
┌─────────────────────┐ ┌──────────────────────────┐
│ The quick brown fox │ │ The quick brown fox      │
│ jumps over lazy dogs│ │ jumps over lazy dogs     │
└─────────────────────┘ └──────────────────────────┘
```

Figure A.   Scaling a bitmap font can produce ugly results.

3.5 Handling text and fonts

3.5.1   The X Font Server

Storing fonts on individual **X** servers makes system administration difficult, especially on a large network. This is overcome by storing the fonts on a 'font server'; the **X** server retrieves fonts from the font server rather than reading them directly itself.

Storing fonts on the **X** server, especially in a server-specific format, causes many problems:

1. Even when fonts are not loaded they take up a lot of storage space, on disk or in ROM. For example, on our MIT server, a typical bitmap font for Roman-language text takes between 10 and 20 kbytes on disk, an outline font takes about 65 kbytes, and a bitmap Chinese-language font takes between 0.5 and 1.0 Mbytes! So on a network of **X** stations, you may be using a vast amount of disk space, storing multiple copies of the same fonts for different servers.

2. Server and application vendors supply different fonts; you may find that when you get a new application which requires a specific font, you have to install this font individually on all your **X** stations.

3. Introducing new font formats becomes very difficult, not just because of the difficulty of upgrading all **X** servers everywhere, but also because the new font format may depend on a proprietary technology not available to all **X** server developers.

4. Formats such as outline fonts consume a lot of CPU power and memory: this may make them unsuitable for low end servers such as PCs and small X-terminals.

To get over these problems, the **X font server** was developed. The basic idea is that the **X** server, instead of reading font files directly itself, requests them from the font server, which provides them in the bitmap format required by that **X** server.

Figure A illustrates three important points about the font server design. First, a single font server can provide fonts for many **X** servers. Secondly, an **X** server can be connected to more than one font server. And finally, font servers can be chained together: if the first font server has been asked for a font which it does not have, it can request this font from another font server it is connected to. Let's see how these features overcome the problems we listed above.

1. Fonts no longer need to be duplicated across every **X** server — the font server can hold a single copy and make it accessible to all the **X** servers on the network.

2. Adding a font to the network is easy — you only have to load it onto one font server and it is available to all **X** servers and therefore to all applications.

3. A new font format can easily be accommodated — only the font server needs to be enhanced to handle it. If the technology for the new format is proprietary, the vendor can supply a complete font server for the new format; this font server can then be chained to existing font servers without any modification at all (Figure B).

4. The font server can be run on a powerful compute server, which is able to handle the demands of complex font formats.

These factors are especially attractive for networks of X-terminals, because they reduce still further the amount of (X) terminal-specific information that has to be stored anywhere.

The font server also provides other facilities for administration. It provides licensing and access control, because many fonts carry a licence or usage fee. It supports grouping fonts into subsets called **catalogues** to help you control who can access which fonts. For example, you might group chargeable fonts into a catalogue and make it available only to specialized DTP users who really need those facilities. The sample implementation of the font server in Release 5 doesn't support these facilities.

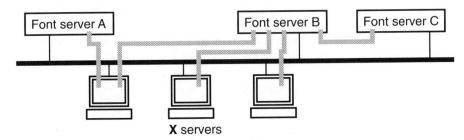

Figure A. Relationship of X servers with font servers.

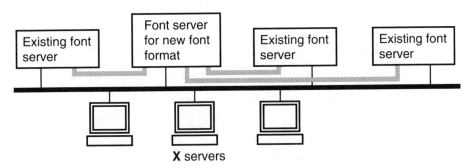

Figure B. Adding a new font format by adding a proprietary font server.

3.5 Handling text and fonts

3.5.2 Graphics requests for text

X provides requests for inquiring about which fonts are available, for loading specified fonts, for drawing text, and for calculating dimensions of text prior to drawing.

(If technical details aren't so relevant to you, you can skip over this module.)

There are relatively few graphics requests for handling text and fonts, because X's text handling is straightforward. This module describes the requests and some more detailed aspects of X's text handling.

- Before you can draw characters from a font into a window you must first issue a request to **load** the font into the server, that is, read the character representations from file into the server's memory.

- As well as the character representations, you also need other information about the font, such as its point size, whether it should be printed left-to-right (as for English) or right-to-left (as for Hebrew), and various dimensions such as the maximum size of any character in the font. You retrieve this information by **querying** the font.

- Instead of loading or querying particular fonts, you can send a request to interrogate the server about what fonts are available on the basis of their full XLFD names. As we mentioned in Module 3.5, an XLFD name itself incorporates a lot of information about its font, so by specifying your query appropriately you can get a list of fonts which meet your requirements without using a lot of resources. You can then load whichever font you choose from this list. For example, if you wanted a bold, roman, 18-point font for Roman-language text, in your query you could specify the name:

    ```
    -*-*-bold-r-*-*-*-180-*-*-c-*-iso8859-1
    ```

    whereas if you required the Korean graphic character set you might specify:

    ```
    -*-*-*-*-*-*-*-*-*-*-*-*-ksc5601.1987-0
    ```

- Having loaded the font, you can write strings of characters from it. In the standard X function XDrawString, used to request text drawing, you specify the string of characters, the window they are to be drawn in, the coordinates where they are to start from, and a graphics context (Module 3.3.2) which contains the identifier of the loaded font you wish to use.

- You can use several different fonts in a single operation using the function XDrawText: instead of a single string you specify a list of many items, each of which contains a string of characters and a graphics context (and the graphics context specifies which font to use for this particular string).

- Before drawing text, you often need to know what size it will be — so that you can position it appropriately, or ensure that some other user interface component is big enough to accommodate it. **X** provides requests for you to query how big a specified text string in a particular font will be.

- When you have finished with a font, you **free** it — unload it from the server so that the memory it occupied can be re-used.

- The server has a list of names of the directories on the server's filesystem in which it looks for fonts you have asked to be loaded. You can add extra directories to, or delete them from, this list. (This list is called the **font path**.)

3.6 Handling colour

X provides support for a very wide range of colour capabilities, from simple mono bitmap frame buffers to elaborate 24-bit colour systems. Colours can be specified by name, in terms of RGB components or device-independent specifications, or as internal values within the server.

In keeping with its design goal of being suited to a wide range of display types, **X** works across the whole spectrum of hardware, from monochrome to 24-bit colour, as well as grayscale.

Internally — that is, within the server — **X** colour specifications consist of three 16-bit values, one each for the red, green and blue components (RGB) of the colour to be displayed. These values are normally written in hexadecimal notation:

pure red	`ffff/0000/0000`	full red, no green or blue
pure green	`0000/ffff/0000`	full green, only
white	`ffff/ffff/ffff`	as much of everything as possible
black	`0000/0000/0000`	nothing at all
yellow	`ffff/ffff/0000`	mixture of red and green

Externally, for example when you specify in a text file a default colour for some item, you can use ordinary colour names like 'pink', 'orange', etc. And most **X** programs let you specify foreground and background colours on the command-line when you run them, as in:

```
xclock -foreground red -background blue
```

You can also use RGB specifications externally in place of colour names, by adding a prefix of 'rgb:'.[2] The command:

```
xclock -foreground rgb:ffff/0/0 -background rgb:0/0/ffff
```

is exactly equivalent to the one above.

The server maintains a simple database of colour names and the corresponding RGB values; internally, using standard **X** functions, the client can request the server to lookup a colour name, and use the value returned, or it can specify a colour directly by name. The MIT program showrgb lists the colour names your server knows about, with their RGB components; for example, Figure A shows a selection of lines in our colour database.

A given RGB specification can result in markedly different colours depending on the monitor and graphics hardware used. As well as being more natural, colour names allow a degree of device independence, by letting you tune the RGB-values allocated to a colour name for the particular hardware you are using. For example, you (or your system vendor) would ensure that the RGB specification corresponding to 'pink' really

---

[2]Release 5 only. Earlier releases had a similar facility, but the rgb: prefix wasn't necessary, because the other types of colour specifications introduced with Release 5 were not supported. In Release 4 and earlier, an explicit RGB colour was prefixed with a hash (#) to distinguish it from a colour name.

does give a pink colour on screen! In Release 5, a much more powerful system for specifying colours in a device-independent way was included, and we describe that in the next module. After that we describe some of the detailed mechanisms available for handling multiple applications which together require more colours than the hardware can display at one time.

```
199   21 133        medium violet red
176 196 222         light steel blue
102 139 139         paleturquoise4
159 121 238         mediumpurple2
141 182 205         lightskyblue3
  0 238 118         springgreen2
255 160 122         light salmon
154 205  50         yellowgreen
178  58 238         darkorchid2
 69 139 116         aquamarine4
```

Figure A.   Some of the entries in our RGB colour database.

3.6 Handling colour

3.6.1 Device-independent colour specifications

Release 5 introduced Xcms, the **X** Colour Management System. This lets you specify colours in a device-independent way, so you can be sure the visible colour will be the same whatever hardware it is displayed on.

(If technical details aren't so relevant to you, you can skip over this module.)

The RGB scheme for specifying colour that we outlined in the previous module relates very closely to colour display hardware. The individual RGB values specify more or less directly the intensity with which the electron guns in the hardware are to fire at the red, green and blue phosphors on the screen. While this scheme may be a convenient way of driving the hardware, it has several deficiencies from the point of view of people:

- As we already mentioned, the visible result produced by RGB specifications varies widely across different systems.

- It isn't easy for the user to specify colours:

  - If you have a colour and its RGB value, and want to get a related colour — for example, a brighter version — it isn't obvious how to change the RGB values. You will often have to change the three RGB components by unequal proportions to get the effect you require.

  - The size of increment needed to get a visible difference in the colour displayed depends upon where you are in the possible range of RGB values. For low intensities you may have to increase a component value by 10 or 20 steps before you can see any difference; elsewhere, one step may be enough.

- There is no unique representation for a colour as perceived by the user: one colour can have many corresponding RGB representations, which can result in you using more colours in the server than necessary. (We'll see the significance of this in Module 3.6.3.)

To overcome these problems, **Xcms**, the **X Colour Management System**, was introduced with Release 5. This makes use of the international colour standards of the CIE (*Commission Internationale de l'Eclairage* — International Commission on Illumination). With Xcms, colours can now be specified using the CIE XYZ, CIE uvY, CIE xyY, CIE L*a*b*, CIE L*u*v*, and TekHVC schemes, as well as the RGB values and colour names we have already seen. These schemes were developed to allow colours to be specified in an absolute and reproducible way, and with the exception of TekHVC were not specifically for addressing colour in computer systems (in fact, most of these systems were developed quite a long time ago). By using one of these representations, you can specify a colour irrespective of the hardware you are using, and with Xcms you can reliably reproduce this colour on any hardware. We won't go into the details of all these specification schemes, but will just outline the principles of Xcms.

With Xcms there are no changes in the server — it still handles colours internally in terms of RGB specifications. All the changes are on the client side, and consist of enhancements to the standard client library, Xlib, and to the applications that want to use it.

Figure A shows schematically how colour specifications are processed with Xcms. Xcms effectively acts as a translator, changing device-independent colour specifications to RGB values to send to the server, and converting RGB values received from the server into the format required by the application.

In the next module we look at how Xcms takes account of the colour characteristics of the particular graphics hardware that your server is using.

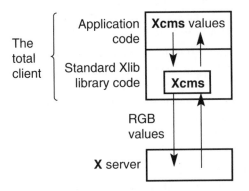

Figure A.   Xcms translates device-independent colour specifications on the client side.

3.6 Handling colour

3.6.2 Calibrating hardware for device-independent colour

The colour and illumination characteristics of the graphics hardware used by the server must be measured, and then stored so that Xcms can access them and take account of the way that your hardware renders colours.

To convert between device-independent and RGB specifications, we must first perform some measurements on the hardware, to find out what its colour and illumination characteristics are. For instance, the illumination from a screen does not increase linearly with RGB value; at low intensities, you need quite a large increase in RGB value to give a small increase in illumination, whereas at higher intensities this isn't so. Separate measurements have to be carried out for each of the red, green and blue components of the screen. All these characteristics are specific to each type of screen and graphics hardware. Figure A shows the characteristic curve of illumination versus RGB value for the red component of a screen similar to our own.

This process of measurement is called **device calibration**. The **contrib** release includes the program xcrtca, to drive a CRT colour analyser so you can perform this function for yourself. (Very few organizations need to do this — tables of characteristics for particular combinations of graphics hardware and monitors are being made available. The **contrib** release already contains some of these in a form suitable for use by Xcms, and as Xcms is more widely adopted, hardware manufacturers will provide the necessary calibration information.)

Having got the device characteristics, we must make this information available to Xcms in a form it can understand; this is called **device characterization**. The colour profile of the screen is stored in two properties on the root window, XD-CCC_LINEAR_RGB_CORRECTION and XDCCC_LINEAR_RGB_MATRICES. You load these properties from a file containing the characterization information using the MIT program xcmsdb. Applications using Xcms can now retrieve the characterization information from the properties when they require it, as shown in Figure B.

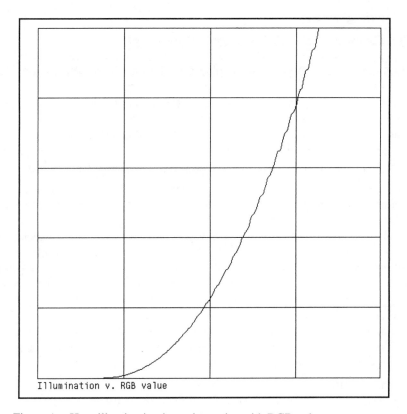

Figure A. How illumination intensity varies with RGB value on our screen.

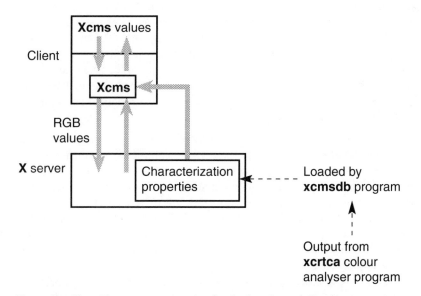

Figure B. How Xcms uses properties for device characterization.

3.6 Handling colour

3.6.3   Colour capabilities and colormaps

The number of colours you can display simultaneously on your screen is determined by your hardware, and is usually quite limited. If you have several applications running, they may require different sets of colours, which would exceed the hardware limit. To get over this, **X** provides 'colormaps' — tables of the colours which are currently to be displayed by the hardware.

(If technical details aren't so relevant to you, you can skip over this module.)

The most common colour systems are 8-bit. That is, each pixel is represented by an 8-bit value, which means that $2^8 = 256$ distinct colours on the screen are possible at any one time. We say that such a colour system has a **depth** of 8. On such a system, while only 256 colours are possible at any one time, we can choose which 256 are to be used out of the total **palette** that the colour hardware makes available, which typically offers $2^{24} = 16777216$ possibilities. It is the software that specifies which set of 256 colours are to be used, by means of a **colormap** — a colour lookup table that says what particular combination of RGB values is to be associated with a given pixel value (Figure A). All pixels containing the same value will show the same colour on the screen, because they all reference the same element of the colormap. If you change the RGB values in the colormap element, then all pixels referencing it will immediately change on screen to reflect the new colour.

This manipulation of colormaps can be very useful in imaging applications, where the user needs to set colours frequently, for instance while trying to adjust the contrast to get the clearest view of some image. Speed is obviously important in this case, and in fact colormap manipulation is very fast; as only a few bytes in the colormap are being changed, the colour on screen changes almost instantaneously. (If it was necessary to cycle through all the video memory, perhaps as much as a megabyte or more for a full-screen colour image, changing individual pixels to contain a different value, it would be very much slower.) In fact, colormaps are often manipulated interactively by means of scrollbar-like sliders, one each for the red, green, and blue components of a colormap element; as you drag a slider the colormap is updated and you see the effect instantaneously on your whole screen. The contributed program cpicker, shown in Figure B, has this facility.

In fact, colormap handling is considerably more complex and sophisticated than we have described here. Some hardware's colormaps are read-only and cannot be modified; other hardware supports multiple simultaneous hardware colormaps. And different systems either themselves interpret the values in the colormap elements in different ways, or let you specify how they are to be interpreted You may come across the terms 'PseudoColor', 'DirectColor', 'StaticGray', 'StaticColor', and 'TrueColor': these are specifications of how the colour mechanism works. The term **visual** or **visual class** refers to which of these colour mechanisms is used. For example, the visual class for the colour scheme outlined in the first paragraph of this module is 8-bit PseudoColor. However, you're unlikely to have to bother with these low-level aspects unless you are programming the system or working with it at quite a detailed level.

Monochrome systems have a depth of 1, and can therefore only display $2^1 = 2$ distinct colours, that is, black and white. Grayscale systems have a depth of greater than one, so they are not limited to black and white, but can also show many different intermediate shades of gray, just like a black-and-white photograph. High-end systems are increasingly providing 24-bit colour, which obviously allows a huge number of distinct colours.

In the next module we see how **X** handles different applications using different colormaps at the same time.

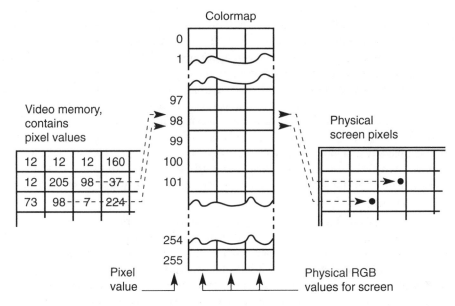

Figure A.   Colormap determines what colour a pixel shows on screen.

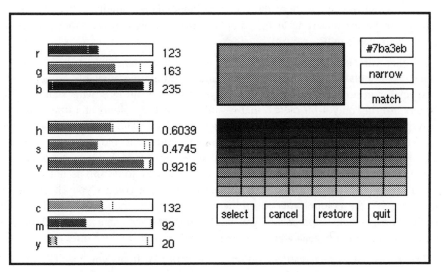

Figure B.   The cpicker colormap manipulation tool.

3.6   Handling colour

3.6.4   Using many different colormaps together

Each application may need to use a set of colours specific to itself, so **X** allows each window to have its own colormap associated with it. The window manager loads this colormap into the colour hardware when the window becomes active so that it shows its correct colours when you are working within it.

Let us consider an 8-bit colour system. This allows you to display 256 colours on the screen. This number of colours is usually more than adequate for decorative purposes (for distinguishing between different windows, for example) and for highlighting particular items within applications. But with applications such as graphics design, CAD, CAE and imaging, which need a great many distinct colours (for example, in photographic images), you start to get problems. First, 256 colours may just not be enough; if so your only option is to buy more capable hardware, such as a 24-bit system. Second, while no individual application might need more than 256 colours, there may be a clash *between* applications, about which particular set of colours they want. For example, you might have two mapping application on your screen; one needs 200 colours, mostly greens and browns, for a terrestrial map, while the other needs 100 shades of blue for a marine map. The total number of colours needed is 300, which is more than the hardware can display.

To get over this problem, **X** provides multiple software colormaps, and each window can have its own colormap associated with it; by **installing** one of these into the hardware colormap you easily change from one set of colours to another. It is the window manager's responsibility to install the appropriate software colormap into the hardware as you move from one application to another. So when you are working in an application, the colours showing are correct for that application, although they may not be correct for other applications on the screen (Figure A). In a situation like this, as you move from one application, the screen colours change rapidly. This 'technicolor' flashing can be disconcerting at first, but it is the only way to use more colours than the hardware can handle.

Another very common problem is that the window manager, which is often one of the first clients to start up, has used quite a few of the available colours. (This is especially noticeable on small colour systems, such as PCs with standard VGA adapters offering only 4-bit colour, that is, only 16 distinct colours at a time.) To avoid this type of problem, programmers are encouraged to share colormaps, within and between applications. By minimizing the number of different colormaps you reduce the flashing technicolor effects, and also maximize the number of windows simultaneously showing their correct colours. (The easiest practical way to do this is not to use any special colormaps, but to restrict the number of different colours you choose to use, and to specify the colours you do use with colour names rather than RGB or other specifications, which helps ensure you really are using the same colours throughout. You can also configure your window manager and restrict it to use only two colours.)

The Xcms colour management system helps here too. It lets you specify clearly the colours you are using. This avoids a common problem with the RGB system, which is that you may specify several colours that have different RGB values (thus requiring several slots in the colormap) but which look the same and are effectively one colour as far as the user is concerned.

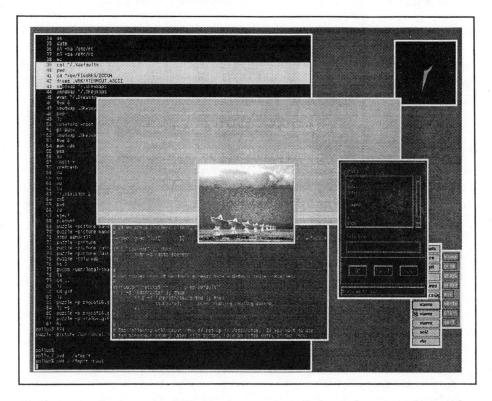

Figure A.   Applications with different colormaps don't display their correct colours at the same time.

3.7   Pictures and images — bitmaps, cursors and pixmaps

Applications can create bitmap images, to be used as icons, as pictures or graphic images, or as patterns for window backgrounds, borders, etc.

We have already seen two of the principal types of graphical objects supported by **X** — text fonts and 2-D graphics. In this module we look at a third type of object — pictorial images. A picture is not described by geometrical formulas as lines or arcs can be; instead it is represented as an array of pixels with the colour of each pixel specified explicitly. As a result, picture representations consume a lot of memory.

The simplest form of picture is a **bitmap**. Each pixel is represented by a single bit: if the bit is zero, the pixel shows in the background colour, otherwise the bit is one and the pixel shows in the foreground colour.

Bitmaps are used for small pictorial images, such as window manager icons, or pictorial labels for pushbuttons. They are also widely used as a very general way of specifying a shape: the shape consists of all the 1-bits in the bitmap. This technique is used for cursors (Module 3.7.2). It is also used to restrict the area affected by a drawing operation; a bitmap is used to specify a **clipping region**, such that only pixels in the specified region are affected. (The bitmap effectively provides a stencil through which the drawing operation is performed, as shown in Figure A.) This technique is how **X** provides non-rectangular windows on screen — windows are fundamentally rectangular, but can have an associated clipping bitmap, so the shape actually displayed is that specified by the bitmap. Note that in a bitmap *any* set of bits can be set on; in particular, the bits do not have to be contiguous but can be disjoint, and therefore by applying a disjoint clipping bitmap to a window, it can be displayed as several disjoint pieces. This is how the MIT program xeyes shows as two separate eyes (Figure B).

X provides a simple external representation for bitmaps. They are described as C-program fragments, as shown in Figure C. They can be incorporated into the source code of C programs, and there are also Xlib utility functions to write out internal bitmaps to a file in this format, to read them in from a file, and to convert them to **X**'s internal representation within the server. Most **X** bitmap manipulation tools use this mechanism, so it is both portable and flexible. For example, the MIT bitmap editor bitmap is shown in Figure D editing the bitmap file of Figure C.

A text-picture representation of a bitmap can also be created with a normal text editor, as shown in Figure E, and converted to standard bitmap form using the MIT program atobm ('ASCII to bitmap').

In the next module we look at pixmaps, which are **X**'s general format for representing images. In the module after next, we look at bitmaps used as cursors.

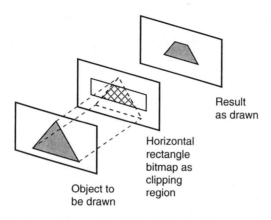

Result
as drawn

Horizontal
rectangle
bitmap as
clipping
region

Object to
be drawn

Figure A.   Bitmap used to specify a clipping region for a graphics operation.

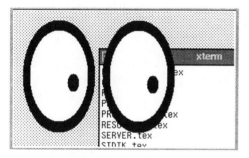

Figure B.   The xeyes windows shows as two
disjoint pieces.

```
#define test5x3_width 5
#define test5x3_height 3
static char test5x3_bits[] =
  {
    0x00, 0x1f, 0x15
  };
```

Figure C.   A bitmap is represented
externally as a fragment of C code.

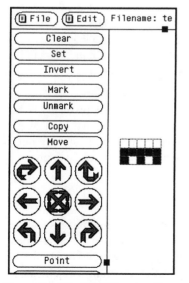

Figure D.   The MIT bitmap editor.

```
venus% cat /tmp/my_arrow
----------------------------------------
----------####----------------
---------#####----------------
---------###-##----------------
-------###-###----------------
------###-###------------------
-----###-###-------------------
----###-###--------------------
---###-####################-
--###-#-####################--
-###-#-#-#-#-#-#-#-#-#-##---
###-#-#-#-#-#-#-#-#-#-##----
-###-#-#-#-#-#-#-#-#-#-##---
--###-#-####################--
---###-####################-
----###-###-------------------
-----###-###-------------------
------###-###------------------
-------###-###----------------
--------###-##----------------
---------#####----------------
----------####----------------
----------------------------------------
venus%
```

Figure E.   Text-picture representation of a bitmap.

3.7 Pictures and images — bitmaps, cursors and pixmaps

3.7.1   Pixmaps — X's most general picture format

X represents pictorial images internally in the server as 'pixmaps', which are rectangular offscreen arrays of pixels. You can draw graphics into pixmaps just like you draw into windows. Client applications support conversion of X images to and from other standard image file formats.

So far we have only been dealing with bitmaps, where each pixel in the picture is represented by a single bit. X's most general internal representation of pictures is the **pixmap**. Pixmaps are similar to bitmaps, but each pixel in the pixmap is represented by a fixed number of bits. In fact an X bitmap is held internally as a pixmap with one bit per pixel. The number of bits used is called the **depth** of the pixmap, and this is analogous to the depth of a colormap in Module 3.6.3.

Pixmaps are often used within programs for **tiling** window backgrounds, borders, etc., that is, as (small) images which are repeated until the specified area is completely patterned.

Pixmaps (and bitmaps) reside in the server, and clients create them by issuing requests to the server. When first created, a pixmap is just a rectangular area of pixels; you must then transfer whatever image you require into the pixmap using the usual X graphics requests as described below.

As we mentioned in Module 3.3.2 pixmaps are drawables, that is, you can perform all graphics and drawing operations into a pixmap instead of into a window. This means you can maintain and manipulate an image offscreen, in a pixmap, and later transfer it rapidly to a window when you need to. This technique is used in complex graphics applications, where the cost of redrawing a window in response to an expose event can be very high, perhaps involving the reprocessing of a display list of thousands of elements. To get over this, when you originally draw the graphics into a window, you also draw the same graphics into a pixmap. Then, when the window has to be redrawn after an expose event, you block-transfer a copy of what is in the pixmap into the window — a relatively fast operation requiring no recalculation on the part of the application.

However, a problem with this technique (and any other use of pixmaps) is that offscreen memory in the server may be very limited. By assuming that a lot of it is available you can reduce the portability of your application; your program may fail to run correctly or at a usable speed on servers which cannot support such large pixmaps.

Other image formats, and applications

What we have outlined here are the standard X facilities for handling images and pictures. The server does provide these basic mechanisms, but to satisfy the requirements of imaging, of CAD, and of comprehensive end-user graphics systems much more is required. This extra functionality is provided by application programs, which convert to and from standard image file formats such as GIFF, TIFF, raster files, etc., so the

X server itself does not need to support foreign file formats directly. For example, the **contrib** program xloadimage lets you display many of these different types of graphics files.

The **X** Imaging Extension which is under development by the MIT **X** Consortium (see Module 15.1) will expand the functionality **X** provides to support imaging applications.

3.7   Pictures and images — bitmaps, cursors and pixmaps

3.7.2   Cursors

The server has its own default set of cursors. Applications can also create their own custom cursors from bitmaps.

X systems normally have a mouse or similar pointing device, and as the mouse is moved so a **pointer** is moved on the screen. The pointer takes a shape called a **cursor**, and each window within an application can have its own cursor shape associated with it.

Internally, a cursor consists of a bitmap, that is, a pixmap of depth one, specifying the shape of the cursor and what colour is to be used to display it. It also has defined a **hot spot** — a single pixel which determines where exactly the cursor 'is'. (Without this, if you had a cursor consisting of 16 x 16 pixels, say, on the boundary of two windows, how could the system know which window the cursor is really in?) A cursor also has another bitmap known as a **mask**, which has its own separate display colour. Why is this needed? Assume that the cursor's display colour is red; when the cursor is in an area which is also red, the cursor would be invisible. So, typically, the mask is defined to extend slightly beyond the basic cursor shape on all edges, and displayed in a contrasting colour, so that the cursor is now visible no matter what the colour of the underlying area is. A cursor bitmap and mask are shown in Figure A.

X provides a standard set of cursors in the special font named cursor; Figure B shows this displayed by the MIT font display program xfd. Applications can also create their own custom cursors from a bitmap, using a special **X** request for this purpose.

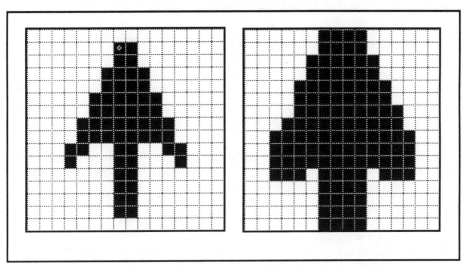

Figure A. A cursor bitmap, showing hotspot, and cursor mask.

Figure B. cursor — the MIT font of standard cursors.

3.8   Extras you may want or need: server extensions

Specialized servers incorporating features such as PostScript, or live video windows or other special facilities are available. These features are extensions to the basic system and are provided using a special extensions mechanism. New functionality is incorporated into new releases of standard servers using this mechanism rather than directly, to give compatibility with earlier releases and to ensure consistent operation on servers from different vendors.

When they developed **X**, its designers realized that for various reasons it was missing certain functionality which would have to be added later on. Either the technology had not yet matured enough (as with 3-D graphics) or the functionality was not crucial and could therefore wait (as with non-rectangular windows) or it was just outside the scope of the **X** development at the time. Moreover, any successful system will to some extent have to grow dynamically over time, requiring the addition of features which were not anticipated at the beginning. Because of this, **X** has a well-defined mechanism for adding extended functionality to the server. (There is no difficulty extending client functionality — you just add it in with extra code and libraries.) Also, it is likely that some extensions will be so popular that they will become almost standard in time so they must be well integrated into the system. (This has already happened with the MIT SHAPE extension, introduced with Release 4, which allows windows to be non-rectangular.)

The **X** extension mechanism is merely a clean way for a server vendor to add something new to a server, and to be able to make this enhanced functionality available in a standard and controlled way on servers from many different suppliers. For example, if you write a program that uses the Display PostScript extension on a server from DEC, that program should also work when displaying to another server with its own Display PostScript extension on a Hewlett-Packard workstation. The mechanism is *not* intended as a means for end-users to add enhancements to their servers themselves. How an extension affects the client programs is covered in the next module.

Common extensions

The following extensions are part of the standard MIT release:

> **Shared memory** (MIT-SHM). When client and server are running on the same CPU, a lot of compute time and resources can be saved by placing certain data structures for images and pixmaps in shared memory. Now, instead of having to explicitly pass a large amount of data between the client and the server, only a pointer need be exchanged. This gives much faster throughput and better performance when a lot of data has to be transferred.

> **Shape extension** (SHAPE): allows windows to be any shape rather than just rectangular.

Phigs extension to X (X3D-PEX): provides support for the Phigs graphics standard within the **X** server. It is necessary to implement this in the server rather than as a library within the client for performance reasons: there would be far too much data to transfer between client and server otherwise.

PEX wasn't included in the base **X** system as it would have taken another year or more to implement, even if Phigs had been a widely accepted graphics standard at the time. A sample PEX extension was first included in the MIT release with Release 5; revisions are likely as Phigs standards are stabilized (Module 15.1).

Other common extensions are:

Input extension: allows the use of additional input devices beyond the pointer and keyboard devices handled by standard **X**.

Video extension to X (VEX): allows windows containing live video to be used as part of the **X** screen (using special hardware).

An example — the Display PostScript extension

For many applications, **X**'s graphical and font capabilities are perfectly adequate. However, the limitations in its text handling (inability to rotate fonts and, except in Release 5, to scale them) and lack of coordinate transformation mean that for sophisticated typesetting and imaging something more powerful is needed. Accordingly Adobe have developed the **Display PostScript** system (DPS), to provide within **X** the same facilities which are available with PostScript printers.

The advantages of the system are resolution-independent imaging. Sizes (of text, lines, etc.) are specified in real-world units such as inches or centimetres, and the system transforms these into the correct number of pixels according to the number of dots-per-inch of your screen. You also get high-quality scalable and rotatable fonts and, most importantly for many users, the fact that what is shown on screen can be printed exactly on a PostScript printer.

DPS is representative of commercial extensions. It is not part of every server, but is widely useful, and has been incorporated by vendors into servers for many different platforms. It is produced by a commercial software company and is not a minor or local change to the server by an end-user organization for its own use, but provides considerable functionality on top of the standard **X** system.

3.8   Extras you may want or need: server extensions

3.8.1   How extensions affect applications

An extension adds extra functions to a server. It is an extension to the **X** protocol, and defines new primitive functions which the server supports. Therefore there must be extra requests for the clients to invoke this functionality, and usually extra subroutine libraries containing functions to issue these extra requests.

(If technical details aren't so relevant to you, you can skip over this module.)

Just as clients don't build standard **X** protocol requests themselves, but use Xlib and other libraries to provide a higher-level interface, so clients making use of extensions will use special extension-specific libraries. As shown in Figure A, there are extra components in both client and server.

To ensure that an extension works consistently across different servers, there must be some way for the client using the extension to identify that the requests it issues relate to the particular extension. We could reserve special request opcodes for each registered extension (and MIT does maintain a register of special names, etc., so this is feasible). However, there is a limited range of opcodes available, so a different scheme is used, based on the *name* of the extension. Each extension is allocated a unique name by MIT. (Figure B lists the names of the extensions registered with MIT when Release 5 was issued.) When an application first wants to use a given extension, it asks the server if it supports an extension of that name. If so, the server returns the **major opcode** for the extension. This is the special code which is included in requests sent to the server to identify what type of request this is, and the application inserts this in each request it issues for functions provided by the extension.

One extension is likely to require many different request types, that is, there are many different functions that the extension supplies, and the program must be able to specify which one is required. Rather than allocate a major opcode to each request, all requests for the one extension use the same major opcode, but use another **minor opcode** to distinguish between them. Effectively, the major output routes the request to the extension-specific portion of the server, and the minor opcode is used by that part of the server to decide which particular action it should perform. Figure C lists the minor opcodes used by the MIT SHAPE extension (which lets you use non-rectangular windows).

As we mentioned above, the application queries the server to see if the extension is present. This is essential, so that applications can decide what action to take if the extension is absent, rather than just failing. The action taken depends on the application, and why the extension was being used. If the application was using the SHAPE extension just to make pushbuttons look nicer by rounding the corners, the sensible course is just to use rectangular buttons if the extension is absent. However, if the application is a PostScript document previewer, and the PostScript extension is absent, the only useful action the application can do is to print an informative error message, and terminate.

Applications can also ask for a list of all extensions supported by the server, rather than explicitly querying in turn if each extension the application knows about is supported. This is how the MIT program **xdpyinfo** lists the extensions available on a particular display.

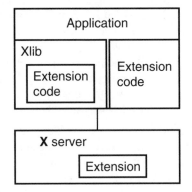

Figure A. Extra components of an X system with an extension.

```
Acorn-Noise                        SGI-MISCELLANEOUS
Adobe-DPS-Extension                SHAPE
AixDeviceControlExtension          SonyKeyboardExtension
AixExtension                       SonySoundExtension
AixEventControlExtension           SonyVideoExtension
AixStatExtension                   SonyPrinterExtension
AixDialExtension                   stellar-cm
AixLpfkExtension                   stellar-db
APOLLO-SHARE                       stellar-im
ARDENT-XDoubleBuffer               stellar-shmLink
ARDENT-XTitan                      stellar-xfdi
bezier                             stellar-xtest
DEC-XTRAP                          TekCms
MIT-SHM                            TeKDisplayListExtension
MIT-SUNDRY-NONSTANDARD             TeKHardCopySupport
Multi-Buffering                    TeKPeerWindows
NCD-SIE                            VEX
ORL-SYNC                           VIT-Image Display List Extension
PanasonicDosEmulatorExtension      X3D-PEX
SGI-GLX                            XTestExtension1
SGI-XGL                            ZoidExtension
```

Figure B. Extension names.

```
#define X_ShapeQueryVersion     0
#define X_ShapeRectangles       1
#define X_ShapeMask             2
#define X_ShapeCombine          3
#define X_ShapeOffset           4
#define X_ShapeQueryExtents     5
#define X_ShapeSelectInput      6
#define X_ShapeInputSelected    7
#define X_ShapeGetRectangles    8
```

Figure C. Minor opcode definitions for the MIT shape extension.

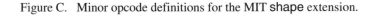

Summary

In this chapter you have seen what the role of the server is, and how the rest of the system is hardware independent because only the server interacts with the display hardware. We looked in detail at how the server is implemented and how it responds to requests from clients — to create and manipulate windows, and to draw text, graphics and pictorial images. We also looked at some of the more sophisticated mechanisms for handling fonts, which are especially useful when you are managing large **X** networks, and for the colour management required by advanced applications. Finally, we saw that the extensions mechanism allows extra functionality to be added to systems, so that **X** can grow organically but in a controlled way nonetheless.

So far we have not dealt with user input. We leave that to the next chapter, which examines what passes between client and server. We shall see that input from the user is processed initially by the server, but that it passes most of the work of input processing over to the client.

4

Communication between the Server and Clients

4.1   Clients send high-level 'requests' to the server
        4.1.1 Requests are transmitted asynchronously

4.2   The server uses 'events' to communicate input and status changes to the client
        4.2.1 The information contained in an event
        4.2.2 Keyboard input is received on the server but interpreted in the client
        4.2.3 Input methods

4.3   Intercepting input and requests for special handling
        4.3.1 The Virtual Screen system

4.4   X can work over many different network types, as well as locally

4.5   What load does X impose on the network?

4.6   X Version and Release numbers, and compatibility issues
        4.6.1 Compatibility and conformance

Introduction

This chapter deals with the second major component of the system — the communication channel between the client and server, and what passes across it. First we look in detail at the requests the clients send to the server, the events the server sends back to the clients, and how these are used to handle user input. Then we go on to look at features of the network itself, how heavily it is loaded, and how special systems can cope with very slow network links.

4.1 Clients send high-level 'requests' to the server

Requests are the fundamental mechanism by which clients specify to the server what graphical, window or management operations are to be performed on the display. Requests are network-efficient — items to be drawn are specified as objects, not just as bitmaps.

The only way a client can perform any graphics or window operation is by sending the appropriate requests to the server. You can think of requests as the interface between client and server, or as the equivalent of 'system calls' provided by an operating system.

We have already dealt with events relating to graphics and text drawing in Modules 3.3.2 and 3.5. **X** provides many other requests to let clients manage windows and other resources. These are some of the classes of request available:

- Creation and deletion of windows.

- Changing window attributes such as the window's cursor, its border, or its colormap.

- Configuring a window — changing its width, height, its position relative to its parent, and its position in the stacking order.

- Requests for information about a window, its attributes, and its configuration.

- Manipulating and retrieving properties. A **property** is a named piece of data which an application can attach to a window. Then any other application can read this or write to it, providing a way for applications to communicate via the server. This is the basis for all communication between **X** clients. (We cover properties in detail in Module 9.2.)

- Listing and loading fonts.

Even if you are programming the system, you don't ever have to deal with requests directly; the standard **X** subroutine library (**Xlib**) insulates you from them by providing convenient functions which do all the hard work of constructing the request and passing it to the network transport software. Moreover, in the last chapter we saw the effects that requests cause — the actions that the server performs handling colours and fonts, and drawing graphics and text, etc. So we won't go into any more detail about individual requests, but there are some general characteristics of requests that need to be emphasized. In the rest of this module we see that requests are relatively high-level, and in the next module we look at how they are communicated.

Requests are high-level

As we have seen with line and text drawing, requests are object-based, that is, instead of transmitting a bitmap or a list of pixels to be drawn, the request merely specifies the character number within the font, or the coordinates of the line, to be drawn.

This means that requests are network efficient — they use little network bandwidth, and the number of pixels affected by a request is typically 10 or 100 times greater than the number of bits comprising the request. As an example, a text request to draw a string ('the quick brown fox jumps over a lazy dog') is shown in Figure A: the string consists of 41 characters, and the total number of bytes in the request is 60, so the request is not much bigger than the absolute minimum possible.

Later on in this chapter (Module 4.5) and again in Module 13.2 we'll see that the load **X** imposes on the network is less than you might expect.

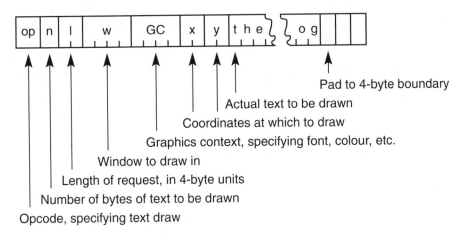

Figure A.   Example of an X text drawing request.

4.1 Clients send high-level 'requests' to the server

4.1.1 Requests are transmitted asynchronously

To maximize throughput, requests are sent asynchronously — in general, the server does not reply to the client to requests have arrived. This makes good use of the available network capacity and allows high throughput.

The client transmits almost all requests to the server **asynchronously**, and the server does not acknowledge that it has received the request. So after the client sends one request it doesn't have to wait for a reply but can send the next request immediately. When you are writing a program, this means that those functions in the standard **X** subroutine library (Xlib), which cause requests to be sent, return immediately and don't 'block', that is, they don't wait to receive until they receive a return value. This contrasts with an Open File system call, which waits until the operating system has replied whether the file has been opened successfully or not, and then it returns this status to the calling program. Figure A shows how three requests are sent asynchronously with no time gap between them.

The effect of this is good utilization of network bandwidth. Because the client can push requests 'down the wire' as quickly as it can generate them, it means there are no occasions when the network is standing idle because the client is awaiting a response from the server. Further, the network transport layer can package many requests into a single network packet, which reduces network overhead.

The reason that a reply from the server is unnecessary is that **X** works over a **reliable stream** network connection; the transport that **X** uses guarantees that the bytes sent from the client arrive correctly at the server. This is also how **X** can be network independent — it relies on the lower layers to deal with the networking problems, so no network-specific handling needs to be incorporated in the system.

Asynchronous operation is necessary to make displaying over a network feasible. If request transmission were synchronous, the client would have to wait for a reply from the server each time it sent a request. The wait time would be:

> *time to travel from client to server +*
> *time for server to process request +*
> *time to travel from server back to client*

that is, the time for a **round-trip**. As shown in Figure B, the time to send three requests synchronously involves three round-trip times. Even on fast networks this could easily be many tens of milliseconds and therefore that less than a hundred requests a second could be sent. This in turn would mean that just scrolling the text in a window would only ever be as fast as over a 9600 bps terminal line! (**X**'s predecessor, the W window system, was synchronous. It worked acceptably on the networks it was developed for, but over standard networks it proved too slow to be usable.)

(One disadvantage of asynchronous operation is that if an error does occur on the server due to your application, it is not easy to work out which request caused the error, as many requests may have been sent since. This complicates debugging. There is no easy answer to this, but using standard toolkits goes a long way to help. You can also explicitly force **X** to operate synchronously, to aid debugging.)

Surprisingly, the performance of the network is rarely the limiting factor in the overall system. In fact, the overall performance of an **X** application is sometimes *better* when working remotely over a network than when running locally on the same CPU as the server. Simply, this is because in the remote case you have two CPUs sharing the work in parallel, they are not contending for resources and they are not causing each other to page or swap in and out of memory. (We examine network performance in more detail in Modules 4.5 and 13.2.)

Some requests do wait for a reply

While synchronous operation is not necessary for most requests because the underlying reliable network software guarantees delivery, there are some requests which do need a **reply**. These functions block (wait) until the reply is received from the server, so their completion does involve a round-trip from client to server and back again. Replies are distinct from events, and are transmitted in their own format, specific to the corresponding request.

Typically these requests ask for information from the server about itself or some of its resources. Such requests include querying whether something is available (a font, a server extension) are supported, asking for details of something (window attributes, the value of a property, size characteristics of a font, etc.) or listing items (properties on a window, available fonts, hosts allowed connect to the server, etc.).

Because round trips can take a considerable time (Figure B), for good performance you obviously want to minimize the number of requests in your program causing round trips. We discuss this further in Module 13.3.

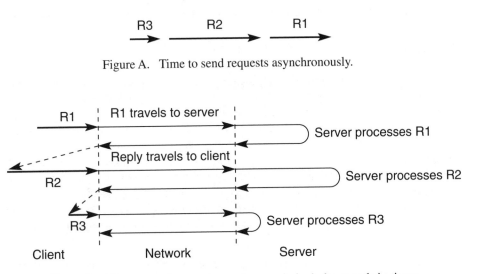

Figure A.   Time to send requests asynchronously.

Figure B.   Time to send requests synchronously includes roundtrip times.

4.2   The server uses 'events' to communicate input and status changes to the client

Events are messages from the server to the client that something has changed. They are the mechanism for obtaining input from the user — pressing keyboard keys, or moving the mouse. Events are also used to tell the client about other changes — in visibility of windows, in keyboard mapping, and in certain internal tables such as colormaps. These events enable clients to maintain the contents of their windows by redrawing when necessary, to communicate with one another, and to operate correctly in the presence of other applications.

So far we have looked at how the client requests the server to perform actions such as drawing graphics or creating a window — essentially how a client gets output onto the screen. Now we are looking at how *input* is handled using events, and also how the server uses events to inform applications about other changes they are interested in, exposure events for example. In a way, you can think of events as the reverse of requests — events are the information sent back from the server to the client (Figure A).

Apart from input from the keyboard and mouse, events are generated in a window when the configuration (size or position) of any of its sub-windows changes, when sub-windows are created or destroyed, or mapped or unmapped. When several applications are running, events are also required to tell one client when another has installed or de-installed a colormap, or when the keyboard mapping (which we discuss in the module after next) has changed. Other events inform a client when the contents of a property has changed and, as we shall see in Module 9.3, this enables clients to exchange information with each other. The selections mechanism of Module 9.4 also uses events for inter-client communication.

In the rest of this module we look at how events in general work, and in the following modules we examine keyboard input events in detail.

The events mechanism

The server informs a client about significant occurrences by sending an event. Events, like requests, are asynchronous — they are sent as necessary, and they are not acknowledged. Events are sent as a result of input from the keyboard or the mouse, or when a previously processed request has caused a side-effect; for instance, destroying a window will cause any windows covered by it to be exposed, and resizing a child window will probably require its parent to take some action, perhaps resizing to accommodate the new size of the child. Events in **X** are analogous to interrupts in an operating system: they allow changes in the system to be processed without forcing the client to poll. That is, the server explicitly tells the client when an event has occurred, instead of the client itself having to repeatedly check some status indicator, to see if something of interest has happened.

Normally, events are relatively infrequent because most events relate to user input, and people only type at a few characters per second. It is only where the motion of the mouse is being tracked in detail — for example, in freehand drawing applications, or when 'rubber-banding' a window during a resize operation — will there be a much higher rate of events, perhaps 50–150 per second.

To minimize the load of processing events, the client has to specify explicitly to the server the types of events it wants to be informed of, and in which windows. The server will send only these specific events to the client, so the client won't waste time processing events that are not relevant to it. Different sets of events of interest can be specified for each separate window in your application. For example, a client will want to process <KeyPress> events in a window dedicated to text input; whereas in a graphics drawing window it will be interested in the motion of the pointer, and will request <PointerMotion> events. When handling text input the application may also want <KeyRelease> events, so it can handle 'chords' consisting of multiple keys pressed simultaneously by noticing if one key is still down when another is pressed. (However, all servers don't necessarily support <KeyRelease> for keys other than Shift, Ctrl, and Alt, so using this feature may make your program non-portable.) Typically the client **selects for** or solicits its various event types (tells the server it is interested in them) just after the relevant window is created, which is often during the initialization stages of the program.

Any events that are not requested by some application are thrown away; for example, many applications ignore the <MotionNotify> events due to the mouse pointer moving in a text window.

It is possible for several clients to request the same event on the same window: *each of them* will be informed when such an event occurs.

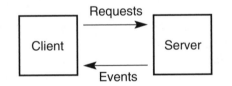

Figure A.   Events are 'the opposite' of requests.

4.2 The server uses 'events' to communicate input and status changes to the client

4.2.1 The information contained in an event

All events contain a common set of basic information, such as where and when the event occurred. Each particular event type also contains information specific to itself, giving more detail about the type of change in the system it relates to. For keyboard events the server only reports to the client that you have pressed or released that particular key, but the server attaches no meaning to it.

All events specify what type of event they are and in which window they occurred. Beyond that, the detailed contents of the event vary with the type of event, reasonably enough. For example, a <KeyPress> event must specify which key on the keyboard was pressed, and which **modifier keys** were also depressed at the time. (The modifier keys are Shift, Ctrl, Alt, etc., which when pressed modify what characters are generated by other alphanumeric and punctuation keys.) On the other hand, a window <Expose> event needs to say which window and what part of it was exposed. Now let us look at the contents of mouse and keyboard events in more detail.

Mouse events

The types of event generated by mouse input are as follows:

- <ButtonPress> and <ButtonRelease> are how mouse clicks are detected. These events also contain the time at which they occurred, so the application receiving them can decide whether two successive clicks constitute a double click if they are separated by a sufficiently short time.

- <MotionNotify> events report that the pointer has moved. Optionally you can request to be informed of these events only when one or more specified mouse buttons are depressed: for instance, to handle mouse drag actions. These events contain which buttons are depressed, and the (x,y) coordinates of the pointer when the event occurred.

- <Enter> and <Leave> events report when the pointer enters or leaves a window. These are used by menu systems, so they can be automatically be told when the pointer enters a window representing a selection panel on the menu — they can then highlight the panel, and un-highlight it when the pointer leaves again (Figure A).

Figure B shows the detailed contents of an event caused by dragging with the middle mouse button (button no. 2).

Keyboard input

When you press a key on the keyboard, the server generates a <KeyPress> event. The event does not interpret the meaning of thekey: instead it contains a number identifying which key has beenpressed. For example, on our workstation, the numeric identifier for the key with `Control` marked on it is 83, and the key marked `c` is 109. These numeric identifiers are called **keycodes**. The event also contains an indication of which modifier keys (Ctrl, Shift, etc.) were depressed at the time the key was pressed. But note that the server has not assigned any meaning to the key, for instance it has not interpreted it as an ASCII character, or an EBCDIC one, or anything else — that's done later, and it is done by the client. Figure C shows the events caused by pressing (and subsequently releasing) `ctl-C`.

When the key is released, a <KeyRelease> event is generated. By using key release events, the application (or the server where appropriate) can realize that one key is already down when another is pressed. This is essential where **chords** of keys are required, that is, a set of keys that must all be depressed together to invoke some (typically special-purpose) action. (For PC users perhaps the best known chord is `ctl-alt-Delete`, which causes the machine to reboot.) However, not all keyboards report the releasing of keys other than Shift, Ctrl, and Alt, so programs which rely on release events with other keys may be non-portable.

Just like other events, <KeyPress> and <KeyRelease> are reported only to clients which have requested them. For example the xclock clock program does not accept textual input, and therefore doesn't select for keyboard events at all.

In the next module we look in more detail at how a meaning is attached to these keyboard events.

Figure A.   Menu pane highlighted, after Enter event received.

Figure B.   Details of event, dragging with middle mouse-button.

```
      event opcode: MotionNotify
     normal or hint: Normal
               time: TIM f5a791b4
     root-window ID: WIN 0000002a
    event-window ID: WIN 03000014
    child-window ID: None
       root-window x: 349
       root-window y: 176
      event-window x: 16
      event-window y: 58
    state of buttons: Button2 pressed
         same-screen: True
```

```
      event opcode: KeyPress
           keycode: 109
              time: TIM f5b2c828
    root-window ID: WIN 0000002a
   event-window ID: WIN 03000014
   child-window ID: None
      root-window x: 155
      root-window y: 462
     event-window x: 80
     event-window y: 33
    modifiers state: Control
        same-screen: True
```

Figure C.   Details of events due to pressing Ctrl-C.

4.2 The server uses 'events' to communicate input and status changes to the client

4.2.2 Keyboard input is received on the server but interpreted in the client

---

When you press or release a keyboard key it is the client that interprets the key and decides whether it means an ASCII 'w', say, or a 'Trademark' symbol, or some Japanese character. This permits multiple applications with different character sets to coexist on the same display at the same time.

(If technical details aren't so relevant to you, you can skip over this module.)

When the keyboard event arrives, how does the client know what it is supposed to mean, as it contains little other than a key number? First, let's consider the simplest case, in which the key is to be interpreted as an ASCII character. The server does in fact contain a table saying which symbols are painted on the caps of each key; these symbols are called **keysyms**. So the table is a mapping of keycodes to keysyms. On some systems the table is obtained from the hardware or operating system. On others it has to be built manually by the server developer, and is compiled into the server, or is supplied as a configuration file which is read by the server every time it starts up. (In this way if a different keyboard type is to be used, only the configuration file needs to be changed to ensure correct keycode/keysym handling.) Taking our keyboard as an example, on the third row we have the keys marked with **Control**, **A**, **S**, ..., and on the numeric keypad a **4** with a left arrow, then a **5**, then a **6** with a right arrow, and finally a plus sign. The server table entries for these keys are:

Keycode	Keysym-1	Keysym-2
83	Control_L	
84	A	
85	S	
...		
98	Left	KP_4
99	F31	KP_5
100	Right	KP_6
132	KP_Add	KP_Add

(The keysym-2 entry relates more or less to the key when Shifted.) When the client starts, it can request this table from the server, and then use it to map the keycodes onto whatever characters are desired. For example, if ASCII characters are required, for the alphabetic keysyms like **A** and **S** the client only has to generate the directly corresponding character, checking the state of the modifier keys (Ctrl, Shift, etc.) to see if the character is to be lowercase, uppercase, or a control character. In fact there is a special function in Xlib specially for this (Figure A). Other keysyms such as the cursor keys (**Left** and **Right**) and function keys (**F31**) are interpreted in a client-specific way; for example, our terminal emulator program maps **Right** onto the 3-character sequence **Escape [D**, whereas in our text editor it is interpreted as the single character `ctl-F`. Later on, in Module 12.1, we'll see how on the client side we can change our keyboard mapping on a per-application basis (or even per window within the application), using the **translations** mechanism of the standard **X** toolkit.

Other, more elaborate ways to interpret the keys are possible. For example, if a client is using a Japanese character set, it may be necessary for the user to press several keys in succession to specify one Kanji character to be input. It is precisely because different applications may want to use different character sets that the character interpretation is left to the client. An extreme example of this would be a translator's workstation, which might have one window in Japanese, another in Hebrew, a third using English in ASCII encoding, and another English window connected to an IBM computer which is expecting EBCDIC characters.

A common problem, especially on PCs where people often swap the physical keyboard, is that the server table doesn't match the physical keyboard. Then the client generates characters according to what the server believes is written on the key caps, not what is actually on them, so you get confusing results. Fortunately, you can print the server table and modify it (using the MIT program xmodmap), so customizing the server to match the keyboard you have. People often use this facility even when the keyboard mapping is correct, to 'rearrange' the keyboard to their particular preference, for example, to alter the location of the `Control` and `Shift` keys on a PC keyboard to match those on a workstation. And as we mentioned above, some servers let you install a different mapping table just by using a different keyboard configuration file.

In the next module we look at 'input methods', which are a more sophisticated way of converting server events into the characters required by the application.

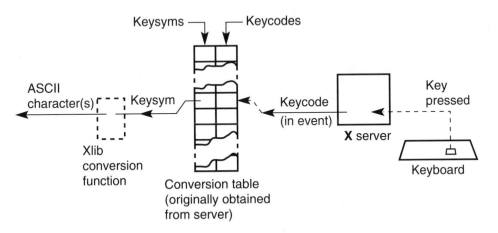

Figure A.   How keycodes are converted to characters.

4.2 The server uses 'events' to communicate input and status changes to the client

4.2.3 Input methods

So that you can enter characters in languages that are not adequately supported by normal (ASCII) computer keyboards, **X** provides 'input methods'. These are algorithms for entering characters in a particular language and can be implemented within the application itself or in a separate process called an input server.

Release 5 extends and simplifies the support of multiple languages, by means of the **input method** mechanism. An input method is an algorithm or mechanism for entering characters other than those on the keyboard. This is necessary for European languages which contain characters other than ASCII, and for oriental languages which contain far more characters than could be accommodated directly on any keyboard. Entering special symbols by using a **compose** key is an example of an input method implemented on many hardware terminals. The input method effectively translates events from the server into characters in the particular language which the application requires (Figure A).

X allows input methods to be implemented either in the client as part of a library (Figure B), or as a separate process known as an **input server** (Figure C). In either case, keyboard events are received by the input method and processed, and the resulting decoded character is passed to the application program. The advantage of the separate process approach is that a single server can handle many applications on several different machines on the network, although there is a communications overhead. Incorporating the input method in the library compiled into the program removes the communication load, but at the cost of reduced flexibility — the program can no longer select its input method dynamically, which it must if it is to be portable to different language environments.

Multi-language support and internationalization are covered further in Module 5.3. The next module looks at a mechanism similar in a way to input methods, where special processing of input is handled by a separate process.

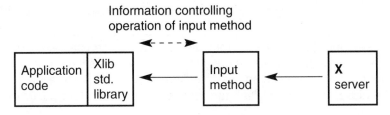

Figure A. The input method receives events and translates them into the language-specific characters for the application.

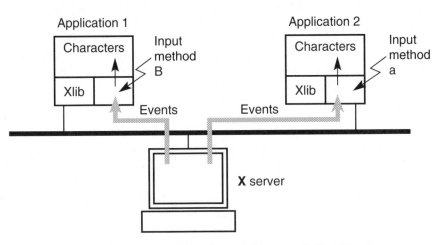

Figure B. An input method implemented as part of client libraries.

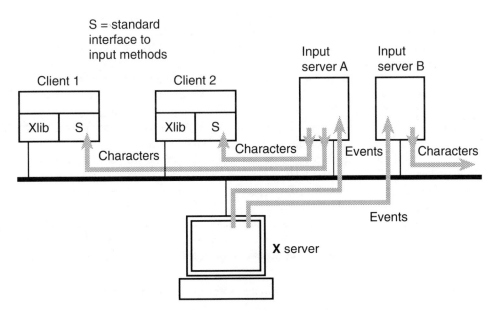

Figure C. Input method implemented as a separate process servicing many applications.

4.3   Intercepting input and requests for special handling

All user input (and requests from clients, too) can be channelled via a separate process. This can be used merely for performance testing and analysing system behaviour, or to provide special handling — for example, to allow voice input, or give disabled users facilities to manage a keyboard more easily, or emulate a mouse.

The simplest type of processing involves a process that sits between client and server. To the **X** server it is just a client, whereas to the user application it appears to be an **X** server and it is to this process that the initial connection is made (Figure A). The process notes all events and requests, but otherwise passes them through transparently, so the client and real **X** server continue to work, and require no alteration. The intercepting process can record or print out details of the events and requests. (See Module 13.4.1 for examples of how this type of facility is used.)

XTrap

The **XTrap** server extension developed by DEC intercepts events from the input devices before they are processed by the server proper, and passes them to a separate client application (Figure B). The application can perform specialized processing on them, and pass them back, perhaps modified, or with some extra events added, back to **XTrap** to despatch them to the server. **XTrap** also intercepts requests and passes them to the separate application before the **X** server processes them. While **XTrap** is a server extension, it is only the interception of events and requests that happens within the server; all special processing is handled within an external client application.

XTrap was developed to allow **X** sessions to be recorded and played back, and for testing and performance measurements. However, it has also been used to allow people with manual disabilities to use the **X** system. Much **X** software implicitly assumes that there is a pointing device such as a mouse or trackball on the system, and that the user can use both the pointer and the keyboard simultaneously; for the manually disabled, this may not be true. The solution using **XTrap** overcomes this by providing emulations for the mouse functions, and allowing one-at-a-time key presses to simulate the use of modifier keys and chords; for example, it allows the modifier keys Control and Alt to be locked, to supplement the standard CapsLock provided by the keyboard. But the **XTrap** control application goes far beyond providing simplistic emulation of mouse functions (vertical/horizontal movement, button-clicks, etc.); it can provide an end-user of standard, unmodified, **X** applications with higher-level replacements of the logical or semantic functions the mouse is used for. For example, it can be set up so that a single key-press can position the pointer in a particular pushbutton within a previously specified application's window; the user doesn't have to move the pointer up and across to the correct position by repeatedly and tediously pressing some keyboard keys emulating mouse motion.

XTrap is included in the user-contributed software of the MIT Release.

In the next module we look at another system that intercepts events and requests and modifies them, but does it entirely within an 'ordinary' client and without any modifications to the server.

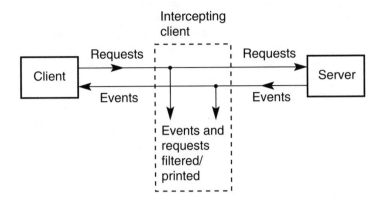

Figure A.   Separate process between client and server, intercepting all X traffic.

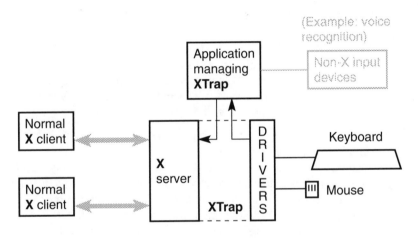

Figure B.   XTrap intercepts events and requests.

4.3 Intercepting input and requests for special handling

4.3.1 The Virtual Screen system

The Virtual Screen system provides a 'virtual root window' by intercepting requests to the X server and modifying them appropriately. Windows on this virtual screen are shown on a normal X window on the real X server. This system has been used for multi-media applications and task management.

(If technical details aren't so relevant to you, you can skip over this module.)

The system we describe here is not available commercially nor is it included in the MIT Release; however, we cover it in some detail not only because it offers a very useful facility, but also because it illustrates the extent to which separating the client and the server allows X to be enhanced without any changes to the server or the Protocol.

Virtual Screen is a client program that provides a virtual screen or virtual root window on which other windows can exist. The virtual root window is just a normal X window on the real X display. To the applications using it, the Virtual Screen program appears to be an X display, but to the real X server it is just another client; so to operate, it requires no modification to the real X server. Like some of the systems we mentioned in the previous module, it is a special client which sits between the normal applications and the X server (Figure A).

However, requests from the applications are not necessarily passed through unchanged. In particular, any requests that refer to the real root window, of the real X server, are modified to refer to the virtual root window provided by Virtual Screen. Thus the system overall is more precisely illustrated by Figure B.

Virtual Screen has been used for two quite different purposes. The first is as a general mechanism for creating multimedia documents. Let's consider a multimedia editor as an example. The basic editor handles text in the normal way. To include a drawing in the document being edited, a Virtual Screen is incorporated into the editor's window (the user presses an insert button to do this), and the user's favourite X drawing application is run displaying its X window onto this Virtual Screen root window. Editing the drawing is performed using the drawing application and in the normal way, except that the drawing area is encapsulated in the editor. Similarly, other types of media such as spreadsheets, video, and animated displays, can be incorporated in the document by running their appropriate applications in an included Virtual Screen.

The other application of Virtual Screen has been to provide the user with 'task management'. You can dedicate a separate Virtual Screen to each major activity you perform, and group all the applications you need to perform that task onto the Virtual Screen. For example, for preparing a financial report, you might have a spreadsheet, a calculator, and a word processor, whereas for programming you might use a couple of editors, a debugger, and the application you are developing. When you are not doing a task, you can just iconify its Virtual Screen (which as we said is really just a normal X window) to keep it from cluttering your screen. Each Virtual Screen can even have its own window manager handling the windows on it, so you can manage the windows within a Virtual Screen just like you do on a real screen! (By contrast, in the multimedia case, each Virtual Screen has only one application connected to it and window management within the screen is therefore not required.)

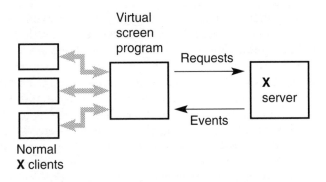

Figure A.   The VirtualScreen client between applications and server.

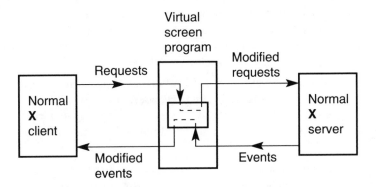

Figure B.   VirtualScreen modifies requests before passing them to the real server.

4.4 X can work over many different network types, as well as locally

---

X is network independent — it can work over any network that provides guaranteed delivery of data in the order sent. Several different network systems can be used simultaneously. However in practice most X systems are TCP/IP based.

X does not use facilities specific to particular networking systems, and so it can operate over many different ones: it is **network independent**. X assumes that the complexities of networking — ensuring reliable delivery of data, acknowledging receipt, checksumming to validate contents of packets, re-sending lost packets, etc. — are all handled by the lower (network) layers of the system, so X itself doesn't have to bother with them. As a result, X does not contain code to handle those aspects, which simplifies its implementation, and isolates it from specific system dependencies. This layering approach is illustrated in Figure A.

X is able to use all these different systems because its networking requirements are fairly simple; it needs a **reliable stream** protocol. Here, 'reliable' is a strict term: it means that bytes sent across the network are guaranteed to arrive at the other end, and are guaranteed to arrive in the order they were sent. This is why X can operate asynchronously, as we described in Module 4.1 — it knows that once it passes requests or events to the network, they will reach the other end.

X prefers a 'stream' connection to a record-oriented one because X can then buffer things more efficiently. As the X loading increases, it can send progressively larger packets, with consequently less overhead. This is a sensible way to operate; be efficient when the load is heavy, but when you are lightly loaded you can afford to waste a few cycles.

In order to support both local and remote operation, X obviously must operate over both types of communication system. In fact, X works over true inter-machine networking systems, such as TCP/IP, DECnet, AppleTalk, and OSI (all of which offer reliable byte streams) and inter-process communication systems (IPCs) for communication within a single machine, such as UNIX sockets, shared memory, streams, and named pipes.

Considering the lower networking levels, it follows that X operates over any of the physical systems supported by the high-level protocols such as TCP/IP or DECnet. For example, X is widely used across Ethernet, token ring, FDDI and X.25 networks. X can also be run over modem-connected serial lines, for instance using TCP/IP in the form of SLIP (serial line Internet Protocol) or PPP (point-to-point protocol). When ISDN becomes widely available as a service, it will be an attractive option for connecting widely spread X stations to central computing resources, such as allowing people to use their office X applications from workstations at home. (However, ISDN is only a fast digital replacement for a modem connection, so you will still have to use a network protocol like SLIP across these links.)

To avoid confusion, it is worth pointing out that a client and server can operate across a particular network system, OSI say, only if both of them have had support for it compiled into them when they were written. In other words, **X** of itself does not provide any new support for any type of networking system; however, **X** systems can be written to *use* any networking support that has already been developed. Thus the network transport system used by your server determines which of the machines on your network you can interoperate with, that is, run clients on. For example, if you have an OSI-only server, you won't be able to use applications running on a TCP/IP-based remote host. However there are **X** servers that have been written to handle more than one protocol simultaneously, for instance both TCP/IP and DECnet as shown in Figure B. Here, cutting-and-pasting from application T's window to application D's is really transferring data from a VMS VAX across DECnet and X.25 to a UNIX machine across TCP/IP and Ethernet, using the **X** server as an intermediary.

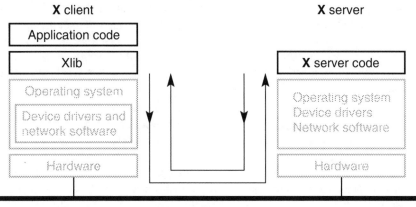

Figure A.   X leaves transport between client and server to lower-down system software and hardware.

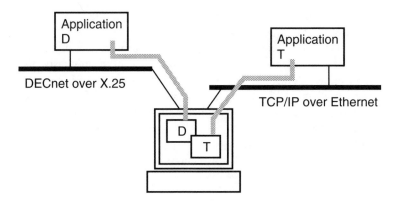

Figure B.   Multi-protocol server simplifies communication between disparate operating systems and networks.

4.5   What load does X impose on the network?

Typically an **X** display uses a very small fraction of the bandwidth of a network with a capacity like an Ethernet, although peak loads may be 30% or more. In some circumstances dial-up phone lines can give acceptable performance. However, executing over the network is not suitable for some data-intensive applications.

When **X** was designed the type of networks then current on university campuses and within organizations were Ethernet or token ring. It was developed with these in mind — its performance on these everyday types of networks had to be acceptable.

Performance studies show that for a typical mixed workload, an X-terminal (which is the worst case, as all its clients run over the network) peaks at about 1% of an Ethernet; because not all the terminals peak simultaneously, a single Ethernet segment should be able to handle hundreds of X-terminals (according to the X-terminal manufacturers). Other measurements, relating to implementing **X** over OSI transports, indicate an average bandwidth requirement of only about 20 kbits per second, that is, about 0.2% of an Ethernet.

Figure A shows network loadings for some common activities. It is clear that activities such as rubber-banding window outlines and tracking the mouse, which are commonly thought to be very consumptive, impose relatively little load. But the figure does show that some activities *do* cause a heavy load. Not surprisingly, dumping the contents of a window — which involves manipulating and transmitting each pixel individually rather than sending just high-level object-based requests — imposes the heaviest burden.

There are some data-intensive applications that are just not suitable for running remotely, and which need to be run on a workstation where the server and client are on the same CPU. Typically these involve images, which have to be specified and manipulated on a pixel-by-pixel basis; this involves transmission of large quantities of data between client and server.

But in normal situations the network is not the limiting factor on performance for remote applications. The limiting factor is often the display hardware — even over the network clients can send requests quicker than the hardware can process them. This is not surprising, considering that requests can be sent asynchronously, that they are high-level and network-efficient, and that the server is not competing with the client for the use of the client's CPU. For similar reasons 9.6 or 19.2 kbits per second phone lines (often used by people working from home) have proven usable. This is especially true for applications which are largely text-based: as we discussed in Module 4.1, the overhead added by **X** to text transmission is quite small. (Module 13.2.1 deals with how performance over slow network connections is being improved.)

Network 'speed': latency versus bandwidth

There are two different aspects of network speed. The first is the obvious and most common measure of **bandwidth**: how many bits can you send down the wire in each second. As we mentioned above, there is a sensible lower limit of several tens of Kbits per second on this; and for some data-intensive applications, the higher the better. But for most applications, very high bandwidth is not essential.

The second aspect of network speed is the **latency** — how long is it before the first bit sent actually arrives at its destination? A long latency will affect the interactive performance of a system. For example, if latency is a quarter of a second, when you press a key on the server, the keyboard event takes 0.25 s to travel to the client, the client responds with a request to draw a character on the screen, and that request takes another 0.25 s to return to the server. This means that you have to wait an absolute minimum of half a second for the first character you type to be echoed. If you were tracking the mouse, for example when drawing freehand, or rubber-banding a window, this latency would be very uncomfortable.

Latency and bandwidth are completely separate. A serial line using copper wires may only have a 19.2 kbits per second bandwidth, but it has tiny latency — once sent, signals travel along the wire at about two-thirds the speed of light, that is, they arrive almost instantly. On the other hand, a satellite link has very high bandwidth, perhaps many Megabits per second, but it has a very high latency because the signal has so far to travel — from earth to the satellite and back down again — and even at the speed of light this imposes a considerable delay.

In summary, bandwidth determines how acceptably you can shift large amounts of data, particularly for pixel-based images, whereas low latency gives you a small round-trip time which is essential for good interactive feel.

(See Module 13.2 for more about network performance.)

Activity type	Peak traffic bytes/s	Peak traffic packets/s	Peak % Ethernet utilisation	Typical packet size, bytes
Continuous page scrolling, xdvi document previewer	75K	90	6	1080
Benchmark tests, xbench, mixed activities	78K	92	6.5	1080
Capture window image (xwd) and redisplay (xwud)	160K	220	13	1080
Position and resize windows with twm window manager	30K	170	2.7	90
Cursor tracking	12.5K	180	1	90
Continuous scrolling, in xterm terminal emulator	20K	50	1.8	1080
Continuous scrolling, in emacs text editor	11K	40	1	1080

Figure A.   Peak network loads imposed by common activities.

4.6   X Version and Release numbers, and compatibility issues

The **X** Protocol definition — the formal description of **X** — has been frozen at 'Version' 11. MIT distributes occasional 'Releases' of implementations of the Protocol, adding functionality or improving performance.

Because the only connection between the client and the server is the communications link between them, it follows that the 'messages' sent across this link are the only factor which determines whether a client will successfully inter-operate with a server. The **X Protocol** is the official MIT standard which determines what these messages are, the format in which they are transmitted (the **encoding** of the requests, replies, and events) and how the client and server are to interpet them.

In a sense, the Protocol *is* **X** — the code from MIT is just a sample implementation of server and clients, which many people find useful. The MIT code includes the basic **X** programming library, Xlib, which is more or less a set of C-language 'function-wrappers' around the basic protocol requests. (We discuss Xlib, and the extra functionality it provides, in Module 5.2.2.)

Version numbering

The **X version number** refers to the Protocol. The version number is incremented when the protocol changes, that is when the new version becomes incompatible with the earlier one, and existing programs will no longer work correctly. The current version number is '11'. When we say a program 'uses X11' or 'conforms to **X** version 11', what we mean is that it is using this version of the Protocol, and that the messages being passed between client and server are in the format specified by that version.

Figure A shows a history of **X** version numbers. **X** went from version 1 to 9 very quickly — in the early days many backward-incompatible changes were made to it as it developed. Version 10 was widely used, and a few commercial products were based on it, but is was not until **X** version 11 ('X11') that **X** became very widely accepted and large-scale commercial product development began. So much has now been invested in X11 that a version 12 is unthinkable — X12 would require just too much redevelopment of existing software.

However, the fact that the Protocol is fixed does *not* mean that the functionality of the system is frozen. Obviously new clients can be written, but by means of the **extension mechanism** designed into X11 from the beginning, new features can be added to the system in a controlled way (see Module 3.8). It is also worth noting that many major improvements to **X**, such as the Xcms colour management system, input methods, and improved internationalization support, are entirely on the client side. And even other features such as the font server and xdm and XDMCP (Module 11.1) which do affect the **X** server's operation, only relate to its system administration and don't affect how requests are processed. (We cover this issue in more detail in the next module.)

Release numbering

Every so often, MIT issues a collection of sample servers, clients, and programming libraries for the current version; these are **releases** of **X**. Releases usually include:

- Performance improvements.

- Bug fixes.

- New client programs, and enhancements to existing ones.

- Improvements or changes to programming libraries, and perhaps new user interface or programming toolkits. For example, Release 5 adds support for internationalization, which is implemented entirely in the libraries and the clients.

- New functionality in the server that does not affect the **X** Protocol, often in the area of system administration. For example, Release 4 introduced the XDMCP system for handling the startup of X-terminals; this is just a convenience tool, and as we mentioned above, it does not affect the requests sent to the **X** server, and therefore is not an extension. Release 5 introduced the font server, to allow fonts to be held on one central machine rather than requiring all fonts to be held on all **X** servers; again, this does not affect the format or content of requests sent to the **X** server, and means no incompatibility has been introduced into the Protocol.

MIT releases typically occur about every 12–18 months. Commercial suppliers often lag about 12 months behind.

In the next module we see how version and release numbers affect compatibility of clients with servers.

Version 1: mid-1984.

Version 6: late 1984. This was the first version to be licenced for use outside MIT.

Version 9: released publicly in September 1985.

Version 10: late 1985. People and organisations outside MIT were now contributing a lot to the software.

First commercial X product: DEC announced their VAXstation-II/GPX in January 1986.

Version 10, Release 3: February 1986.   **X** was spreading, and being ported to many new systems.

Version 10 Release 4: November 1986. During 1986 it was clear that Version 10 could not evolve to satisfy all the requirements that were being asked of

it. MIT and DEC undertook a complete redesign of the protocol. The result was **X**, Version 11.

Version 11 Release 1: September 1987.

MIT X Consortium founded: January 1988, to foster development of **X**, and to control the X standards.

Version 11 Release 2: March 1988.

Version 11 Release 3: October 1988.

Version 11 Release 4: January 1990.

Version 11 Release 5: August 1991.

Version 11 Release 6: Not released at the time of writing, but expected in late 1993.

Figure A.   Summary of X version and release numbers.

4.6 X Version and Release numbers, and compatibility issues

4.6.1 Compatibility and conformance

Applications are forward-compatible with later releases of the server, and many are backward-compatible too. However, problems arise in applications when new 'standard' extensions are used, and in system administration areas which depend on functionality available only in later releases.

How, if the **X** Protocol is now frozen at version 11, can X11 clients be incompatible with earlier or later servers? What do manufacturer's claims like 'Fully conformant to Release 5 of X11' mean?

For development systems, and for software packages that include client programs, conforming to a release means providing all the updated library facilities, plus at least the new client programs essential to using new system administration features. Ideally all the other new and modified MIT clients would be included, but as many manufacturers have provided their own replacements for various applications such as terminal emulator, clock, editor, etc., these may be omitted. (After Release 5, it is likely that many of the standard MIT will no longer be part of the **core** release, but will be included as part of the **contrib** software instead, emphasizing that the MIT Release is just a sample.)

In practice, manufacturers must continually track the features of the latest MIT releases if they are to remain competitive, because the new features are so important to users and system managers.

Compatibility of clients between releases is not usually a problem, because what they are sending to and receiving from the server is determined by the **X** Protocol, which is unchanged. Typically, you can be using one release of the server today and switch over to a new release tomorrow without any change whatever to your applications. (This is just as well, as the new X-terminal you plug into your network may be using a later server release, and you don't want to be forced to upgrade all your applications everywhere else on the network just because you bought one new terminal.)

However, difficulties can arise with a program when you recompile it, because often the interfaces to the programming libraries used by the program change with a new release. Similarly, the internals of the libraries may have altered, so that relinking may give problems, or the final program may not work as intended. This is most common when you are using an **X** toolkit in your program. Toolkits are continually being enhanced, and so change relatively frequently. Even so, an existing toolkit application will continue to work OK unless you recompile it. The solution in both cases is to amend the source-code to bring it into line with the new library interface, and rebuild. You should also keep the old version of the program and the old libraries available, so that you can maintain the program based on the earlier **X** release, until porting to the new release is complete and has been tested. (Even if you don't recompile, you may also get problems if the original application was built using shared libraries, because these effectively involve dynamic relinking of the program every time it is run. The solution here is to keep the old shared libraries available as well as the new ones. For more about shared libraries, see Module 14.1.)

In Release 4 a bug in the server was corrected, causing stricter checking of unused data fields in certain requests. Many applications had been built which now failed; a special bc (backward compatibility) option is provided in most servers now to disable this strict checking, to allow the erroneous programs still to work.

For a server product, conforming to an MIT release is simply a matter of ensuring all the new functionality, including extensions and non-extensions, is present. While the new features may not affect the **X** Protocol, they can still affect either how an application works, or how you administer the system. Let's look at each case in turn.

New application functionality in a release can be included as an extension, or in some other way; we'll illustrate this with two examples. First, Release 4 introduced the SHAPE extension to allow non-rectangular windows. Servers prior to Release 4 don't include this, so if your applications insists on having non-rectangular windows, it just won't work with Release 3 servers or earlier. (See Module 3.8.1 for how applications ought to query the server to see if an extension is present.) Second, font scaling was introduced in Release 5, not as an extension, but as a change in how the XLFD name of a font is interpreted — by using the correct font name you specify that a font is to be made available at some (scaled) point-size. If your application implicitly assumes that font scaling is available and that it will therefore it dynamically request fonts at different and unusual sizes, your program is unlikely to work properly with pre-Release 5 servers. To summarize, if your application assumes and depends on functionality that was not available in earlier releases, that application will have backward-compatibility problems.

The second type of functionality included in a new release relates to system administration. These changes won't affect individual client applications but, because they affect how you manage your **X** network as a whole, they may actually be much more important than application-related changes. Two examples are the introduction of XDMCP in Release 4, and the font server in Release 5. With XDMCP (described in Module 11.1.3) you can add **X** stations very simply to your network, and manage all startup configuration information centrally instead of holding it on each individual station. Once your network management is based on this, going back to Release 3 servers that don't provide it becomes a real headache even though all your applications programs will work OK. The other example is the Release 5 font server. Not having it won't cause applications to fail, but once you configure your whole network to share and access fonts using the font server, incorporating an **X** server without it into your network probably costs more effort than it's really worth.

Summary

This chapter has dealt with the second of the three major components of the system — the information exchanged between client and server over the communications link between them. We looked at the events sent from the server, their contents, and the format in which they are transmitted over the network. We saw that events are the mechanism for receiving input from the user, but the processing of user input is left to the client as only it can decide how input is to be interpreted, perhaps relying on input methods for sophisticated processing. Then we looked more closely at how **X** can operate over many different types of network, and the issues of network performance. Finally we saw that the **X** Protocol is the formal definition and standard of what is communicated between client and server, and saw how **X**'s version- and release-numbers affect compatible operation of client and server.

In the next chapter we look at the third component of the system — the client program — having already covered here how it handles user input.

5 Clients — the Application Programs

5.1   An overview of the client and its role

5.2   What **X** clients consist of, and how they are built
    5.2.1 **X** programs are event-driven
    5.2.2 Basic **X** client functions are provided by the Xlib library
    5.2.3 Listing of a program based on Xlib
    5.2.4 Most **X** applications use a high-level toolkit

5.3   Internationalizing and localizing applications — Xi18n
    5.3.1 Internationalized text input, and input methods
    5.3.2 Internationalized **X** text output

5.4   Examples of **X** application programs
    5.4.1 Some common **X** applications

Introduction

So far we have covered the server and the communications channel between server and clients, and in the last chapter we saw how clients respond to and process events sent to them, to handle user input and other functions. Now we are going to look at the other functions which a client program has to provide, how it is constructed, and some representative examples of applications. The emphasis here is on a single client working more or less in isolation; later on, in Chapter 9, we'll consider multiple applications and how they interact.

5.1 An overview of the client and its role

X clients are application programs. They contain the application code — for example, to process the payroll, send electronic mail messages, or handle queries and updates to a database. They also include code for X support.

The function of the client is to give you the application functionality that you need to do your job as a user, and so the main part of the client is the application code. For example, typical clients include spreadsheet programs, accounts packages, electronic mail programs, database systems, network management packages, program debugging tools, medical imaging systems, etc.

However, because the client is an X program, it also needs to contain all the code to handle the various aspects of X operation, many of which we have already seen:

- Establish the connection to the server.

- Set up parameters to indicate preferred size and aspect ratio of the application's window, to be used by the window manager.

- Issue requests (as we described in Module 4.1) to create/destroy windows, load fonts, decode colour specifications, draw graphics and text, etc.

- Select for and handle exposure, mouse, and other events (Module 4.2).

- Provide all the components of the user interface, including menus, scroll-bars, pushbuttons, etc. and any special event handling they require. For example, enter/leave events are used to detect when the pointer enters a pane in a menu, and mouse motion events are used to control scrollbars.

- Handle keyboard input events and interpret input in terms of appropriate character sets, by mapping keysyms to characters — either directly or via an input method.

- Read in defaults and preferences from defaults files, and process command-line options.

- Handle cut-and-paste mechanisms, the Selections Service (see Chapter 9) and any other client-to-client communications.

So the client (in fact, each client) has to include a large amount of code to make use of X and, when running, it will contain all the data structures describing the user interface of the program, how it interfaces with the application code, and so on (Figure A). This contrasts with other window systems, where most of these functions are provided either directly by the operating system, or by the base window system itself. In X much of this functionality is provided by the Xlib library, and in most cases the user interface components are provided by a toolkit. Even so, these libraries and toolkits are actually built into the client at compile-time (as we'll see in more detail in the next chapter).

Very little is contained in the server — only the very basic data structures it needs to maintain its windows on screen, use the fonts it has loaded, etc.

In many ways the situation is similar to an application written for an ordinary, character-based terminal. The application doesn't run on the terminal itself, but on the remote host. Everything to do with the application and all its data structures — even those relating to the layout of windows and graphics on the screen — are contained in the application itself. The only information in the terminal is the low-level data relating to the display on the screen, such as the bitmaps of the characters, their colour, and style (underline, bold, etc.). (Recall the comparison we made of X-terminals and character-based terminals, in Module 3.2.1.)

Minimizing what's held in the server is a deliberate design feature. The server needs to be small and stable, whereas applications (and the libraries and toolkits they are built on) are more easily changed. Moreover, functions provided by the server are limited by the speed of the server's CPU, whereas if a client function isn't fast enough, it can be speeded up (for everybody on the network) by running it on a faster machine. (If the function were in the server it would involve changing the machines on all the users' desks.)

The rest of this chapter covers in detail many of these aspects of the client.

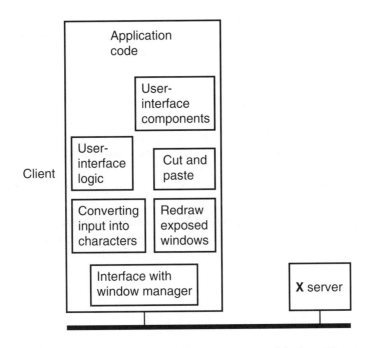

Figure A.   In X most application functions are not part of the base X systems.

5.2 What X clients consist of, and how they are built

Clients are usually built with libraries, to simplify coding and encourage good programming practice and 'playing by the rules'. The program structure of **X** clients is 'event-driven'.

As we saw in the previous module, applications include a lot of code to handle **X**. The most basic way to build an application is to use the Xlib library, which provides the fundamental interface to **X**; it contains elementary functions for issuing requests to the server, and receiving and processing events.

However, the interface provided by the standard **X** function library, Xlib, is very low level. It is more suited to systems programmers than applications programmers. So, most applications are built with a toolkit. Simply, a toolkit is a library of higher-level functions which is layered on top of Xlib, as shown in Figure A. As well as hiding some of the detailed internals of **X**, a toolkit typically provides a consistent user interface, with standard functions to create and use user interface components such as menus, scrollbars, pushbuttons, etc. However, this layered structure is not like the ISO seven-layer reference model for networks, in which a layer can only talk to its immediate neighbours above and below. Instead, in **X** a layer can communicate with any other as necessary, as show in Figure A. The application code needs to access the operating system directly for services such as file handling, time-of-day, etc., for surely such facilities are none of **X**'s business. For detailed graphics the application will probably need the low-level but powerful graphics primitives provided by Xlib and will bypass the toolkit, while the toolkit layer may require access to the operating system, for example to write temporary data to a work file. (Xlib is described in detail in Module 5.2.2, and toolkits in Module 5.2.4 and Chapter 6.)

Applications also contain other libraries. For example, a typical large graphical application might contain libraries of functions related to the user-problem it addresses (for example, chemical, financial, or statistical functions), functions which encapsulate organization- or project-defined standards, or facilities, third-party libraries for standard graphics functions (for example, GKS-to-**X** conversion), and so on, as already shown schematically in Figure A.

In the next module we look at how an **X** application must be structured to be able to handle all the different events that the server may generate for it; in the three modules after that we look at the Xlib and toolkit libraries for building **X** programs.

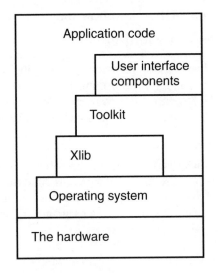

Figure A.   X applications have a layered structure.

5.2   What X clients consist of, and how they are built

5.2.1   X programs are event-driven

Because the user can interact with any component of the graphical user interface presented by an X application, the program does not know which actions it will have to perform next. Instead it is driven by events — caused by user input or other external factors. This largely determines the internal structure of an X program.

X programs, in common with those for most other window systems, are **event-driven**, whereas most programs for character-based terminals are **data-driven**. Let us see what these terms mean, by taking as an example a hypothetical program to let the user enter contact details for a customer. The data-driven program asks (prompts you) for the data it requires, and will not allow you to proceed until it gets what it wants. You have no choice about which field may be entered; the program has complete control and therefore knows exactly in what order information will be entered.

On the other hand, the event-driven program has no control over what you are going to enter. You can start not only by entering the phone number first, but by entering half of the address, then skipping to the name, then modifying the phone number, not to mention being able to access the pull-down menus. In other words, the application must be prepared to handle whatever *you* choose to do — it must base its processing on external *events*. (To some extent, applications which make use of forms-based input on character-based non-X terminals, have a similar event-driven structure.)

The structure of data-driven programs is straightforward, as illustrated in Figure A. However, event-driven programming requires a very different style. The program must be always ready to receive an event (typically user input), and once an event is received work out what sort of event it is, what it means, and how to process it. This structure is shown schematically in Figure B.

Event-driven programming constrains how you write your programs. In particular, you have to ensure there are no long computations — processing must be done in small pieces so that the program is always ready to respond to an event very soon after it has arrived. This can be difficult enough when you are writing a new program from scratch, but may be almost impossible if you are trying to change an old program to use X. The best approach may be to write a separate X event-driven front end which runs as a separate process, communicating with a more or less unchanged old program. Indeed there are a number of development tools available precisely for this type of work (see Module 14.3).

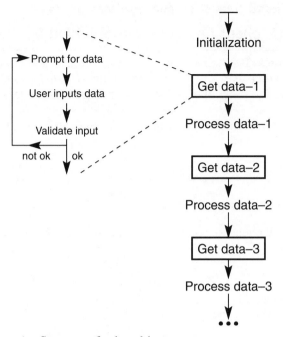

Figure A. Structure of a data-driven program.

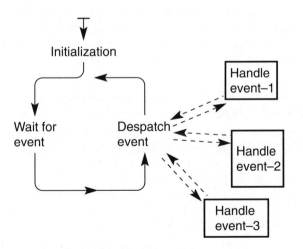

Figure B. Loop structure of an event-driven program.

5.2 What X clients consist of, and how they are built

5.2.2 Basic X client functions are provided by the Xlib library

The Xlib library provides the client with a set of subroutines for issuing requests to the server and receiving and processing events. It is the lowest level interface to the X system, and most applications use it as their low-level foundation.

The standard **X** library, Xlib, is just a library of subroutines, providing the following functions:

- Opening connections to servers.

- A convenient way of issuing **X** requests.

- Despatching the requests to the transport software, to be sent to the server.

- Receiving events and information from the server.

- Convenience functions for **X**-related tasks.

- Performance enhancements.

In a way you can think of Xlib as the **X** 'operating system'; calls to the subroutines it contains are analogous to system calls. Now let us look in turn at each of the facilities it provides.

Xlib **makes the X protocol requests available** to the applications programmer as a series of C-language functions. ('Xlib is a C-language binding of the protocol.') Originally Xlib provided functions that were little more than wrappers around the requests. However, with time Xlib has been improved and now it offers a lot more, as we see below.

Xlib handles the client side of the **communications between the application and the server**. When the application calls a function to issue a request, **X** passes the request to the necessary transport software so it can be sent to the server. This will be network software if the client is running remotely, or inter-process communication (IPC) software if client and server are on the same machine. Xlib also provides all the functions necessary for the application to select for particular event types and to inform the server of this selection. When events are sent by the server over the network or IPC software, Xlib receives the events and queues them until the application is ready to retrieve and process them using other Xlib functions.

Xlib provides many **utility** or **convenience functions** for **X**-related tasks, including reading in default values for various components of the program, parsing default values to see what they mean (for example, for **geometry specifications** of window size and position), handling **regions** (arbitrary sets of pixel locations), interpreting colour specifications, manipulating bitmaps and images, and translating keyboard events to ASCII strings. In other words, Xlib gives you a wide range of facilities for managing those data structures within your application which are related to **X**, but which need to be processed by the client and not just by the server. For instance, reading a bitmap from a file must be done on the client machine and using the client machine's file system, before the bitmap can be sent to the server for drawing.

Xlib has grown to include many **performance-enhancing features**. Xlib buffers requests, collecting several together before it passes them to the network software for transporting to the server, so that network traffic is reduced. Multiple requests for drawing single items into the same window are merged into a single 'poly' request. For example, multiple successive calls to draw lines in a particular window are merged into a single poly-line draw request which draws multiple line segments in a single operation. Not only does this batching reduce the network traffic, it also reduces the number of requests the server has to handle, and the amount of processing it has to perform.

Using Xlib in a program

The next module shows a listing of a very simple **X** program using only the basic functions provided by Xlib. The program displays the string 'Hello, world' in a window, and correctly handles events when the window is exposed or resized, re-displaying and re-centring the string in the window (Figure A). The program is compiled and linked with the commands shown in Figure B.

In the program listing, all the functions with names beginning with an uppercase 'X', such as XOpenDisplay() and XDrawString(), are provided by Xlib. You can see from this example that programming using Xlib is long-winded and excessively detailed. The toolkits described in Module 5.2.4 help overcome this problem.

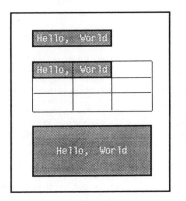

Figure A.   The X 'Hello, World' program.

```
cc -c xhello.c
cc -o xhello   xhello.o -1X11
```

Figure B.   Compile and link commands for a simple X program.

5.2 What X clients consist of, and how they are built

5.2.3 Listing of a program based on Xlib

The program listed here is a simple X program to display a string in a window. It handles events when the window is exposed or resized, re-displaying and re-centring the string in the window. It also allows customization using the standard X defaults or resources mechanism (described in Module 12.2).

```c
#include <stdio.h>
#include <X11/Xlib.h>
#include <X11/Xutil.h>
#define STRING  "Hello, world"
#define BORDER  1
#define FONT    "fixed"
#define ARG_FONT                "font"
#define ARG_BORDER_COLOR        "bordercolor"
#define ARG_FOREGROUND          "foreground"
#define ARG_BACKGROUND          "background"
#define ARG_BORDER              "border"
#define ARG_GEOMETRY            "geometry"
#define DEFAULT_GEOMETRY        ""

XWMHints        xwmh = {
    (InputHint|StateHint),      /* flags */
    False,                      /* input */
    NormalState,                /* initial_state */
    0,                          /* icon pixmap */
    0,                          /* icon window */
    0, 0,                       /* icon location */
    0,                          /* icon mask */
    0,                          /* Window group */
};
main(argc,argv)
    int argc;
    char **argv;
{
    Display     *dpy;           /* X server connection */
    Window      win;            /* Window ID */
    GC          gc;             /* GC to draw with */
    char        *fontName;      /* Name of font for string */
    XFontStruct *fontstruct;    /* Font descriptor */
    unsigned long ftw, fth, pad;/* Font size parameters */
    unsigned long fg, bg, bd;   /* Pixel values */
    unsigned long bw;           /* Border width */
    char        *tempstr;       /* Temporary string */
    XColor      color;          /* Temporary color */
    Colormap    cmap;           /* Color map to use */
    XGCValues   gcv;            /* Struct for creating GC */
    XEvent      event;          /* Event received */
    XSizeHints  xsh;            /* Size hints for window manager */
    char        *geomSpec;      /* Window geometry string */
    XSetWindowAttributes xswa;  /* Temporary Set Window Attribute struct */

    if ((dpy = XOpenDisplay(NULL)) == NULL) {
        fprintf(stderr, "%s: can't open %s\n", argv[0], XDisplayName(NULL));
        exit(1);}
    if ((fontName = XGetDefault(dpy, argv[0], ARG_FONT)) == NULL) {
        fontName = FONT;}
    if ((fontstruct = XLoadQueryFont(dpy, fontName)) == NULL) {
        fprintf(stderr, "%s: display %s doesn't know font %s\n",
                argv[0], DisplayString(dpy), fontName);
        exit(1);}
    fth = fontstruct->max_bounds.ascent + fontstruct->max_bounds.descent;
    ftw = fontstruct->max_bounds.width;
    cmap = DefaultColormap(dpy, DefaultScreen(dpy));
```

```
if ((tempstr = XGetDefault(dpy, argv[0], ARG_BORDER_COLOR)) == NULL ||
    XParseColor(dpy, cmap, tempstr, &color) == 0 ||
    XAllocColor(dpy, cmap, &color) == 0) {
    bd = WhitePixel(dpy, DefaultScreen(dpy));}
else {
    bd = color.pixel;}
if ((tempstr = XGetDefault(dpy, argv[0], ARG_BACKGROUND)) == NULL ||
    XParseColor(dpy, cmap, tempstr, &color) == 0 ||
    XAllocColor(dpy, cmap, &color) == 0) {
    bg = BlackPixel(dpy, DefaultScreen(dpy));}
else {
    bg = color.pixel;}
if ((tempstr = XGetDefault(dpy, argv[0], ARG_FOREGROUND)) == NULL ||
    XParseColor(dpy, cmap, tempstr, &color) == 0 ||
    XAllocColor(dpy, cmap, &color) == 0) {
    fg = WhitePixel(dpy, DefaultScreen(dpy));}
else {
    fg = color.pixel;}
pad = BORDER;
if ((tempstr = XGetDefault(dpy, argv[0], ARG_BORDER)) == NULL)
    bw = 1;
else
    bw = atoi(tempstr);
geomSpec = XGetDefault(dpy, argv[0], ARG_GEOMETRY);
if (geomSpec == NULL) {
    xsh.flags = (PPosition | PSize);
    xsh.height = fth + pad * 2;
    xsh.width = XTextWidth(fontstruct, STRING, strlen(STRING)) + pad * 2;
    xsh.x = (DisplayWidth(dpy, DefaultScreen(dpy)) - xsh.width) / 2;
    xsh.y = (DisplayHeight(dpy, DefaultScreen(dpy)) - xsh.height) / 2;}
else {
    int         bitmask;

    bzero(&xsh, sizeof(xsh));
    bitmask = XGeometry(dpy, DefaultScreen(dpy), geomSpec, DEFAULT_GEOMETRY,
        bw, ftw, fth, pad, pad, &(xsh.x), &(xsh.y), &(xsh.width), &(xsh.height));
    if (bitmask & (XValue | YValue)) {
        xsh.flags |= USPosition;}
    if (bitmask & (WidthValue | HeightValue)) {
        xsh.flags |= USSize;}}
win = XCreateSimpleWindow(dpy, DefaultRootWindow(dpy),
        xsh.x, xsh.y, xsh.width, xsh.height, bw, bd, bg);
XSetStandardProperties(dpy, win, STRING, STRING, None, argv, argc, &xsh);
XSetWMHints(dpy, win, &xwmh);
xswa.colormap = DefaultColormap(dpy, DefaultScreen(dpy));
xswa.bit_gravity = CenterGravity;
XChangeWindowAttributes(dpy, win, (CWColormap | CWBitGravity), &xswa);
gcv.font = fontstruct->fid;
gcv.foreground = fg;
gcv.background = bg;
gc = XCreateGC(dpy, win, (GCFont | GCForeground | GCBackground), &gcv);
XSelectInput(dpy, win, ExposureMask);
XMapWindow(dpy, win);
while (1) {
    XNextEvent(dpy, &event);
    if (event.type == Expose && event.xexpose.count == 0) {
        XWindowAttributes xwa;      /* Temp Get Window Attribute struct */
        int         x, y;
        while (XCheckTypedEvent(dpy, Expose, &event));
        if (XGetWindowAttributes(dpy, win, &xwa) == 0)
            break;
        x = (xwa.width - XTextWidth(fontstruct, STRING, strlen(STRING))) / 2;
        y = (xwa.height + fontstruct->max_bounds.ascent
            - fontstruct->max_bounds.descent) / 2;
        XClearWindow(dpy, win);
        XDrawString(dpy, win, gc, x, y, STRING, strlen(STRING));}}
    exit(1);
}
```

Figure A.   Listing of 'simple' **Xlib** program.

5.2   What X clients consist of, and how they are built

5.2.4   Most X applications use a high-level toolkit

Because the Xlib library is low-level, most applications also use higher-level libraries or toolkits to simplify coding by handling many of the complex details, and to ensure consistency in the user interface.

It is obvious from the sample program in the previous module that applications written using Xlib are complex and long-winded (and therefore will be error-prone, and difficult to maintain.) The **X** developers realized this, and have always intended that applications programmers should use a higher-level interface to the system — they should use a **toolkit** — layered on top of Xlib as illustrated in Figure A. Most of the lower-level Xlib facilities need to be used only by developers of toolkits or specialist window system programmers. This approach has many benefits for the end-user of the application as well as the programmer:

- The toolkit can provide standard user-interface 'building blocks'. This reduces the applications programmer's work, and leads to a uniform and consistent interface for the end-user.

- Consistent user interfaces make programs and systems easier to learn and easier to use, as we described in Module 2.3.

- Many toolkits allow the end-user to customize various aspects of an application's operation by specifying preferences and configuration options in a text file (a defaults file).

- Programs written with a toolkit contain fewer lines of code, and therefore are likely to be quicker to develop and easier to maintain.

- The toolkit can hide many low-level aspects of the system from the applications programmer. This reduces the requirement for programmer training, as well as ensuring that complex low-level details are handled correctly. For instance, a toolkit can handle most of the processing required for exposure events, for handling different types of display capabilities such as monochrome versus colour, and for the interaction of the application with the window manager (Module 8.4.1).

You can think of an **X** toolkit as analogous to the 'standard libraries' provided by an operating system, for example the C-language stdio for input/output, or curses for handling character-based screens. They are provided to simplify, to standardize, and to optimize performance for the machine they are running on; it *is* possible to write programs without them and just use the lowest-level interface, but it is much more difficult. In other words, Xlib is the equivalent of the raw operating system interface (Figure B).

There are now many different **X** toolkits available, and we'll deal with them in detail in Chapter 6.

Figure C shows a listing of a program written using the standard **X** Toolkit. Like the program in the previous module, it displays the string 'Hello, world' in a window, and in fact has much greater functionality that the earlier (**Xlib**) program as now we have a whole range of customization facilities and other options provided by the Toolkit. Even so, the Toolkit version is very much shorter, and this degree of improvement is typical.

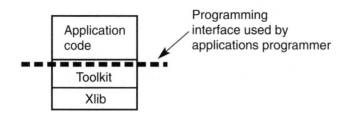

Figure A.   A toolkit layered on top of the basic **Xlib** library.

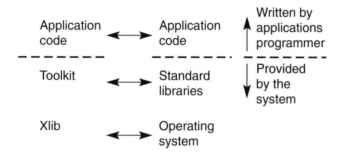

Figure B.   Analogies of **X** and operating system layers.

```
#include <stdio.h>
#include <X11/Xlib.h>
#include <X11/Intrinsic.h>
#include <X11/StringDefs.h>
#include <X11/Xaw/Label.h>

#define STRING  "Hello, World"

Arg wargs[] = {
    {XtNlabel,  (XtArgVal) STRING},
};

main(argc, argv)
    int argc;
    char **argv;
{
    Widget      toplevel, label;

    toplevel = XtInitialize(argv[0], "XLabel", NULL, 0, &argc, argv);
    label = XtCreateWidget(argv[0], labelWidgetClass,
                        toplevel, wargs, XtNumber(wargs));
    XtManageChild(label);
    XtRealizeWidget(toplevel);
    XtMainLoop();
}
```

Figure C.   Listing of a simple X Toolkit program.

5.3   Internationalizing and localizing applications — Xi18n

It is important for both vendors and users of software that the same application is usable in many different countries. It must be able to handle different natural (human) languages, both for input and for output, and address other country-dependent aspects such as the format of dates and times and numbers. Release 5 of **X** has introduced many internationalization features which let you write programs that are not specific to any country or natural language, but will operate correctly in each country and obey the local conventions. **X** internationalization (Xi18n) is based on the ANSI C concept of the 'locale', which defines what the localized behaviour of the program is to be.

Being able to use a piece of software in more than one country is becoming more and more important to users. Organizations increasingly have to work in an international context, with offices or personnel or at least associates in other countries, and they also tend to standardize on third-party software for their whole operation worldwide. For example, the same spreadsheet and word processor will be used in an organization's London, Chicago, Frankfurt, and Tokyo offices, and it must work correctly according to each country's local conventions. Moreover, users in Tokyo will probably have to process documents in English, as well as Japanese. For software vendors too, it is important that their product be usable across the world, so that the product has as wide a market as possible.

What are the requirements of a program which has to operate in many different countries?

- **Inputting and printing the national language** is the most obvious requirement. The application has to be able to display all the characters of the user's language, and it must also allow the user to *input* each of those characters from the keyboard. Most software can do this only for English-speaking countries, where the ASCII characters are adequate. Even for other European languages, while printing characters with diacritical marks (accents, etc.) is straightforward, special processing is needed to allow these characters to be input from a standard (ASCII) keyboard. For other languages, the requirements for input are even more complex.

- **Displaying messages and menus**. As well as just allowing the language to be input and printed, the program must also display all messages, menus, and dialogs in the user's language. Therefore, these cannot be hard-coded into the program, but must somehow be retrieved from a country-dependent file or elsewhere.

- **Number and decimal formats**. English-speaking countries use commas and periods in the style 1,234,567.8901, whereas most European countries display the same number in the style 1.234.567,8901.

- **Currency format.** Both the name of the local currency, and how many decimal digits are shown, vary from country to country. For example, in

Japan and Italy, amounts are shown without decimal points, whereas in the USA and England two decimal digits are included (for the number of cents and pence).

We want the application to be able to handle these country-specific customs and language. But we don't want to have to write (and maintain) a different version of the program for each country. First, that would be very expensive. Second, different languages may be required simultaneously; for example, a person translating from French to Japanese would want two versions of a word processor on-screen at the same time, one in Japanese and one in French. What we really want is for the program itself to be adaptable so it uses different languages without recompiling or relinking. We want to be able to write generic code, and let the user (or system administrator) use environment variables or other configuration controls to select the particular language and country conventions required; then when the program is run, a specific database is loaded which gives the required behaviour for the specified environment. **Internationalization** is the process of enabling the program to do this. It involves removing hard-coded logic and information specific to one language, and replacing them with mechanisms that allow the program to be tailored, at run-time, to one particular language.

Localization is the process of tailoring an already internationalized program for use in a particular country. It must ensure that the user can input the characters in that language, and that all messages and labels are displayed in that language also.

Internationalization is often called i18n (because there are 18 letters between the initial 'i' and the final 'n' of 'internationalization'). The specific **X** implementation of internationalization is referred to as Xi18n.

Locales

ANSI C defines the concept of **locale**. A locale is a name to describe how an application is to behave dealing with a particular language or other country-specific conventions. The locale to be used is specified at the start of the program (usually by means of an environment variable so it is not hard-coded into the program). It causes locale-specific messages to be loaded from a database, and it specifies how various input and output functions behave, to match the specified local requirements. This ANSI locale model really only allows single-language programs: it lets your program work with any natural language, but only with one at a time — it is internationalization but not a 'multilingual' facility.

X internationalization is based on this ANSI locale model.

In the next two modules we look at the mechanisms **X** provides for internationalization and localization.

5.3 Internationalizing and localizing applications — Xi18n

5.3.1 Internationalized text input, and input methods

X supports localized text input using 'input methods'. Internally characters can be stored in 'multibyte' or 'wide-character' storage.

(If technical details aren't so relevant to you, you can skip over this module.)

As we outlined in Module 4.2.3, an input method is a mechanism to let you enter from your keyboard characters which are not directly available on that keyboard. The simplest example of this is the compose input method for entering special symbols and characters specific to some European languages; this facility is available on many non-**X** systems. It is suitable where the written language is based on an alphabet of a small number of symbols (letters) which are used in different combinations to form words; examples are the English (Latin) and Cyrillic alphabets.

However, many oriental languages are **ideographic** — instead of building up words from a small, fixed, set of letters, each word is represented by its own special symbol which is often a semi-graphical representation of the idea it relates to. As a result, these languages have very large numbers of symbols — many tens of thousands — so some special methods are needed for inputting them, that is, for specifying from the keyboard which symbol is to appear on the screen or in a file. This is what input methods allow you to do, and because of the size of the problem, they can be quite complex. Let's consider Japanese as an example.

Japanese has both ideographic symbols (Figure A) and a phonetic writing system using an alphabet. The phonetic characters are shown on the keyboard, and the user types particular sequences of these to generate a single ideograph. However, the same sequence of phonetic symbols corresponds to several different ideographs (in the same way that in English many words that sound the same have completely different meanings, for example 'right', 'write', 'rite' — and even 'right' has several distinct meanings of its own). So, the input method must let the user resolve the ambiguities, for example by presenting a menu of the ideographs, and letting the user choose the required one; this is called **pre-editing**. Pre-editing may be done 'on the spot', in the window where the text is being input, or 'over the spot', in a special window on top of where the text is being input, or in a window elsewhere specially reserved for pre-editing ('off the spot'). The input method may also require other status and auxiliary windows, to show the user what is happening, and for any other special dialogs the method requires.

Coding all this into an application is a lot of work. Even worse, to build an application to work with all different natural languages would require many different input methods, and further, there are several different input methods available for some languages. So **X** allows the input method to be run as a separate process, called an **input server**, and the application communicates with this process, passing to it the input events from the server, and getting back the composed (converted) text. However, setting up and using this communication is handled within the Xlib functions for using input methods and is transparent to the applications programmer. So, while this architecture does mean there is a communication overhead for handling input, it also allows the application to use other input methods (and therefore natural languages) without recompiling or relinking. Unfortunately, different vendors' implementations of Xlib use their own different **X**-based protocols to communicate with the input server, so users don't have the freedom to choose from all available input methods. The MIT **X** Consortium is working on ways to overcome this, with the goal of providing a portable way to add support for new locales not already provided the Xlib vendor, so the user can select locale dynamically.

Storing characters internally

Traditionally, programs have internally stored characters one per byte, as ASCII (or EBCDIC). For internationalized programs this is no longer adequate as one character may require several bytes. There are two ways of handling this:

1. **Multibyte characters** are stored in a variable number of bytes, each character occupying only the minimum storage required. While this gives optimal use of storage, it complicates string processing. For example, to access the nth character in a string, you cannot index to it directly because you don't know what size the preceding n−1 characters are; so you always have to start at the beginning of the string, and read from there. This character type is supported by ANSI C.

2. **Wide characters** are each stored in a fixed number of bytes, the number being that required by the biggest character. This uses more storage, but allows strings to be handled in much the same way as single-byte characters. (For example, programming constructs such as s++ still work.)

In the next module we look at **X**'s mechanisms for internationalized output.

```
      -JIS-Fixed-Medium-R-Normal--24-230-75-75-C-240-JISX0208.1983-0
 Quit  Prev Page  Next Page
                         Select a character

 range:  0x2121 (33,33) thru 0x747e (116,126)
 upper left:  0x3100 (49,0)
```

Figure A.   Oriental languages contain large numbers of ideographic characters.

5.3 Internationalizing and localizing applications — Xi18n

5.3.2 Internationalized X text output

Localized text output is supported with 'font sets' and context-dependent text drawing. Localized messages and menu labels are loaded from a locale-dependent database.

(If technical details aren't so relevant to you, you can skip over this module.)

X version 11 has always supported both 8-bit and 16-bit fonts. That is, a character or symbol is represented by either an 8- or 16-bit number, depending on the font. In Figure A a string of 8-bit bytes is shown interpreted as characters in an 8-bit ASCII font. This also illustrates that the **encoding** of the string — how a numeric value on the string is translated to a printed character — is determined by the font and is specific to a font. The last component of a font's XLFD name specifies what the encoding for the font is; for example '-iso8859-1' specifies 'Latin-1' encoding, which includes the printable ASCII characters as well as almost all the accented characters needed for European languages.

16-bit encoding allows fonts to contain large numbers of characters, and this is almost adequate for drawing the text characters of most languages. However, there are still problems. First, some languages contain more than the 65536 symbols which can be accommodated in a 16-bit font. Second, multiple fonts are needed to cover the requirements of some languages. For example, for Japanese you might have one font for ASCII characters (for computer-related work), another 8-bit font for the phonetic 'kana' characters, and a 16-bit font for the ideographic characters.

In Release 5, the concept of a **fontset** was introduced. A fontset is a list of the fonts which the X text-drawing functions may use when drawing a particular string in the language, taking different symbols from the different fonts as required. A fontset is specified by a list of XLFD font-names. Allowing multiple fonts to be used solves both the problems above.

A third problem with text output is context-dependence, that is, where the appearance of a symbol to be drawn depends on what symbols are beside it. The simplest example is ligatures in certain fonts in English: if the letter 'i' is preceded by an 'f', the two characters are not drawn individually and separately but as a single composite symbol. Two 'f's followed by an 'i' are treated similarly. For other languages, the symbol used for a character can depend on the surrounding ones, even when it is not drawn as a composite symbol with them. The text-drawing routines in Release 5 can now handle these cases.

Note that all these changes, both for text input and output, are exclusively within the client and don't affect the server, even though they appear to be an intrinsic part of the system. The code necessary to support these facilities is within the application code or in Xlib or another library. The fontset list is used exclusively on the client side, by Xlib. Xlib decides which font should be used for each character to be drawn; then it sends to the server a standard text drawing request, which includes (via a graphics context) which single font is to be used for this piece of text. Thus the server sees no change, and thus the **X** Protocol is unchanged. This is a good example of how putting as little functionality as possible in the server allows **X** to grow organically while still maintaining upward compatibility.

Localized messages, labels, and other text

Being able within the program to draw the characters of the user's language is only a partial solution. As part of localizing the program you must also provide translated versions of messages, menu labels, and all other text.

Therefore, internationalized programs must not hard-code any text that will appear in the user interface. Instead, all strings must be stored in a local-dependent configuration file or database; when the program is run, it loads the appropriate database for the given locale, retrieves the individual messages and labels from the database, and uses them when drawing the user interface components.

Supporting locale-related databases is not part of **X**, but is a standard facility which is provided by the operating system (or ought to be), which **X** then just uses.

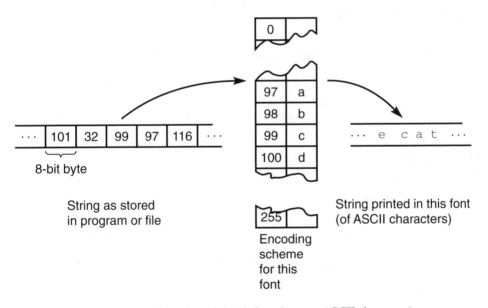

Figure A. Encoding of an eight-bit font (here, as ASCII characters).

5.4   Examples of X application programs

X applications cover a very broad spectrum. The simplest are small 'desk accessories', such as clocks and calculators. At the other extreme of complexity are programs such as industrial control applications, CAD systems, etc., which merely use X as the interface to the application code that is the main part of the program. There are also specific tools for developing with, and administering, X systems.

In X, everything apart from the fundamental mechanisms of the base system is handled by client programs. As a result we have clients offering a very wide range of functionality. In this module and the next, we describe a few applications, just to give you an idea of what is available.

Desk accessories

Most X systems give you several little convenience tools to help you with small day to day tasks. Typical examples are clocks, calculators, calendars, etc.

Tools for the user to control the X system, and utility programs

These are the X applications that provide much of the basic functionality included as part of the base system with other window systems. The most important of these are the window manager, terminal emulators, and desktops and file managers.

Utility programs provide facilities for killing off X applications, capturing and printing screen images, and creating and editing icons.

Office automation

Window systems are especially good for office automation applications because of their good graphics and sophisticated font handling. Functions such as word processors, desktop publishing (DTP) systems, spreadsheets, electronic mail, and text editors are provided either as standalone applications or as integrated program suites.

Vertical end-user applications

The real purpose of computer systems is to provide tools and applications to help the end-users do their job more effectively. X is a fundamental technology, in the same way that database systems are applied to almost every application area, so there are now X clients for medical, scientific, commercial and financial areas, etc.

However, because of X's graphical facilities, it is particularly popular for systems such as CAD and CAE, imaging, mapping, and any other application where input or output is largely graphical in nature.

Program development and migration tools

Standard program development using Xlib and **X** toolkits requires no special facilities. However, special systems to allow programs to be developed graphically, and which provide very high-level programming facilities are becoming common. These UIMSs (user interface management systems) not only generate programs that use **X**, but they are themselves **X** applications in their own right as well.

Most existing programs were not developed to use **X**, so special facilities are needed to run these programs on **X** systems. Special functionality may be included in servers, for example to run applications developed for other window systems running on the same processor type. However, other special emulation systems, for emulating a PC on a RISC workstation, for instance, are usually written as **X** clients.

X-specific tools for system administration

Managing a complex system like **X** with its many different capabilities such as font servers, server options, and customization facilities requires special tools, especially where the environment is on a large multi-vendor network. Most **X** systems include system administration tools for simplifying the management of these aspects of the system, primarily for the system manager rather than the end user.

5.4 Examples of X application programs

5.4.1 Some common X applications

This module illustrates the wide range of functionality provided by **X** clients, from simple convenience tools to complex applications.

Desk accessories

xcalc: is a typical desk calculator.

xclock: is a clock (analogue or digital); oclock is a round-faced variant.

xbiff: tells you when fresh electronic mail has arrived in your mailbox.

xcalendar: displays a calendar a month at a time, and lets you mark on it appointments, etc. (Part of the **contrib** release.)

Office automation

desktop publishing (DTP): commercial packages include FrameMaker and InterLeaf.

spreadsheets: commercial packages include Lotus 1-2-3 and Wingz

electronic-mail: programs such as xmh, cc:Mail, etc.

text editors: such as xedit and emacs.

word processors: commercial packages include Aster*x, WordPerfect, etc.

Graphics applications

The **contrib** release contains xloadimage which understands a wide range of standard picture formats.

Tools for the user to control the X system, and utility programs

Window managers: are the tools most people use to manage their screen layout — sizing and positioning windows, changing them into icons and back again, stacking them, and so on. There are now dozens of **X** window managers. (See Chapter 8.)

Desktop managers: provide an easy-to-use and a system-independent way of using your operating system, to run programs, manage your files and directories, and so on. These are covered in Module 9.6.

File managers: are often provided as part of a Desktop, but are also available as separate applications.

xkill: kills off the application that owns the window you click on.

xwd: dumps an image of the window you click on to a file.

xwud: reads a file containing an image already dumped by **xwd**, and displays it on the screen.

xpr: prints, on a hardcopy printer, a window image already dumped using **xwd**.

bitmap: lets you create and edit bitmap images for use by other programs and utilities.

Program development and migration tools

SoftPC: is a complete software emulation of a DOS PC, so you can run a DOS program with its full graphics output, on the client machine and display it to any **X** station on your network.

UIMSs (user interface management systems): let you build the user interface of your application interactively and graphically, rather than having to program it using a conventional language. (See Module 14.2.)

X-specific tools for system administration

xdm: the **X** display manager, which makes an **X** terminal behave similarly to a character-based oned, by presenting you with a login window to begin with. When you login, you start your **X** 'session' and do your work. When you finish and logout, **xdm** resets the server, and presents the login window again, ready for the next user. As we'll see in Module 11.1.3, **xdm** combined with the XDMCP facility is essential for administering large networks of **X** stations.

xmodmap: allows you to print and modify your keyboard and mouse mappings.

xfd: is the **X** font display program, which we illustrated in Module 3.7.2.

xset: lets you configure options of your server, such as whether keyboard autorepeat is enabled, how loud the bell should sound, where the server should look for its fonts, etc.

xlsfonts: lists the names of the fonts available the server, optionally showing only those matching a wild-carded font name specification.

Summary

In this chapter we have looked at the third major component of **X** — the client application program — and what its overall role is, having seen in the previous chapter how it processes events. We looked in detail at what the client's principal components are and how it is constructed using the standard Xlib library, toolkits, and other function libraries. We looked at how internationalized applications can be built, allowing them to work with different locales specifying the language and other local conventions the program is to work with, and how an internationalized program is localized, to work in a particular locale. Finally we looked at a wide range of example applications, to give an indication of the breadth of function provided by **X** clients.

In the next chapter we continue with the client, and explain in detail what an application's 'look and feel' is, how the user interface is built into the application, and how a standard user interface or look and feel is provided using toolkits.

Many other important aspects of clients are covered later. Chapter 9 (Inter-Client Communications) explains how clients can communicate and interact with each other, Chapter 10 (Writing **X** Programs) includes more information on programming a client, and client performance is covered in Chapter 13 (Performance Factors).

6

'Look and Feel' Part 1 — Toolkits for Application Programs

6.1   'Look and feel' means how the user sees the system
      6.1.1 Look and feel requirements

6.2   **X** allows many different look and feels

6.3   Motif and OPEN LOOK — the standard look and feels

6.4   How look and feel is implemented: toolkits
      6.4.1 What else a toolkit provides

Introduction

Up to now we have been describing the mechanisms that **X** provides to the system builder, but not how these mechanisms are put together to build graphical user interfaces. In this chapter we look at how a consistent user interface is provided in **X**; unlike other window systems, this part of the system is handled entirely within the client, usually using toolkits. We also look at some standard interfaces that have evolved.

6.1 'Look and feel' means how the user sees the system

The visual appearance of an application, and how the user interface behaves and how the user has to interact with it, comprise the application's look and feel. Different user interface systems provide different look and feels.

The 'look' of a program is its visual appearance — how the various controls are laid out, what the components such as menus, scrollbars, buttons and so on look like, and the overall style.

The 'feel' of a program is how it behaves — how the scrollbars operate (can you drag them with the mouse, what happens when you click in certain areas with the left mouse button, with the right?), whether you can 'press' pushbuttons by hitting the keyboard's space-bar or return key instead of clicking with the mouse, etc.

It is the combination of the look and the feel that makes up the overall user interface. It is not only windowed computer programs that have a look and feel: other programs, especially DOS PC applications such as spreadsheets or word-processing packages, have their own recognizable and distinctive look and feel.[1] Computer keyboards have a look and feel. Keys are labelled 'QWERTY...' along the top row, 'ASDFGH...' along the middle row, etc., and that is the look; when you press the key marked F, say, you get the character 'f' printed, and that is the feel.

Even the controls of a motor car have a look and feel: the look for a car with manual transmission is shown schematically in Figure A. This is quite a good example of why you want look and feel to remain consistent even in products from different manufacturers, and how nasty it can be if they don't. For instance, you expect that a car's accelerator (gas) pedal is on the right, and the brake pedal is to its left. What would happen if Volkswagen used that convention, but Ford decided to use the opposite? How easy would it be to drive a car of the other type — a car which has the same look (two pedals) but a different feel (the pedals have opposite 'meanings')?

So, while look and feel is a general term, it is increasingly used to mean *consistent* appearance and style of operation. In the next module we list what we require of look and feel for applications.

---

[1] The distinctiveness of a system's look and feel is the basis for the recent vogue of lawsuits alleging infringement of copyright or other intellectual property rights.

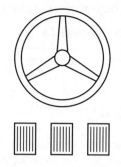

Figure A.   The 'look' of motor car controls.

6.1 'Look and feel' means how the user sees the system

6.1.1 Look and feel requirements

Users are now demanding standard, consistent interfaces, to make applications easier to use and easier to learn.

What we want from the look and feel of an application is:

- **Consistency of appearance**, for example, scrollbars should look the same in all the programs you use. It ought to be obvious that some component *is* a scrollbar just by looking at it, even if you have never used this particular application before. Similarly, the function of other user interface components ought to be obvious from their appearance.

- **Consistency of behaviour**. All the scrollbars in all your various applications should work in the same way. Scrolling up ought to be controlled just the same in your mail program as in your spreadsheet. In other words, it ought to be obvious how to *use* each user interface component.

- By combining consistency of look *and* feel we can **leverage** or **multiply people's knowledge**. Just by looking at a new **X** application you ought to get quite a good idea of what it does and how to use it. Figure A shows a Motif program with some standard components. Once you have used a few Motif applications, you *know* you can pull down menus from the menu-bar, you *know* that the option to Open a file will be in the File menu, that the box to the right of the figure is a 'file selection box' and that you can use it to select a file as well as displaying those files which are available for selection.

There are many other features that we want from a windowed application, that people often attribute to look and feel, but which are really due either to just having a graphical user interface, or more often to having a *consistent* look and feel:

- **Ease of use**. Graphical applications are (when well designed) easier to learn and easier to use. In Module 2.1 we gave an example of this, comparing an **X** calculator program, xcalc, with its UNIX equivalent, dc.

- **Simplicity**, especially for the non-expert. One example is desktop managers (Module 9.6) which let non-computer-experts manage their files and run programs without having to know about the underlying operating system. Another example is menu systems, icons and so on, which can give users access to all the facilities they require without having to know which programs are being run and, in the case of **X**, which remote CPU they are on, or even that a network is involved at all.

- **Standardization and compatibility**. The user interface of the program ought to be compatible with other programs the user already knows. For example, OPEN LOOK has been marketed as a de facto standard, and Motif was designed to be very similar to Presentation Manager and the interface provided on Microsoft Windows for DOS.

In fact most of these are user demands. Vendors have not automatically provided these features, but they are now being forced to listen to what their customers want, to remain competitive.

In the next modules we'll see that **X** lets developers build many, very different, look and feels. We'll look at what they are like, and how they are implemented.

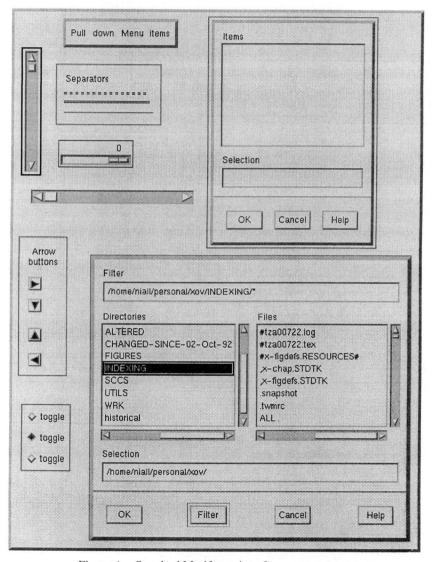

Figure A.   Standard Motif user interface components.

6.2 X allows many different look and feels

The base **X** system deliberately does not provide a standard user interface, so individual application developers have produced their own interfaces. The designers of **X** did not include a standard look and feel in the system for many reasons. This gives great flexibility — for developing new interfaces, or emulating the interfaces of other systems to obtain compatibility. Unfortunately it may also mean you have to deal with many different interfaces.

As we described in Module 1.2, the look and feel of an **X** program is not part of the base system — it is not determined by the server, but is part of the individual application. So, it is possible that each application can have its own distinct look and feel! In the old days, this is more or less what happened: each applications programmer or group of programmers wrote their own. This was bad for users, first, because the user ended up with many different and inconsistent look and feels, and second, because programmers are not necessarily good user interface developers, and some of the look and feels produced were very bad indeed.

However, not building a standard interface into the system does have its advantages. New developments and advances are possible; as the user interface is part of the applications program, researchers have complete freedom to alter it and experiment with new ways of working. This is not possible with most other systems. The source code of **X** is freely available, which also makes **X** the obvious choice for experimentation, in the same way that UNIX has often formed the basis for operating system R & D.

Not specifying a look and feel also means that **X** systems can provide a user interface that is compatible with some other system. For example, Motif is very similar to Presentation Manager and the interface available on Microsoft Windows. It would also be possible to duplicate the interface of the Macintosh (but you would need good lawyers to defend you in case of a law suit from Apple).

This freedom of development leads to an organic evolution of the system. Many new interfaces or look and feels are produced, the best of which form the springboard for future work, leading eventually to the adoption of the best technologies as de facto standards. Ideally this occurs only after the technology has matured enough for a really good system to be available.

Unfortunately, there are disadvantages too. Several viable look and feels have emerged, and each vendor is trying to make their own one the single universal 'standard', resulting in the 'GUI wars'. In practice, we end up with multiple standards, which means confusion for users, and extra work for developers who have to work with all the different systems. (For example, Figure A shows some of the variants of scrollbar offered by different user interfaces.) This diversity is paradoxically a result of the need for the large commercial software marketplace to have a standard; the demand is so great that some common look and feel needs to be defined now, even though it may be premature, and that there just has not been enough time or work done to give the richness of choice necessary before some single interface is chosen and cast in stone. But the user community is demanding standards, so standards are being provided.

In the next module we look at some of these emerging standards.

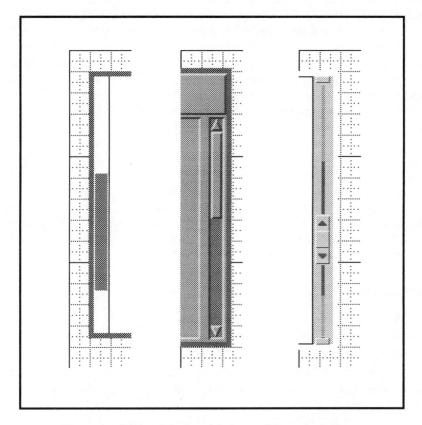

Figure A.   Different look and feels use different scrollbars.

6.3   Motif and OPEN LOOK — the standard look and feels

Standard look and feels are emerging. Motif and OPEN LOOK are the two most widely used. They are very similar in function, but differ considerably in detail.

MIT provide a sample implementation of a look and feel, with their Athena toolkit. This is a relatively simple and unsophisticated system, but it does provide a model for other developers. It is used only in sample applications provided by MIT and in very few other cases. An example of an application using this look and feel is shown in Figure A.

Motif

The Motif look and feel (Figure B) was developed by the Open Software Foundation (OSF) and is based on Digital's DECwindows system and work done by Hewlett-Packard. In appearance and function it is very like IBM's Presentation Manager and Microsoft Windows for DOS. This is very important for users who wish to integrate their new **X** applications with existing IBM or DOS software.

OPEN LOOK

The OPEN LOOK look and feel (Figure C) was developed by AT&T and Sun. It is derived from the user interface developed by Xerox in the early 1980s.

Both Motif and OPEN LOOK have a 3-D appearance, and they offer more or less similar functionality. However, they differ in visual detail, as you can see from the Figures. They also differ in the way the user interacts with them, particularly as to the extent to which you can control an application using the keyboard instead of the mouse. Also, OPEN LOOK provides **drag and drop** facilities, and a push pin to force pop-up menus to stay popped up (Module 8.3); also, a full implementation comes with a file manager application, which provides many of the facilities required from a desktop manager (as described in Module 9.6).

In the next module we discuss how **X** can have so many different user interfaces, and not insist on a single standard.

Which 'standard' do I choose?

There is no easy answer to the question of which look and feel you should use. Your decision is likely to be based less on technical factors (because there is little to differentiate between the two standards) and more on marketing and pragmatic considerations. For instance, which look and feel has more applications available in your application area? If you are a software vendor, what's important is which look and feel do *your customers* want, not which you prefer yourself.

For now, many people hedge their bets and use both standards, perhaps helped by a toolkit which allows you to develop applications capable of providing either look and feel (see Module 7.5).

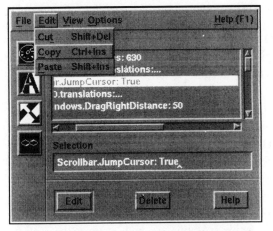

Figure A.   An application with the MIT Athena look and feel.

Figure B.   Example of the Motif look and feel.

Figure C.   Example of the OPEN LOOK look and feel.

6.4   How look and feel is implemented: toolkits

The look and feel is implemented within the application itself, not in the base X system. The components of the look and feel — the elements of the user interface and how they are controlled — are usually provided by a toolkit which gives consistency and isolates the application developer from the details of user interface programming.

A **user interface toolkit** (or just a **toolkit**) in **X** usually provides a set of user interface components from which the applications programmer can assemble the user interface, that is, a set of ready-made building blocks. Figure A shows that the user interface code is actually contained in the application, and also that the toolkit provides a higher-level programming interface.

It was always intended by the designers of **X** that applications would be written with a toolkit. Writing an application using a toolkit rather than basic Xlib functions is analogous to using a high-level language instead of assembler, or writing a C program using the stdio I/O library instead of raw operating system calls. Initially programs *were* written using only Xlib; toolkits are a later development, and represent a maturing of the technology, overcoming many of the earlier problems and simplifying the programming task.

The toolkit provides the applications programmer with a set of ready-made user interface components, which are used in different ways to build up the complete user interface, in much the same way that a house is built from pre-manufactured components such as bricks, doors, electrical sockets, etc. The toolkit also contains the functions necessary for creating, assembling and managing these software components.

By using the standard components we get a consistency within all applications built with that particular toolkit, whether they are written in-house or are bought in from an independent vendor, and irrespective of which platform the application has been written for. So, Motif applications running on a DEC VAX are look and feel consistent with Motif applications running on a Sun; you can't tell them apart. (However, the fact that two applications have the same look and feel does not mean that they were built with the same toolkit. Remember, look and feel defines how the application appears to the user. The same external behaviour in a program could be provided in several different ways internally. For example, you could have three functionally similar programs, written respectively in C, Lisp, and Ada, with each using a toolkit written in its own language.)

Toolkits usually also provide special functions for tasks related to the user interface. For example, to use an application principally via the keyboard and minimize the need for the mouse, we need special keyboard handling to replace normal mouse functions. We want to be able to define **mnemonics** — special key sequences — so that we can pull down menus and select one of the menu options using only the keyboard. We would also like **accelerators** or **short-cut keys** to let us invoke frequently-used menu options directly without having to call down the menu, move to the option, and select it explicitly. (For example, in a word processing system you want to be able to save the document easily. Often ctl-s is used as an accelerator for this, that is, as a quick way to invoke the **save** function.) Additionally, for form-based applications we need a mechanism to let us navigate from one field to another. Toolkits often provide these mechanisms.

There are many toolkits available. Some are standard (for instance, the MIT **X** toolkit, **Xt**, described in the next chapter) with provision for enhancements or for building your own user interface components using the existing pieces or even starting from scratch just using the framework the toolkit provides. Others are specialist toolkits for particular purposes: for example, a basic graphics toolkit for students starting with graphics programming, or advanced toolkits purpose-designed for CAD and CAE systems. There are language-specific toolkits: for example, to allow **X** programming in Lisp or Ada. (And you can even write your own toolkit if you have a particular need: for example, to address the problem domain that your organization specializes in, but this is a little extreme!) Module 7.6 deals with other toolkits.

Many toolkits also provide high-level functions to simplify programming; these are covered in the next module.

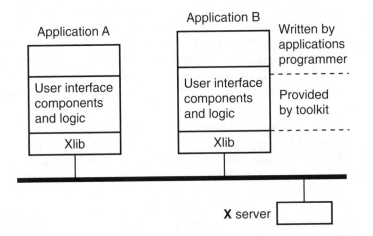

Figure A.   A toolkit provides a higher level interface to the programmer.

6.4 How look and feel is implemented: toolkits

6.4.1 What else a toolkit provides

Toolkits often provide many high-level functions to simplify programming, so that the applications programmer can concentrate on the application-specific aspects of the program, and avoid the low-level details of **X** programming (which are best addressed by a systems programmer or other specialist).

Using a toolkit also provides high-level functions that are not addressed by the basic Xlib library. For example, **X** is a pixel-oriented system: all dimensions are expressed in numbers of pixels on the screen, so the physical length of a line will depend on the resolution of your screen. Some toolkits let you express dimensions in inches or centimetres, and convert to pixels internally, so you can write resolution-independent programs. (If you don't use some system like this, or go to a lot of trouble to provide similar functionality yourself, when you produce an application which looks fine on a low-resolution PC screen, then as soon as you run it on a very high-resolution screen it will be about the size of a postage stamp — see Figure A.) Resolution-independence can be particularly important in DTP applications; the text displayed on the screen must accurately represent what will be output on the printer, even though the resolutions of screen and printer are likely to be very different. To give the necessary control over appearance, some toolkits process individually each character to be drawn, computing its size and optimal screen position, rather than relying on the standard **X** text drawing mechanisms.

Usually a toolkit will handle many routine but essential tasks in an **X** program. Most components of the user interface, such as pushbuttons, labels, scrollbars, menus, etc. will have been created using the toolkit, and therefore the toolkit can redraw them whenever they have been obscured and re-exposed. In other words, the toolkit can automatically handle expose events for most of its components, saving a lot of tedium for the programmer. Similarly, input event handling can be greatly simplified; for example, pushbuttons can be 'pre-programmed' so that they automatically handle mouse <ButtonPress> events (that is, the pushbutton is activated when you click on it), and text components can have keyboard event handling built in so that when you type in them, that is, generate keyboard events in them, the corresponding text is shown. Typically a toolkit provides general mechanisms for event handling like this, and then the specific components in turn use these basic toolkit mechanisms.

Other functions provided by toolkits include:

- Reading-in and processing option settings on the command-line.

- Reading-in default values and user-specified preferences for various components in the program, for example, which server to connect to, what size the application window should be, colours and fonts to use, etc.

- Automatically opening and closing the connection to the chosen server.

- Finding and loading fonts.

- Handling colours and colormaps, and graphics contexts, so the applications programmer rarely has to deal with them explicitly.

- Handling any necessary communication or interfacing to the window manager (Module 8.4.1).

- Supporting communication such as cut-and-paste between client applications (Chapter 9).

In the next chapter we look at the standard **X** way for providing a toolkit, and Module 7.3.1 outlines the extra functionality it includes.

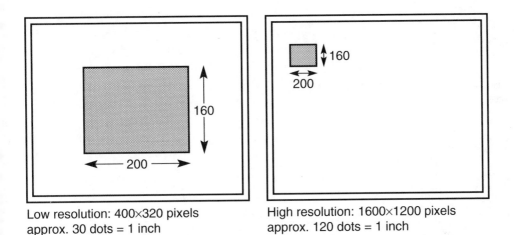

Low resolution: 400×320 pixels
approx. 30 dots = 1 inch

High resolution: 1600×1200 pixels
approx. 120 dots = 1 inch

Figure A. Different screen resolutions affect the size of an image on screen.

Summary

In this chapter we have see that the look and feel of **X** applications — the interface they present to the user — is implemented within the application itself and is not determined by the **X** server. As a consequence, **X** can support different look and feels or graphical user interfaces. We considered what people want from a GUI, to make applications easier to use but also to give consistency of usage across all the user's applications. Then we looked at the de facto standard GUIs, Motif and OPEN LOOK. Finally we saw that the user interface in general and GUIs in particular are almost always implemented by means of toolkits. In the next chapter we examine this in depth, concentrating especially on the mechanisms **X** includes for supporting toolkits.

7 The Standard X Toolkit — Intrinsics and Widgets

7.1   The standard X Toolkit, 'Xt'
    7.1.1 How the Toolkit is related to Xlib

7.2   Widgets and widget sets are building blocks
    7.2.1 Composite widgets
    7.2.2 Primitive widgets
    7.2.3 Gadgets — windowless replacements for widgets

7.3   The 'Intrinsics' lets you manipulate widgets
    7.3.1 Functions provided by the Intrinsics

7.4   Event handling and 'callbacks'
    7.4.1 Callbacks simplify event-driven programming
    7.4.2 Non-X callbacks — file input, and timers

7.5   Some implementations of Motif and OPEN LOOK use Xt
    7.5.1 Motif's User Interface Language — UIL

7.6   Other X toolkits

Introduction

This chapter describes the X standard toolkit, Xt, in depth. We look at the basic user interface components or 'widgets' that it provides, and the different types of widgets there are to perform different functions. We describe how vendors have developed sets of widgets and management functions to provide a particular graphical user interface, for example, Motif or OPEN LOOK. We also examine the X Toolkit 'Intrinsics', which is the framework for creating and manipulating widgets, and which provides a lot of functionality to simplify writing X applications. To finish, we look at some special-purpose toolkits.

7.1   The standard X Toolkit, 'Xt'

X provides a standard basic mechanism, the 'Intrinsics', for building toolkits of
user interface components such as scrollbars, buttons, menus, etc. These components are called 'widgets'. The combination of the Intrinsics and a set of
widgets makes up a toolkit. Many different toolkits, with different look and feels,
have been built using the same Intrinsics.

The **Intrinsics** is officially part of **X** — it is a standard laid down by the MIT **X** Consortium. The Intrinsics is not a toolkit in itself — instead, think of it as a construction
kit for building toolkits. Like the rest of **X**, it is 'policy-free', so it doesn't impose a
look and feel. It provides mechanisms to create and manage user interface components,
but it doesn't specify which components these are, or what they look like, or how they
are to behave.

The Intrinsics defines a new type of object called a **widget**. A widget is a user interface component built within the framework of the standard **X** Intrinsics. The Intrinsics
allows different types of widgets to be created, both 'simple' visible objects such as
buttons, labels, text-entry fields, etc., and 'composite' widgets which are containers for
other widgets — so they can be maintained in rows (as in a menu-bar) or columns
(as in a pull-down menu), or laid out in other programmer-defined ways.   Figure A
shows a very idealized picture of how we would like to use widgets: the cut-outs on
the table-top and in the programmer's hand are how we would like to think of widgets!

It is the individual widgets that provide look and feel. For example, the pushbutton,
scrollbar, and menu widgets will determine a lot of the appearance of an application,
and a good deal of its user interface behaviour as well. More complex aspects of
its behaviour — how you can use the keyboard to navigate from button to button or
invoke specific menus, for example — is determined by the composite widgets, which
incorporate special event processing code for this purpose. Because of this, it is possible
to build many toolkits, each with a different look and feel, by building up different sets
of widgets, even though all use the same standard Intrinsics. For example, the Motif
toolkit, and the **Xt+** and OLIT toolkits which implement the OPEN LOOK look and
feel, are all Intrinsics-based.

In the next module we look at the relationship between the Toolkit and the Xlib
standard **X** library.

Figure A.   How we would like to think of widgets.

7.1 The standard X Toolkit, 'Xt'

7.1.1 How the Toolkit is related to Xlib

The Toolkit complements rather than supercedes Xlib. The Toolkit primarily addresses fairly high-level user interface issues, whereas Xlib provides the fundamental support for all **X** operations, including much low-level processing.

The **X** toolkit (or rather, the many toolkits that have been based on the foundation provided by the Intrinsics) doesn't supersede Xlib. It doesn't duplicate the low-level graphics and other functions which Xlib provides; as shown in Figure A, the application still has access to Xlib, and can continue to use Xlib functions where necessary. This approach is used because many of the Xlib functions are needed for full flexibility of graphics operations: to provide these in the toolkit as well would just be 100% duplication. Instead, toolkits concentrate on the user interface, which is a higher level of abstraction and an area that Xlib doesn't address at all.

As we mentioned in the previous module, the relationship of the toolkit to Xlib is similar to that of standard I/O libraries to the raw operating system calls. The higher-level functions are usually quicker to learn[1] and easier to use because they present the programmer with a simpler application program interface or API (Figure B). They frequently give better performance as well. In fact, the programmer doesn't need to know *anything* about Xlib at all for many applications; where all the **X** programming is for building and handling the user interface, this can be done using the Toolkit exclusively. It is usually only for detailed and specific control of low-level graphics operations that the programmer would need to use Xlib.

The Intrinsics is written in C, so it can be ported to as many different systems as possible.

Now we go on to look at what widgets really are, and how we use the Intrinsics to handle them.

---

[1] **X** Toolkit (Intrinsics) programming has often been criticized for being *difficult* to learn. This was mainly because the Toolkit documentation from MIT was very brief and highly technical, emphasizing the internals of the Toolkit, rather than how to use it. This problem has been addressed since, with the publication of many excellent books on programming the Toolkit, many of which assume no prior knowledge of **X**.

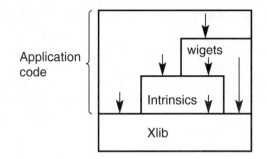

Figure A.   The toolkit does not supersede **Xlib**'s functionality.

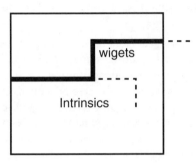

Figure B.   Using a toolkit presents a simpler API to the programmer.

7.2   Widgets and widget sets are building blocks

Toolkit widgets are basic user interface components which are used either directly, to build the user interface of the application, or combined, to form more complex objects which in turn are used in the application. Widgets are usually provided in 'widget sets' — consistent packages of widgets designed to work well together.

Widgets are building blocks which the applications programmer uses to assemble the user interface of the application. A widget consists of an **X** window plus some data structures and procedures. Widgets come 'ready-made' — just like standard functions provided in subroutine libraries, they have usually been written by somebody else (your system's vendor, or a third-party software provider) and you just use them as they come.

The reason you can use widgets from different suppliers is that they are **objects**, in the **object-oriented programming** sense. Widgets hide details of their implementation from the programmer using them, by **encapsulating** much of the information and the procedures necessary for them to operate correctly. For instance, when the window of a pushbutton widget is covered up and re-exposed, it will receive an exposure event; however, as all the graphics in the button window have been drawn there by the widget itself, it knows what needs to be redrawn and the widget has within it an expose procedure which is automatically called for the expose event, so the applications programmer doesn't have to worry about exposures. Similarly, widgets have procedures built-in to handle other occurrences such as resizing, and keyboard or mouse input where appropriate.

There are two broad classes of widgets, **composite** and **primitive**. Composite widgets are containers or boxes for other widgets and usually don't display any visual information in themselves. Primitive widgets perform some function, and display it graphically; they cannot act as containers for other widgets. Within an application, widgets are organized in a tree structure, as shown in Figure A. The leaves of the tree are usually primitive widgets, and the higher-level nodes of the tree must be composite widgets, as only they can have **child** widgets.

You can write your own widgets if you wish, either starting from scratch, or by **subclassing** your widget from an existing one which provides some of the functionality you require. (For example, if you had a histogram widget, you might subclass a pie-chart widget from it. The new widget provides much of the same function as the old, and will be very similar to it in many ways, but it will need new internal procedures built into it to display data in pie-chart rather than histogram format.) However, writing widgets of any type is advanced work, and should really be left for specialist programmers.

We cover composite widgets and primitive widgets in more detail in the modules after this.

Widget sets

While the design of the Toolkit is such that you should be able to use widgets from different vendors in the one program, widgets usually come in sets. A widget set will normally provide:

- A consistent look and feel for all the widgets it includes.

- A broad range of the widgets and functions most commonly required for building a user interface. These include primitive controls such as buttons and scrollbars, widgets to allow input of text, numerics, and perhaps some special items such as filenames, plus composite widgets to provide a range of management or layout options, and some special widgets or functions for building and using menus.

MIT provides the **Athena** widget set as a sample implementation. It is used for MIT's own applications, but isn't widely used commercially. The predominant Motif and OPEN LOOK look and feels have toolkit-based implementations (as well as others) and each provides a large set of widgets.

You buy widget sets from your workstation manufacturer or your **X** software vendor, or from third parties. There are also many useful widgets available free on the public networks.

This module and the next three modules describe what widgets are; Module 7.3 explains how we manipulate them using the Intrinsics.

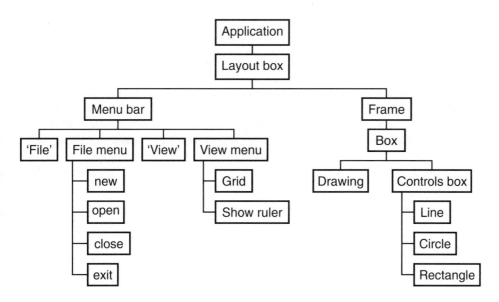

Figure A. Widgets are organized in a tree structure within an application.

7.2 Widgets and widget sets are building blocks

7.2.1 Composite widgets

Composite widgets are basically containers for other widgets — boxes to put them in, and perhaps keep them in some specified form of layout. They vary greatly in the functionality they offer, and their degree of sophistication. Toolkits often provide 'complex' widgets consisting of a container and child widgets pre-configured to perform some specialized function.

The simplest type of composite widget lets you position the child widgets in it initially: you must specify their size and location, and they stay like that forever. If the container widget gets smaller, the position of the children is not adjusted, and they may get truncated. Conversely, if the container gets bigger, the children are left as they were, with a large expanse of space beside or below them (Figure A).

A more advanced container widget automatically resizes its children, often on a per-child basis, as it gets bigger or smaller itself. For example, in the application illustrated in Figure B, the small buttons remain fixed in size and location, the menu bar remains constant in height, but its width stretches or shrinks so that it is always the full width of the application's window, and the large work area containing the graphics expands so that it always uses the maximum area of the application's window available to it.

Other composite widgets perform functions specialized for certain tasks. Some will lay out child widgets in a horizontal row to form a menu-bar, and will perform special keyboard-input handling to enable menu items to be selected by typing rather than by clicking with the mouse. Others will lay out their children vertically and resize them so they are all the same width, to form pull-down menus. Still others will manage collections of buttons, and ensure that if one is pressed 'in' to denote selection of one item, all the others are 'out' and not selected, to form a set of 'radio buttons', giving mutually exclusive selection.

There are still other composite widgets which consist of a container plus some specific children all made up into one pre-configured building block. For example, the Motif selection box shown in Figure C consists of a composite widget and many child widgets, including a list widget with the list of words, a scrollbar, a text widget for the 'selection', plus a separator (the horizontal line) and three buttons. However, to the applications programmer this appears more or less as a single object and can be manipulated as such. Other examples of these compound objects are simple dialogs which prompt for confirmation, give information, or issue warnings.

In the next module we go on to look at primitive widgets in detail.

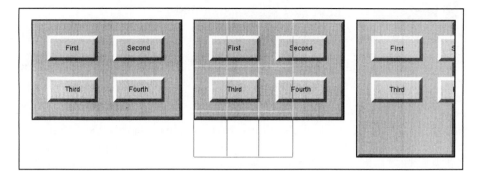

Figure A.   A simple manager widget can truncate its children.

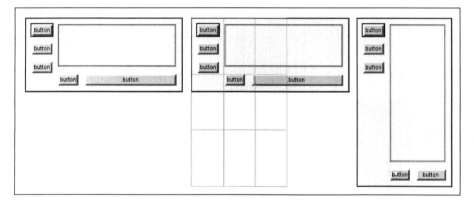

Figure B.   How an advanced manager widget allows sophisticated layout policies.

Figure C.   A Motif selection box widget.

7.2   Widgets and widget sets are building blocks

7.2.2   Primitive widgets

Each primitive widget provides a single, specific type of function, usually for controlling some aspect of the user interface. Primitive widgets cannot contain children.

Most primitive widgets are controls of some kind, and usually have a 'look' or graphical appearance indicating what type of object the widget is, how it works, and giving feedback about what is happening as you use the object. For example, a scrollbar widget controls motion of something, perhaps scrolling a piece of graphics, or a set of items in a list. Its visual appearance, with arrows at either end (in the case of the Motif scrollbar shown in Figure A) suggests that it allows movement in two directions, and the 3-D appearance of the arrows and the slider suggests that you can do things to them (like pull at them, or click on them); and when you use the scrollbar, the slider does indeed move, giving you feedback, both that motion is actually happening, and on the nature of that motion.

Other typical primitive widgets include pushbuttons, labels, slider widgets, single-line or multi-line text widgets, 'blank canvas' widgets for drawing your own graphics into, arrows, and separators (Figure B).

In the next module we consider 'gadgets', which are replacements for simple widgets, and which may offer improved performance.

Figure A. The widget graphic indicates what it is and hints how it works.

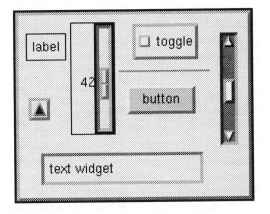

Figure B. Examples of some primitive widgets.

7.2 Widgets and widget sets are building blocks

7.2.3   Gadgets — windowless replacements for widgets

A 'gadget' is a replacement for a primitive widget; it performs the same function but has no **X** window associated with it. Gadgets are supposed to improve performance, but this may not always be the case. Gadgets cannot have children.

Gadgets are defined by some toolkits, and are used a lot in Motif in particular. They are similar to widgets, but they do not have any **X** window associated with them, and therefore require no memory in the server. They are used by the applications programmer in exactly the same way as widgets, but because they don't have a window of their own, there are some restrictions on what you can do with them:

- Gadgets replacements are provided only for primitive widgets, typically buttons, labels, and separators — all the small common items that you use lots of in most programs.

- Gadgets cannot have any children.

- Their visual characteristics are limited, because these are inherited from the parent widget. For example, if you have a blue menu pane with buttons attached, all the buttons will have the same colour. If you want only one of the buttons to be red, then it cannot be a gadget. (But you could use gadgets for all the blue buttons, plus a single widget button, and explicitly specify red as its background colour.)

Figure A shows a menu built with widget button children, Figure B shows the same menu with gadget children, and the corresponding window trees are shown in Figures C and D.

Gadgets were invented for performance reasons. Early studies showed that the performance bottleneck with widgets was in the basic handling of their associated windows in the server; also, each window you use requires some memory in the server, so if your application contains many widgets, you are using a lot of windows and therefore server memory. Accordingly, gadgets were developed. However, later studies indicate that the servers used for this work were particularly bad at manipulating windows, so a better solution would have been to fix the server. Moreover, recent releases of **X** have dramatically improved window manipulation performance within the server, and have reduced the amount of server memory required per window by a factor of three (to about 100 bytes). And finally, more recent studies indicate that the extra event-handling load imposed by gadgets often outweighs any other performance benefit they may have.

Gadgets in detail — implementation and performance

A gadget is like a widget, but has no **X** window of its own. Thus it has most of the data structures of a widget, but the area of the screen where it is drawn is actually part of the window belonging to the gadget's parent (which must of course be a widget, as gadgets can't have children). For simplicity, let us consider a pushbutton gadget which is a pane on a menu, that is, the gadget is a child of a menupane widget.

When you press the gadget pushbutton, this <ButtonPress> event occurs in the menupane widget (because an event occurs in, and is related to, a window). The menupane widget has to tell the gadget to repaint the area of the menupane window that 'belongs to' the gadget. And when the button is released, again the menupane widget has to process the event and inform the gadget. Thus some of the functions that would normally be done by a pushbutton widget child cannot be handled by a gadget child, but become the parent's responsibility. This is the reason why the number of composite widgets that can handle gadget children is limited.

Now let us look at the performance implications. Any pushbutton — widget or gadget — needs to know when the point crosses its boundary and enters, or leaves, the button (so it can highlight/un-highlight itself; in a menu, for example). A widget pushbutton handles this by selecting for <EnterNotify> and <LeaveNotify> events, so the server automatically informs the button about these. However, with a gadget, because it has no window, this isn't possible. Instead, the parent widget must keep track of the pointer all the time (using <MotionNotify> events) and constantly check its position to see if it has entered the gadget's area. This continual generation of motion events by the server, transmission across the network, and checking of them by the client, is usually much more resource-consumptive than handling the few enter/leave events required by a widget.

Probably the best advice about gadgets is that before using gadgets extensively, especially in applications run remotely, you should check on your system to see if they really do give you any better performance; if they don't, use widgets because that is easier, more flexible, and less error-prone.

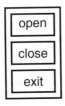

Figure A. Menu, with widget buttons.

Figure B. Menu, with gadget buttons.

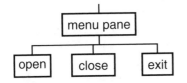

Figure C. Window hierarchy for menu
built with widgets.

Figure D. Window hierarchy for menu
built with gadgets.

7.3   The 'Intrinsics' lets you manipulate widgets

The Intrinsics provides an object-oriented programming system, and widgets are objects in this system. The Intrinsics contains mechanisms for creating and manipulating widgets, plus a very large collection of utility functions which simplify and standardize writing **X** applications.

As we said, an important design goal of the Toolkit was that once widgets were written they should be reusable in other applications. The best software technology currently available to do this is object-oriented programming. We already saw in the previous module that widgets are objects, which we manipulate in the Toolkit environment. However, the **X** Toolkit is written in the C language, which is not object-oriented, so the Toolkit itself must provide the object-oriented programming framework. [2]

Because of a widget's object nature, to use it you only need to know its external behaviour (for example, that it is a pushbutton and handles the tasks that you expect of a button) and the 'messages' you can send to it, both to set its parameters and to tell it to perform its tasks. You don't have to know how it has been implemented, or how its internal data structures are organized. This in turn means that the applications programmer can treat widgets as black boxes or building blocks, and slot them together without much trouble.

Object orientation is also crucial in making the system flexible and extensible. For example, a manager widget which lays its children out in neat rows doesn't need to know in detail what type of widget each child is. Each child is 'just a widget', and the manager widget knows that to resize the child (to fit in neatly with its neighbours, say) it need only send the child a resize message with the desired dimensions as parameters, rather than having to know anything in detail about the child. So when we develop new widgets (or buy them from somebody else), and use them in our programs, our existing manager widgets will continue to perform their function correctly, and will be able to manage the new widgets properly, even though their author never anticipated the new widget type.

Object orientation also helps in controlling the complexity of programs, in increasing their reliability, and in creating new widgets based on existing ones. It does this by means of **classes** of objects. It allows new classes of objects to be based on existing ones, inheriting all but specified behaviour, with extra functionality added as well. Ideally, it ought to be possible to subclass widgets for which you don't have the source code, but at the current point of maturity of the Toolkit, this is not often feasible in practice.

Figure A shows the class hierarchy for a selection of Motif widgets. A class which is connected to one above it by a line in the Figure is said to be a **subclass** of the one above; the class above is said to be a **superclass** of the one below. Most of the classes near the top of the hierarchy, which define the fundamental characteristics of all objects and widgets, and characteristics specific to Composite, are defined by the MIT Toolkit

---

[2]Some of the original **X** developers have remarked that had C++ been as widespread then as it is now, it would have been chosen as the implementation language because it would have simplified the work considerably. However, at that time choosing C++ would have seriously restricted the adoption of **X**.

itself and are used by all other Intrinsics-based toolkits as well as Motif. Thus all widgets in all widget implementations are descended from (subclassed from) the Core class, and manager widgets are subclasses of Composite. However, the XmPrimitive class is specific to Motif; in most other toolkits, primitive widgets are subclassed direct from Core.

Note that in Figure A gadgets separate out into their own distinct class tree at a very early (high-up) stage. This is because they do not have windows associated with them, and so cannot be subclassed from the WindowObj (window object) class, which adds window characteristics to its immediate superclass, RectObj (rectangular objects). Because of this early separation, the gadget classes have to duplicate much of the functionality they would otherwise have inherited from the Primitive widget class.

In the next module we look at the functions the Intrinsics provides.

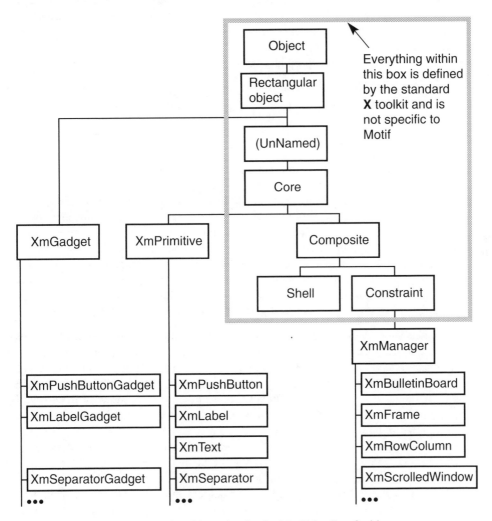

Figure A.   The class hierarchy for the Motif family of widgets.

7.3   The 'Intrinsics' lets you manipulate widgets

7.3.1   Functions provided by the Intrinsics

The toolkit Intrinsics provides two broad classes of functions, those for dealing with widgets, and other more general utility functions.

Widget-related operations

The Intrinsics obviously must provide the whole framework and the programming functions necessary to manage widgets throughout their existence. These include creation and destroying, telling container widgets which children they are to manage, and how they are to be laid out, etc. There is also the important basic mechanism of being able to send a message with some arguments to a widget to change some of its parameters dynamically, for example, to change its background colour, or its size, or the text displayed in it, etc. Also included are functions for controlling which children a manager widget is to display, and to pop-up and pop-down menus.

A large part of the Toolkit is devoted to handling events within widgets. This is covered in the next module.

General utility functions

The Intrinsics handles much of the 'boilerplate' of writing an **X** application. Simple functions are provided which hide much of the complexity of the low-level operation. For example, a simple call to initialize the Toolkit will also parse command-line options, read in default settings from various files, open the connection from the application to the server, and perform all the work necessary to interface the application to the window manager. There is support for writing applications that connect to more than one display, which for example you might use in an interactive messaging program, with two users communicating with each other remotely over a network (Figure A). The Intrinsics also supports the Selections Service used to exchange information and data between applications, as in cut-and-paste operations, for example (see Module 9.2.1).

Facilities for easy handling of colours and fonts are embedded in standard functions so that the applications programmer never needs to call them directly. For example, to set the background colour for a pushbutton, the colour value 'Red' could be specified in a defaults file (a text file containing default settings for one or more applications.) The toolkit reads this file and automatically knows to convert the string of three ASCII characters R, e and d to a reference to **X**'s colour database, and then convert that value to an internal colour value. This Intrinsics facility to handle default and preference settings is very powerful, but here we'll just mention that it can be used for customizing a program according to personal preference, or to match requirements of particular customers, or localize it for use with different national languages. Almost anything can be customized in this way, from simple colours through to keyboard mappings, to the layout of various items within the application. Chapter 12 deals in depth with customizing applications, using the Toolkit's so-called 'Resources' mechanism.

As a result of all this, many applications programmers can completely avoid the details of low-level **Xlib** programming, and work entirely with Toolkit functions. Toolkit programming is, in general, much easier than **Xlib** programming.

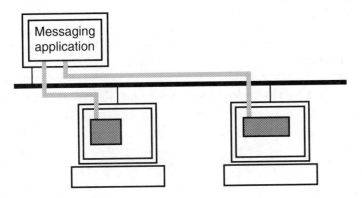

Figure A.   The Toolkit supports connecting a single client to many displays.

7.4   Event handling and 'callbacks'

The Intrinsics contains code to handle events in widgets and to make event-driven programming easier. The Intrinsics handles the low-level **X** events and transforms them into high-level logical occurrences called 'callbacks'. This allows the programmer to specify in a simple way that a particular procedure in the application is to be called whenever a change occurs in a particular component in the user interface.

(If technical details aren't so relevant to you, you can skip over this module.)

As we described in Module 5.2.1, an **X** application is event-driven and must be prepared to process events that may occur in any part of the user interface. With Xlib programming, the applications programmer has to specify explicitly which events are to be watched for in which window, and then handle each of these more or less on a one-by-one basis.

The Intrinsics minimizes this complexity by processing all events for all widget windows itself. It maps low-level **X** events into high-level 'logical events' or 'callbacks' which are much easier for the applications programmer to handle, because a lot of the trivial programming details have been avoided. For example, the Motif pushbutton defines the Activate callback, which is invoked whenever you 'press' the pushbutton. For each callback/widget combination, the programmer can specify (or **register**) a procedure (a **callback procedure**) which is to be executed whenever this logical event occurs. The callback procedure is written by the applications programmer and it usually carries out some application-related functionality; for example, the callback procedure for a Save button in a File pull-down menu might save the current contents of the application's window to a file on disk. How a callback procedure is registered and later invoked, is shown schematically in Figure A. If no procedure is specified for a particular callback, no special action is taken, so the programmer only has to handle events or callbacks which are specifically of interest.

Each type of widget defines its own set of callbacks to suit the type of actions that it is designed to perform. For example, a scrollbar might have a valueChanged callback, called whenever the position of the scrollbar (and therefore the value it represents) changes. A widget for text input might have a modifyVerify callback to allow the programmer to check that text typed by the user is valid, before it is actually entered into and displayed in the text widget, to allow for validated forms-based input.

The mapping of which **X** event (or sequence of events) is to cause a particular callback to occur in a widget is defined by a **translation table**. As we shall see in Module 12.4, you can modify these tables, and so customize the keyboard and input characteristics of your application.

Some events are processed automatically by the Toolkit and don't need to be passed to the application part of the program at all, so no callbacks are defined for them. For example, as we described in Module 6.4.1, exposure events for almost all widgets are handled by the Toolkit itself because it knows what it drew in the widgets window and so can redraw the contents itself instead of calling a programmer-specified procedure.

Explicit exposure callbacks are only provided for widgets that contain graphics drawn directly by the application and not via the Toolkit, and which have to be redrawn by a programmer-specified application function.

In the next module we look at the relationship of callbacks and events in more detail, and at non-user interface 'events' in the module after that.

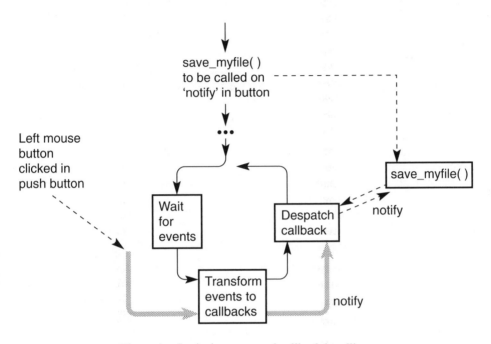

Figure A. Intrinsics event and callback handling.

7.4 Event handling and 'callbacks'

7.4.1 Callbacks simplify event-driven programming

The internal processing of events, even for a simple component like a pushbutton, can be very complex. Callbacks simplify this by removing the need for the applications programmer to deal with low-level events at all.

(If technical details aren't so relevant to you, you can skip over this module.)

The best way to illustrate the idea of callbacks is to use an example — the pushbutton widget. At first glance, the event handling for a pushbutton is easy: when you receive a <ButtonPress> event, the program should invoke the action related to that button — for example, save the file being worked on, by calling the function save_myfile() written by the programmer. But many buttons are more complicated, to make them easier and safer to use. When you press on an Athena pushbutton, it reverses colour to show that it has been pressed; the button is now 'set' and only when you release it again is its action to be invoked. More precisely, only if you release the mouse with the pointer still inside the button will it be activated; if you move the pointer out of the button before releasing the mouse button, the pushbutton 'resets' — goes back to its normal state — and no action is invoked. To make things more complicated, what if the program is being used on a machine that doesn't have a mouse, and the pushbutton has to be invoked from the keyboard?

So, event handling really is quite complex; we need to process <ButtonPress> and <ButtonRelease> events, and be prepared to notice <Leave> events in case the pointer is moved out of the button (and <Enter> events in case it comes back in again). We have to process keyboard events to allow activation from the keyboard, but only invoke the action if the user presses the **Space** or **Enter** key.

Imagine having to write all that code for each button in your application! What the Intrinsics does to get over this is define a set of **callbacks** for the button, to represent the high-level occurrences that you are interested in, and let you specify one or more functions in your program which are to be executed whenever these occur. The Intrinsics handles the low-level events and notices when these indicate that the callback should be executed. For example, the Athena pushbutton widget defines the notify callback, which is called when the button is activated. Thus, all the applications programmer has to do, having created the button widget, is call a subroutine once to tell the Intrinsics that the function save_myfile() is to be executed whenever the notify callback occurs — on other words, register save_myfile() as the callback procedure. After that, the Intrinsics manages all the events and automatically invokes the callback functions as required. A code fragment illustrating this is shown in Figure A.

You can register several callback procedures for a single callback. When the callback is invoked, these procedures are executed in the order they were registered.

Even if the programmer doesn't specify a callback procedure, when a callback occurs the widget may still perform many functions. However, these typically relate only to the widget itself or its near relatives, performing internal 'housekeeping' tasks rather than application-defined functions. For example, with a pushbutton, even if you haven't specified a callback procedure, when you push the button it 'moves in' and reverses its colour; when you release it again, it springs back again and reverts to its normal colour. Similarly, if you select from a pull-down menu an item that has no callback procedure, the button changes colour as usual, and causes the menu to disappear. In Module 12.4 we cover actions linked to callbacks in more detail.

```
void save_myfile(w, pfilename, call_info)
     Widget      w;               /* widget id        */
     caddr_t     pfilename;       /* I passed this info */
     caddr_t     call_info;       /* from the Toolkit   */
        {
        /* write contents of buffer to *(char**)pfilename */
        ...
        }

main (argc, argv)
     int argc;
     char **argv;
        {
        ...
        this = XtCreateWidget("Save", commandWidgetClass, parent, NULL, 0);
        XtAddCallback(this, XtNcallback, save_myfile, &filename);
        ...
        XtMainLoop();
        }
```

Figure A.   Using a callback procedure in a program.

7.4   Event handling and 'callbacks'

7.4.2   Non-X callbacks — file input, and timers

The Toolkit provides three special types of callback to handle occurrences outside the user interface. 'Alternate input sources' take input from a file or a serial line or another process. 'Timers' let you execute a procedure at a specified time in the future, and 'workprocs' let you do useful background work when the Toolkit would otherwise be idle.

The mechanisms we described in previous modules all relate to events and input coming from the user interface — from some type of **X** component. However, some programs need to process input that does not originate within **X**. In UNIX the input is read from a file descriptor, so it can in fact be from a normal file (which is rarely used — normal file processing is usually adequate) or from a hardware input port such as a serial line, or from another local or remote process. Let us look at some examples of these.

Many **X** applications read input from other programs. Terminal emulators need to read the input from the program they are running in the emulator window. The MIT program xconsole takes the input that would normally be printed on the workstation's console screen and displays it in a window, instead. And often, **X** is used to provide a graphical front end to an existing application running in the background, to make it easier to use; these front end programs need to input whatever the background application prints as its output.

Reading from hardware devices and serial lines can be used to add some types of new input device. For example, a dial for specifying how on-screen objects are to be rotated can be integrated this way. (However, this makes the device available only within this single toolkit application; integrating a new device to act as the main pointer would require the Input server extension of Module 3.8.) Similarly, the output of instruments, perhaps connected via an analogue to digital convertor on a serial line, can be processed.

Using the Toolkit, you handle these inputs in a uniform way just like normal callbacks, by registering them as **alternate input sources** using a specific Toolkit function, and specifying a callback function to be executed whenever input is available to be read on the particular file descriptor. Within the callback function, a read is usually performed to retrieve the available data, which is then processed according to the application's requirements.

Timers

The Toolkit allows you to register a timer callback function which is to be executed after a specified time interval. These are very like normal callbacks, but they are initiated by time elapsing rather than window or user-input events.

Typical applications of this type of function are alarms, or to update some display regularly (for example, update the hands on a clock every minute or every second), or to check the status of something regularly (for example, e-mail programs typically look in your mailbox every so often to see if any new mail has arrived). Many Toolkit programs also use timers with very short intervals, to make items flash on screen: for example, the flashing outline in xmag, and editres's flashing of widgets. These timer callbacks function by drawing or displaying the items in the reverse of the colour they are currently drawn in, each time the callback function is executed.

Background work procedures

When the Intrinsics is in its main event-loop waiting for an event to arrive, it is doing nothing. You can register a **work procedure** or **workproc** which is to be executed when the Intrinsics has nothing else to do, to make use of spare CPU cycles. Again, this procedure is very similar to a callback procedure, but is triggered for different reasons.

If the workproc returns the value False when it completes, it remains registered, and will be executed again when no events are pending; if it returns True, indicating the task is completed, the Intrinsics unregisters it and removes it. This lets the programmer control the use of the workproc, typically leaving it in place doing a small piece of its task each time it is called, only returning True when there's nothing left to do.

Because events that arrive while a workproc is executing are queued until it has finished, workprocs should be written so that they only take a short time to execute if they are not to impair the application's interative response. They should do a little work often, rather than a lot at one time.

Workprocs are often used to save time by creating the widgets within pop-up menus and dialogs before they are actually required, while and when the application is waiting, doing nothing else. When the dialog is finally required, it can be displayed quickly because there is no delay while its widgets are created, so the response of the program is improved. Workprocs are also used to update part of the user interface which can be allowed to get a little bit out of date. For example, in a DTP system or text editor, updating or scrolling the image on screen can be done by a workproc. The result is that keeping the image current has less priority than reading and processing user input; this is a reasonable strategy because what the user is typing may render obsolete the image that the program was about to re-display. For example, if you have moved to the middle of a document, completing the scrolling and painting of the current page is a waste of time if the user has subsequently just pressed the goto-end-of-file key.

Another major use of workprocs is performing large computations, while still allowing the application to respond to user input (see Module 14.1.2).

7.5   Some implementations of Motif and OPEN LOOK use Xt

Most Motif implementations and some OPEN LOOK ones use the standard Intrinsics. These 'toolkits' are really widget sets, with some extra functions, specific
to the look and feel, provided in additional libraries.

The principal implementation of the Motif 'standard' look and feel — the source code
distributed by the Open Software Foundation — is Intrinsics-based. Most Motif development and user systems, from both hardware vendors and third-party suppliers, are
founded on this released code. There are some other systems that provide the Motif
look and feel which do not use this code as a basis. Of these, most are special toolkits
that aim to provide GUI-independent programming, where the programmer can write
one source program which when compiled on different systems (typically Microsoft
Windows, Macintosh, and UNIX with Motif) will use the native GUI of that system.
(See Module 7.6 for more detail.)

The OPEN LOOK GUI is also available as an Intrinsics-based toolkit, called Xt+ or
OLIT. However, its most common implementation is probably the one called Xview,
which was specifically designed to simplify porting applications to **X** from Sun's proprietary SunView system; Xview doesn't use the Intrinsics. Figure A shows how the
same look and feel is provided by two very different internal program structures.

The fact that very different GUIs can be based on the same toolkit Intrinsics shows
how flexible the **X** toolkit mechanism is. It also means that even if an organization
chooses to adopt one particular look and feel, Motif, say, all the programming techniques
and skills gained by programmers are equally applicable to Motif and OPEN LOOK,
because they are provided by the Intrinsics. So, later on, migrating to or porting to OPEN
LOOK would not be a difficult task (although it would be long and tedious, because all
the widget names, the widget parameters, and how they interact are different).

In the case of the Intrinsics-based toolkits, what the toolkit vendor is really providing
is a set of widgets, because most of the basic functionality is provided by the standard
system. Vendors do supply some extra libraries of functions as well, to augment the
standard Intrinsics functions. Many of these are simple convenience functions — just
'wrappers' around standard Intrinsics functions. For example, Motif provides a special
function to create a pushbutton window, but it is just as easy to call the standard
Intrinsics widget-create function with an argument specifying that the widget type is to
be a pushbutton. However, other functions perform more complex tasks. For example,
a menu creation function not only creates the basic widget that forms the menu pane,
but also configures it for correct operation — so that all the menu items are aligned
vertically (for a pull-down menu) and the event processing is correctly initialized to
allow the menu to be invoked, and items selected from it, via the keyboard.

The toolkits also provide enhanced support for communication between applications.
Motif provides a clipboard for cutting and pasting. OPEN LOOK includes support for
drag and drop — selecting an item in one program, and communicating this selection
to another application or a different part of the same one, by dragging the item with the
mouse pointer, and dropping it onto some other appropriate object. (For example, you

might print a file by dragging its icon and dropping it onto a printer's icon.)   Other features included are support for localization of applications, so that one application may be produced which is suitable for use with many different national languages and character sets. (See also Module 5.3.)

Toolkits providing both Motif and OPEN LOOK look and feel

Many software developers, especially those developing software for sale rather than in-house use, don't want to choose just Motif or just OPEN LOOK — some of their customers will want an OPEN LOOK product, whereas others will have standardized on Motif and will want a Motif version.   Intrinsics-based toolkits are now coming available which let you write your program using 'generic' user interface components (for example MooLIT from UNIX System Laboratories). You specify just a scrollbar or a pushbutton, not a Motif scrollbar or an OPEN LOOK pushbutton, and compile your program with the Intrinsics and 'dual-look and feel' toolkit libraries, giving you a single executable (binary) program. Then at run time you specify which look and feel you want to use. Thus you can have two instances of an application running on the same CPU from the same program-file on disk, one offering the OPEN LOOK look and feel, the other Motif.

Similar facilities are provided by several non-Intrinsics toolkits (Module 7.6).

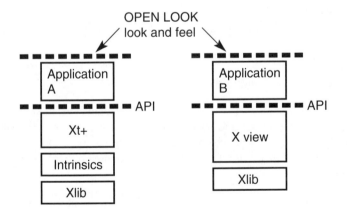

Figure A.   The same OPEN LOOK look and feel is offered by two very different toolkits.

7.5 Some implementations of Motif and OPEN LOOK use Xt

7.5.1 Motif's User Interface Language — UIL

The standard Motif system includes a special language for specifying the user interface of the application. This is called UIL — the User Interface Language. You specify in a text file the tree-like hierarchy of widgets your application needs, and compile it separately from your main program. The main program interprets this file at run time using special Motif functions. This lets you alter the user interface easily, changing only the UIL file, without having to change, or even recompile or relink, the main program.

UIL is a special-purpose language for describing a hierarchy of widgets in an application, plus the various parameters for each widget, such as position, size, text to be displayed in labels, menu composition, etc. You write the widget descriptions in a text file, called a .uil file. Then, using a special UIL compiler, you convert this text file into a .uid file.

Separately, you write and compile and link your main program (Figure A) but you omit all the code you would normally include to create widgets, position them, specify their parameters, etc. Instead, you include a few special functions ('Motif Resource Manager' or MRM functions) provided in a Motif library; at run time these functions read in the already prepared .uid file, and dynamically create and configure the widgets specified in that file. (Figure B)

The advantages of this over programming the user interface by hand, using C calls, are:

- UIL code is more compact than C.

- The UIL compiler can perform extra error checking, as it knows about widgets and what values and data types may be specified for widget parameters. For example, if you try to specify a font parameter for a scrollbar, UIL knows scrollbars don't have any font parameters, and gives you an appropriate error message.

- Most of the user interface code (in the .uil file) is separated out from the application code (in your .c source file) which makes the code more modular.

- This separation makes it easier to develop the two parts of the program in parallel, reducing development time as well as allowing early prototyping of the user interface.

- The user interface can be changed, by editing and recompiling the .uil file, at any time, without recompiling the main program. So software vendors can ship the .uil source file with the executable program, allowing customers to tailor the user interface to their own requirements as much as they like, without having access to the (presumably proprietary and valuable) source code of the main program.

While UIL makes it easy to specify the layout and appearance of your program's user interface, it only allows you to provide a static (fixed) description of the interface. It is really a layout specification, and UIL has no programming facilities for specifying the time-dependent (dynamic) aspects of the interface. For example, you cannot write some UIL code to perform a function like 'if the user pressed pushbutton A, then call up dialog B, but if they pressed button C as well, don't show options X, Y and Z on the dialog, and expand widget W'. You have to program sequences such as this in your main program, probably with callback procedures.

Many **X** interface development systems and program generators output UIL code from which the final program is built.

This concludes our look at the **X** standard toolkit facilities. In the next module we look at some other toolkits that are *not* based on the Intrinsics.

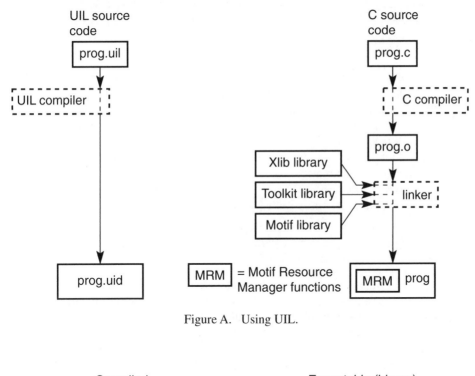

Figure A.   Using UIL.

Figure B.   At run time the Motif program reads in the user interface description from the .uid file.

7.6   Other X toolkits

Many toolkits do not use the Intrinsics at all, often because they are implemented in a language other than C. Some of these provide the same look and feel as Intrinsics-based toolkits.

The Intrinsics is the **X** standard mechanism for building toolkits, but it is not the only mechanism. There are other toolkits which do not use the Intrinsics, for many reasons listed below. The schematic structure of these is contrasted with a standard Intrinsics-based application, and one using only Xlib functions, in Figure A.

- **Toolkits to support languages other than C.** The Intrinsics and widgets are written in C: toolkits for other languages, such as Lisp or C++ are often written in their own language. Examples are Interviews and Solbourne's OI toolkit. Many of these toolkits provide both Motif and OPEN LOOK look and feels, because providing such dual features is much easier in a true object-oriented language.

- **Special purpose toolkits — for porting.** When you use the Intrinsics, your program has a particular structure that reflects how the Intrinsics processes events and despatches them to invoke callbacks, etc. This structure may be very different from that used for other window systems. Some toolkits, Sun's Xview for example, are specifically designed to simplify porting an application to **X** from some other environment, and are structured so that the program source code needs as little modification as possible. As a result, the program structure will not fit into the pattern needed for the Intrinsics, so these toolkits are specially built using their own low-level layers.

  There are other toolkits for UNIX systems to let you compile Microsoft Windows source programs, producing a program running on the UNIX system with the Motif look and feel.

- **Special purpose toolkits — GUI-independent programming.** Often a software developer needs to provide the same application on many different hardware and software platforms. While **X** is obtainable for a wide range of machines and operating systems, there are environments where **X** is either not available or is not what the user wants, for example in dedicated Macintosh or PC environments. In order to make all their applications available under several different graphical or window systems with the minimum of work, some vendors have developed special toolkits. Typical systems let the programmer write a single source program which is then compiled on the chosen platform to produce an application with the appropriate look and feel. Platforms most often supported are Motif or OPEN LOOK on VMS or UNIX, Microsoft Windows, Macintosh, or Presentation Manager. Examples of such toolkits are XVT and Neuron Data's Open Interface.

  Because these toolkits must provide a generic program framework, they are not Intrinsics-based.

(See Module 14.4 for more on special toolkits.)

As we mentioned previously in Module 6.4, the fact that an application has a particular look and feel does not necessarily mean that it was implemented with a particular toolkit. Remember, look and feel is the appearance and external behaviour of a program: internally, an application can provide the same look and feel in many different ways, and there are many common examples of this:

- The OPEN LOOK look and feel is provided both by the **Xview** toolkit, and the Intrinsics-based **Xt+** toolkit. So programs using these different toolkits will have the same look and feel, but will have a very different internal structure.

- The GUI-independent toolkits usually provide a particular look and feel, for example, Motif or OPEN LOOK, not by including standard implementations of those systems, but by writing their own code which produces the same visual and behaviour effects.

And of course with toolkits such as **OI** which we mentioned above, and the dual-interface toolkits of Module 7.5, the reverse is the case: a single internal program structure is capable of providing more than one distinct look and feel.

			LISP toolkit	Other language toolkit
	widget set	non-Intrinsics toolkit		
	Intrinsics		LISP **X** bindings	Other language **X** bindings
Xlib	Xlib	Xlib		

Figure A. Schematic structure of applications based on **Xlib** Intrinsics, and other toolkits.

Summary

In this chapter we have looked at how **X** supports user interface toolkits.

We saw that most applications use the standard Xt Toolkit, which consists of a basic object-oriented framework provided by the Intrinsics, with widgets created using this framework. Primitive widgets are typically single-purpose user interface components, while composite widgets are containers to manage the layout of other widgets, for example in menus. The Toolkit offloads most of the event-handling complexity from the application programmer, and by means of callbacks simplifies integrating the user interface with the application-related code. We also looked briefly at non-Intrinsics toolkits.

In fact we have dealt with only one part of the overall user interface the user sees — the part relating to how you interact with the graphical interface components within a particular application which we call the 'application interface'.

The other part of the total user interface is how you control the layout of your screen as a whole — how you position one application's window relative to another, how you move and resize the applications on your screen, and how you move control from one application to another. In the next chapter we move on to look at this other major part of the whole user interface — the 'management interface', which is determined by the window manager.

Chapter

8

'Look and Feel' Part 2 — Window Managers

8.1 What you need a 'window manager' for

 8.1.1 Optional and advanced window manager functions

8.2 Using the window manager

8.3 The window manager's look and feel

 8.3.1 The management interface and application interface are totally separate

8.4 How a window manager works

 8.4.1 Communication between window manager and applications — properties

Introduction

So far we have been dealing only with a single application, and have concentrated on how the user interface within that application is built up. However, to make the most of any system we need to be able to use several applications simultaneously on screen, and even for a single application we often need to have multiple windows — for control panels, or dialogs, or to be able to view several sets of information simultaneously. We need a way to control the initial placement of these windows and to manage them as we proceed with our work; this function is provided by the window manager. In this chapter we look at what the window manager is, and how its appearance and behaviour form the second major part of the overall look and feel that the user sees. This introduces the scenario of multiple simultaneous X clients, which we expand on in the chapter after this.

8.1   What you need a 'window manager' for

The window manager is what you use to instruct the system to configure your screen as you want it — to move or resize windows, turn them into icons, etc. The interface the window manager presents is the second part of the total look and feel which the user sees.

As we mentioned in Modules 1.2 and 3.1.1, the base **X** system — the server — has no in-built means for you to tell it how the windows on the screen are to be laid out and managed. So you need an 'agent' which performs actions on your behalf, in response to commands (in some form which we have yet to discuss) from you.

At its very simplest, the problem is: if you have a window on the screen and you want to make it bigger (or smaller), how can you tell the system to do that? What if you need to move windows to different positions on the screen, or bring a particular window to the top of the stack if it's obscured by some other windows? Unlike the application interface, this function cannot be provided by the application itself, because a change in one application may require changes in another; for example, if your application windows are to be **tiled** (Figure A), expanding one window requires that one or more others be reduced.

The answer is, you need a special program called a **window manager** which will interpret some special actions you take and manage the windows on your screen accordingly. Any **X** program that performs these functions for you is a window manager. So, many different window managers are possible, and in fact many have been developed by different organizations over the years. Facilities the window manager should usually provide include:

- **Configuring application windows** on screen as mentioned above, including moving, resizing, stacking, and initial placement when a new window is created.

- Changing windows into **icons** — small, often pictorial, representations of windows — to save screen space when the window isn't required, and changing icons back into windows again. Not all window managers use icons; others do, and support a special **icon box** which keeps the icons arranged neatly, while still others let the icons be positioned anywhere.

- Maintaining particular **window layouts** on the screen. For example, a **tiling** window manager will not allow application windows to overlap, but will always try to use as much of the screen as possible, as illustrated in Figure A.

- Directing the keyboard input to different applications, that is, **controlling the keyboard focus**. There are two types of focus policy:

  1. **Click to type**, where you click with the mouse on a particular application, and all keyboard input goes to that application, no matter where the mouse pointer is.

2. **Pointer-driven** focus, where the input is sent to whichever application currently contains the mouse pointer. (If the pointer isn't in any application window, the input is just thrown away.)

- **Handling colormaps.** As we discussed in Module 3.6.3, some applications need to use so many colours that they have to have a special table of colours — a colormap — which has to be installed into the colour graphics hardware each time that application is active, so that it shows its graphics in the correct colours. If an application does use a special colormap, the window manager installs that colormap when the application receives the keyboard focus (and of course de-installs it when another application received focus and has *its* own colormap installed), as we described in Module 3.6.3.

  The window manager has to perform this task because there is a deficiency in the **X** protocol: a race condition can arise if more than one client installs colormaps, so to overcome this the **X** convention is that only a window manager may install colormaps.

In the next module we look at some facilities provided by more advanced window managers.

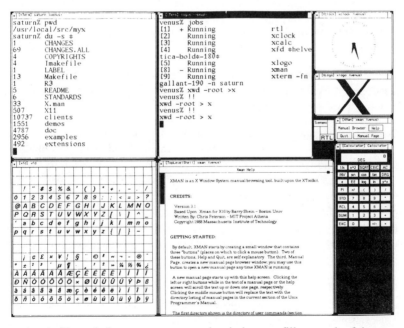

Figure A.   A tiling window manager expands windows to fill as much of the screen as possible.

8.1   What you need a 'window manager' for

8.1.1   Optional and advanced window manager functions

Extra functionality and more sophisticated features have been added to window managers as the number of window managers available has increased.

In the early days of **X**, many window managers were developed, because people were investigating how best window management ought to be addressed. Many of the best features of these early window managers have been incorporated into more recent implementations, and in fact new prototype window managers are still continually produced. As a result, many window managers now offer a range of features far beyond the necessary minimum, such as:

- **Pop-up menus**. Most window managers now let you define your own pop-up menus, both to invoke functions the window manager itself provides, and to run other **X** and non-**X** programs (Figure A).

- **Configurability**. Early window managers had fixed ways of invoking their window configuration functions, or at best somewhat limited facilities for customising them; for example, to move a window you had to press the `Meta` key and drag the window with the left mouse button. However nowadays most let you choose your own set of keyboard and mouse sequences for invoking the functions, and you can configure them for use on systems which don't have a mouse at all.

- **Operating on groups of windows**. More sophisticated managers let you select several windows and perform an operation on them as a group, for example moving them or iconifying them as a unit.

- Providing a **virtual desktop** — effectively a virtual screen which is much larger than the physical one; the physical screen is a viewing port onto this larger area, and you can move the port around to access different sections of the overall desktop (Figure B). This lets you group together sets of windows required for a particular activity. You place different sets in different areas of your virtual desktop, so that most of the time they are not visible and don't clutter up your screen space. However, when you want to perform that particular task, you move the viewing port to that area, so you have all the applications you need group together exactly as you left them before.

- **Programmability**. Some of the more recently developed window managers are programmable, especially those emerging from the research community. For example, gwm is programmable in Lisp.

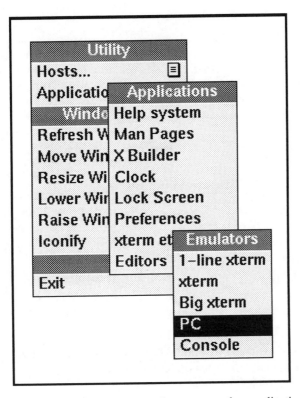

Figure A.   Configurable pop-up menus let you run other applications easily.

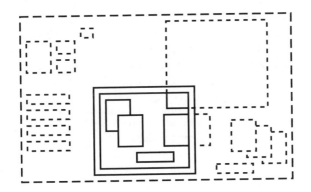

Figure B.   Window manager 'virtual desktop' controller.

8.2 Using the window manager

Because the window manager is not part of the server, but is a separate **X** client, you can easily replace it. While only one window manager can be in use on a display at any particular time, many different window managers can be in use on the same network simultaneously.

The window manager is not built into the server nor into the operating system, but is 'just another' client program. This feature has many important consequences for the system as a whole:

- It is easy to change the window manager. If you don't like one, you can choose a different one. (You can even do this halfway through a session — just kill off one window manager, using whatever operating system command is required, or the window manager's **Quit** or **Exit** function if it provides one — and start the other.)

  This flexibility was one of the design goals of **X** — rather than giving a single fixed interface, to provide mechanisms that can be used to build any desired interface. (Another example of the 'mechanism, not policy' philosophy.)

- You don't always need a window manager, although for normal working, one is almost essential. (Otherwise you may find that all new windows are created in the top left corner and cover up other things you are working on, and that it is impossible to place a control panel where you need it.)

  However, if the user only ever works with a single application, with a fixed configuration, it may actually be more convenient not to have a window manager. For example, a data-entry clerk might work with the same part of the same application all day, and no changing of window configuration is ever needed. Or, for a critical application such as a power-plant control system, you certainly don't want the user to be able to iconify the application's window or cover it up with another one, just in case an important warning message alert appears on the system.

- Each user on a network can choose their own window manager which suits them best — there is no requirement (other than ease of administration and training, and cost) for everybody in an organization to use the same window manager. Different window managers may suit different classes of users. For example, programmers may prefer something different to secretaries.

- As the window manager is just a client program, it can run remotely over a network. Figure A shows a window manager executing on machine 'A', but managing the windows on the display of machine 'B'. Where the display is an X-terminal, which can only execute the server and no clients, the window manager *must* be run remotely. (Although, as we mentioned in Module 3.2.2, some X-terminals do have a window manager built in now.)

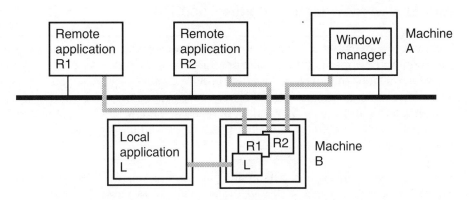

Figure A.   The window manager can manage a display on a different machine to the one
it's executing on.

8.3   The window manager's look and feel

Each window manager has its own distinctive appearance and its own way of providing window management functions; therefore each has its own look and feel which is independent of the interface provided within the application windows by the applications themselves. Because managing screen and window layout is such a large and visible component of using a window system, many people identify the look and feel of the window manager with the look and feel of the whole system.

You use different window managers in different ways. Some add **title-bars** and other **decorations** around the edge of the application window, as shown in Figure A. (You use these to configure your window; for example, to resize you drag on one of the edge- or corner-decorations, and to iconify you click on some particular part of the title-bar.) Other window managers add only title-bars, and still others add nothing to the window, so that to perform an action on a window you have to use a pop-up menu, or press a particular combination of mouse and keyboard strokes. (For example, to move a window you might have to drag with the left mouse button, with the `Alt` key pressed down all the time.) As we mentioned in Module 8.1, different window managers handle icons in different ways, perhaps keeping them in a neat icon box; Figure B shows two styles of icon box, one of which uses scrollbars to allow you to get to the icon you want, whereas the other expands to accommodate the number of icons it has to hold, and assumes that you have enough screen space for the whole of the box to be visible.

So, window managers have distinctive visual appearances, and you use them in different ways because the commands they respond to are different. In other words, each window manager has its own look and feel. Because configuring windows and managing your screen space is such a frequent activity, it is the look and feel of the window manager that most people regard as the dominant characteristic of a window system. For example, it is largely because the Motif window manager's title-bars and borders (shown in Figure A) are so like those of Presentation Manager, and behave in the same way, that Motif and Presentation Manager are regarded as providing more or less the same look and feel. (There are many other similarities as well, but window management is the most important.) And one of the most striking features of OPEN LOOK is its 'push pin' feature, which lets you 'pin' dialog boxes and menus to the screen (Figures C and D) inhibiting the menu popping down when you've made your selections. You use this feature where you want to invoke a function repeatedly, and popping up the menu each time as well as selecting the function from it would be awkward.

It is very important to realize that the window manager's look and feel is completely separate from the look and feel of the user interface within a particular application, and we deal with this in detail in the next module.

Figure A.   Decorations added around a window by the Motif window manager.

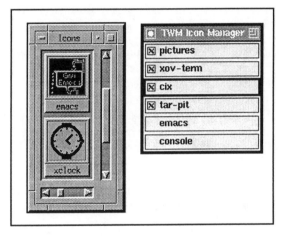

Figure B.   Different styles of iconbox used by the Motif and twm window managers.

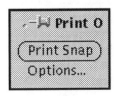

Figure C.   OPEN LOOK
menus and dialogs have a pushpin.

Figure D.   Menu kept 'popped-up' with a pushpin.

8.3 The window manager's look and feel

8.3.1 The management interface and application interface are totally separate

The overall interface as seen by the user consists of two separate parts — the application interface built into the application program, and the management interface provided by the window manager. The two are completely separate even though the user may not notice this.

The two distinct components of the total interface a user sees are:

1. The application's user interface (the **application interface**) which is built into the program and remains fixed. This is usually provided by means of a toolkit as we discussed in the last chapter. To change this interface you would have to modify and recompile the source code of the program.[1]

2. The window manager's interface (the **management interface**) is determined by the window manager, and if you run a different window manager, then you get a different management interface. This is illustrated in Figures A, B, and C which show the contributions made by the application and the window manager to the overall interface. Everything within the window border 'belongs to' the application, whereas everything outside — the decorations, etc. — belongs to the window manager.

A different way of thinking of this is to consider that the window manager treats windows as pieces of paper on your desktop without looking at what is written on the pieces of paper; it is the applications themselves that know what is on the pieces of paper, what they mean and how you work with them.

How does the window manager gets its look and feel? The answer is clear when you remember that the window manager is just another client application — so it too has its user interface built into it, with the toolkit or other libraries it was compiled with. For example, the Motif window manager mwm is compiled with the standard Motif toolkit, and so the look and feel of its menus, scrollbars, etc. are the same as for all other Motif applications. As a result, for someone using only Motif programs, the whole interface including both management and application parts is very consistent and the user will not realize how the various aspects of the interface are being provided internally. Of course, if you use a Motif window manager with OPEN LOOK applications, the interface won't look so homogeneous. Other window managers are built using non-standard toolkits and will have a completely different, non-standard, appearance.

This separation of management and application interface is an explicit design goal of **X**. In general, applications should be independent of window manager policy, so they can work correctly on as wide a range of systems as possible. An application can be

---

[1] While this is no longer 100% true for applications built with dual-interface toolkits (Modules 7.5 and 7.6), the argument remains broadly correct: an application can only provide the interface or interfaces that were built into it when it was compiled. For example, to add a Macintosh-like look and feel, even OI and MooLIT applications would have to be extensively modified and re-compiled.

written to take advantage of special facilities provided by a specific window manager, and will work particularly well with that window manager, but it should still be written to operate satisfactorily and adequately with other window managers in general. For example, the OPEN LOOK window manager includes a status/error message area in the decorations it adds to an application window — an application can reasonably display its error messages here. Other window managers don't provide this feature, so when running with a different window manager the application should explicitly display the message in some other way, probably as a pop-up dialog window (rather than just not giving the message to the user at all!)

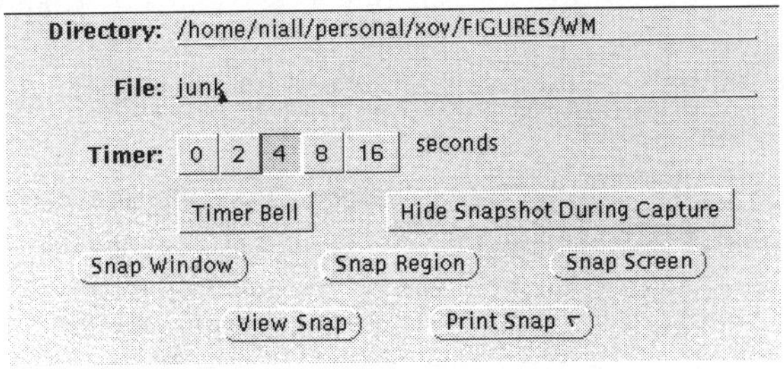

Figure A.   The application interface.

Figure B.   The window manager's contribution – the management interface.

Figure C.   The overall user interface.

8.4   How a window manager works

The window manager is not part of the server, but is a separate **X** client. Most of the mechanisms it uses to manipulate the windows on your screen are not special, but are the same mechanisms any application uses to handle its own windows and sub-windows.

(If technical details aren't so relevant to you, you can skip over this module.)

In **X** there is no protection mechanism on a per-window basis: if an application has access to one window on a display, it has full access to *every* window on that display. Because the window manager is just another application connected to your display, it has full access to all the windows on your screen, and can resize them or move them or whatever else it needs to do.

So, the window manager is not using any special system mechanisms to manipulate the windows. Instead, it is just using the ordinary **Xlib** function calls which any program may use to configure any of its windows. This means that writing a very primitive window manager of your own is not too difficult (although writing one that works correctly and adheres to all the necessary standards is a *very* big job).

However, there are a few functions that are used most often by window managers, although other applications occasionally need them, too:

- **Redirecting configuration operations.** When a new application is created and is about to be shown on the screen, the window manager needs to know what its size and position are going to be; the window manager must also be able to change these if it needs to. (For example, a tiling window manager will often want to force a new window to be a particular size in a particular location which the window manager chooses.)

  The window manager can specify that configuration operations on the (top-level) application windows (resize, move, and change of stacking order) should not actually be actioned but instead should cause an event to be sent to the window manager. The window manager receives the event, and itself performs the action, either as the application wanted, or as the window manager thinks fit. Effectively the window manager is getting between the application and your screen, and intercepting the configuration requests. This is how it can enforce a layout policy — tiled or overlapping windows, preventing windows being moved partially offscreen, or whatever.

- **Grabbing keys and buttons.** We want the window manager to receive some special events — those key or button sequences that are to be interpreted as commands to the window manager — no matter which window they occur in. Normally the server sends a keyboard or mouse event to the application which owns the window in which the event occurred. To ensure that the window manager will get the events it needs it **grabs** them, that is, it tells the server that it has a special interest in these events, and that they are always to be sent to the window manager whenever and wherever they occur.

Of course, this means that the other (normal) applications will never see these particular key/button sequences. So when you are using configurable window managers which let you specify which keyboard and button sequences you want to use for window configuration, you have to be careful you don't specify some keys that one of your applications might need. (You can reduce the risk of a conflict by specifying keys or buttons in conjunction with one or more modifiers such as `Shift` or `Control` or `Alt`.)

- **Reparenting windows.** We saw in Module 8.1 that the decorations around an application window are not part of the application, but are added by the window manager. **X** does not allow grouping of windows, so to 'attach' the decorations to the window, the window manager uses the mechanism known as **reparenting**. In the absence of a window manager, the application windows are children of the root window; Figure A shows the window tree for this case. When the window manager starts up (or when the window manager is already running and a new application window is created), the window manager creates another window as a child of the root window; this window is made big enough to contain both the decorations and the application window. Then the decorations are created in this new window, and the application window is reparented, that is it is made a child of the new window instead of the root window. The window tree after reparenting is illustrated in Figure B. The reparenting process is effectively shown schematically in the figures of the previous module; the original top-level application window is shown in Figure A, the window its reparented to and containing the decorations is Figure B, and the final reparented result in Figure C.

Note that this whole procedure emphasizes that the management interface — the appearance and behaviour of the window manager — is definitely not part of the application program.

In the next module we look at the mechanisms the window manager and application use to communicate with one another.

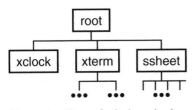

Figure A.   Tree of windows in the absence of a window manager.

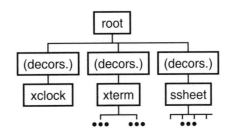

Figure B.   Tree showing application windows reparented by window manager.

8.4   How a window manager works

8.4.1   Communication between window manager and applications — properties

The client needs to communicate with the window manager, especially when the client starts, to give information about its preferred size and location, names to be used for window labels and icons, etc. Client and window manager communicate using the standard mechanism of properties.

There are strict conventions about how applications should behave in relation to a window manager. Basically, as the window manager represents the desires of the user, an application should accept whatever configuration a window manager gives it. An application should never 'fight' with the window manager about the size it has been made, because that is the size that the user wanted, and the application should do the best it can to work at that size. If an application is written correctly like this, it will be 'management independent', that is, it will work with many different styles of window manager, and in many different environments. These conventions are laid down in the **X** standard document *Inter-Client Communication Conventions Manual*, which we discuss in more detail in the next chapter.

In the previous module we saw that the window manager can decide to make a window any size it chooses. In order to decide how to configure an application sensibly, the window manager needs more information: how big does the application want the window to be, does it have any preference about aspect ratio (does it need a tall thin window, or would it really prefer a square one), what is the minimum size that the application can use, what is the maximum, etc.

To give this information to the window manager, the application uses **properties** (Module 4.1).   A property is a named piece of data which a client can attach to a window, and which any other client may read or overwrite. Here, the application places information about its desired configuration in a number of properties with specific names, attached to the application's top-level window. (The property names are standard — they are defined in the *Inter-Client Communication Conventions Manual*, and all begin with the prefix **WM_**). The window manager looks at these properties when it needs the information. These properties are also used to pass other information the window manager needs, for example the name of the application as it is to be shown in its title-bar. An example of the window manager-related properties of our text-editor window is shown in Figure A.

Once the application has started and its top-level window (or windows) has been configured, there is normally very little communication between application and window manager. An exception is where the application sets the **WM_PROTOCOLS** property on its window. The value of this property is a list of functions or actions which the window manager may ask the application to perform, and which the application is able to perform. The actions include:

- **WM_DELETE_WINDOW** tells the application to delete this top-level window. This is particularly useful where the application has several windows;

for example, an editor might have a separate window for each file being edited, and WM_DELETE_WINDOW lets you selectively remove any of these you don't need any more.

- WM_SAVE_YOURSELF tells the application to save its current state so that it can be restarted later, ideally in exactly the same state as it is in now, and record the command necessary to restart itself in the WM_COMMAND property. For example, a text editor would save or checkpoint all files being edited, and record which files it has in its buffers, and other status and configuration information about those files.

(If the application can't perform a particular action or doesn't know about it, that action's name is not included in the WM_PROTOCOLS property; if the application can't perform any of the standard functions, it doesn't set the property at all.) When the window manager wants the application to perform an action, it sends a <ClientMessage> event to the application, with an indication in the event specifying which action is to be performed.

We discuss properties in detail in Module 9.2, and the way that one client can send events to another in Module 9.3.1.

```
WM_STATE(WM_STATE):
                window state: Normal
                icon window: 0x0
WM_ICON_NAME(STRING) = "printtool       "
_OL_WIN_ATTR(_OL_WIN_ATTR) = 0x8e, 0x8f, 0x90
_OL_DECOR_ADD(ATOM) = _OL_DECOR_FOOTER
WM_NAME(STRING) = "Print Tool"
WM_NORMAL_HINTS(WM_SIZE_HINTS):
WM_HINTS(WM_HINTS):
                Client accepts input or input focus: False
                window id # to use for icon: 0x280000b
                window id # of group leader: 0x280000c
WM_PROTOCOLS(ATOM): protocols  WM_TAKE_FOCUS,
                WM_DELETE_WINDOW, WM_SAVE_YOURSELF
```

Figure A. Sample set of properties for communicating with a window manager.

Summary

In this chapter we have seen that the role of the window manager is to act as agent for you, the user — it is the way you control the layout and other aspects of the application you are using on your display. We have looked at the functionality the window manager must provide, and how it provides it. In particular, the window manager is just another client, so it has its own look and feel which can differ from that of the applications it controls, and many different window managers are available. We looked at the mechanisms the window manager uses to perform its tasks, and we saw that it uses the same **X** functions as any other **X** application.

This chapter has concentrated on how a single application interoperates with the window manager. In the next chapter we go on from here and see how multiple clients can work together, allowing a set of separate programs to cooperate in order to provide a more integrated environment for the user.

Chapter

9

Using Many Applications Together — 'Inter-Client Communications'

9.1   Why applications need to communicate with each other

9.2   'Properties' — the basic mechanism for inter-client communications
        9.2.1 Examples of the use of properties

9.3   Advanced communications mechanisms
        9.3.1 Sending events from one client to another

9.4   The Selections Service — a high-level communications mechanism
        9.4.1 The detailed data transfer mechanism using Selections
        9.4.2 Selection clipboards, and Selection data formats

9.5   ICCCM — the rulebook for inter-client communications

9.6   Desktop managers

Introduction

In the last chapter we saw how a window manager and a single client operate together. Here we move on to look at the mechanisms any applications can use to communicate with each other, and how multiple clients interwork with one another. We cover the issues involved in making very different clients — perhaps running on different operating systems and networks — interwork together; of necessity this is quite complex, and if technical details are not so relevant to you, you can skip over this chapter.

9.1   Why applications need to communicate with each other

User applications interact with one another to provide cut-and-paste facilities, and to exchange data within a suite of related applications. **X** user applications also have to communicate with the window manager, to indicate preferred size, position, etc. The **X** server must provide communication mechanisms because clients may not be able to communicate directly.

X is a multitasking environment, so you can expect to have many different applications working onscreen simultaneously. To get the maximum benefit from multiple applications you must be able to exchange information between them. We can divide the information which needs to be exchanged into three broad classes:

1. **Information that the user explicitly transfers.** When you are using several programs for different parts of some overall task, you often want to move information around. For example, if you are sending an electronic mail message concerning some budget information, you might query an accounting application, transfer the result into a spreadsheet program, use a calculator on some of the spreadsheet data, and finally incorporate the results into your mail message.

   The most common way to move information explicitly is to cut-and-paste. You specify which data you want to transfer (usually by clicking or dragging with the mouse within one application) and then include it in the other application either by mouse clicking or by selecting a special **paste** menu option. In Modules 9.2.1 and 9.4 we'll see two different mechanisms **X** provides for cut-and-paste.

2. **Information transferred automatically by the applications themselves.** Some applications operate together automatically. For example, a 'talk' application which enables one user to have an interactive dialogue with another running a similar application will require automatic transfer between the two programs of the text each user types in.

   Other suites of programs may be divided up functionally, so that one program in the suite manages the data, another is the front end used to interact with or control the system, and one or more other programs display views of the current state of the system. In these cases the applications would initiate their own communications with each other.

   Some **X**-specific applications such as user interface builders and rapid development tools also need to send information to each other. As a simple example, the standard MIT program editres (see Module 12.5) allows you to interactively edit various settings of the widgets in a running Toolkit program. editres runs as a separate program, but it sends messages to the application you are editing, and also receives information from it.

3. **Information transferred for system functions.** We have already seen that user applications and the window manager need to communicate with each

other. Other system-like functions requiring communications facilities are desktop managers, discussed in Module 9.6.

The window system itself — the server — must provide the mechanisms for applications to communicate with each other, and all communication between the applications must be via the server. This is essential because the applications may not be able to talk to each other directly; as shown in Figure A, the applications may be on different networks or using different protocols on the same network.

In the rest of this chapter we look at the general mechanisms **X** provides which are used for clients to communicate with each other, in particular properties and send events. We then go on to see how higher-level communications services, in particular the **X** selections mechanism, can be built using these, and look at the standards laid down for these functions. Finally we look briefly at some desktop managers, which require these features.

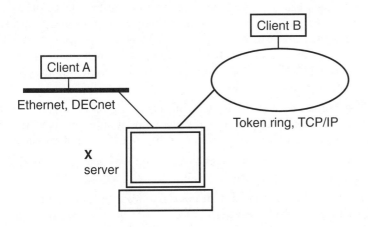

Figure A. Applications may not be able to communicate directly, so information is sent via the server.

9.2 'Properties' — the basic mechanism for inter-client communications

An application can store arbitrary data in named locations called 'properties' on the server, and other applications can retrieve the data from there. This simple mechanism is used for almost all communication between applications, and it can be used to construct sophisticated inter-client communication protocols.

X's properties provide the basic mechanism for most communication between applications. The idea of a property is that it is a named piece of (arbitrary) data related to (or attached to) a particular window. An application stores information in a property, using the Xlib function XChangeProperty(). After that, any other application which knows the name of the property (and the window it's related to) can retrieve that information, using the Xlib function XGetProperty().

Several windows each can have a property of the same name, but because each of these properties relates to a different window, each of these properties is distinct, can contain different data, and can be accessed separately. This fact is commonly used: for example, each application window typically has its own group of properties (WM_CLASS, WM_NAME, etc.) containing information needed by the window manager to handle that particular application.

Any application can access and modify the contents of a property — not just the one that created or first wrote data into it. Also, the property lives on even after the client that created it has terminated. So properties really are truly shared resources.

Retrieving the value of a property involves a round-trip: the client sends the request asking for the value, and the server sends the value back as a reply.

The typical use of properties combines all the above features. Applications which need to exchange information with each other agree on (or have hard-coded into them) the name of a property which they will use to pass the information, and to which window the property will be attached. Again, applications passing information to the window manager are a good example of this: both applications and window manager know that the property names are WM_CLASS, WM_NAME, etc., and that they are attached to the application's main or top level window. Figure A shows the properties on an OPEN LOOK menu, listed using the MIT program xprop.

In the next module we look at some examples of how properties are used in an **X** system.

```
venus% xprop

WM_STATE(WM_STATE):
                window state: Normal
                icon window: 0x2001a0
_OL_PIN_STATE(INTEGER) = 1
_OL_DFLT_BTN(INTEGER) = 45, 13, 4, 4, 82, 19
WM_NAME(STRING) = "Print Options"
_OL_WIN_ATTR(_OL_WIN_ATTR) = 0x61, 0x66, 0x62
_OL_DECOR_DEL(ATOM) = _OL_DECOR_RESIZE
WM_NORMAL_HINTS(WM_SIZE_HINTS):
                program specified location: -131240464, 113032
                program specified size: 146656 by -134221188
WM_HINTS(WM_HINTS):
                Client accepts input or input focus: False
                window id # of group leader: 0xa0000c
WM_PROTOCOLS(ATOM): protocols  WM_TAKE_FOCUS, WM_DELETE_WINDOW,
                WM_SAVE_YOURSELF
```

Figure A.   Listing properties on a window with xprop.

9.2 'Properties' — the basic mechanism for inter-client communications

9.2.1 Examples of the use of properties

Properties are used widely, for communicating default values to applications, and to allow cut-and-paste between applications.

A simple example of the use of properties is the standard MIT program xrdb. This stores default settings for programs in a special property, RESOURCE_MANAGER, on the root window. Each application as it starts up looks for this property, and if the property exits, the application reads the default settings from the property rather than from a file, as illustrated in Figure A. The settings in the file myresf are usually loaded into the RESOURCE_MANAGER property with the MIT program xrdb as soon as the server has started, and the value is then checked by listing all the properties on the root window with the xprop command, as shown in Figure B.

Settings have to be stored in a property rather than a file, so that all applications using the particular display can access these settings; if they were stored in a file on one particular machine, they might not be accessible to applications on other machines which may be on a different network or using different network protocols or different operating systems. The root window is used because it's always present once the system has started, so every application can always access it.

Example — cut-and-paste of text using cut-buffer properties

Another example of the use of properties is cut-and-paste using **cut buffers**. When you 'cut' some text, that is, select it, the application you used to select that text copies it into a property called CUT_BUFFER0 on the root window. (Again, the root window is used because it's always present and accessible to every application.) To help the user, applications typically highlight or show in reverse video the text that has been selected.

When the same or another application wants to 'paste' the previously selected text, it just retrieves the data from CUT_BUFFER0 on the root window. The information is cut and pasted as a stream of text characters or bytes.

Figure C shows some text selected in an xterm window, with the corresponding value of the CUT_BUFFER0 property shown beside it.

While these cut buffers are still available in the standard MIT release of **X**, they are historical, and should not be used by newly developed applications. The Selections Service (Module 9.4) should be used instead.

In the following modules we look at the more sophisticated mechanisms for handling properties and see how they can be used to build more elaborate communications, for dynamic data interchange.

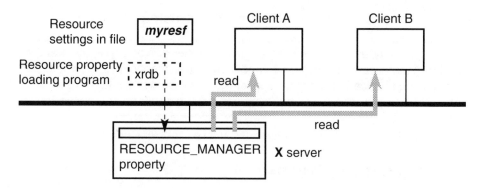

Figure A.   xrdb stores values into the RESOURCE_MANAGER property.

```
venus% cat myresf
  xclock*background: pink
  xterm*font: 9x15

venus% xrdb -m myresf

venus% xprop -root
  _XSETROOT_ID(PIXMAP): pixmap id # 0x1400001
  RESOURCE_MANAGER(STRING) = "xclock*background:\tpink
                             \nxterm*font:\t9x15\n"
  CUT_BUFFER1(STRING) = "/tmp/f"
  ...

venus%
```

Figure B.   You load properties into the RESOURCE_MANAGER property with xrdb, and check them with xprop.

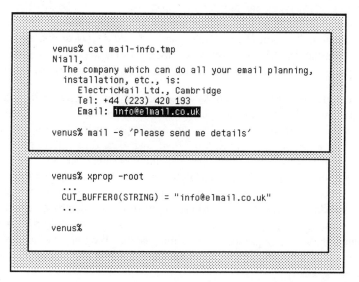

Figure C.   Selected text is highlighted, and stored in the CUT_BUFFER0 property.

9.3   Advanced communications mechanisms

When a property is changed, the server generates a PropertyNotify event, so that applications can be informed immediately of the change; this allows efficient dynamic communication between applications. Properties contain 'typed' information, so complex data can be exchanged among cooperating applications.

(If technical details aren't so relevant to you, you can skip over this module.)

Advanced property mechanisms

The first mechanism relates to how an application finds out when the value of a property it is interested in has changed. For simple exchange of information driven by the user as with cut-and-paste, just looking at the property when its value is required is both adequate and efficient. However, where the transfer of information must be dynamic something better is needed and **X** does provide it: when a property is changed by an application, the server generates a <PropertyNotify> event. Applications which need intimate communication select for <PropertyNotify> events on some mutually agreed window, and thus they are more or less automatically notified when the property they are interested in changes. (In fact, they are told when *any* property on that window changes, so the applications do have to check which property it was that changed.) Then they can perform any actions required by the change. This mechanism is analogous to an operating system handling I/O in an interrupt-driven way, as opposed to polling the hardware periodically to see if any change has occurred.

The second feature of properties is that they are *typed*, so they can contain information in the representation most convenient for the applications that are using it.

- Many standard types are pre-defined. For example, CUT_BUFFER properties are of type STRING as they are used to contain text. Other built-in types include INTEGER to contain numbers, WINDOW to contain a window identifier, WM_HINTS and WM_SIZE_HINTS to contain the information passed between application and window manager, and many others.

- You can define your own property types, as complex as you wish, in much the same way that in a language like C you can construct arbitrarily complex data structures from the fundamental data types (using typedef struct). Thus, for example, you could have your own data type for interchanging 'objects' if you are building an object-oriented user interface. Or in an office automation suite, you might define a property type to hold all the information about a customer, and this property would be used to pass customer details in a standard format to the various applications — database, electronic mail, word processing, fax, etc. Then each application would incorporate the information it required, for example the fax program would use the customer's fax number, name and organization, but would ignore the postal address details.

9.3   Advanced communications mechanisms

9.3.1   Sending events from one client to another

Applications can construct 'synthetic' events and send them to each other via the server, providing another level of inter-client communication. Any type of event can be sent, but 'ClientMessage' events are provided specifically for applications to exchange information.

The final mechanism for applications to communicate is for one application to request the server to send an event to the other. The exact details of the event to be sent are specified in the request. The other application processes this event when it receives it (Figure A).

ClientMessage events

One type of event, <ClientMessage>, is provided specifically for clients to pass information to other clients. These events have a slot of 20 bytes which can be used for any information whatever to be sent to another application. (If you want to send more than 20 bytes, you have to send several events.) For example a talk program has been implemented which transmits all the text of a dialogue between two users via events sent from one running copy of the program to the other. The editres program of Module 12.5 uses <ClientMessage> events to communicate with the application you are editing; these events are processed by **X** Toolkit code within the application, interrogating or changing parameters of the widgets in the application. Window managers also use <ClientMessage> events, to send messages to applications requesting them to perform the WM_PROTOCOLS actions we described in Module 8.4.1 (and for some other obscure purposes relating to reconfiguration of application windows).

Sending other types of event

<ClientMessage> events are not the only type of event one client can send to another — *any* event-type can be sent. The receiving application receives the event exactly as though it had come directly from the server, with the exception that a status indicator in the event is set ON to say this is a send-event. The most common example of this is the way some window managers (including twm) process keyboard input that is typed in an application's icon or window decorations. The server sends these events to the window because it is the owner of the window where the input took place; the window manager then passes these events on, as send-events, to the corresponding application window.

However, send-events can be a security hole; by sending <KeyPress> events to the application you are running, an intruder can effectively type anything into your application, bypassing all your password and other security mechanisms. For this reason, applications should allow you to specify that send-events are to be ignored. (For example, the MIT program xterm has an option controlling send-event processing, so you can specify in a defaults file that it is to be disabled; it also has a menu selection, shown in Figure B, allowing you to interactively enable or disable the send-event processing.)

Send-events can be very useful in testing a system. If you can capture all events when you are running the system interactively (and there are facilities to let you do this — see Module 13.4.1) then you can later 'replay' the events to run the system automatically just by re-sending all the events which were recorded, either by having a special application, or by a special modification to the server to allow this.

Finally, send-events are used extensively by the Selections Service covered in the next module.

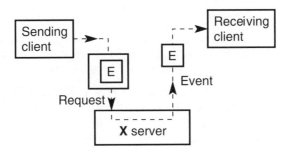

Figure A. One client can cause an event to be sent to another client.

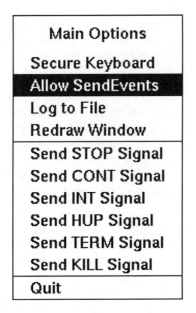

Figure B. **xterm** menu lets you enable or disable send-event processing.

9.4   The Selections Service — a high-level communications mechanism

---

The Selections Service uses properties and send-events to pass data between applications. The applications can negotiate dynamically about the format the data is to be sent in. The mechanism is extensible — sets of applications can define their own private and sophisticated conventions for exchanging data between themselves.

(If technical details aren't so relevant to you, you can skip over this module.)

Like a property, a selection is a name on a server. However, unlike a property it doesn't have any data attached to it, and it is not related to a particular window. Instead, the selection is a place-holder for information that can be obtained from somewhere else.

X defines three standard selection names, PRIMARY, SECONDARY, and CLIP-BOARD, which are used by the Selections Service. X provides for **ownership** of selections. Only one client at a time **owns** a selection, and then any other client can find out who the owner is. Having found out, the second client can ask the owner for the value the owner associates with the selection. Any client can request ownership of any selection when it wants to make some data available. Thus a selection just acts as a type of flag — an abstract token which allows 'ownership' to be shared and controlled amongst the different applications, as we describe below.

The most common example of selections is the use by all (up-to-date) clients of the PRIMARY selection as the principal means of exchanging information, typically as a cut-and-paste mechanism. The SECONDARY selection is intended for tasks which require two pieces of information — for example, 'swap this selection with that one'.

The fundamental difference between this use of selections and the cut buffer mechanism we described in Module 9.2.1 is that no information is transferred when ownership is asserted (that is, when you 'cut' or select some information in an application). Instead, the transfer of information is deferred until another application requests the information from the selection owner. This allows the owner to send different data, or the same data in different formats, depending on the requesting client and what it needs to receive; this decision by the owner about what to send is made each time the selection is requested.

Why is it necessary or useful to delay passing the information until it has actually been requested? Let's consider 'cutting' a portion from a spreadsheet, and pasting it to another application: what information should be transferred? Should a bitmap of the spreadsheet, with all its graphics, multiple fonts, etc. be transferred, or just the ASCII characters representing the values in the selected spreadsheet cells? Or should it be the spreadsheet's internal representation of the data? It is impossible to give a single 'correct' answer; what should be transferred depends on the particular *pair* of clients involved. And even for the same two clients, different formats may be required at different times: if I am using a DTP system to prepare a manual for the spreadsheet program, when I paste the information I'll probably want an exact graphic representation of the screen image, whereas if I am using the spreadsheet to generate information to be included in a report I am writing with the DTP system, I may only want the spreadsheet information as columns of ASCII characters. By waiting until another application requests the value of the selection, the owner can at the time of transfer decide what information and which format is to be used. By contrast, with a cut buffer, once the 'cut' has been performed the information has been stored, and the 'owner' no longer has any control over it. Figure A shows schematically how the same selection is transferred in very different formats depending on which application requested the value; the next module discusses in detail the precise mechanisms involved when the Selections Service is used.

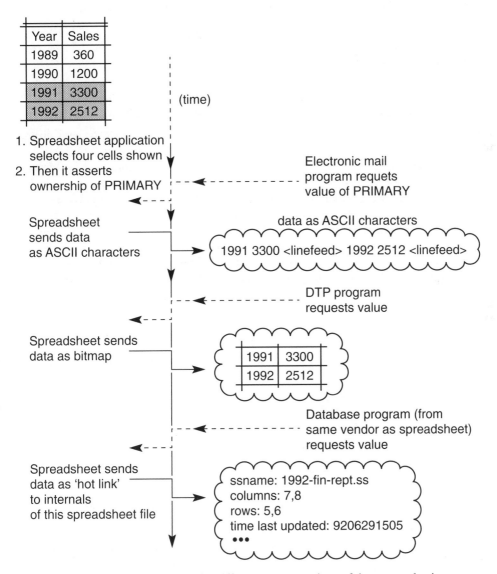

Figure A.   The owner can transfer different representations of the same selection to different requestors.

9.4   The Selections Service — a high-level communications mechanism

9.4.1   The detailed data transfer mechanism using Selections

An application requesting the value of a selection can specify the format it wants the data in, by specifying the type of the property to be used to receive the data. Therefore the data format, and even which data is sent, can be decided dynamically for each transfer requested.

(If technical details aren't so relevant to you, you can skip over this module.)

The process used to transfer information using selections is quite long-winded. Figure A shows the steps for cutting (or selecting) information in application A, and pasting it into application B, and then later into application C.

This illustrates how events are used to inform the owner that some other application requires the value of the selection, and in turn to tell that requestor who the owner is. It also shows that all the data transferred goes via properties, and therefore via the server.

Note that the process is dynamic and active rather than passive: the owner converts the data and transfers it explicitly *each time* the selection is requested, even if it is the same information and the same format as before. Different values and formats can be transferred even when the selection as seen by the user remains the same. In the previous module we gave an example of pasting from a spreadsheet. Another example is a window manager where clicking on a window adds that window to a list accessed via the PRIMARY selection. If you 'paste' this selection, it is converted to a list of names of the windows as text; but if you perform a move operation, the selection is converted to a set of window identifiers, and then each window is moved in the way you specified, so that the overall effect is that the windows are moved as a group.

1a. User selects text in Application-A (a text-editor, say)
  b. Application-A issues request
    SetSelectionOwner(selection=PRIMARY)
    (Previous owner, if any, loses ownership.)
  c. Application-A issues request
    GetSelectionOwner(selection=PRIMARY)
    to check that it really does own the PRIMARY selection.
  d. If it owns the selection, Application-A highlights the selected text.

    2a. User selects Paste menu option in Application-B.
      b. Application-B issues request
        · **ConvertSelection(selection=PRIMARY, format=TEXT, replyprop=MyBProp, replywin=MyBWin)**

3a. Application-A receives event
    SelectionRequest(selection=PRIMARY, format=TEXT, replyprop=MyBProp, replywin=MyBWin)
  b. Application-A can provide **format=TEXT**, so it copies the selected info as text into MyBProp on MyBWin.
  c. Application-A sends event
    SelectionNotify(selection=PRIMARY, format=TEXT, replyprop=MyBProp, replywin=MyBWin)
    to the owner of MyBWin (which we know is Application-B).

    4a. Application-B receives SelectionNotify event indicating success.
      b. Application-B retrieves the data from MyBProp on MyBWin, using GetProperty request.
      c. Application-B deletes MyBProp on MyBWin.

    5a. User selects Paste menu option in Application-C, which is a DTP system, say.
      b. Application-C issues request
        ConvertSelection(selection=PRIMARY, format=POSTSCRIPT, replyprop=Prop-C, replywin=Win-C)

6a. Application-A receives event
    SelectionRequest(selection=PRIMARY, format=POSTSCRIPT, replyprop=Prop-C, replywin=Win-C)
  b. Application-A doesn't understand **format=POSTSCRIPT**, so it signals this by sending the event
    SelectionNotify(selection=PRIMARY, format=TEXT, replyprop=None, replywin=Win-C)
    to the owner of Win-C (which we know is Application-C).

    7a. Application-C recives SelectionNotify event; the fact that
      replyprop=None means that C's request failed, so:
      b. Application-C tries another format, and issues request
        ConvertSelection(selection=PRIMARY, format=TEXT, replyprop=Prop-C, replywin=Win-C)

8. Application-A receives the event. It understands **format=TEXT**, and the transfer proceeds as in Steps 3 and 4.

Figure A. Transferring data using selections.

9.4   The Selections Service — a high-level communications mechanism

9.4.2   Selection clipboards, and Selection data formats

If the owner of a selection terminates, other applications can no longer obtain the value of the selection; a 'clipboard client' can overcome this problem, but the dynamic nature of the selection transfer is lost. Applications can define their own selections as well as the format to be used for selections, and can even ask the owner of the selection which data formats it can support. Large data transfers via selections are handled in many pieces.

A side-effect of the dynamic nature of the transfer is that if the application which is the owner of the selection terminates for any reason, other clients can't paste the information any more — it isn't held in an (intermediate) clipboard. (You can see this for yourself if you run the standard MIT program xfontsel, press its Select button, and paste the value into another application. Then quit from xfontsel, and paste again: you don't get the same value any more, as xfontsel is no longer the owner of the selection.)

This drawback can be overcome to some extent by using a special 'clipboard client' program, which continually monitors the CLIPBOARD selection. As soon as it changes, the special client requests the value of the selection from the owner, and then takes ownership of the selection itself. The value of the selection the clipboard client will supply to any requestor is the same information as it retrieved. Now if the initial owner of the selection terminates, the clipboard client still retains the information. (The MIT release contains the MIT program xclipboard which works in this way; relatively few MIT applications use the CLIPBOARD selection by default, but Motif and OPEN LOOK use it for copy/cut/paste operations.) The advantages of this scheme are the stability it gives, and that the special client can constantly display the contents of clipboard as an aid to the user. However, the disadvantage is that we have lost flexibility; by converting the data 'early'— as soon as it is selected — we have lost the dynamic and adaptive behaviour which is the main benefit of selections.

Selection format

Data is transferred by storing it in a property, from which it is then read; the format of the data is determined by the type of the property. All the standard property types can of course be used, but as we mentioned in Module 9.3, applications can define their own property types, and so arbitrarily complex typed information can be exchanged using selections. A requestor can even ask the selection owner for a list of the formats it supports, and then choose the format it likes best for the owner to use for the actual data transfer.

Obviously, the amount of data you can store on a property on a window is limited — by the amount of memory available in your server if by nothing else. If a very large amount of information has to be transferred, the Selections Service includes a mechanism whereby the information is passed in successive small chunks, so that the server isn't swamped.

As well as defining your own data formats, you can also define your own selections (that is, create new selection names) which you might use in a suite of applications which need to communicate among themselves. (However, all selections are public — if an application knows the name of a selection it can access it, and there is no way to restrict this access.) For example, specific selections like this are used to communicate between the various processes involved in some of the more complex input methods for Oriental languages.

The standard **X** Toolkit contains a lot of code to handle selections and simplifies their use. Even so, programming selections correctly is quite complex, and many earlier **X** programs don't use them but rely on the historical CUT_BUFFER mechanism.

9.5   ICCCM — the rulebook for inter-client communications

The 'Inter-Client Communications Conventions Manual' (ICCCM) specifies conventions for client/window manager and client/client interactions. These conventions are necessary to ensure that applications and window managers from different developers can co-exist on the same system, and inter-operate correctly.

(If technical details aren't so relevant to you, you can skip over this module.)

The ICCCM lays down the rules for how clients — both user applications and the window manager — communicate with each other. Of necessity it is complex and obscure, because it is specifying general mechanisms for how clients cooperate, but as far as possible without artificially limiting what can be done. In a way one might think that the ICCCM is breaking the **X** ideal of 'mechanism not policy', but if the user is to be able to operate applications and window managers from very diverse sources satisfactorily, then some rules must be laid down.

Fortunately, only programmers need concern themselves with the ICCCM, and even then the standard toolkits help a lot, and do most of the work. (In itself, this is a very good reason to use a toolkit.)

An outline of the ICCCM table of contents is shown in Figure A. The parts of most interest to us are Section 2, dealing with Selections, and Section 4, dealing with the interacting of window manager and client. In fact we have already covered Section 2, as the mechanism we outlined in the previous module for data interchange using the Selections Service was exactly as specified by the ICCCM.

How window manager and application interact is probably the most frequently quoted part of the ICCCM. It gathers together many of the aspects of window management that we have already mentioned so far, including:

- The requirements that applications should be independent of window manager policy (Module 8.3) and that the application should accept the window configuration the window manager has given it (Module 8.4.1).

- The properties WM_HINTS, WM_INFORMATION, WM_ICON_NAME, etc., which we covered in Module 8.4.1, and how they should used by the application when it starts, to indicate its preferred size, layout, etc.

- The WM_PROTOCOLS mechanism for specifying which publicly or privately defined messages or function-requests the application will obey if the window manager sends them (WM_SAVE_YOURSELF, etc., described in Module 8.4.1).

- Focus handling (Module 8.1).

- Handling colormaps (Module 8.1).

Other window manager-related ICCCM topics are:

- How pop-up windows are to be managed. They must be handled specially — imagine how awkward it would be if every time you popped up a menu you got a rubber-band outline, and had to use the mouse to position the menu before you used it!

- Managing icons.

- Managing groups of windows as a single unit, although this is currently not handled by many window managers.

Prior to Release 4, most window managers did *not* comply with all the ICCCM rules, especially in the area of colormap management. Since then, most widely-used window managers have been brought into line. The ICCCM continues to evolve, both as experience shows that its scope must be extended, and as new requirements develop. For example, colour management was included with Release 5, and in future we can expect sections covering 'drag and drop', session management, and anything else which relates to how a set of applications can cooperate closely to produce a more unified environment.

<table>
<tr><td>

1. Introduction
   Evolution of the Conventions
   Atoms

2. Peer-to-Peer Communication by Means of Selections
   Acquiring Selection Ownership
   Responsibilities of the Selection Owner
   Giving Up Selection Ownership
     Voluntarily Giving Up Selection Ownership
     Forcibly Giving Up Selection Ownership
   Requesting a Selection
   Large Data Transfers
   Use of Selection Atoms
     Selection Atoms
       PRIMARY, SECONDARY, CLIPBOARD
     Target Atoms
     Selection Targets with Side Effects
       DELETE, INSERT_SELECTION,
       INSERT_PROPERTY
   Use of Selection Properties
     TEXT, INCR, DRAWABLE, SPAN Properties

3. Peer-to-Peer Communication by Means of Cut Buffers

4. Client to Window Manager Communication
   Client's Actions
     Creating a Top-Level Window
     Client Properties
       WM_NAME, WM_ICON_NAME,
       WM_NORMAL_HINTS, WM_HINTS,
       WM_CLASS, WM_TRANSIENT_FOR,

</td><td>

       WM_PROTOCOLS,
       WM_COLORMAP_WINDOWS
     Window Manager Properties
       WM_STATE, WM_ICON_SIZE
     Changing Window State
     Configuring the Window
     Changing Window Attributes
     Input Focus. Colormaps
     Icons. Pop-up Windows
     Window Groups
   Client Responses to Window Manager Actions
     Reparenting. Redirection of Operations
     Window Move. Window Resize
     Iconify and Deiconify
     Colormap Change. Input Focus
     ClientMessage Events
     Redirecting Requests
   Summary of Window Manager Property Types

5. Client to Session Manager Communication
   Client Actions
   Client Responses to Session Manager Actions
   Summary of Session Manager Property Types

6. Manipulation of Shared Resource
   The Input Focus. The Pointer. Grabs.
   Colormaps. Keyboard Mapping, modifier Mapping

7. Device Color Characterization
   XYZ RGB Conversion Matrices
   Intensity RGB value Conversion

</td></tr>
</table>

Figure A. Topics addressed by the ICCCM.

9.6 Desktop managers

Many end users need to interact with the operating system on their computer. Desktop managers provide a graphical and easily learned interface to the operating system, hiding much of the underlying technical detail.

Some end-users of computer systems are provided with the single application, or set of applications, they need to perform their job; they work only within these applications and don't use the machine's operating system directly at all. Clerks in an accounting or shipping department, or travel booking agents, will often fall into this category.

However, many other users who are not computer specialists *do* need to work with the operating system, to manage their files, run programs, administer the system, and so on. (For example, a secretary will maintain separate word processing files for letters, DTP files for presentation graphics and charts, spreadsheet files for reports, and so on.) Users like these can benefit from having a good graphical interface to the operating system, to make the system easier to use and hide its complexities. A **desktop manager** provides such an interface.

Typical facilities offered by a desktop manager are:

- A **file manager** — a graphical representation of the files and directories you are working with. Often this is shown as a tree structure, with files at the lowest level shown as individual icons, as illustrated in Figure A, and you can select files by pointing rather than by typing their name or selecting them from a menu.

- **Drag and drop** facilities. For example, you can copy or move files by manipulating them with the mouse, and you might e-mail a file by **dragging** its icon and **dropping** it onto a picture of the person you want to mail to, or print it by dropping its icon onto the icon of a printer.

- **Menus** and **dialogs** for selecting commonly required functions such as printing, copying, renaming and so on. (In fact, many of these facilities are what made the Macintosh system so attractive to its users.)

More sophisticated managers offer customization and programming features, so you can tailor the environment you provide to your users. For example, you might limit the commands you make available to clerical staff to a subset containing only basic file manipulation, editing and DTP facilities; this reduces the amount of information they have to deal with and minimizes the risk of unauthorized use of other facilities.

A big advantage of desktop managers is that they can provide some degree of operating system independence. For example, by having your files and directories shown in tree form, you don't have to know whether the command to list a directory on your system is ls or DIR; to look at the contents of a text file you click on its icon and don't have to know what program is being used to display it (whether it's cat or more or TYPE or TYPE/PAGE). For non-specialist users who have to switch between different operating systems this can be a great benefit.

Don't confuse the desktop manager with the window manager (even though the term 'desktop' may often be used ambiguously, to mean either the set of windows on your screen, or the files, programs, and other operating system objects you are working with). While there is some overlap — as both let you build menus which you can use to run other applications — the two managers are addressing different things:

- You use the **window manager** to manipulate your windows on the screen just as though they were pieces of paper. You are performing purely mechanical operations like moving, resizing or (de)iconifying windows.

- The **desktop manager** is a graphical front end to the operating system, giving you access to files and the various facilities your system offers. Often the desktop manager is just another application with one or more windows; these windows are onscreen with other applications' windows, and are of course managed by your window manager.

However, in other systems, for example the Macintosh, it is difficult to distinguish between the two, as both sets of functionality are integrated into the base system.

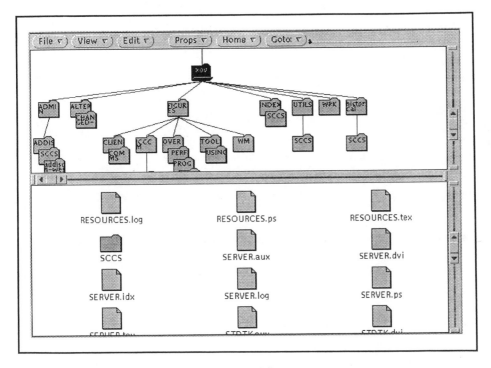

Figure A. A typical file manager.

Summary

In this chapter we have looked at why separate applications need to communicate — essentially to provide a more homogeneous environment for the user, and to allow some system functions such as window management to take place. We saw that properties form the basis of most inter-client communications, and when coupled with the ability for one client to send events to another, they allow sophisticated mechanisms to be used; in particular, the very powerful Selections Service is built on these facilities. We looked broadly at the scope of the ICCCM, and finished off with an overview of desktop managers which simplify for the user the task of handling many applications and files.

This chapter ends this Part of the book on how **X** works, and we have finished looking at **X**'s internal mechanisms. In the next part we go on to see how you actually use the system in practice.

3

Using the System, System Administration, Performance, and Programming

Up to now we have concentrated on the architecture of the system and its internal mechanisms. In this Part of the book we move on and look at how you use the system in practice — what you need to get started, what tools are available, programming issues, administering and tailoring your system, and evaluating its performance.

10 Using the X System

10.1   What you need to get started
    10.1.1 What the MIT system comprises

10.2   How you use the network facilities
    10.2.1 How applications are started remotely

10.3   Using character-based applications — terminal emulators
    10.3.1 Terminal emulators and applications on different machines
    10.3.2 How a terminal emulator works
    10.3.3 How the terminal emulator handles output

10.4   Integrating X with other systems

10.5   Where to get the software

Introduction

This chapter outlines how you use the X system, especially in a network environment. We also look at how you can use programs for character-based terminals and for other window systems in conjunction with X.

10.1   What you need to get started

The realistic minimum system is a server, a window manager, the basic **X** client applications, and ideally some **X** administration tools. The easiest way to start is to use a multitasking workstation, and initially avoid the complexities of running over a network.

The easiest way to get started using **X** is with a workstation running a multitasking operating system such as UNIX or VMS. Your system is self-contained, with all the components on a single machine (Figure A). If you start with a networked configuration (Figure B) not only do you have to work out which components go where, but you also have to ensure the network is properly set up, and you need to use network commands to run applications remotely. While most of this is relatively straightforward, it is a complication the newcomer can do without.

To use **X** you need:

The X server for your particular hardware and operating system. The server is supplied with the fonts it needs, and the colour database (typically just a single file) which it uses to translate colour names into internal colour values.

As shown in Figure B, all these components reside on the machine where the server is running. (Later, if you need to, you can store fonts elsewhere on your network using the font server we mentioned in Module 3.5.1.)

Basic applications programs and tools to let you perform the work you use your computer for. If you have been able to obtain **X** software for your particular applications, you can start using it immediately. More often, however, you will have existing, non-**X**, applications, so you need a terminal emulator program such as the MIT program xterm, to let you use your character-based applications (see Module 10.3). A terminal emulator is almost essential for system administration work too. Other convenient but non-essential tools are small applications such as a clock, a desk calculator, etc.

These applications can run on the same machine as your server, or elsewhere on the network.

A window manager to manage your application windows.

Just like your other client programs, the window manager can run on the same machine as the server, or remotely.

Standard defaults files which are supplied as part of your applications, to specify the default layout, fonts and colours used, etc. by the applications. These files usually reside on the same machine as the application they relate to, or at least are accessible from that machine using a networked file system such as NFS. (We cover these files in detail in Module 12.2.)

Shared libraries. If your system supports shared libraries and your application uses them, you will need the libraries on each machine the applications run on. (See Module 14.1 for details.)

In the next module we describe the contents of the MIT Release of **X**, which is representative of many commercial **X** systems.

Using X in a networked environment

If you are going to run applications remotely over a network, then as well at the network itself you will need for both the server machine and the machine(s) on which the applications are to run:

Network hardware to connect the machine onto the network, for example an Ethernet interface card.

Network software to drive the network interface and transfer data to and from it, to provide the basic transport which **X** requires: for example, TCP/IP software. On the server end you will also need software to allow you to start applications running on remote machines: for example, the rsh or telnet programs which work over TCP/IP.

Of course, if you are using an X-terminal and not a workstation, these components will already be incorporated, and most of your work will relate to configuring the host machine elsewhere on the network, which the **X** clients are to run on.

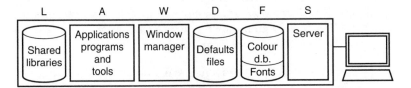

Figure A. A standalone workstation containing all the components of the X system.

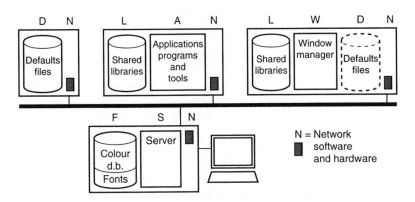

Figure B. Networked X is more complex, as system components are distributed.

10.1   What you need to get started

10.1.1   What the MIT system comprises

The MIT release of **X** contains source code for servers and clients for several different Unix platforms, with installation scripts and complete documentation. The range of applications provided is typical of many commercial **X** systems.

The MIT release of **X** provides source code for a complete working system, plus everything needed to build it. We include details here to give you an indication of what a typical system contains.

The release includes many basic clients, such as the **xterm** terminal emulator, the **xedit** text editor, bitmap editors, desk accessories such as clocks, tools to read and send e-mail, and of course a window manager. There is also a comprehensive set of administration tools for configuring your system and checking its status, covering aspects such as fonts, preferred settings and defaults both for your display and individual applications, keyboard mapping, etc.

The following is an extract from the release notes for Release 5:

> ***clients*** *This directory contains most of the sample applications. See the program man pages for details.*
>
> ***config*** *This directory contains configuration files and the imake program used to build the release. Details are covered in other sections below.*
>
> ***demos*** *This directory contains a small collection of graphics demonstration programs, a few utility/test programs, and some performance demonstration programs. These are by no means the 'best' demo programs around, they just happen to be ones we try to maintain.*
>
> ***doc*** *This directory contains troff sources to X Consortium standards, server internals documentation, documentation for various utility libraries, some useful tutorial material.*
>
> ***extensions*** *This directory contains implementations of X server extensions, both the server internals and the application programming libraries, and some test programs. Of particular note here, new in Release 5, is PEX, the PHIGS Extension to X used for 3D graphics, and the PHIGS programming library which interfaces to the PEX protocol.*
>
> ***fonts*** *This directory contains bitmap fonts in source form, some outline fonts, a sample font server, a utility font library used by the X server and font server, a client font library for interacting with the font server, and programs for building fonts and querying the font server.*
>
> ***hardcopy*** *This directory contains pre-generated PostScript files for the client man pages and for most of the documentation found in the doc directory. The files are compressed with compress to save disk space. If*

you do not have compress on your system, you will find a version in the mit/util/compress directory.

include *This directory contains various library-independent C header files and a collection of bitmap files.*

lib *This directory contains programming libraries and support files. Of note are Xlib (the lowest-level C programming interface to X), Xt (the X Toolkit Intrinsics), Xmu (an eclectic set of utility functions), Xaw (the Athena Widget Set), and CLX (a Common Lisp interface to X).*

man *This directory contains a few top-level man pages about the release (general information, server access control mechanisms, the X Consortium, and X Consortium standards), and man pages for some of the programming libraries.*

rgb *This directory contains a program to generate the color database used by the X server and sample databases.*

server *This directory contains the X server sources, both device-independent (dix) and device-dependent (ddx). In this release, there is support for building the following servers:*

> *DECstation 2100/3100 monochrome and color displays*
> *DECstation 5000 CX and MX displays*
> *IBM RS/6000 skyway adapter*
> *Apple Macintosh monochrome and color displays*
> *MIPS monochrome and color displays*
> *OMRON LUNA monochrome displays*
> *Tektronix 4319 color display*
> *VAXstation QVSS and QDSS displays*
> *Sun monochrome and 8-bit color displays (with GX support)*
> *Various VGA displays under System V/386*

If your favorite hardware is not listed above, please do not blame us at MIT, we ship what Consortium members provide. Only in a few cases do we try to maintain device-specific software for our own development needs.

util *This directory contains miscellaneous utility programs and shell scripts used to build, maintain, and install the release.*

10.2 How you use the network facilities

Running applications on remote hosts but displaying to your **X** station lets you create a very flexible and rich user environment. Using remote applications is easy.

When using an X-terminal, which cannot run any of its own applications, you have to run your **X** clients remotely over the network. Even when running with the **X** server on a multitasking workstation which *can* run applications locally, many users frequently use **X**'s remote execution facilities. This is because on most real-life networks, there are facilities — special hardware, or a particular software package — which are available only on specific machines; having a window open onto that machine or running that package is very convenient. Using **X** like this, to share expensive or limited resources among many users across the network, can be very cost-effective. (Even for inexpensive resources, it is often cheaper to provide them centrally to save on administration costs.)

Figure A shows a typical scenario, of an X-terminal (mars) and two workstations (venus and pluto) on a network. There are several points to note, which are typical of real-life use:

- The two workstations and the X-terminal are using applications from several different remote hosts at the same time.

- A workstation often runs local applications for its own server as well as applications for other remote servers.

- The window manager, mwm, is always run from venus (presumably because Motif has been licensed only for venus). It is run locally for the display on venus itself, and remotely for mars and other displays.

- pluto is running a different window manager, olwm, locally.

- Whereas the X-terminal has to run all clients remotely, the workstation will normally run locally any 'standard' widely available clients such as the xterm terminal emulator and 'small' applications such as the clock and calculator.

- pluto is running xterm remotely on venus as well as locally, giving pluto's user a terminal session on venus. This type of setup is particularly useful to system administrators who need simultaneous access to many machines on the network when configuring, troubleshooting, or just monitoring the performance of the systems.

- Applications that are using files intensively are best run remotely on the machine where the files are resident, rather than on the user's own machine with the files shared using a networked file system like NFS. (For example, the database is shown running on neptune rather than on venus.) In this way the network load is minimized (see Module 13.2 for more details).

In the next module we describe how to run remote applications.

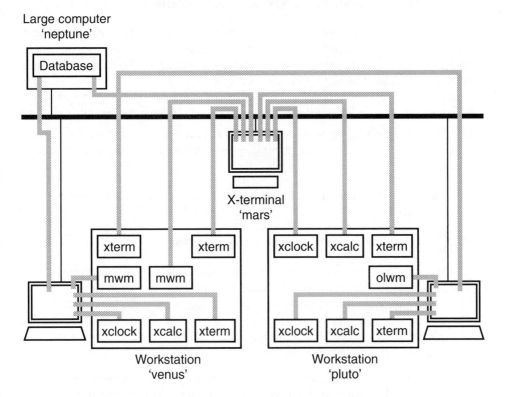

Figure A.   Running programs remotely over the network to an xterminal.

10.2   How you use the network facilities

10.2.1   How applications are started remotely

Networking software systems provide commands that make it easy to start single programs running on machines elsewhere on the network, or to run a whole session on a remote machine. You use these commands to run your applications remotely, displaying back to your own **X** server.

(If technical details aren't so relevant to you, you can skip over this module.)

With suitable networking software it is very easy to start a program on a remote machine displaying back to your own. For example, with a TCP/IP system the usual commands you use are:

> **rsh.** To start a program running on a remote machine you enter a command of the form:
>
> rsh   *remote-machine-name   program-to-run* ...

Figure A illustrates how, from the workstation venus, you would start a clock locally, and then a window manager, calculator, and xedit text editor running remotely. You can see that each rsh line starts a single command, and the line must specify the command completely; no information or status persists from any previous command, which is why you have to repeat the display-name specification '-display venus'.

rexec is similar to rsh, and is usually provided on System V implementations of UNIX, whereas rsh is part of the Berkeley UNIX implementations.

telnet lets you login to a remote host and run an entire session on that machine, terminating only when you explicitly log out. Figure B shows a telnet session from venus onto saturn, starting the same commands as in the previous example. (The setenv line stores the name of the display to use, venus, into the standard environment variable DISPLAY, to avoid having to type -display *name* for each command.) When you have a lot of work to do on one particular machine telnet is probably the easiest option, because you can customize aspects of your environment in this way. The alternative is to use rsh to start an xterm running on the remote machine, and then within that xterm window do the rest of your work.

Being able to connect applications on remote machines to your display has its disadvantages too: it allows other people on those hosts to use your display and possibly interfere with your work or steal your password. **X** does provide security mechanisms to control access to your server, which we cover in Module 11.4.

```
venus% xclock -display venus:0 -geometry 100x120-0+0 < /dev/null &
venus% rsh saturn /usr/bin/X11/twm    -display venus:0 < /dev/null &
venus% rsh saturn /usr/bin/X11/xcalc -display venus:0 -geometry +50+600 < /dev/null &
venus% rsh saturn /usr/bin/X11/xedit -display venus:0 -geometry 300x280+400+420 < /dev/null &
```

Figure A. Starting remote applications using rsh.

```
venus% xclock -geometry 100x120-0+0 &
venus% telnet saturn
   Trying 192.9.200.132 ...
   Connected to saturn.
   login: niall
   Password:
   Last login: Thu Oct 15 17:20:22 from saturn
saturn% setenv DISPLAY venus:0
saturn% twm &
saturn% xcalc -geometry +50+600 &
saturn% xedit -geometry 300x280+400+420 &
saturn% logout
   Connection closed by foreign host.

venus%
```

Figure B. Starting remote applications using telnet.

10.3 Using character-based applications — terminal emulators

Terminal emulators let you use non-**X** character-based applications on any **X** display, without any change to the application.

Most programs and applications have not been written specifically for **X**. So how can you use them on an **X** display? As we said in Module 2.2.3, the answer is: via a special program called a **terminal emulator**.

Simply, a terminal emulator is a program that 'pretends to be' a real terminal: it gives you a window which in almost every respect behaves like a physical terminal. Starting the emulator is analogous to switching on a real terminal and logging in. After that, you have a normal terminal session with your normal system prompt, and you run programs and receive their output as normal (Figure A, top left window). In UNIX terms, a shell or command-line interpreter is running in the window; it receives the input you type in the window just as though it had been typed on a normal terminal keyboard, and it runs the programs you command it to. Output from the shell and the programs you run appears in the window just as though on a terminal's screen.

Thus, a terminal emulator lets you run all your old programs written for character-based terminals. This of course includes all the standard operating system commands such as ls, cat, pwd, vi (or DIR, TYPE, SHOW DEF, and TPU), as well as all the compiler, linker and debugger programs for your system. (So in a way, you can consider that your terminal emulator is a virtual terminal, something which is 'giving you back the old world' or providing you with a 'gateway to history', that is to old, non-windowed, programs.)

As an example, let's look at the DEC VT102 emulation provided by the MIT xterm program. The real VT102 terminal supports many features, including cursor addressing, character underlining, inverse video, etc. xterm gives you exactly the same facilities. In addition it provides extras, such as the ability to change the font size on the fly by means of pop-up menus. xterm also provides emulation of the Tektronix 4014 graphics terminal (Figure A, bottom right window). Many other emulators are available commercially, especially of the Tektronix graphics and DEC terminals. There are also programmable or customizable emulators available, described in Module 14.3.

Advantages of terminal emulators

Running character-based applications via an **X** terminal emulator gives you many advantages even though you are still using a character-based program:

- You can cut-and-paste between your emulator and other **X** windows, giving some degree of communication between your old application and other clients.

- You can have multiple 'terminals' on screen at once in different windows, allowing you to perform various parts of an overall task easily, and cut-and-paste between them, instead of having to stop one program, start another, and then go back to the first. And of course you can run several copies of one program if you want to.

- You can customize your keyboard, and map function keys on a per-window basis.

- You can scroll your output, to look back at output that has gone by. You can also log your session to a file.

- You can dynamically change fonts, for example to select a very small font to display the maximum amount of information in your window. You can make the emulator window very large to show even more information, or very small if that's all you require.

- Multiple terminal emulators can be connected to different hosts, allowing you to use old applications on many different machines together.

In the next module we describe how emulators can handle applications running on other hosts, and in the module after that we look at the internal operation of a terminal emulator.

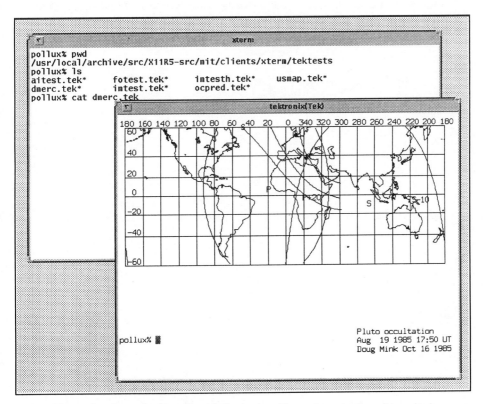

Figure A.   A terminal emulator behaves just like a character-based terminal.

10.3   Using character-based applications — terminal emulators

10.3.1   Terminal emulators and applications on different machines

Using facilities such as telnet allows the **X** terminal emulator to run on one host while the character-based application it is handling runs on another host elsewhere on the network. Thus, with terminal emulators you can even use applications running on machines which have no **X** support.

While non-windowed applications are often run on the same machine as your emulator, especially standard utilities such as mail programs, editors, directory listings, etc., the non-**X** application doesn't have to run on the same machine. Instead it can run elsewhere, and be connected to the emulator via telnet or something similar (Figure A). This is often necessary where the old application is on a platform which doesn't support **X**, but as long as that platform has some network remote execution facilities like telnet or SET HOST, you can still use the application from your **X** station.

We shall see in Module 14.3 how this same principle is used by programmable terminal emulators to provide an **X** front-end to character-based applications on systems which don't support **X**.

In the next module we look at the internals of the terminal emulator's operation.

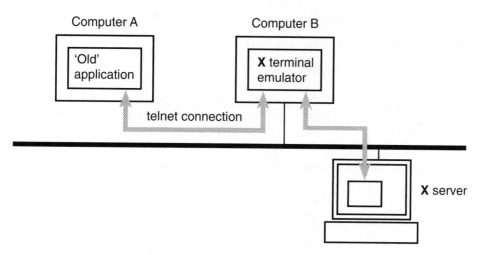

Figure A.   Application running remotely from a terminal emulator.

10.3   Using character-based applications — terminal emulators

10.3.2   How a terminal emulator works

The non-X application runs on its normal machine and operating system, but is connected to a 'pseudo-terminal' instead of a real terminal. The terminal emulator captures the character output and draws it in an X window, and transforms X keyboard input into characters which it sends to the application as though it were connected directly to a normal terminal keyboard.

(If technical details aren't so relevant to you, you can skip over this module.)

The non-X application, which for simplicity we are assuming uses ASCII characters, is run as normal but, instead of being connected to a real terminal (Figure A), it is connected to a **pseudo-terminal** (Figure B).

A pseudo-terminal is a facility provided by the machine's operating system. It is just a terminal communications channel, but instead of being attached to a physical terminal with a human at the the other end, it is controlled by some other application. All normal input and output handling which occurs on a physical terminal also occurs on a pseudo-terminal. For example, sending a Delete character will remove from the input buffer the last character typed; and most terminal characteristics can be set as usual, for example whether input is to be echoed, whether characters are 7-bit or 8-bit, etc. So the application takes its input from the input side of the pseudo-terminal instead of taking it direct from a terminal keyboard; what it receives will be whatever the application controlling the pseudo-terminal sent. And instead of writing its output direct to a terminal screen, the original application writes it to the output side of the pseudo-terminal, where the controlling application reads it and can do with it whatever it decides is necessary.

Here the application controlling the pseudo-terminal is an X terminal emulator program. Internally, the terminal emulator is taking in X events from the server, and translating them into characters (ASCII for simplicity) which it sends to the 'old' program. The terminal emulator is also receiving ASCII characters output by the program over the pseudo-terminal, and translates these into the appropriate X requests to make the output appear in the terminal emulator window in the same place as it would on a real terminal. The flow of events, characters and requests in the system is shown schematically in Figure C.

The next module deals with how the emulator handles output to the 'terminal' screen.

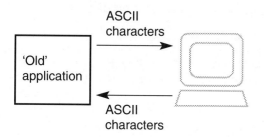

Figure A.   Application connected to a physical terminal.

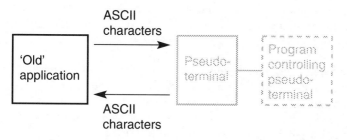

Figure B.   Application connected to a pseudoterminal.

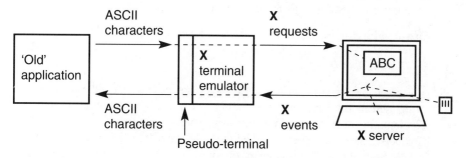

Figure C.   The flow of information when a terminal emulator is used.

10.3   Using character-based applications — terminal emulators

10.3.3   How the terminal emulator handles output

The terminal emulator program must duplicate the functionality of the physical terminal it is emulating, to handle functions such as cursor addressing, character-underlining, inverse video, etc.

(If technical details aren't so relevant to you, you can skip over this module.)

The output stage of the emulator is crucial, as it determines what physical terminal is emulated. The functions normally performed by a physical terminal's hardware or firmware must now be mimicked by the emulator to produce the same result. So the emulator must watch the stream of input characters and handle all the escape sequences and mode changes that the target terminal-type supports. As an example, let's look at some of the features of the DEC VT102 emulation provided by xterm:

Elementary character printing. Handling of output to the 'terminal screen' is straightforward. The first string of printing characters is printed in the first 'row' and first 'column' of the screen with an XDrawString() request. As further characters arrive, the emulator prints them on the same row (same Y-coordinate in the **X**-window) as the previous character string, but the print position is moved successively to the right (increased **X**-coordinate in the **X**-window) each time. If an incoming string contains a newline character, it has to be split in two; the parts before and after the newline are drawn by separate XDrawString() requests on separate 'rows'.

Cursor addressing. When the character sequence:

ESC [*num* A

is received by the terminal emulator, the cursor is to be moved *num* lines up the screen (in fact, up the window). To do this xterm must keep a representation of the screen in its memory; when it next draws a character in its window, the coordinates specified to the XDrawString() function should be *num* lines above the previous position.

Character underlining. The VT102 can be switched via an escape sequence into a mode where all characters printed are underlined. **X** does not have special fonts with underlines included. Therefore xterm, as well as having to recognize the escape sequence requesting underlining, has to underline the characters explicitly. Thus, when the emulator is in underline mode, whenever it draws a character string in its window, it immediately afterwards performs an XDrawLine() function in the row of pixels immediately below the characters just written (Figure A).

Inverse video is handled by reversing the foreground and background colour settings for the XDrawString() function used to draw the characters on the screen.

Figure A.   How the terminal emulator prints underlined characters.

10.4   Integrating X with other systems

You can use **X** on machines already running other window systems by means of special servers. These let you mix applications for **X** and for the system's native window system on the same screen. Other facilities let you run Macintosh and Microsoft Windows applications remotely, but display their output and interact with them on your **X** screen just as if they were remote **X** applications.

As mentioned in Module 2.2.4, for computers running some other window system, special servers enable you to work with both **X** and the native window system. There are special servers available for SunView, Microsoft Windows, NeXT and Macintosh systems.

Figure A shows a Microsoft Windows screen, with both **X** and DOS applications simultaneously on screen. This system is typical of what these special servers provide. You can run your **X** applications as shown, with each as a separate window in the native window system, and with the window management being done by the native system and not by **X**. If the **X** programs use the Motif toolkit the integration achieved is particularly good, as the Motif and Microsoft Windows user interfaces are very similar. Alternatively, you can have a single native window which acts as a virtual **X** screen (shown as the shaded window in Figure B) with all the **X** applications running within it and under the control of an **X** window manager. However, this does not provide such seamless integration — the user has to operate in two different 'worlds', and it's obvious which programs are native and which are **X**.

The advantages to the user are illustrated by Figure C. The **X** server is effectively bridging the DOS and UNIX operating systems, giving the user access to the best application for the tasks to be done. This setup is also bridging the Novell and TCP/IP networked file systems, again making use of the facilities best suited to the particular task.

The systems we have described so far allow you to add **X** to the system already on your desktop machine. There are other systems that work almost in reverse, by giving you access from any **X** screen to applications written for other systems. Figure D shows this facility linking a Macintosh (running on its own AppleTalk network) into a TCP/IP-based **X** network. The hardware bridge is necessary to convert the two network protocols, and it also contains special software which gives the remote user access to the application running on the Macintosh. What the user gets is the ability to use Macintosh applications without having a Macintosh on their desk. (In a sense, the Macintosh is acting as a 'Macintosh-application server' to the rest of the network.)

Similar facilities are available for DOS applications. There are also complete DOS emulators that are entirely software-based, to run on many different types of workstation and minicomputer, which use **X** to display the virtual PC screen and to receive the keyboard input to be sent to the DOS application.

M = Microsoft Windows program   **X** = **X** applications

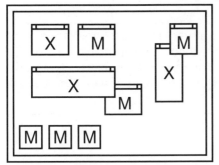
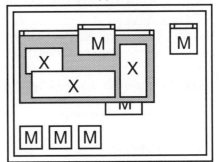

Figure A. Microsoft windows and X applications running simultaneously on a DOS screen.

Figure B. All X applications running in a single Microsoft window.

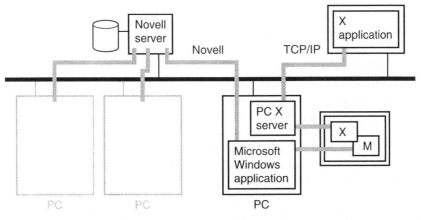

Figure C. The special X server bridges Novell and TCP/IP, DOS and UNIX or VMS.

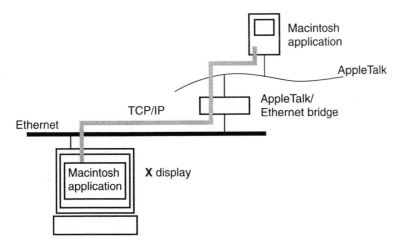

Figure D. Using a Macintosh application from an X station, via a TCP/IP AppleTalk bridge.

10.5   Where to get the software

The MIT Release of **X** is available free, or at very little cost. It contains much useful documentation and code, but is unsupported. While it can be used to build a complete working system, organizations starting with **X** are better off buying a supported implementation elsewhere. A lot of other useful software is available free, too.

The MIT Release

The MIT **X** Consortium makes the full source release of **X** available on a variety of tape formats for a small distribution cost. (Figure A gives the contact details for the Consortium.) The same software is available completely free via ftp file transfer from MIT (but you need suitable networking facilities). There are also a number of archive sites which can provide the software via electronic mail over various public networks.

The MIT software is the starting point for most commercial implementations, and it includes a lot of documentation and some example programs. The user-contributed software included in the release contains many useful tools for system administration and programming, as well as applications for image processing and other tasks.

The MIT Release also provides a very cheap system — it includes everything required to build a fully functional working system. Because it is provided at no cost, it is of course unsupported and provided without any warranty. It is only suitable (without modification) for systems running UNIX. Moreover, installing the MIT Release involves a lot of work and needs a lot of disk space; while many (primarily academic or research) sites do use the MIT software directly, organizations new to **X** should, at least initially, either use the **X** system provided by their hardware vendor, or purchase a supported **X** system from a third-party supplier. (However, should you require it, some consultancy houses do offer support for the MIT software.)

Other **X** implementations

Most hardware vendors now also supply **X** for their systems, and often their versions are specially tailored and optimized for the particular platform. There are also many third-party suppliers that supply versions of **X** for common workstations; such companies are particularly useful for providing the latest software very soon after release, and for providing and supporting additional software such as toolkits.

Other sources of **X** software include user groups (see Module 15.3) and the various interest groups on the public networks which make available a huge amount of free software (of varying quality).

```
MIT X Consortium
Laboratory for Computer Science
545 Technology Square
Cambridge, MA 02139
USA

email: rws@expo.lcs.mit.edu
```

Figure A.   Contact details for the MIT X Consortium.

Summary

This chapter has described how the **X** system is seen by a user and how its various features are used in practice, from getting started, through using the network to integrating applications for character-based terminals and for other window systems into your **X** environment. For fuller details about using the system, see this book's companion volume, *The X Window System: A User's Guide*, or any of the other user handbooks now available.

In the next chapter we look at the system from a different perspective, and see how it is set up and administered.

Chapter

11

System Administration

11.1 Starting up the system
  11.1.1 xdm, the **X** Display Manager
  11.1.2 Sessions and session management
  11.1.3 XDMCP — the **X** Display Manager Control Protocol

11.2 Customizing server settings

11.3 Administering fonts

11.4 Security
  11.4.1 The Magic Cookie authorization scheme
  11.4.2 The Kerberos authentication system
  11.4.3 Basic principles of Kerberos
  11.4.4 Kerberos in detail

11.5 A summary of **X** system administration

Introduction

In this chapter we concentrate on those aspects of the system that most concern the system manager. We first look at how you start up the system, and how a workstation, X-terminal, or PC can be configured to bring the user automatically into **X** at switch-on time. We then look at how you can customize your overall environment. We see how fonts are administered to overcome problems caused by dependence on the resolution of users' displays, and by limited font availability. We consider the security aspects of **X** systems, and some of the emerging security mechanisms. Finally, we summarize the elements of system administration required for **X**, and the administration tools available.

255

11.1   Starting up the system

Well-engineered **X** servers give you an easy way to start an initial client at the same time as the server, so you can 'bootstrap' the complete environment you require. More sophisticated startup systems are continually being developed, which greatly simplify the system administration of **X** networks.

What the **X** Protocol covers is specific and relatively limited — how the server should respond to requests from clients, and how it should handle input from the hardware, and other events. This doesn't address a lot of things that are vital to someone using the system — in particular, how do you start the first client?

This is a problem (especially on an X-terminal) because once the server starts without a client, no application is connected to the display. Therefore, while all input from the keyboard and mouse is handled by the server, it is immediately thrown away because no client has registered an interest in these events. Figure A shows a screen with only the **X** server running — there is nothing for the user to interact with!

The primitive and cumbersome solution is to walk over to another terminal or workstation and from there run a client displaying to your **X** server. You start an xterm or some other program that enables you to issue further commands to your operating system. Then you can walk back to your **X** display and from within the xterm start any other programs you want (now, or later on as you need them).

A simple and better solution, but suitable only for a multitasking system, is provided by the program xinit. This starts the server as a sub-process, and once the server is running xinit starts a (specified) client connected to that server. By default the client started is xterm, so that you can then run any other programs you wish.

For X-terminals and PC **X** servers a similar approach is used. However, because an X-terminal can't run any clients locally, the initial client to be started *must* be on a remote machine, and so the command used to start the client must be a network command connecting to that remote machine. As we described in Module 10.2.1, you can use a non-interactive command like rsh to start a single remote program and go on from there. Or you can use an interactive program like telnet giving you a full interactive session, allowing you to start as many clients as you want. In practice, most people use rsh to run a shell script or command file, which in turn starts all the clients required, in the desired configuration. Figure B shows a configuration file for a PC **X** server: it specifies that the initial program my_startx is to be run on the remote machine saturn by executing the rsh command as user niall. (The other lines are configuration options specific to this particular server.) With a suitable script file, a setup like this can start up your **X** environment exactly as you want, automatically. PC users can even include the server start up commands in their AUTOEXEC.BAT file, so that their **X** session comes up as soon as they switch on. Figure C shows a simple script to start up **X** with our usual applications.

However, the most recently developed, and best, way to start up your **X** system is with xdm, described in the next module.

Figure A.   An X screen with only the server running.

```
arch 2
type MSWIN
fp fonts\misc,fonts\100dp
net PCTCP2
host saturn
xdm indirect
set bd
syskeys cehstf
tftpRootDir c:\XVIEW
log
wm local
virtual 1024x768
XSelection 0
```

Figure B.   A typical startup configuration file for a PC X server.

```
#!/bin/csh

source .login
source .cshrc

xrdb ~/.Xdefaults
xhost +
xset m 12 5 c on s blank s 300
xset +fp /usr/local/lib/X11/our-fonts
xmodmap ~/.Xkeymaps
xsetroot -solid gray -cursor_name iron_cross -fg red

xclock  -geom   100x100-0+0      -update 1                                   &
xbiff   -geom   100x100-0+100                                                &
xcalc   -geom   -0-0                                                         &
xterm   -geom   80x63+400+0      -iconic -name pictures -sf -title pictures  &
xterm   -geom   115x59-10+10     -iconic -name cix                           &
emacs   -geometry 108x61+250+15  -i -in emacs                                &
twm                                                                          &
exec xterm -geom +0+0            -C -ls -name console -title console
```

Figure C.   Shell script to start our usual applications.

11.1 Starting up the system

11.1.1 xdm, the X Display Manager

xdm manages your display by starting your server, and giving you a window in which you log on to the system. It then starts a specified application or script and, when you have finished your work session, xdm resets the server and presents the login window again, ready for the next user.

xdm gives you a clean way to start up your **X** system. It allows you to start your server, and just like xinit starts a client also. However, the client it starts initially gives you a login window (Figure A). Once you have logged in, xdm runs either an xterm (the default), or a program specified by you. Often the program you specify is a shell script or command file which starts up your usual applications and configures your **X** environment, as we described for rsh in the previous module. Alternatively, the script can be a standard one set up for your whole site by your system manager. The sample script provided with xdm lets the system manager define standard facilities for all users, but allows individual users to customize their own environment if they want (see next module).

xdm is the best way to start **X** on a workstation because it gives the cleanest and most obvious interface. If the workstation is to be used as a dedicated **X** station, xdm can be run from the operating system's startup script, so that as soon as the machine is fully booted the **X** server is up and running, with xdm waiting for a user to log in (just as a character-based terminal gives a login prompt when it is switched on). You as user don't have to know what programs are necessary to run **X** — you just log in! xdm makes starting an **X** session similar to and just as easy as starting a session on a character-based terminal.

xdm can also be used with X-terminals and PC **X** servers to provide the same login-window facility. As the xdm program itself cannot be run on the terminal or PC, it is run remotely from elsewhere, and one running copy of it can handle multiple terminals or PCs.

Prior to Release 4, in this basic configuration xdm periodically polled the X-terminals it knew about (their names or network addresses were listed in a configuration file), and when it found a terminal that had an **X** server which it was not already managing, it started up a login window and continued as normal. On the X-terminal side, the server was started with no initial client, and it waited for xdm to notice that the server was now running. With Release 4, the facility XDMCP (**X** Display Manager Control Protocol) was introduced which lets xdm handle X-terminals in a much more sophisticated way. We cover that in the module after next, but in the next module we look at what an **X** 'session' is.

Figure A.   xdm's login window.

11.1   Starting up the system

11.1.2   Sessions and session management

A 'session' is everything between when a user logs on and logs off the system — typically a continuous period of work by one user. You can tailor your startup configuration to set up your complete environment automatically, instead of having to start manually the applications you want, each time you begin an **X** session. If the terminal or workstation is public, a session by one user will often be followed by a session by another user. Only rudimentary session managers are currently available.

xdm's login window facility effectively defines the start of your **X** session, but what is the end of the session — how do you log off? In fact your session ends when your initial client terminates, that is, when the application that runs just after you have successfully logged in to xdm ends. Then all other applications are killed off, the server resets, and you get the xdm login window again to start the next session, either for you, or for some other user if the **X** station you are using is a 'public' resource within your organization.

If your initial client was an xterm, it means that when you close down that window (by typing logout or exit or ctl-D, or by using an option from an xterm menu) your session is ended. If it was a script, your session ends when the script program terminates (which is when the last program in the script exits). People usually configure their script so the last program is either an xterm as above, or else is the window manager: then, when they exit the window manager, the session ends. As most window managers provide a convenient way to end — usually a menu option — this gives you a neat way to finish off your session. The Motif window manager, mwm, asks for confirmation before exiting. (You really need this if exiting the window manager is going to end your session too, because then all running applications will be killed off forcefully and you won't get a chance to close them down gracefully.)

As we mentioned in Module 11.1, by specifying a script or command file as your initial client, you can have your standard environment set up for you automatically at the beginning of each session. A script typically sets any specific server features the user wants (Module 11.2), starts the usual applications the user wants (for example, our own script starts four xterms, a text editor, our own screen configuration program, and a clock), plus a window manager.

If written properly, a script lets the system manager provide a standard default environment for the site as a whole, but which individual users can refine for themselves if they want to and know how. Thus end users do not have to concern themselves with technicalities, but at the same time programmers have the freedom to set up the facilities they need without affecting anyone else. Figure A shows a very simple xdm script: if the user has a file .xsession in their home directory, it is taken to be the script to be executed. Otherwise, the default setups for the site are performed — load the user's defaults settings if the file .Xresources exists, run an xterm, and finally start the MIT window manager twm. Our own .xsession file (Figure B) illustrates how the starting position and size of applications can be specified with the -geometry flag.

Session managers

There are no session managers publicly available, but the ICCCM defines standards for what they should do — be able to start a collection of clients as a group, remember the current state of running clients so they can later be restarted in the same state, and be able to close down clients in a controlled way. In Module 8.4.1 we saw how window managers used **WM_SAVE_YOURSELF** message and **WM_COMMAND** property for some of these functions, and some of the more complex window managers and desktop managers provide part of the functionality we expect from a session manager. More capable session managers will be commonly available soon.

```
startup=$HOME/.xsession
resources=$HOME/.Xresources

if [ -f $startup ]; then
        exec $startup
else
        if [ -f $resources ]; then
                xrdb -load $resources
        fi
        exec xterm -geometry 80x24+10+10 -ls &
        twm
fi
```

Figure A. **xdm** lets you customize your startup environment via a simple command script.

```
#!/bin/sh

xhost +
xset m 12 5 c on s blank s 300
xset +fp /usr/local/lib/X11/our-fonts
xsetroot -solid gray
xsetroot -cursor_name X_cursor -fg red
xclock   -geometry 100x100-0+0    &

xterm    -geometry  80x63+400+0 -sf              \
         -iconic -xrm "*iconX:1000" -xrm "*iconY:60"   \
         -name demos -title demos &

xterm    -geometry 115x59+235+25                 \
         -fg yellow -bg gray                     \
         -name xov-term                          \
         -xrm '*cursorColor: pink'               \
         -xrm '*vt100.translations: #override    \
         <Leave>: string(clear) string(0xd)' &

xterm    -geometry 80x16+0-0 -sf                 \
         -iconic -xrm "*iconX:1000" -xrm "*iconY:80"   \
         -name tar-pit -title tar-pit &

emacs    -geometry 88x61+350+15 -i &
screenmenu -geom -0+580 -fg gray85 -bg lightslategray
xterm    -geometry +0+0 -C -ls                   \
         -xrm "*iconX:1000" -xrm "*iconY:140"    \
         -name console -title console    &
twm
```

Figure B.   Our own startup script for use with **xdm**.

11.1   Starting up the system

11.1.3   XDMCP — the X Display Manager Control Protocol

XDMCP lets you connect X-terminals into a network and have them automatically managed by an xdm program running on a remote host. You don't need to maintain any special tables or configuration files for xdm or XDMCP, so managing large networks of X-terminals is made easier.

(If technical details aren't so relevant to you, you can skip over this module.)

The simple way that xdm handles displays on X-terminals and PC **X** servers, described in the previous module, has a big problem — xdm has to be configured so that it knows which terminals it is to manage. While that may not seem very important, for large networks especially it would be very much better if you could just connect your X-terminal into the network and let the terminal itself request an xdm service from some other machine without any pre-configuration. This is what XDMCP, the **X Display Manager Protocol**, does.

As before, you have to have one or more machines running xdm and prepared to provide service for terminals, but now these xdms listen on the network for XDMCP requests for server. Now when a terminal starts up and wants xdm service it goes through the process shown in detail in Figure A. Briefly, what happens is:

1. The terminal broadcasts a request on its network, saying that it wants an xdm session. This request is in the format specified by XDMCP.

2. Any machine running xdm which is prepared to handle the terminal replies, saying it is willing.

3. The terminal decides which xdm-provider it wants, and replies to that provider (and only that one) saying it has been chosen.

4. The chosen provider replies saying that it accepts this. (The other providers do nothing.)

5. The terminal says that, yes, it really does want to be handled by this provider. (The seeming redundancy in these steps is necessary for reliable handshaking.)

6. The provider starts an xdm sub-process to manage the terminal, and display the login window. The main xdm just goes back to where it started, and waits for requests from other terminals.

The beauty of this is that the terminal and the xdm provider don't need any configuration to tell one about the other. You can just plug in an X-terminal onto your network, and with XDMCP you can be running an **X** session almost immediately. (You do of course have to set up the *network* configuration for the provider and the terminal — ensure that they have valid network addresses, etc.) Now connecting a new X-terminal into a network is easier than connecting a character terminal to a minicomputer. (Another benefit of having the terminal initiate the xdm session is that it removes the need for xdm to poll the terminals constantly, thus eliminating some wasteful network traffic and CPU activity.)

If more than one machine is prepared to provide xdm for the terminal, at step 3 above the terminal can use any mechanism it wishes, to decide which offer to accept. For terminals that don't have any special mechanism of their own, xdm can run the program chooser to display a menu of hosts from which the user (rather than the terminal) picks which one to use.

While xdm and XDMCP are part of the standard MIT release, they are *not* part of the base **X** system — they are not part of the **X** Protocol. Rather, they are extras which make systems easier to use and administer. Changes like these — new facilities which improve real-life implementations of the system but don't involve any change to the Protocol — are typical of the differences between one release and another. (XDMCP was perhaps the most significant functional enhancement in Release 4.)

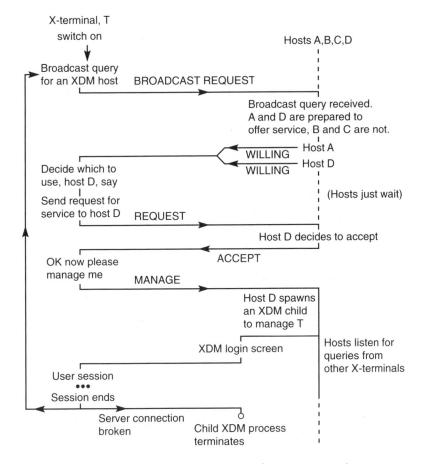

Figure A. How an xterminal requests xdm to start a session.

11.2 Customizing server settings

You can customize many aspects of the server — for example, the keyboard mapping, whether the keyboard keys auto-repeat, where fonts are to be searched for, etc. The server is reset to its default settings at the end of each session, so you must re-invoke your customizations each time you start a session.

You can configure or customize many server parameters, to match your personal preferences, or to take account of any special configuration required by you or your site. The most significant settings are:

Keyboard mappings. As we described in Module 4.2.2, each key on the keyboard has a unique keycode which identifies it, and the server has an internal table which maps these keycodes onto keysyms — symbols representing what is painted on the key top. The client uses the keysyms to interpret the key event as a character in whatever character-set it is using (ASCII, EBCDIC, or whatever).

You can change the keysyms associated with a particular keycode and so remap your keyboard. (The MIT program xmodmap is an easy way to do this.) As you are changing this mapping within the server, the changes will affect all clients on your display. You can use this facility to customize function keys, or to redefine which keys are to be used as the modifiers (Ctrl, Alt, etc.) This is convenient when you use different machines with different keyboards: you can remap the keyboards so that they are all consistent, for example, changing the relative positions of the Shift, CapsLock and Ctrl keys on a PC to match those on a workstation. Another common requirement in Europe is to change the layout of the alphabetic keys on the left side of the keyboard to match the national convention.

Keyboard parameters. The MIT program xset lets you customize such characteristics as key click, and auto-repeat, as well as determining their current settings.

Directories for storing fonts. Also with xset you can add to or change the list of directories in which fonts are stored for your server. You often use this to specify a directory of your own which contains fonts specific to you or your workgroup.

Bug compatibility mode. Most implementations of **X** up to Release 3 ignored incorrect values in the unused bytes in some server requests. This was corrected in Release 4, with the result that some earlier programs now fail. These can be made to work again by enabling this compatibility mode (which requires the extension MIT-SUNDRY-NONSTANDARD).

Screen saver. To prevent your screen burning out when the same image is displayed for long periods, you can enable the **screen saver** which either blanks out the screen or displays a moving pattern, after your server has been idle for a specified time (10 minutes by default).

Root window settings. Using the program xsetroot you can change the background and foreground colours of your root window, and the shape of the cursor and its colour. You can also specify a bitmap to be used to pattern the window (Figure A) rather than having just a plain coloured ground.

Any changes of settings you make to your server persist only for the length of this session, that is, until the server is reset or restarted. So if you want these settings every time you use the display, you should incorporate in your startup script for xdm (or whatever startup system you use) the xset, xmodmap, etc. commands to make the changes. Examples of such settings were shown in Figure 11.1.2B.

Chapter 12 describes how you customize individual applications.

Figure A. Customized colours and pattern in the root window.

11.3   Administering fonts

X fonts are often supplied in a portable form which you then compile into the specific form required by your server. Font converters and editors may be useful when you are migrating from other systems. Correct definition of font search paths can give you display-resolution independence even with bitmap fonts.

Server vendors usually provide a large set of fonts for use with their server. Many of these are part of the MIT release of **X** and may be used freely, but some fonts are proprietary and you may have to license them for use on other machines. (For example, 'Times' is a trademark of Linotype, and the Times-Roman font in the MIT distribution is copyrighted by Adobe.) You can also obtain fonts from many public-domain sources, or buy them from font developers (or 'foundries', as they call themselves).

Fonts are normally provided ready for use with your server. They may also be distributed in a portable, plain-text, format called **BDF** (**Bitmap Distribution Format**) which you then have to convert into the format your server needs, using a font-compiler provided with your server. (All the fonts in the MIT Release are supplied in BDF.) In Release 5, the server's internal format is **PCF** (**Portable Compiled Format**): this stores the font information in an efficient internal form, but it is portable across all servers from Release 5 onwards. In Release 4 and earlier, the internal format was **SNF** (**Server Natural Format**); while the specification did allow this to be platform-specific, in practice it was often portable across platforms which had the same byte-ordering; however BDF was the only guaranteed portable form.

Many conversion utilities are available (especially in the MIT user-contributed software release) to convert vendor-specific font formats to BDF, so you can continue to use fonts that you have on another window system. There are also font editors if you need to create or modify fonts.

As we described in Module 3.5, **X** uses XLFD (**X** Logical Font Description) for naming fonts, and this includes a lot of information about the font in the name. A full XLFD name for a Times Bold font is shown in Figure A. **X** applications can get a 'directory listing' of fonts (of all fonts, or those matching a specified name which may contain wildcard characters), and so obtain a list of fonts matching a desired set of criteria. For example, instead of specifying one explicit font in an application, the programmer can give a wildcard specification:

```
-*-*-bold-*-*-*-*-240-*-*-*-*-*-*
```

to select a **bold** font, at **24** point size. (The size is expressed in tenths of points, 240 here, to make it easy to specify decimals of point-sizes.)

Using wildcard specifications like this makes the application independent of specific fonts to some extent. (The alternative would be for the application to check that the font requested is available, and if it isn't, use some fallback or default font). Programmers and system administrators need to be careful when specifying fonts because there is no standard set of **X** fonts — you cannot assume that a particular font will be available, or even if it is, that it will be available at the point-size you want. However, the introduction in Release 5 of scalable fonts will make this less of a problem in the future.

Because fonts are stored as bitmaps, they are not resolution independent: a specific '10-point' font will show up three times bigger on a 40 d.p.i. screen than on a 120 d.p.i. (the characters are drawn with the same number of pixels on each screen, but on the 40 d.p.i. screen the pixels are three times bigger). To overcome this problem, **X** stores its fonts on the server in different 'directories', with fonts intended for use at a particular resolution stored in a directory of their own. So, we might have two directories, called dpi40 and 120dots, say, each containing fonts that are very similar, but designed for use at the particular resolution. The fonts' names will be very similar too: the only components of the names that will differ are those indicating the resolution the font was designed for. We can tell the server to search the directories in a particular order when it is looking for a font. If we specify the search order correctly, and use suitably wildcarded names to specify fonts, being careful to omit the resolution-related parts of the XLFD-name, we can get resolution independence. Using the example above, and assuming we told the server to look in dpi40 first, if there is a bold font there with a point-size of 24 (that is, 24 point when printed on a 40dpi screen) then the server will use that font. Only if there is no suitable font there will the server continue by looking in the other directories.

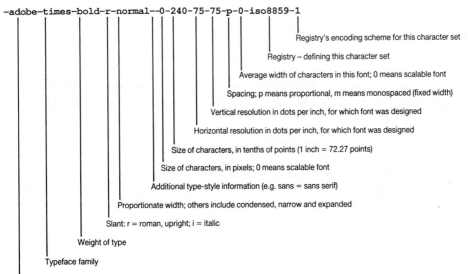

Figure A.   The full **XLFD** name for a Times Bold font.

11.4 Security

Typical **X** systems provide rudimentary facilities for securing displays against unauthorized connections, and for securing connections against tampering. More sophisticated and secure systems are now becoming available.

X doesn't provide any protection on a per-window basis: if an application is connected to a display it can access any window (or other server resource) on that display.   As we described in Module 8.4, the window manager depends on this to be able to manage the windows of all your applications. The disadvantage is that anyone connected to your display can (without your knowledge) capture images of any of your windows, or change their contents, and if your application accepts send-events, someone else can effectively type directly into your application (Module 9.3.1).

To provide some protection, **X** does let you control whether or not a request to open a connection onto your server is to be allowed, that is, if an application run by a particular user from some machine is allowed to use your display. The **X** Protocol doesn't specify which authorization scheme should be used, but it lets you use anything suitable that is supported by your server and applications.

Currently, most systems only provide a basic protection system — you specify which remote hosts you 'trust', and connections are allowed only from those hosts. It doesn't matter who the user is — access is decided exclusively on the host name (or network address). By default, your own host is included in the trusted list. Using the MIT program xhost you can modify the list of trusted hosts interactively. But even allowing 'my host only' isn't secure unless my host is properly secured in other ways. For example, prohibiting **X** applications on other machines connecting to my display won't help much if people can telnet or rlogin or rsh to my machine and run **X** applications from there.

The Protocol does have **hooks** (provision in the code for adding extra facilities) for including more sophisticated authorization mechanisms. The MIT sample server implements three other access control systems that allow connections to be controlled on the basis of the user who is connecting, not just the machine the application is running on:

1. **MIT-MAGIC-COOKIE-1:** MIT's own system. As this is a representative facility, we discuss it in more detail later.

2. **XDM-AUTHORIZATION-1:** a DES-based authorization system, similar to MIT-MAGIC-COOKIE-1. However, it uses DES to encrypt the authorization keys (passwords) so that they are never sent 'in clear' over the network. This gives extra security where network snoopers could be monitoring the network traffic looking for passwords, etc.

3. **SUN-DES-1:** this is based on a public-key secure remote procedure call system available with Sun's operating system.

Another increasingly common security system is Kerberos authentication, which we describe in Module 11.4.2.

What we are discussing here is how to prevent other unauthorized people connecting to your server. If you succeed in doing this, then the threat of intruders capturing images of your windows or changing their contents, or of using send-events to interfere with the input to your application (Module 9.3.1) is removed, because these actions can only be performed by a client connected to your server.

As an aside, commercial vendors are now providing **X** servers that meet military security requirements.

In the next module we describe the Magic Cookie scheme in a little more detail.

11.4   Security

11.4.1   The Magic Cookie authorization scheme

The MIT Magic Cookie system restricts connections to your server by insisting that applications requesting a connection present a secret password-like token to the server. This token is stored in a file that only you — and therefore the applications you are running — are allowed access. Thus the scheme is using the file-system security mechanisms to secure your **X** server.

The Magic Cookie scheme (Figure A) is simple. The user who starts up the server is trusted, because it is 'their' server. xdm puts a randomly-generated key (the magic cookie) into a file (.Xauthority) which xdm makes accessible only to this trusted user, by setting the file's access permissions appropriately. Later, when this user starts a program connecting to this server, the XOpenDisplay function provided by Xlib reads the key from the file, and includes it in its request to the server to be allowed connect. If the key sent by the client matches the one the server started off with, the connection is allowed, as it will be in the case we've just described. Otherwise, the server reverts to the host-based system described in the previous module, and uses that to decide whether to allow the connection or not. If another user's application tries to read the key from your file, it will not succeed because xdm has set the file permissions so as not to allow access.

If an application on another machine needs to connect to this server, then either the user on that machine must have access to your .Xauthority file via NFS or similar network file system, or else the user (which we hope really is you) has to explicitly copy the authorization information to that machine. (The MIT program xauth lets you edit and manage authorization files for this purpose.)

Essentially Magic Cookie is based on the security of your file system: if someone else can read your .Xauthority file, then they can steal your cookie and gain access to your server. However, this scheme provides a simple and usable security system, especially where snoopers can't get at the network easily. It is widely available because it is included in the MIT Release, and unlike DES, there are no export restrictions placed on it by the US Government. Even though MIT provide it, it is *not* an **X** Consortium standard.

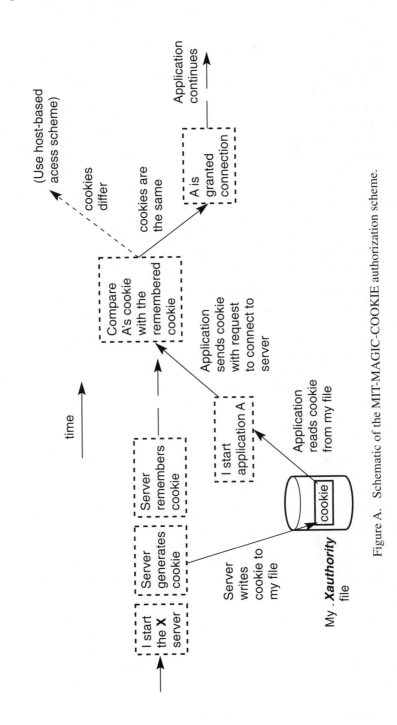

Figure A. Schematic of the MIT-MAGIC-COOKIE authorization scheme.

11.4   Security

11.4.2   The Kerberos authentication system

Kerberos securely identifies a user who is requesting the use of some service, that is, it 'authenticates' the user's identity. Kerberos can be used merely to control initial connection to a server, or if necessary to authenticate each request and message passed between client and server. It issues 'tickets' to the client, to allow use of a particular server. Kerberos authentication is secure even on a non-secure network.

The Kerberos security system was developed at MIT as part of Project Athena. It is becoming popular for managing the security of large networks with large numbers of machines. It is not included in the MIT release, but commercial vendors are now starting to supply it as part of their systems. It is a general authentication system, and isn't limited just to **X** systems. (It gets its name from Kerberos or Cerberus, a three-headed dog who guarded the entrance to Underworld in Greek mythology.)

The function of Kerberos is to identify a user who is asking to use some service, that is, to **authenticate** the user's identity. In 'the old days', knowing which workstation a program was running on was a fairly reliable way of identifying its user, because workstations were a limited resource and available only to a restricted (supposedly responsible) group of people. As networks get larger and more difficult to control, and as access to workstations gets easier, you can't rely on a workstation's identity as proving its user's identity any more. (For example, in a UNIX environment, if the user on a remote workstation is called root, who is really out there?)

As shown in Figure A, Kerberos is a 'third party' authentication system: there is a Kerberos authentication server which is used both by the provider of a service (in this case the **X** server), and the user of that service (an **X** application). The details of how Kerberos authenticates a connection are long-winded: we describe them fully in the next module, but here you just need to appreciate the main features.

Like many operating system security systems, Kerberos relies completely on secret passwords as being the only way for someone to prove they are who they say they are. If the person at the other end claims to be 'Mary' and uses Mary's secret password, Kerberos believes the person really is Mary. (So as usual, users must ensure nobody else learns their password.) Kerberos also relies on the security of the Kerberos server and other authentication servers that may be required. However, it does *not* rely on the security of the client or requesting machine. Kerberos doesn't rely on the network being secure either, because it takes appropriate precautions:

- Passwords are never sent over the network in an unencrypted form, so network snoopers can't steal passwords easily.

- The messages Kerberos uses include time-stamps so that snoopers can't just capture all the Kerberos messages, and 'replay' them later: the time-stamps will show that these are old messages, and Kerberos will not accept them.

- When you ask to use a particular service, such as an **X** server, a file-server or whatever, Kerberos gives you a **ticket**. A Kerberos ticket is just like a real-life ticket for a train or an aeroplane — it is only valid for the service for which it was issued (you can't travel on an aeroplane using a train ticket), you have to send it to the right place to get the service you want, and it has your name on it and can't be used by anyone else. But unlike a travel ticket, a Kerberos ticket doesn't give you permission to use the service: it merely proves you are who you say you are. When you want to connect to the service you need, you send your ticket to the service with your request to connect, and now that it knows who you really are, the service decides whether to allow you or not.

Our discussion of Kerberos here and in the next modules deals with authenticating only the initial connection to the service. Kerberos can be extended so that *each message* between client and service is authenticated, and in turn this can be enhanced so that the message is not only authenticated (that is, that the server knows the message came from the particular client or user) but encrypted also (so that nobody else can see the contents of the message).

In the next module we look at the basic ideas behind Kerberos, and in the module after that we describe its operation in detail.

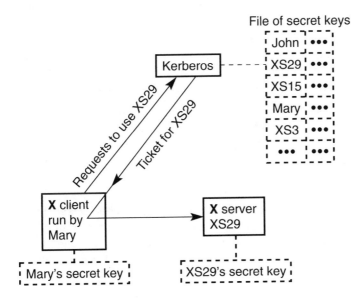

Figure A. Kerberos is separate from both the user and the server used.

11.4   Security

11.4.3   Basic principles of Kerberos

Kerberos uses double encryption to preserve security. Messages between the Kerberos server and the client are encrypted with a key or password known only to Kerberos and the user; messages between client and the requested service are protected by encrypting with a key known only to that server and to Kerberos. 'Tickets' are issued to prove the identity of the client.

(If technical details aren't so relevant to you, you can skip over this module.)

This module introduces the basic ideas used in Kerberos; the full procedure is described in the next module.

The basic principle of Kerberos is that you and Kerberos both know a secret key (password) which identifies you; if you can give the correct password for your user-name when you are asked, Kerberos believes you are that user. In addition, Kerberos and the service you want to use both know (share) a different password, so the service also can prove its identity to Kerberos.

Let's say your name is 'Mary'. When someone signs onto the system and enters their user-name as Mary, the login program sends a message to Kerberos containing the name 'Mary' and the name of a service this program wants to use. So far, no password has been entered.

When Kerberos receives the message from the user, it builds but doesn't yet send a reply authenticating you (that is, proving that you are who you say you are — Mary). Kerberos then doubly-encrypts this reply, first using the service's key, and secondly using your password, and sends it back to the login program.

The login program asks the user for their password. If the user really is you, you enter your (Mary's) password, and you can decrypt the reply from Kerberos. If the user is somebody else pretending to be Mary, they don't know Mary's password, thus they cannot decrypt the reply or get at the authenticating information, so they cannot proceed any further.

At this point, you (or in fact your login program) has a piece of information that proves you are Mary; we'll call this information your **initial ticket**. Later on, you, or rather the applications you are using, will present your initial ticket to the service you want to use, to prove you are who you say you are. You can present it many times, as you may want to use the service more than once. From the ticket, the service knows that you are who you say you are, and can decide whether to allow you access to the service or not. The whole process is outlined in Figure A; however, the picture isn't complete, because there are complications, which we describe in the next module.

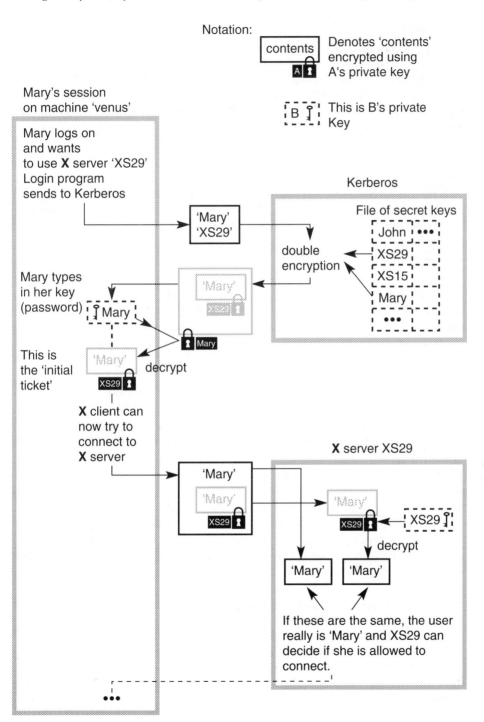

Figure A.   Simplistic view of obtaining and using a Kerberos ticket.

11.4 Security

11.4.4   Kerberos in detail

Kerberos uses 'authenticators' to prove that the ticket was presented to the service by the person it was issued to, and wasn't stolen by someone else. So you don't have to enter your password each time you request a service, Kerberos uses a 'Ticket Granting Service'.

(If technical details aren't so relevant to you, you can skip over this module.)

There is a problem in what we have done so far: as you send your ticket over the network, someone else may snoop and take a copy of the ticket, and then present it themselves to the service, pretending to be you. To avoid this problem, Kerberos is slightly more complicated than we outlined earlier; as well as possessing the ticket, you must also have some way of proving that you are the person it was given to in the first place. Kerberos uses **authenticators** for this.

When building the reply to the login program, Kerberos generates a random **session key** which will later allow you to communicate securely with the service you want. Kerberos includes this session key in the initial ticket itself, and also in the overall message, which is encrypted with your password and sent to you (Figure A). So when you decrypt the reply from Kerberos you have a copy of this session key as well as the initial ticket. Now when you request a service, you build an authenticator consisting of your user-name (Mary) and your machine's network address. (Other information is included too.[1]) You encrypt this authenticator with the session key, and send it with the initial ticket to the service you are requesting.

When the service receives your request (Figure B) it decrypts the initial ticket using its own password, because that is what Kerberos encrypted it with originally. Now the service has the information proving who you are, but it also has a copy of the session key that was included in the initial ticket. It now uses the session key to decrypt the authenticator your program sent, and checks the information in the authenticator: is the user-name the same as in the ticket? Is the network address actually the one we received the request from? If so, the service is happy that the sender of the ticket is the person to whom it was given in the first place, because only that person ever had access to the randomly generated session key, which was never transmitted 'in clear' (unencrypted) over the network.

Using Kerberos to access an X server

If Kerberos used only the mechanism outlined above, the user would have to enter the password each time a service was requested, because the ticket obtained is valid only for a single service. This would be very tedious, so Kerberos uses another phase in the whole process. Your initial ticket gives you access not to an **X** server, or file-server or whatever, but to a Kerberos **Ticket Granting Service** or **TGS**. As before, you have had to enter your password.

---

[1]Timestamps are used so that if a network snooper copies your messages and tries to replay them later this can be detected. However, for simplicity we'll forget about these details.

Now, you ask the TGS and not Kerberos itself to give you further tickets to use specific facilities such as **X** servers, etc. These tickets are just the same in form as the initial ticket, but the key used for the internal encryption is one shared only by the TGS and the requested service. This full sequence is illustrated in Figure C.

Figure A.   A Kerberos ticket contains the sessionkey, both singly- and doubly-encrypted.

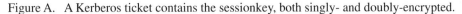

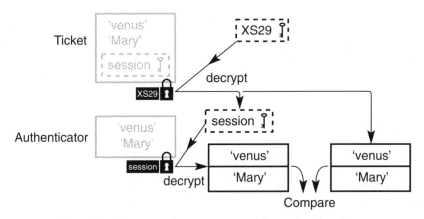

Figure B.   How a service processes a ticket and authenticator.

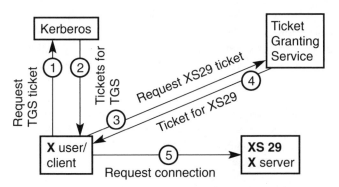

Figure C.   The full sequence of accessing an X server.

11.5   A summary of X system administration

This module outlines all the aspects of system administration required for **X** systems.

Depending on your system (for example, if you have only workstations and no X-terminals) some of the tasks listed below will not be necessary, and many others will be performed automatically when you install a complete **X** 'package' supplied by a vendor. Even so, this list should give you a clearer picture of what is happening at a detailed level.

Resource/capacity planning

1. Provide adequate CPU power on your hosts to run applications for X-terminal users.

2. Ensure there is enough disk space for fonts and for the applications you will be using.

3. Make sure hosts running applications have adequate swap or paging space, because **X** applications are relatively large.

4. Ensure that your hosts have enough memory to run all the applications expected of them, without having to swap excessively. (See the next chapter.)

Installing the server

1. Install the X-terminal hardware.

2. Configure the X-terminal for your network. Allocate its network address, and if necessary tell it from which machines it will download any files (such as fonts) or programs (for example, the **X** server), and how it will access them (for example, via explicit file transfer, or using NFS).

   Ensure that any necessary network services software is available to service remote terminals and hosts, and is configured. (For example, rarpd and others are necessary for booting many X-terminals, and will require configuration information in the /etc/ethers file; file transfer requires a tftpd or an ftpd daemon.)

3. Install the server software on workstations running **X**. If you are upgrading to a later release, keep your earlier version accessible for some time, in case you run into problems with applications and need to check whether they are due to the change of server.

4. Ensure the keyboard mappings are correct for your hardware.

5. Install your fonts. Make sure they are accessible to any other machines that need them, probably using NFS. Compile any special fonts you require. Remember, fonts are used by the server, not the client, and each different type of X-terminal you use will probably need its own specific fonts. Configure your font server(s) if you are using them.

Installing the client software

1. Install the standard clients on a machine accessible to any other workstations or X-terminals that will need to run the applications remotely.

2. Build any clients you require from the MIT **contrib** user-donated software release. Install them.

3. Install third-party and in-house developed applications.

4. Ensure all the window managers required by your users are available somewhere on your network and are accessible.

Application configuration

1. Install all the application-defaults files in the standard directories.

2. Modify any resources files necessary, for site-wide or per user customization.

Session management

1. Make sure one or more machines provides xdm (with XDMCP facilities for X-terminals) and starts xdm automatically at boot time.

2. Set up default scripts for xdm.

Enabling and restricting access — UID administration

1. Configure system hosts.equiv files, or users' .rhosts files, so that they can easily run applications on those remote machines they are allowed to use.

2. Configure your access control system (xhost, Kerberos, etc.).

3. Make sure that unauthorized users cannot get root or system privileges on any system, so that they cannot bypass any **X** access controls.

4. Set any environment variables necessary in users' .profile or .login file, in particular those specifying the location of resource files, and the PATH variable so they can access the **X** programs.

5. Ensure you have enough licences to let everyone have access to the applications they require. Ensure any networked licence management software is started automatically.

Summary

In this chapter we have described the most important aspects of setting up an **X** system. We covered how a user starts up the system, and how by using xdm and XDMCP the system manager can easily control the startup to provide the environment necessary for the users. We saw how you can alter various server settings according to preference. We then looked at how fonts can be administered to provide some resolution independence, and we dealt with aspects of security in an **X** environment. Finally we summarized the steps necessary to manage a complete system.

In the next chapter we move on to the related topic of how individual applications can be customized.

12 Customizing Applications

12.1   Customizing applications

12.2   The Resources mechanism for customizing applications
    12.2.1   How resources are named
    12.2.2   Wildcards and class names in resources

12.3   How the Toolkit uses resources

12.4   Translation tables resources and keyboard mapping
    12.4.1   Translation tables, actions, and callbacks

12.5   Tools for customizing resources

Introduction

In the previous chapter we saw how you or your system manager can tailor your user environment to match your own requirements and preferences. In this chapter we look at the 'resources' mechanism provided by the basic **X** system, which allows initial and default values to be specified for parameters in an application. After that we describe how the **X** Toolkit builds on this foundation, and allows you to customize almost any aspect of a Toolkit program by using resources.

12.1 Customizing applications

X makes it easy to write applications that the user can customize by specifying the initial values for many aspects of the program. You can set colour preferences, positions of applications and items within applications, fonts, key mappings, etc. You can customize third-party applications as well as those developed in-house.

It is very easy to make **X** programs customizable by the user, using standard functions provided by the standard **X** library Xlib, and the **X** Toolkit. A great deal of the program's behaviour can be altered: changing simple visual characteristics such as the colours and fonts used is straightforward, and offered by almost every window system. However, **X** goes much further, and lets you specify different keyboard mappings for each window in the application, whether functions can be invoked from the keyboard or using the mouse, the placement of items in the user interface, the text on labels and buttons, which bitmaps are to be used for images, etc. You can (if the program is written appropriately) even customize non-**X** aspects — for example, the names of files, numeric values of any kind, chemical formulae, stock names and prices, and so on; the possibilities are literally endless. First, let us look at why it is useful to be able to customize an application (and some of the problems it creates, too), and then in the rest of the chapter we will look at the mechanisms **X** provides for doing this.

Why do we need to customize applications?

At the simplest level, people like to tailor applications to match their own preferences, especially regarding the visual characteristics such as colour, fonts used, and so on.[1] Beyond this simple matter of taste, there are many other reasons why we want applications to be customizable:

> **Keyboard differences.** Keyboards vary a lot from system to system and country to country. Users may need to customize an application to make it easier to use on their computer.

> **Internationalization.** Not everyone in the world lives in the USA or Europe. As we discussed in Module 5.3, the language used, and therefore the text displayed in messages and in the user interface components such as labels and buttons, must be modifiable, which in turn may require changes in the size and layout of the components.

> **Customizable programs are easier to integrate** with other applications. Visual characteristics and keyboard and mouse usage can be made consistent across all the applications used in an organization. This reduces the load on the application vendor's development and support staff: they don't have

---

[1] An extreme example of this is one programmer we know who aways uses the most garish colours on his screen: the reason is that he wears sunglasses when programming, and his colours show up nicely though the glasses!

to anticipate everything anybody could possibly want — instead the users (or their system managers) have the flexibility to change the application as they require.

Multiple copies of the same application need different settings.   For example, if you need several xterm windows, you want different names for each window so you can distinguish between them when they are iconified. You also want them to start up automatically in particular positions with particular sizes (which is perhaps the most common customization required for any program). Occasionally it is helpful to colour code your windows, too, for quick identification.

Physical disabilities of the user. People with a visual handicap may need to use very large fonts, which in turn may require layout changes. For colour-blind users, letting them choose their own colours is a good idea. Users with motor control disabilities may find it very difficult to use the mouse and prefer to invoke functions using the keyboard instead.

Applications are used in different circumstances. In a demonstration environment, people will need to use (very) large fonts. In a process control environment, certain colours may be reserved (such as red for danger, orange for warning) and if you have used these colours for aesthetic purposes, the program must be changed. If your application is being used in an astronomy observatory at night, the users will probably want to change the colours used to dark ones and especially reds, so the dark-adaptation of their eyes isn't much affected. You just don't know who will want to use your software, or where.

However, making programs very customizable can cause its own problems. First is the question of documentation: how do you document a program if the user has changed it? And even more difficult, how do you provide on-line context-sensitive help? (There's no easy answer to this, though we may eventually see programs which are self-documenting by means of adaptive help systems, which provide information based on the current configuration, examined dynamically, rather than just printing fixed help messages stored in a file.) The second difficulty is that the user may customize the program incorrectly, but then blame the developer for incorrect operation. Examples are changing colours so that the application is writing white characters on a white background (not noted for its readability), specifying keys for use within the application which have already been reserved by the toolkit or the window manager being used, or changing the position of items so they are off-screen or hidden behind others. A partial solution is to structure the way customization is done within the program so that items are grouped and are automatically altered together: for example, preventing ill-considered positioning of single items in a menu.

In the next module we look at the basic mechanisms Xlib provides for customizing programs, and later we'll see how the Toolkit develops that into a very flexible and powerful customization facility.

12.2   The Resources mechanism for customizing applications

Xlib provides the 'resources' for specifying parameter values in an application. Resource values are specified in text files or in properties, are read in by the application when it starts running, and are stored in a table within the program. The program can retrieve values from this table when it requires them.

X uses the concept of a **resource** for customizing applications. (Resources in this sense are default values or parameter settings, and have nothing to do with server resources; unfortunately, **X** uses the same word for both.) At its simplest, a resource is just an item which has a name and a value, and you can retrieve the value associated with a given name. When the program starts up, values are loaded in from various **resources files** (or **defaults files** as they are also known) and are stored in a table held in memory within the application. This table of names and values is often called the application's **Resource Database**. When the program requires a value, it queries the database for a resource of a particular name, and the value is returned if found. The returned value is just a text string at this level of operation, and the application must then process this text and convert it to the appropriate internal form.

Resources are implemented by **Xlib**. The set of functions within **Xlib** which handle resources and manage the Resource Database are often called the **Resource Manager**. In Module 12.3 we'll see how the Toolkit adds extra functionality to this.

Resource names

A resource name can be viewed as consisting of two main parts, the first specifying an 'object' and the second specifying some **attribute** of that object, such as its foreground colour, its width, or the text string displayed within it. In practice, the object to which a resource specification refers is typically a user interface component or widget. For example, in xterm, the terminal emulator window is called:

```
xterm.vt100
```

The attribute of the resource is appended to the object name; thus the full resource name for the foreground colour of this window is:

```
xterm.vt100.foreground
```

which is the name you use in a resources or defaults file. To make a full resource specification you append a colon and the value required. So to specify green as the foreground colour, use:

```
xterm.vt100.foreground: green
```

When xterm starts, this line is read by the Resource Manager, and stored in the Resource Database. If the application queries for the foreground attribute of the drawing window (by specifying the full resource name exactly as above), the value green will be returned as a text string containing five characters; the application can then manipulate this as required — for example, converting it to an internal representation of the colour.

The resource database mechanisms are part of Xlib, but to use them the Xlib programmer must explicitly call the Resource Manager functions and write the code to make use of the returned values. If this isn't done, the program will not be customizable via resources.

Here we have described the simple use of resources. In fact the resources mechanism is very sophisticated, and in the next module we look at resource naming in more detail, and see how resources are applied to widgets in a Toolkit application.

Where and when resources are specified

When each application starts, the Resource Manager within that application loads its Resource Database by reading in resource specifications from several places. These include files specific to the application, files specific to the host the application is running on, and to the user running it, and from the RESOURCE_MANAGER property on the root window of the display the application is using. The user can also specify particular files to be used, and specific directories to be searched for resources files with the environment variables XAPPLRESDIR, XFILESEARCHPATH and XUSER-FILESEARCHPATH. In this way very precise tailoring of resources is possible, taking account of which operating system the application is running on, and the capabilities of the server — whether it supports colour, what its resolution is, etc. The MIT program xrdb is very useful for conditionalizing settings like this. Again because resource settings are loaded from many places, it is easy to set up site-wide default settings for the system as a whole and/or for particular applications, and then let individual users selectively override them according to their own personal preferences.

Figure A shows a defaults file with several resource specifications. (The meaning of these should be fairly clear, but the next module explains the precise format used.)

```
XTerm*saveLines:        630
XTerm*scrollBar:        true
XTerm*background:       alice blue

*font:                  -*-gallant-*-*-*-*-19-75-*-*-*-*-*
*cursorColor:           DeepSkyBlue
*pointerColor:          red

xclock*update:          5
xclock*Foreground:      white
xclock*background:      slate gray
xclock*hands:           red

xcutsel.selection:      CLIPBOARD

emacs.BitmapIcon:       on

xedit*enableBackups:    yes
xedit*backupNameSuffix: .tmp
```

Figure A.   A defaults file containing several simple resource specifications.

12.2   The Resources mechanism for customizing applications

12.2.1   How resources are named

Resource names are hierarchical, consisting of one or more sub-names. The **X** Toolkit also uses a hierarchical naming scheme for widgets, and so it is easy to link resource names to widget names. In turn this allows values for attributes to be specified on a per-widget basis, so it is possible to customize almost anything in a Toolkit program.

(If technical details aren't so relevant to you, you can skip over this module.)

The naming scheme for resources has evolved to meet the requirements of toolkits, by allowing a single object to have many different attributes. For example, the vt100 widget in xterm has several attributes specifying the various colours it is to use, and their full resource names are:

```
xterm.vt100.foreground
xterm.vt100.background
xterm.vt100.cursorColor
xterm.vt100.pointerColor
xterm.vt100.pointerColorBackground
```

This fits in well with the idea of widgets: a widget is an object, and it has many characteristics or attributes governing its appearance and behaviour.

The full name of an 'object' from the point of view of the Resource Manager actually consists of one or more sub-names concatenated together and separated by a dot. Xlib attaches no meaning to the sub-names,[2] but in fact this scheme has been influenced by the requirements of the Toolkit, because concatenated names easily lend themselves to hierarchical, tree-structured, naming. The Toolkit defines the full name of a widget to be the widget's own specific or sub-name, preceded by the full name of its parent. (So widget names reflect the tree structure of the application's widget hierarchy, which we described in Module 7.2.) Using the Toolkit's widget full names gives us a simple way of providing unique object names to the Resource Manager for resources. Let's use the MIT text editor, xedit, as an example.

Figure A shows a typical xedit window, which you can see is made up of many components that are in fact widgets. Figure B shows the widget tree. The xedit is the application's top-level window; its full name is xedit. Its only child is the widget called paned, which is a composite widget managing the overall layout; its full name is:

```
xedit.paned
```

This is turn has children, one of which is buttons, itself a manager, with full name:

```
xedit.paned.buttons
```

---

[2]Even the attribute is itself just another sub-name; as far as the Resource Manager is concerned it is not special. However, we have given it a special name, not only to make the explanation simpler, but also to follow the **X** Toolkit's terminology.

This manages three button widgets and one text widget. The full name of the save button is:

```
xedit.paned.buttons.save
```

and to specify red for the background attribute of this button we say:

```
xedit.paned.buttons.save.background: red
```

Thus, the basic Xlib hierarchical resource naming scheme allows us to use concatenated sub-names to specify a Toolkit widget precisely and, by appending an attribute name, to specify one out of the many possible attributes for that particular widget.

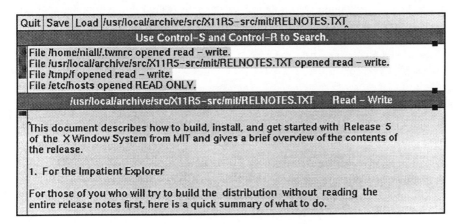

Figure A. The xedit text editor's window.

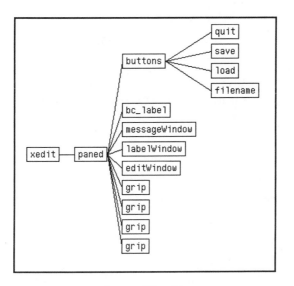

Figure B. xedit's widget tree.

12.2   The Resources mechanism for customizing applications

12.2.2   Wildcards and class names in resources

Resource specifications can contain 'wildcards' and widget and attribute class names, so many values can be set at once. If many different resource specifications apply to one attribute of an object, precedence rules determine which single specification is actually used.

(If technical details aren't so relevant to you, you can skip over this module.)

When you specify values in resources files the name of the resource does not have to be specified exactly — the Resource Manager lets you use **wildcards**. To specify that red is to be the foreground colour and black the background throughout the application, you can use the specifications:

```
xedit*background: black
xedit*foreground: red
```

where the '*' is the wildcard, taking the place of zero or more sub-names. Thus the effect of the second line in the example above is to specify red as the value for each of:

```
xedit.foreground:
xedit.paned.foreground:
xedit.paned.buttons.foreground
xedit.paned.buttons.save.foreground
```

as well as all the foreground for all other widgets in the application. (Below we see how such broad specifications are kept manageable, through resource precedence rules.)

Using class-names in resource specifications

You can also specify objects and/or attributes by their class names instead of their own specific names, which is effectively a more specific form of wildcarding. Thus, to specify that all menu buttons are to have a yellow foreground, without affecting the foreground settings of any other objects, use:

```
xedit*Command.foreground: yellow
```

(This is an Athena application: Command is the class name for Athena pushbuttons.)

Even the application or program can be specified by class name rather than its own specific name. There are no rules on how application class names should be formed — they are merely hard-coded into the application, although often the class name consists of the application name with the first one or two letters capitalized. For example, xedit's class name is Xedit, xclock's is XClock, and xfontsel's is XFontsel. (You can see what the name actually is by running xprop on the application's window and looking at the WM_CLASS property.) Application class names are useful because you may run

several copies of a particular application, each with a different application name, set
with the command-line flag —name. You can set resources for all these applications as
a group using the application class name, and set resources specific to an instance using
its particular application name:

```
XTerm*cursorColor: DeepSkyBlue
console*cursorColor: red
```

How conflicting resource specifications are resolved

What we are doing is giving the Resource Manager more or less imprecise keys on
which to retrieve a single value from the Resource Database each time it performs
a query. Often, more than one of the specifications you have entered can apply to
a single object; for example, each of the last two or three examples above specify a
foreground colour for the Save button in our application. When the application queries
the Resource Database for the value for this resource, what will be returned, red or
yellow? The Resource Manager returns only a single value ever — the specification that
is the most specific match to the object queried for. Above, red applies to everything
in the application, but yellow is specific to buttons, so the value returned in this case
will be yellow. (There are many other rules for deciding which one value of many is
to apply, but we omit the details here.)

Combining hierarchical naming with wildcarding, and using class-names in resource
specifications, gives you great flexibility and power in specifying resource values. For
example, the three specifications:

```
xedit*Command.foreground: orange
xedit*search*foreground: blue
xedit*foreground: pink
```

set the default foreground colour for everything in the xedit program to pink; however,
all pushbuttons will be orange, except those that are descended from the search widget
(which is a pop-up dialog) — this widget and all its descendants including pushbuttons
will have a blue foreground. (For reasons we won't go into, the second resource
specification above takes precedence over the first and third; but the order in which the
specifications are listed in the file doesn't matter.)

A resource specification is really a pattern, and the Resource Manager will use it and
the value it specifies only if it matches the full name of the object and attribute for which
a value is being queried. If a sub-name or attribute in the specification is misspelled, it
will be ignored, because when the Resource Manager looks at it, it won't match what is
being looked for. And, because the Resource Manager attaches no meaning to names or
sub-names, it can never detect such misspellings, so errors like this can be very difficult
to find. Of course, if you misspell a *value* for a resource, the Toolkit may not recognize
it when it tries to convert it, and will give you an error message:

```
venus% xclock -fg geern
Warning: Color name "geern" is not defined
```

12.3   How the Toolkit uses resources

The Toolkit uses resources for all values relating to widgets, giving you the ability to customize without having to write any code yourself. The Toolkit adds a lot of extra functionality to resources, and defines the semantics of many resource types, including common data-types such as strings and numerics, but also many X-specific types such as colours, geometry specifications, colormaps, etc.

The resource mechanisms we have considered so far are those provided by Xlib. Xlib doesn't have a pre-defined set of resource types, or any view of what they relate to: values are returned as text strings and the programmer can do what she wants with them. However, the Intrinsics uses resources for *all* values relating to widgets in the Toolkit, and it adds a lot of extra meaning to resources. It defines how values represented as text strings (ASCII characters in a defaults file) are to be converted to the internal type needed, as well as providing functions called **resource converters** for performing these conversions. Each widget class defines the types of values each of its resources needs (or can accept).

Let's take an example. If the foreground colour is specified as red, then the value returned by the Resource Manager to the Toolkit will consist of a three-character ASCII string containing r, e, and d. The Toolkit must then look up this string in the colour database, to find what RGB value it represents, and then convert this to the internal pixel value used by the server. A simpler example is how Boolean (on/off or true/false) values are handled: the two-character string On and the three-character string Off have to be recognized (and others rejected) and then converted to their internal values (probably one and zero respectively).

The Toolkit contains converter functions for almost every type of **X**-related data needed in an applications program, so you can specify a value in a resources file for almost anything you require. Resource types defined include numeric values (for sizes, positions, etc.), string values (for labels and buttons), font names, and of course colours and Boolean values which we have already mentioned. There are other more complex types that are used internally, such as pixmaps, geometry specifications, callback functions, and colormaps. And in the next module we look in detail at another type of resource, the translation table.

Because the **X** Toolkit uses resources internally for all widget values, Toolkit programs are automatically customizable: the programmer doesn't have to write any code for the customizability to be included. As a result, you can customize third-party Toolkit applications and those you develop in-house, in exactly the same way. The only limitation is that values which are hard-coded into the program cannot be overridden; developers should bear this in mind, and wherever possible place even basic values required by the program in a resources file. To make this easier, the Toolkit uses the concept of the **application-defaults file**. This file is stored in a system-wide standard directory, derives its name from the application it relates to, and is read by the Resource Manager only when that application is run. Thus it can contain settings exclusive to that application. When taken to its full extent, the 'app-defaults' file can contain *all* the application's parameters, so that it really is an integral part of the application, and should be shipped with the binary (executable) program. The advantage of separating parameters out into a separate text file is that the application is now highly customizable, and major changes such as localization for use in another country are possible, without the involvement of the developer and without having to ship source code.

Another good reason for keeping values in a file rather than hard-coding them into the program, is that you reduce your coding work very considerably. Data checking and conversions are being done by the Toolkit converters instead of by code which you would otherwise have had to write yourself. For instance, in the 'red foreground' example above, you would not have had to include *any* colour-handling code for it to work correctly. Moreover, as new facilities are added to later releases of the Toolkit as device-independent colour specifications were in Release 5, your application will be able to make use of them without requiring any programming changes.

Customizing applications from the command-line

The **X** Toolkit provides command-line options or flags for setting commonly altered resource values, which is another form of customization. For example, the flags –fg, –bg, –fn and –ic specify the foreground and background colours, the font to be used, and that the application should be iconified immediately it starts up. This makes it easy to start several instances of the same program with distinctive visual characteristics, in the configuration you want, as in:

```
xterm -fg yellow -fn '*-courier-bold-*-18-*' -bg gray
xterm -bg black -fg white -ic
```

Internally, the operation of these flags is simple. Using conversion tables provided by the programmer, the Toolkit merely textually converts the strings on the command-line into full resource specifications which are then processed as normal. For example, the flags:

```
-fg white
-ic
```

are transformed by xterm into:

```
xterm*foreground: white
xterm.iconic: On
```

(Notice that the application name is included in the expansion, and the delimiter for iconic is a dot, not a star, so there is no wildcarding — the iconic resource is being set only for the main xterm application window, not for each widget within it.)

The Toolkit provides specific flags only for setting resources which the user will often want to change from one instance of the program to the next. However, you can include *any* resource specification on the command-line by quoting it and prefixing with the –xrm flag (for 'X Resource Manager'), as in:

```
xcalc -xrm "*ti.button5.pointerColourBackground: RGB:00/aa/aa"
```

12.4 Translation tables resources and keyboard mapping

One of the most useful resource types is the 'translation table' which lets you customize the bindings of your keyboard and mouse buttons on a per-window or per-application basis.

(If technical details aren't so relevant to you, you can skip over this module.)

A complex resource type that is used frequently is the **translation table** (or just **translations**) which provides application-specific or even window-specific keyboard mappings. In Module 7.4 we explained that callbacks are 'high-level' or 'logical' events, and that procedures written by the applications programmer can be invoked when these callbacks occur — for instance, on the 'activation' of a pushbutton. Here we describe how real **X** events are mapped onto these logical occurrences.

What happens is that each widget has a translation table, which specifies that certain **actions** are to occur (more precisely that certain **action procedures** are to be executed) when particular sequences of **X** events occur in this widget. Using the Athena pushbutton as an example, the default operation is that the widget is set when the left mouse button is pressed, and it is activated when the mouse button is released again. (The button activates on release rather than press to make it easier to use. First, the set action inverts the button colours, so you get visual confirmation of which button you have pressed. Second, if you have pressed the button by mistake, you can avoid activating it, by moving the pointer out of the button before releasing; the button then just unsets and reverts to its normal colours, without ever activating.) The button's partial translation table is:

Event sequence	Action(s)
Left button pressed	set()
Left button released	notify() unset()

The notify action just calls the callbacks registered for activation (and some other minor functions which we discuss in the next module). Using a table like this gives a level of indirection between **X** events and the actions executed by the widget as a result: by changing the table, we can invoke the same actions with different events, or invoke different actions with the same events. For example, we could use the keyboard to operate the pushbutton by changing the table to:

Space-bar pressed	set() notify() unset()
Return key pressed	set() notify() unset()

Thus translation tables let you tailor keyboard and mouse-button bindings (and even use other events, such as <Enter>, <Leave>, <Expose>, etc.) to invoke functions within the application. By including the default bindings for the application in an application-defaults file, not only is the default clearly documented, but it is easily accessible to the system manager who might need to change it. Figure A shows a resource specification for a translation table for the manualPage widget in the MIT program xman.

In the next module we look at how translation tables and actions relate to callbacks.

```
Ctrl<Btn1Down>: XawPositionSimpleMenu(optionMenu) MenuPopup(optionMenu)
Ctrl<Btn2Down>: XawPositionSimpleMenu(sectionMenu) MenuPopup(sectionMenu)
Ctrl<Key>q:     Quit()
Ctrl<Key>c:     Quit()
Ctrl<Key>r:     RemoveThisManpage()
Ctrl<Key>n:     CreateNewManpage()
Ctrl<Key>h:     PopupHelp()
Ctrl<Key>d:     GotoPage(Directory)
Ctrl<Key>m:     GotoPage(ManualPage)
Ctrl<Key>v:     ShowVersion()
Ctrl<Key>s:     PopupSearch()
Shift<Btn2Down>,<Btn2Up>:       GotoPage(Directory)
```

Figure A.   Specifying a translations table for the manualpage widget in the xman
program.

12.4 Translation tables resources and keyboard mapping

12.4.1 Translation tables, actions, and callbacks

Translation tables specify that certain action procedures are to be called when a particular sequence of events occurs in a widget. Most action procedures are defined by the widget in which they are used, to implement the callbacks for that widget. Applications programmers can also write their own action procedures.

(If technical details aren't so relevant to you, you can skip over this module.)

What is the relationship between actions (or action procedures) and callbacks? In the example from the previous module:

> *Event sequence*   *Action(s)*
> Space-bar pressed   set() notify() unset()

when are the activation callbacks called, if ever? The answer is that the notify action procedure includes code to call any callbacks registered for activation. By contrast, the set action[3] has no callbacks associated with it: the action merely changes internal state variables, to allow a subsequent notify to go ahead, and changes the appearance of the button so that it's clear that is has been set. (We referred to this briefly in Module 7.4.1.)

Figure A shows the relationship of **X** events, translation tables, actions, and callback functions. This shows that our schematic diagram in Module 7.4 was in fact a simplification and omitted the translations mechanism. The figure here also illustrates the point we made above, that some actions defined by the widgets themselves have related callbacks, whereas others have no relation to callbacks at all.

Where action procedures are defined

Action procedures are provided by the widget (precisely, the widget class) and can be used only within that type of widget. For example, you can't use an unset action in a translation table for a scrollbar widget, because unset is meaningful only for pushbuttons.

The applications programmer can also write action procedures of her own, and these can be used in translation tables just like a widget's own action procedures. Programmer-defined actions are crucial in allowing the user of the application to customize how certain tasks within the application are to be invoked, for two reasons:

1. These actions typically perform application-oriented tasks. For example, in an e-mail program, actions defined might include send-this-message, move-to-next-message, etc. By contrast, widget actions tend to be rather low-level, and concerned with the internal operation of the widget or the user interface. Figure B shows just some of the programmer-defined actions provided by xterm.

---

[3]We are talking about the **Athena** pushbutton here. The equivalent action for the Motif pushbutton is arm, which does have callbacks associated with it, though they are rarely used in practice. Another difference is that a Motif button can be activated even if there hasn't been a prior arm action.

2. Programmer-defined actions can be included in the translation table for *any* widget, and therefore they can be invoked from any place in the user interface. For example in our e-mail program, forwarding a mail message to another person might normally be invoked from a menu; but by using translations, the user (or system manager) could specify that it could also be invoked by pressing key **F7** in the main edit window, or by clicking the middle mouse button in the 'read message' window.

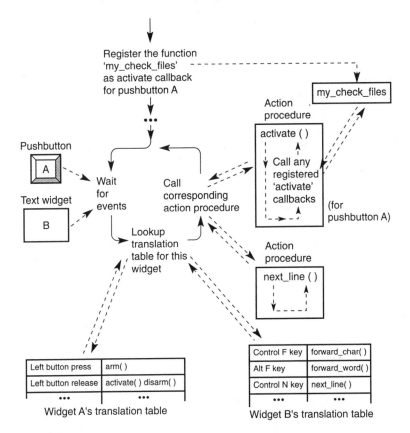

Figure A.   Relationship of translation tables, actions, and callbacks.

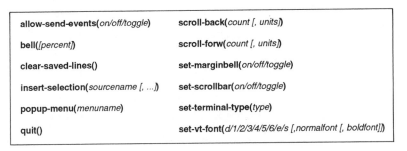

Figure B.   Some of the actions defined in xterm.

12.5   Tools for customizing resources

Recent MIT releases of **X** include tools that simplify customizing an application. Some tools list which resources apply to the application, and their values. Another tool lets you interactively edit the resource settings for a running program: the tool's 'point and click' interface makes resource editing fairly simple, and it lets you see immediately the effect your changes have had.

The MIT release contains several tools to help you customize programs. **viewres** shows graphically the tree of widget classes it knows about, and lets you display which resources (attributes) each class provides, as shown in Figure A. (By default **viewres** supports only the MIT **Athena** set, but it can be re-compiled to include others.) **listres** performs a similar function but prints out resource names rather than showing them graphically.

   Two other MIT programs let you work with resources for a specific application. **appres** ('application resources') prints out the resource value settings that the Resource Manager would return for the components or widgets in the application you specify. The program **editres** ('edit resources') lets you interact with a running **X** Toolkit application, and dynamically edit resource settings on the application's widgets, so you can see exactly the effect they have (Figure B). You can save the modified resource settings for future use, too. **editres** is particularly useful when you need to set resources for a program where the widget hierarchy isn't listed clearly in the documentation, because the widget tree is shown so clearly. As with **viewres**, **editres** by default knows only about the **Athena** widget set, but can be re-compiled to support others.

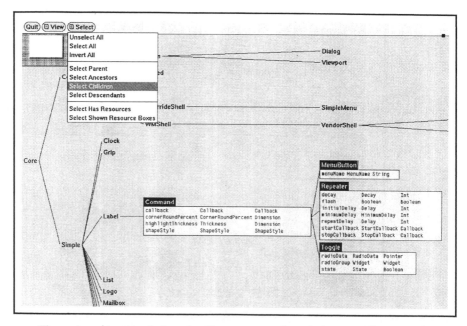

Figure A.   **viewres** window showing resources for subclasses of **Command**.

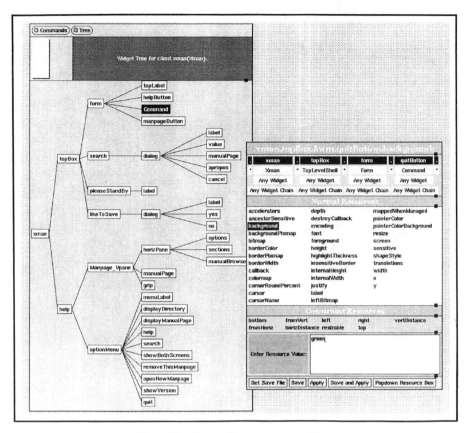

Figure B.   The editres resource editor.

Summary

In this chapter we introduced the basic resources mechanism provided by Xlib, and described how an application can use resources to retrieve values to use within that program. We saw how resources are named, and that objects and attributes in the program can be specified not just by name but also by class, and by using 'wildcard' specifications as well. Then we looked at how the X Toolkit uses resources for all values relating to widget, thus letting you customize a large portion of a Toolkit program's interface. You get this customizability 'for free' — it is a fundamental part of the Toolkit — so you can customize third-party applications as well as your own. We looked at a specific type of resource specification, the translation table, and how it relates to callbacks and widget actions, and we finished off with a brief description of some tools you can use to manage resource customization.

In the next chapter we move on from customization, and consider the performance of **X** systems.

Chapter

13   Performance Factors

13.1   Server performance
     13.1.1   Standard server facilities: backing store and save-unders

13.2   Network performance
     13.2.1   Performance of local versus remote clients

13.3   Client performance
     13.3.1   Effect of memory usage and CPU on client performance

13.4   Benchmarks and tests
     13.4.1   Profiling applications, and replaying sessions

Introduction

In this chapter we examine the three main components of the **X** system — the server, the network and the client — to see what factors affect the performance perceived by the user. We also describe some of the measurement tools available, which can help you choose a server suited to your application mix, or perhaps tune your existing **X** system.

13.1 Server performance

The speed of **X** servers varies widely, and is very dependent on the hardware used. Memory usage in the server can be critical for satisfactory operation. Most servers offer standard facilities that can improve the performance of graphics-intensive applications.

The speed for a given **X** operation can vary by up to a factor of 100 between different servers. Some of the many aspects of the performance of a server are:

- **The speed of the server's CPU.** The faster the CPU the better, especially for operations that involve manipulating a lot of data in memory. (Operations mostly use integer arithmetic, so the floating point performance of the CPU isn't so important.)

- **Server graphics hardware.** Clearly, performance can be affected by any special graphics hardware used by the server. However, what is crucial is how much of its graphical manipulation and computation the server can delegate to the graphical hardware, instead of having to perform it explicitly itself in the main server CPU. For example, there is a wide range of graphics boards available for DOS PC **X** servers, but what appears to be a wonderfully fast board from its specifications will do you no good unless your server software can make use of the board's fast facilities, and has in fact been written to do so. **X** lays down strict standards for the results of graphics operations, and if the special graphics hardware doesn't match these specifications, the facilities it provides won't be much use to you.

  You should really try out any special hardware with the applications and servers you will actually be running before you invest heavily.

- **Special optimizations for local operation.** Applications running locally on the same machine as the server can improve performance by bypassing some or all of the standard Xlib code and going direct to the hardware. For example, Sun take this approach with the XGL software (Figure A). Simply, the system can bypass both the code needed to package requests in the standard format, and the code in the server which interprets and executes these requests. Instead, when the application is aware of the local hardware and its capabilities, it can take a short cut and communicate directly with the hardware to perform the operation. (This functionality is of course transparent to the applications programmer, and is hidden in the standard development libraries provided with the particular system.)

  Another example of local-execution optimization is the MIT-SHM shared memory extension described in Module 3.8.

- **Platform-specific optimization.** Many vendors start off using the MIT Release code as a base. (This is not surprising, considering that new releases come out relatively frequently.) However, to get the best performance from a particular machine, the developers should not just port the server but should optimize it and change it to take advantage of any special features that are available in the hardware or operating system. (Alas, not every server developer does this in practice.)

You should also note that servers are not uniformly fast over the whole range of **X** functions: a server may be fast in one area and slow in another. To find the best server for your purposes, you should consider benchmark tests (see Module 13.4). And in the next module we look at standard facilities that can greatly improve a server's effective performance.

Memory usage

X servers need memory for fonts, for pixmaps, bitmaps, windows, backing store (see next module), etc., and in Module 13.3 we'll see how a client can, at the expense of a good deal of server memory, improve its own performance.

The server's memory requirement is dynamic, and it is quite possible that at some point your server will run out of memory. (This is a major difference between X-terminals and normal ones — you can't imagine your VT220 terminal failing because of lack of memory!) What happens depends on your server. Some servers will just crash, others will give an error message and let you kill off clients to free memory or abandon the client that had requested the memory, so that at least your whole session isn't lost.

Many servers now use virtual memory, which more or less eliminates this problem in practice. Virtual memory is of course available on most multitasking workstations, but X-terminals are increasingly making use of it too.

X doesn't provide any way for an application to ask the server about memory availability or usage, but some servers do let the user get this information manually, for instance by pressing some special key sequence. You can use this information to get a profile of the memory requirements for the different applications you run, and so configure your **X** stations accordingly, to avoid memory problems.

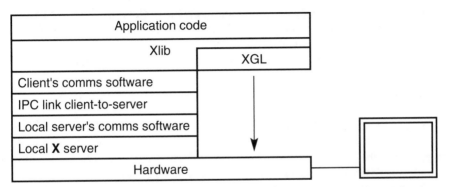

Figure A.   Some special applications can bypass the local server and access the hardware directly.

13.1 Server performance

13.1.1 Standard server facilities: backing store and save-unders

'Backing store' and 'save-unders' are two facilities that cause the server instead of the application to maintain the contents of windows which have been obscured. Backing store is typically used for large or complex graphics windows, whereas save-unders are used for transient windows such as pop-up menus and dialogs.

With Release 3, two new facilities were introduced to minimize the load of handling exposure events — **backing store** and **save-unders**. They both cause the server instead of the application to maintain the contents of windows which have been obscured, so the server can redraw the window when it is exposed, without imposing any load at all on the client. However, the two serve quite different purposes.

Backing store

When backing store is enabled on a window the server will maintain the contents of this window even when it is covered up (Figure A). When the window is exposed again, the *server* can redraw the window immediately and doesn't have to send an expose event to the client. Not having to redraw can save some clients a lot of computation and other resources.

Backing store can be quite consumptive. The server can easily require a megabyte or more to store an obscured full-screen window on a colour system. Moreover, the window may remain covered for a long time, so the memory is required for a long time. If there are many windows with backing store enabled, the server could run out of memory, so **X** allows the server either to refuse to enable backing store on a window when requested, or if it is enabled, to disable it dynamically at any time, forcing exposure events to occur as normal again. In fact a server does not have to implement backing store at all to comply with the **X** standard, but in practice virtually every server now provides it.

Backing store is enabled on a per-window basis. Typically in an application the programmer would enable backing store on the main working windows which involve a lot of graphics and take a long time to redraw. Other windows, such as the menus, labels, text widgets, etc., would not have backing store enabled: they don't take long to redraw, and enabling backing store would use up memory in the server.

Save-unders

When save-unders are enabled on a window, the server maintains the contents of any window *which this window obscures* — not the contents of this window itself. Save-unders are normally enabled on menus, pop-ups, and other short-lived items, to avoid causing potentially very expensive expose events on other windows. Save-unders generally require less memory than backing store, as the menus, etc., they are typically used for are fairly small. And because save-unders are usually used for transient windows, their requirement for memory is usually short-term.

When a window enables backing store, it is effectively saying 'I am an important window and the server should maintain my contents'. By contrast, when a window enables save-unders, it is saying 'I am unimportant, but I want to cause as little disruption as possible to other windows'. So save-unders are social-minded citizens, whereas backing storers are hogs.

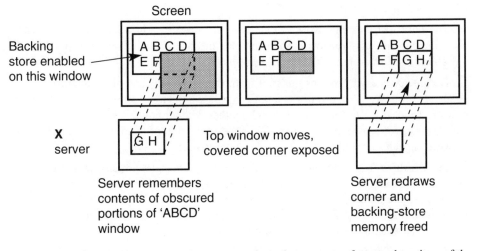

Figure A.   With backing-store, the server remembers the contents of covered sections of the window.

13.2   Network performance

Network bandwidth is not normally a performance bottleneck.

As we discussed in Module 4.5, there are two measures of the speed of a network — its bandwidth and its latency — and these affect performance in different ways. **Latency** relates to how long a round-trip on the network will take, and primarily affects response time, as we discuss in the next module.

The **bandwidth** of a network is a measure of capacity — how many bits per second you can transmit and receive. For example, the bandwidth of many serial lines is 9.6 kbits/s, and that of an Ethernet is 10 Megabits/s.

Because **X** is asynchronous, most of its traffic is one-way and not 'round-trip'. As a result, **X** can make good use of the available bandwidth: for example, once a client has sent one request it can immediately send another without any delay, because it doesn't have to wait for a response. In turn, **X**'s good utilization of bandwidth means that the network capacity needed is less than you might expect.

Studies show that on average an X-terminal uses about 1% of an Ethernet when the terminal is active. As terminals are idle quite a lot of the time, it means the effective average requirement per terminal is a good deal less than 1%, so a typical network can handle many many **X** stations without overloading. (X-terminal vendors claim an Ethernet can support hundreds of X-terminals.)

These data tie in well with investigations of **X** over X.25 networks: it was found that for a typical application mix, an average bandwidth of about 20 kbit/s was adequate. There are of course transient requirements for much higher bandwidth, so this figure doesn't mean that a single user with a 19.2 kbit/s line would have perfect response. But it does suggest that ten users sharing a network with 200 kbit/s capacity would be OK, because of the statistical spread of their usage. Nonetheless **X** has been run over 9.6 kbit/s serial lines (usually by people at home connecting to their office) and performance is just about tolerable. Vendors and the **X** Consortium are working on developing a standard for using **X** over slow lines, using compression or other techniques (see Module 15.1).

Traffic patterns have been measured for different types of operation (Figure A), and show surprisingly low network loading, usually with a large number of small packets. Even window management, which for many users of office-automation type systems is the most demanding interactive activity they carry out, isn't very heavy. Resizing a window, which involves dragging with the mouse, gives lots of very small packets, and even rapid mouse motion still uses only 1% of the Ethernet; however, resize can be jerky if the CPU or network is heavily loaded. (As we mentioned in Module 3.2.2, using a local window manager can get over this problem.) Some applications can impose high intermittent network loads. A typesetting previewer, which is drawing whole pages at a time, generates big packets, and the utilization increases, up to about 10% of an Ethernet.

When applications start manipulating images, loading can increase a lot. The network packets are often of maximum size, and as we mentioned in Module 4.4, **X** becomes more network-efficient with larger packets. For example, when transferring the image of a window with the MIT program xwud, there are spikes of around 25% Ethernet utilization, as a lot of data is being transmitted. If an application is transferring a lot of images all the time, it can result in very bad performance and heavy loading of the network; applications like this are better run locally on a multitasking workstation, as described below. Higher bandwidth networks, such as FDDI with a bandwidth of around 100 Megabits/s, can improve the performance of data-intensive applications. However, for most **X** applications, where the traffic consists of many and small packets, these networks don't give as much a benefit as the numbers would suggest, as the networks are less efficient with small packet sizes.

Fast wide area networks

The bandwidth of wide area networks (WANs) is increasing dramatically, as bandwidth-on-demand systems, ATM (Asynchronous Transfer Mode), frame relay, and SONET (Synchronous Optical Network) technologies are being widely developed and deployed. These networks are making bandwidths of 10, 100, or even 1000 Megabits/s fairly common. Moreover, ATM allows you to control, and if necessary minimize, the variability of transmission time of separate network packets; this is important to avoid a deterioration in interactive response. Experiments are being conducted on the use of ATM even for links to the desktop.

Availability of such networks will surely affect which applications can viably be run over long-haul WANs, or even on your LAN; systems will become very much more distributed.

In the next module we consider the performance implications of running applications remotely.

Activity type	*Typical traffic bytes/s*	*Typical traffic packets/s*	*Typical % Ethernet utilisation*
Continuous page scrolling, xdvi document previewer	50K	60	4.6
Capture window image (xwd) and redisplay (xwud)	80K	110	7
Position and resize windows with twm window manager	10K	100	0.8
Cursor tracking	12.5K	180	1
Continuous scrolling, in xterm terminal emulator	9K	10	0.8
Continuous scrolling, in emacs text editor	4K	14	0.3
Eight hour user session, all activities	0.25K	1.6	< 0.1

Figure A.   Representative performance figures for intensive phases of typical X activities.

13.2   Network performance

13.2.1   Performance of local versus remote clients

Running a client remotely may not degrade its performance, and sometimes may even improve it. However, some intensive applications benefit considerably from running locally. High network latency (as in a satellite link) can cause problems by increasing response times.

Surprisingly, running a client remotely over the network can often be faster than running it locally. There are several factors involved:

- Running remotely, there are two CPUs working in parallel, one generating the graphics, and the other drawing them on the screen, rather than a single CPU doing everything.

- On many servers the graphics hardware's performance is a bottleneck; by running the client elsewhere the server CPU can be dedicated to keeping the graphics hardware fully utilized. And if graphics hardware is limiting the throughput, any delay caused by using the network isn't likely to be very significant.

- With local execution on a workstation, not only are the server and client competing for the CPU, but also they may cause swapping or paging (as **X** servers and clients are often quite large in memory), and other non-**X** applications may also be contending for machine resources.

However, to avoid network congestion and slow performance, certain data-intensive applications need to be run locally on the same CPU as the server, that is, in a workstation environment. This is especially the case for applications dealing with images, as they are transferring each individual pixel between client and server. As an example, an image on an 8-bit colour system requires one byte per pixel, and therefore approximately a million bytes for a full-screen image. Thus to transfer the image, we must transfer a million bytes or 8 Mega*bits*; now the nominal bandwidth of an Ethernet is 10 Megabits/s, so we can see that the minimum transfer time is almost a second, theoretically, and will be a good deal more in practice. (By contrast, when we are dealing with graphics specified as objects such as lines, arcs, polygons, etc., **X** uses high-level requests which require relatively few bytes to be transmitted.) Running the application locally we avoid the network completely. Moreover, the use of shared memory can result in very high effective bandwidth between client and server (see Module 3.8) and in addition local clients may be able to make use of optimizations for local running, for example bypassing the server and addressing the hardware directly, as we described in Module 13.1.

The response-time of remote clients

In Module 4.5 we defined the latency of a network as a measure of how long it takes for a bit you transmit to arrive at the other end. The latency affects operations which require a round-trip— transmission from client to server and back again. Many window management tasks, such as manipulating a rubber-band outline of a window when resizing or positioning a window, generate a lot of round-trip traffic. Low latency is important for interactive working like this, and on high latency connections it is beneficial to run at least the window manager locally.

Special communications methods for slow network links

For low bandwidth networks special **X** systems are available which compress the data sent between the clients and the server. Current implementations require special, non-**X**-standard software on the host that is communicating with the server. In some cases the host-based software is providing little more than data compression and decompression, whereas in other cases it is almost as though part of the server has been moved to the host.

Systems such as these let you use distant **X** stations over modem connections (Figure A) or even connect stations on-site over serial lines such as RS-232 links instead of over a LAN.

An MIT **X** Consortium working group has been set up to address this requirement for better **X** performance over slow links, and provide a standard solution. (This is often referred to as **LBX** or **Low Bandwidth X.**)

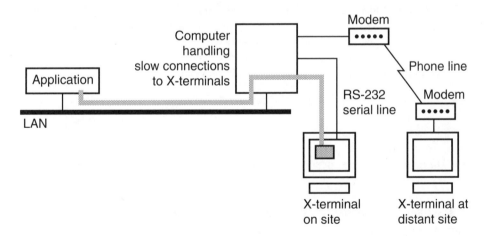

Figure A.   Using an X-terminal connected via modems or serial line.

13.3   Client performance

Many factors affect client performance, including use of particular programming techniques and whether the application has been built with the standard **X** Toolkit. Complex graphics applications may benefit from drawing indirectly to an off-screen image in memory and then to the screen, rather than directly, to simplify redrawing after expose-events.

Like all applications, **X** programs benefit from good coding and optimization, but there are several factors specific to **X**.

Because an application should always be ready to respond to incoming events, it should contain **no very long non-interruptible tasks**, as we describe in Module 14.1.2. If a program breaks this rule it will give a bad interactive response — you will have to wait a long time before the application notices what you have just done (pressed a button, or typed some text) and actions it. The least the programmer should do is give some visual feedback that the program is busy, so the user can see what's happening: for example, by changing the cursor to a clock or the 'hour-glass' shape.

Exposure event handling can be very costly for applications that have very complex graphics. It can be improved in two ways:

1. **Enabling backing store** on the windows containing the complex graphics results in fewer expose events, although there is no guarantee that the server will always be able to provide backing store. (But if an application is sufficiently important to you and it *really* needs backing store, make sure you have a server which provides what you need.)

2. As well as writing the graphics directly to the window on the screen, you can also **write** exactly the same thing **to an off-screen image**, to a pixmap in fact, thus maintaining an exact copy in memory of your window. When the application receives an expose event on the window, instead of having to regenerate the graphics, it only has to copy the image from the pixmap to the window (Figure A).

Enabling save-unders on your application's pop-up windows won't directly improve its performance, but it reduces the load on other programs, which may benefit your application, especially if it is running on the same host as the other programs.

Minimizing round trips makes your application more responsive, especially when run remotely over a network where the round-trip time can be very considerable. The section below discusses how the Toolkit helps you in this. Query-requests (asking for information about fonts, pointer position, colours, etc.) require round trips; where possible, they should be cached in the client once they have received. Module 7.2.3 discussed how using gadgets can increase the number of pointer motion events generated for an application; while these don't directly involve round trips, any requirement on a client to wait for a particular event before issuing the next request effectively requires a round-trip time, so having to process a stream of such events will degrade performance.

Using the X Toolkit

One of the goals in the design of the **X** Toolkit was to reduce the amount of traffic to the server, and the number of round trips in particular. The Toolkit meets this aim well. Two versions of the 'Hello, world' client program (Modules 5.2.2 and 5.2.4) were studied, one built with Xlib, the other using the **X** Toolkit. The communications traffic between server and client was monitored: for initial setup the traffic generated is roughly the same for both, but for resizing the window under control of a window manager, the Toolkit version transfers less data and involves very few round-trip messages.

However, you need to be careful about widget creation. Widgets do consume resources, so you shouldn't use too many; tens and even a few hundreds of widgets in a program perform acceptably, but when you have thousands, you are likely to suffer performance problems. If your program really does need a large number of widgets, you are in a dilemma. Either you create them all at once when the program starts, giving you a long startup time, or else you create them as needed, which may give you bad interactive response time. You can overcome this to some extent by caching things like dialogs for reuse where possible. Another approach is to use gadgets instead of widgets. As we discussed in Module 7.2.3, opinion is divided on this, but it is worth experimenting with your particular application and server to see if you get an appreciable benefit.

Memory allocation is one of the most time-consuming activities in the Toolkit internals, so if your standard libraries don't provide fast and efficient versions of the memory allocation functions, you should consider replacing them with better ones.

We look at memory usage in a little more detail in the next module.

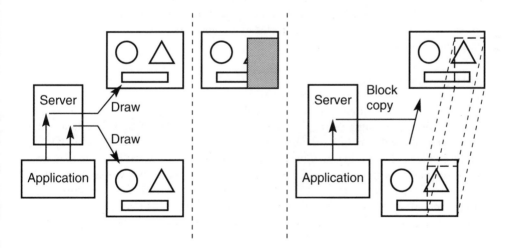

Figure A.   Using a pixmap as an off-screen image, to improve expose event handling.

13.3   Client performance

13.3.1   Effect of memory usage and CPU on client performance

Providing adequate memory on the hosts running the **X** applications is one of the best ways to avoid performance degradation. Providing more CPU power may overcome some problems, too.

Just like any other programs, **X** applications consume memory and their performance degrades if there isn't enough. However, with **X** the problem is more common. First, because both **X** clients and server are quite large; second, because with a window system you run many applications simultaneously; and finally, because with X-terminals and PC **X** servers you often end up running all the applications for many users on a central machine.

In fact, lack of memory on the hosts running the applications is probably the single most common cause of performance problems with **X** systems. The effect you see is a great deal of swapping and paging, resulting in poor response and inefficient utilization of the CPU.

There are two answers. The first is to buy more physical memory. Often this is cheaper than any other change you can make to your system. (As an example of how effective this can be, when we upgraded one of our workstations from 4 Mb to 8 Mb of memory, elapsed time to run one sequence of **X** programs reduced from 250 seconds to 45 seconds.)

Another answer is to use shared libraries if your operating system allows. As we describe in Module 14.1, this can reduce memory requirements dramatically, especially for small applications, as well as reducing the amount of space required to store the programs on disk.

CPU considerations

If, in spite of all the improvements you make, your application still runs too slowly, you can consider running the application on a more powerful CPU. This solution may not be popular, with you or your customers, but it is an option that many other systems won't give you. Depending on your configuration, only one central machine may need to be upgraded, with users accessing it remotely from their own workstations or X-terminals. If you compare the cost of the extra hardware with the total cost of the system including software, management time, and training, this may be a better option than it first appears. (It at least has the advantage that it's very quick to implement!)

13.4   Benchmarks and tests

As **X** matures, benchmarks are being continually developed for evaluating servers. These are best used in conjunction with tools which profile how your application mix loads the server. The MIT **X** Consortium has also developed a suite of tools for testing servers.

The basic purpose of benchmarks is to provide a comparison on paper of servers, to save you having to run real-life evaluations of many different machines to which you probably don't have easy access. To be of most value, these comparisons ought to be representative of real-life performance of the applications and environment you will actually be using. In particular, you want to identify what will be the slowest part of the system, to see if it will still give acceptable response time and adequate speed.

Several benchmark tools have been developed; here we'll mention only those which are widely available and are free. (There are some commercial benchmark systems available too.)

xbench

The user-contributed program **xbench** runs about 40 individual tests consisting of different **X** operations; typical output is shown in Figure A. It combines the results of these tests into a single measure using a set of arbitrary weightings; the final number is the rating of your server in **Xstones** (by analogy with Whetstones and Dhrystones). The higher the number of Xstones, the faster the server.

There are some problems interpreting **xbench** results. First, the weightings of the various aspects of the server may be inappropriate for your task or application mix; you can quite easily get a variation of a factor of two between **xbench** results and actual elapsed-time measurements of the same task on the different servers. Secondly, **xbench** doesn't measure everything, and some of the features it omits may be important for your work, or may even be those parts of the server under test which have the worst performance. Finally, your actual performance and response times may be heavily influenced by other factors that will swamp the server, no matter how good it is — for example, problems on your host (maybe not enough memory), or the effect of the network.

x11perf

The MIT program **x11perf** tests over 150 different aspects of the server, covering virtually every feature in **X**. It gives a separate time for each feature tested (see Figure B) and does *not* combine all the figures into a single 'representative' benchmark figure, because, according to **xbench**'s authors: *"We consider such numbers to be uninformative at best and misleading at worst. Some servers which are very fast for certain applications can be very slow for others. No single number or small set of numbers are sufficient to characterize how an X implementation will perform on all applications. However, by knowledge of your favorite application, you may be able to use the numbers x11perf* *reports to predict its performance on a given* **X** *implementation."*

In other words, you have to decide which aspects of the server matter to you for your work; then you can measure them directly with **x11perf**. (The companion program **x11perfcomp** merges output into a convenient tabular form for comparisons.) How do you decide which server features are most important for your applications? Use **xscope**, described in the next module.

The MIT test suite

The **X** Consortium has commissioned a suite of programs to test how faithfully an **X** implementation conforms to the **X** Protocol. It is based on Test Environment Toolkit from X/Open, the OSF and UNIX International. It has been designed to allow automated and extensible testing, without having to have a real person clicking mouse buttons, typing at the keyboard and so on, and it uses a special server extension, XTEST, to allow synthetic or simulated events to be used instead.

The suite was released publicly in September 1992. The tests uncovered many detailed bugs in a wide range of servers, typically relating to exactly which pixels should be affected by a given drawing operation. Now that the suite is widely available we can expect improved servers, and vendors will probably publish the results of tests on future releases of their servers.

```
========= line10 =========
LINES

1290240 vectors of len. 10 in 10 secs
rate = 129024.00 vectors/sec
========= line100 =========
LINES

417792 vectors of len. 100 in 10 secs
rate = 41779.20 vectors/sec
...
RECTANGLES
...
TILE-FILLED RECTANGLES
...
FILLED ARCS
...
COPYAREA (SCREEN->SCREEN)
...
```

Figure A. Typical output from a run of the xbench benchmark.

```
...
 90000 reps @   0.0574 msec (17400.0/sec): Fill 1x1 equivalent triangle
...
 2000 reps @   3.0567 msec ( 327.0/sec): Fill 100x100 161x145 tiled trapezoid
...
 3000 reps @   1.9888 msec ( 503.0/sec): Fill 100x100 216x208 tiled trapezoid
...
 84000 reps @   0.0645 msec (15500.0/sec): Char16 in 7/14/7 line (k14, k24)
...
160000 reps @   0.0325 msec (30800.0/sec): Char16 in 40-char image line (k14)
...
 80000 reps @   0.0966 msec (10400.0/sec): Copy 10x10 from pixmap to window
...
```

Figure B. Typical output from a run of the x11perf benchmark.

13.4 Benchmarks and tests

13.4.1   Profiling applications, and replaying sessions

You can profile any application to see what mix of requests it generates, by using a special program which appears to the application as a server, but in fact is just a client that captures details of the requests and passes them on to a real server. This lets you find out what features of the server are most important for performance of that application. Modified servers let you capture and record all the requests in a session, so that you can replay it later, for demonstration or testing purposes.

xscope **and** xrecorder

The user-contributed program xscope monitors *all* traffic between a client and the server. It does this using the technique we outlined in Module 4.3 — by pretending to be a server as far as the client is concerned: when you start the client you connect to xscope, not to the real server. xscope receives all requests from the client, prints out the request contents in more or less detail, and then passes on the requests, completely unaltered, to the real server, which actions them. Similarly, all events and replies from the server are passed via xscope, which prints them out and sends them on to the client. This is shown schematically in Figure A.

Note that you can use xscope with any **X** station, as it just another client as far as the real server is concerned — it can even run remotely from the real server (Figure B). (You can think of xscope as a protocol analyser for **X**.)

xscope lets you specify the level of detail you want printed, from just the names of the requests, to every byte involved. Figure C shows the least detailed output, of an xclock starting up. From this you can see how it is possible to analyse what **X** operations are dominant in the application, by post-processing the text printed out.

xrecorder is another user-contributed program. It is effectively an enhanced version of xscope which lets you filter out any particular types of event you are interested for printing or recording in a file.

xghost

The user-contributed xghost software is a set of modifications to the standard MIT server, so that all requests sent to the server are captured, and recorded in a file. Later, you can replay these events to the server, with their time-separation maintained, so that your whole session is re-run almost exactly as before — you can see the mouse pointer moving, pushbuttons being depressed, scrollbars moving, etc. This is obviously useful for demonstrations of software, but also for regression testing — to check that the current version of some software still works correctly after changes have been made, and that no new bugs have been introduced.

Even if you are not using MIT software for production work on your machines, if you need this type of facility you could make it available on a single workstation with the MIT server, and dedicate that to testing and profiling. The alterations are only to the server, so you can run your own or third-party applications unaltered.

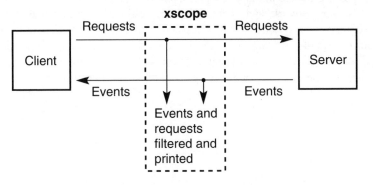

Figure A.   xscope sits between client and server, intercepting all traffic.

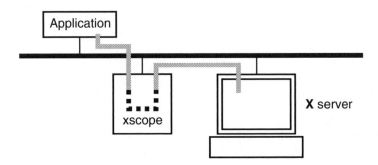

Figure B.   xscope, the application being profiled, and the real server, all running remote from one another.

```
0.00: Client -->    48 bytes
0.04:                                272 bytes <-- X11 Server
0.21: Client -->    48 bytes
           ...........REQUEST: CreateGC
           ...........REQUEST: GetProperty
0.24:                                 32 bytes <-- X11 Server
                               ..............REPLY: GetProperty
0.32: Client -->    24 bytes
           ...........REQUEST: InternAtom
0.33:                                 32 bytes <-- X11 Server
                               ..............REPLY: InternAtom
0.53: Client -->    28 bytes
           ...........REQUEST: InternAtom
0.54:                                 32 bytes <-- X11 Server
                               ..............REPLY: InternAtom
0.54: Client -->    16 bytes
           ...........REQUEST: InternAtom
0.66:                                 32 bytes <-- X11 Server
                               ..............REPLY: InternAtom
0.66: Client -->   932 bytes
           ...........REQUEST: CreatePixmap
           ...........REQUEST: CreateGC
           ...........REQUEST: PutImage
           ...........REQUEST: FreeGC
           ...........REQUEST: CreatePixmap
           ...........REQUEST: CreateGC
           ...........REQUEST: PutImage
           ...........REQUEST: FreeGC
           ...........REQUEST: InternAtom
0.77:                                 32 bytes <-- X11 Server
                               ..............REPLY: InternAtom
```

Figure C.   Output from xscope.

Summary

In this chapter we looked at the factors affecting each of the major components of an **X** system — server, network, and client. We have outlined some practical steps you can take to examine your system, and if necessary to re-configure or change it to improve performance. Finally, we looked at the benchmarking tools available to characterize server performance, and for analysing applications to see which aspects of the server performance are the most important for your particular application mix.

14 Writing X Programs

14.1   Programming the system, and development tools

14.1.1 Compiling and managing X source programs

14.1.2 X programming techniques

14.1.3 Other programming techniques

14.2   User interface management systems and other development tools

14.3   Migrating old applications to X — enhanced terminal emulators

14.3.1 How enhanced terminal emulators work

14.4   Porting from other window systems, and multiple-platform applications

14.5   User interface design, and programming

Introduction

In this chapter we look at how you write X programs. This is not a programming tutorial, and we don't look at any coding details. Instead, we outline the factors that are specific to X programming, and some aspects requiring special consideration. First we look at some techniques that are typical of many X applications. Then we look at some specialist tools for developing new applications, and for porting existing applications to X. Finally, we briefly consider how the user interface should be developed.

14.1   Programming the system, and development tools

To write **X** programs you need at minimum the basic Xlib library (or equivalent) for the host on which the application is to run. Ideally you should also have a toolkit. Specialist tools such as User Interface Management Systems and migration and porting tools are becoming increasingly common.

What you need for programming with X

If you are going to write programs using **X** (or build any user-contributed software, from the MIT **contrib** release or elsewhere), you will need, as well as the basic components we listed in Module 10.1, some extra software:

> **Libraries of X functions.** The Xlib function- or subroutine-library is essential (except on some systems using exotic languages which provide their own equivalent of Xlib). In addition you need the function libraries for whatever toolkit you are using.
>
> Note that these libraries are collections of object files compiled for the particular hardware and operating system that the *application* is to run on, so you need a version of the libraries for each target platform. When writing your program, you are not concerned at all with what type of server you expect to be using the application with, other than ensuring the correct network transport protocol is supported.
>
> **Header files,** the *.h files to include system definitions, etc. in your source program. (These files often include definitions specific to the target platform for the application.)

This is the absolute minimum you need. However, when writing applications it is almost essential that you use either a toolkit as we described in Chapter 6, or an even higher-level programming system such as the user interface management systems and porting tools that we describe in Module 14.2.

Shared libraries

Shared libraries are a way of reducing the run-time memory requirements of a system. Instead of linking a copy of a library into each application which uses it, only a pointer is linked in, so that the size of the executable file is very much smaller. At run time the library is loaded into memory if it is not already resident, and the running program accesses the functions it requires. If the library had already been loaded, then the application can immediately access it. The overall effect is that only one copy of the library is ever resident, no matter how many programs are using it (Figure A) whereas with normal 'static' libraries there is one copy resident per program (Figure B). The **X** libraries are large (on our machine Xlib is about 450 kbytes, and the Toolkit library is about 300 kbytes), so reducing the number of copies can save a lot of memory when you are running several **X** applications. Because a copy of the libraries are not linked into the application, the size of the executable file stored on disk is very much smaller too.

However, shared libraries can cause problems, too. If the libraries are updated, for example with a later release of software, but the applications remain the same, you may get some incompatibility between the two. This is sometimes called **version skew** — the version of the libraries in use doesn't match the version the application was built with. If you get this problem, you must either relink the application to use the new libraries, or make sure the older versions remain available as well. Some people refuse to use shared libraries because of this problem, and always use static linking, especially for applications that are shipped to customers. The compromise is to provide two versions to customers, one statically linked which you know will always work, the second linked with shared libraries that customers can use if they wish, to save on memory and disk space.

size of programs in memory

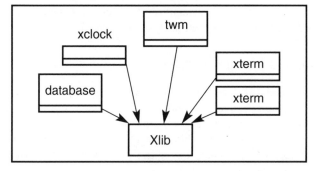

Figure A.   Only one copy of a shared library is in memory at run-time.

size of programs in memory

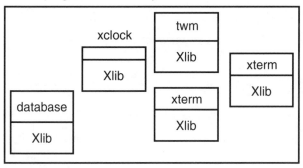

Figure B.   Each running program has its own copy of a static library.

14.1 Programming the system, and development tools

14.1.1 Compiling and managing X source programs

Xlib and Toolkit libraries are incorporated into the program when it is compiled and linked. The MIT program imake helps manage building and maintaining large software developments.

Modules 5.2 and 5.2.4 described what a typical **X** application consists of, with layers of software providing basic **X** functions, toolkit and widget functionality, and at the highest level the application code. Here we look at how these various components are brought together.

The compilation process is shown schematically in Figure A. The UNIX commands to build the simple 'hello world' **X** program mentioned in Module 5.2.2 are shown in Figure B, illustrating that the locations of the include files and libraries mentioned above are specified if they are non-standard. For more complex programs, there would of course be many source files, and probably libraries specific to the problem-domain addressed by the application (for example, a graphics program might have a GKS library) as well as in-house and operating system standard libraries.

Configuration management — imake

Large-scale development with **X** can be administratively complex, because of the many parameters and development-administration tools which may be site- or machine-specific. To overcome this problem, and to make its own release as portable as possible, MIT uses the imake program, which is included in the MIT Release. This is an enhanced version of the UNIX make program which automates the building of software components. imake uses a site-wide set of configuration and template files to isolate the vendor- and site-dependent parameters, so that the files specifying how to build a particular program are brief, portable, and site-independent. Figure C shows a sample imake file.

We strongly recommend that you use imake for **X** development.

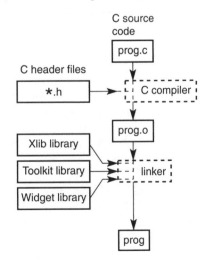

Figure A. Block diagram for the compile and link process.

```
venus% cc -I/usr/X11R5/include -c  xhw3.c
venus% cc -o xhw3 xhw3.o  -L/usr/X11R5/lib  -lXaw -lXmu -lXt -lXext -lX11
```

Figure B.   The commands used to compile and link a typical X program.

```
...
LibraryObjectRule()

SpecialLibObjectRule(Intrinsic.o,$(ICONFIGFILES),$(SRCH_DEFINES))
SpecialLibObjectRule(Error.o,$(ICONFIGFILES),$(DB_DEFINES))
SpecialLibObjectRule(Alloc.o,NullParameter,$(ALLOC_DEFINES))
SpecialLibObjectRule(Converters.o,$(ICONFIGFILES),$(BC_DEFINES))
#if DoSharedLib
SpecialObjectRule(sharedlib.o,,$(SHLIBDEF))
#endif

#if DoSharedLib
#if DoNormalLib
SharedLibraryTarget(Xt,$(SOXTREV),$(OBJS),shared,..)
#else
SharedLibraryTarget(Xt,$(SOXTREV),$(OBJS),.,.)
#endif
SharedLibraryDataTarget(Xt,$(SOXTREV),$(UNSHAREDOBJS))
InstallSharedLibrary(Xt,$(SOXTREV),$(USRLIBDIR))
InstallSharedLibraryData(Xt,$(SOXTREV),$(USRLIBDIR))
#endif
#if DoNormalLib
NormalLibraryTarget(Xt,$(OBJS))
InstallLibrary(Xt,$(USRLIBDIR))
#endif
#if ProfileLibXt
ProfiledLibraryTarget(Xt,$(OBJS))
InstallLibrary(Xt_p,$(USRLIBDIR))
#endif
#if DebugLibXt
DebuggedLibraryTarget(Xt,$(OBJS))
InstallLibrary(Xt_d,$(USRLIBDIR))
#endif

LintLibraryTarget(Xt,$(SRCS))
InstallLintLibrary(Xt,$(LINTLIBDIR))

BuildIncludes($(HEADERS),.,.)
InstallMultiple($(HEADERS),$(INCDIR))

DependTarget()

NormalLintTarget($(SRCS))
```

Figure C.   The imake file to build the MIT server.

14.1 Programming the system, and development tools

14.1.2 X programming techniques

The event-driven programming style required by **X** demands that no task should take very long, in order that events are handled promptly and the time to respond to an action of the user is short. However, 'modal' dialogs and other techniques let the programmer inhibit user-input, forcing the user to give a reply to an important question, or confirm a particular action is required, before the program can proceed.

The event-driven nature of **X** has several important consequences. **X** programs are usually written in an 'event loop' style (Module 7.4). The main routine of the program consists of a loop which waits for an event, and when one arrives despatches it to a separate event-specific routine for processing. While this routine is executing, any further events which arrive are kept in a queue. When this routine completes, it returns to the main routine, where any queued events are despatched in turn, and the cycle repeats forever. The Toolkit simplifies writing programs in this form, by providing the event loop functions, and easy mechanisms to cause callback functions to be executed when particular events occur in specified widgets. Thus, almost all event processing and despatching can be handled automatically by the Toolkit.

This program architecture imposes constraints: the program must always be ready to handle events. However, while the program is in an event-processing function, other events which arrive for the program are being queued and not processed immediately. Now as long as the program returns to the main loop quickly, events will be handled promptly. But if a long period elapses, events remain in the queue for a long time, unprocessed (Figure A). This causes problems when you are using the program: it appears that the program is doing nothing, or hasn't noticed your mouse or keyboard input, and you may repeat your last actions. But then, when the time-consuming function completes and event processing is resumed, your original actions (events) are still in the queue, and both those and the repeats are processed, usually causing results that you didn't want or expect. So ideally, callback and other functions that process events should be quick and shouldn't involve any long computations or very time-consuming I/O. If a lot of processing really is necessary, either structure your program so that the large tasks are broken into small subtasks which are executed in workprocs (Module 7.4.2) and other events can be handled between subtasks, or else delegate the large task to a sub-process, so that the main program can continue to handle events. Alternatively, at least set the program into a mode where further events can't be generated, and give a visual indication that the program is busy: for example, change the cursor to a clock or an hour-glass shape.

Fortunately, the callback structure of the Toolkit encourages a style of programming where each event (in fact each callback) is processed by its own specific function, and it is easy to write your program using a lot of small (and hopefully quick) functions. Also, the MIT **X** Consortium is working on multi-threading for clients and servers (Module 15.1) which may overcome some of the problems of long callbacks.

Dialogs, blocking input and inhibiting events

Some dialogs also require special handling, and they block input so the user can't do anything else while the dialog is on-screen. The program is no longer fully event-driven; instead of letting the user drive the application as normal, invoking whatever menu or action they want, the application is demanding some specific information from the user. The Toolkit addresses this requirement by providing **modal** dialogs, which stop you using the rest of the application until the dialog is finished. For example, when you try to exit a word processor without first saving your file, you are often given a modal dialog asking whether you want to save your change, and you have to reply. (The Toolkit also provides **modeless** dialogs, which don't affect the operation of other parts of the application. A typical example of a modeless dialog is the printer-setup within an application — it is taking in information specific to one area of the program's function, and has no need to inhibit the operation of other parts of the application.)

Motif further distinguishes between the types of modal dialogs it provides. The type described above is **application modal** — it suspends the operation of the rest of this application, but you can use all other applications as normal. **System modal** dialogs prevent you using this and any other application while the dialog is on-screen. For example, when you want to exit or reset the Motif window manager, it gives you a system-modal dialog asking if you really want to perform this action.

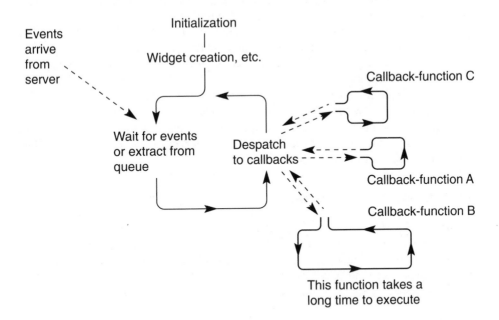

Figure A.   The toolkit event-loop, showing how events may be queued when a callback function executes for a long time.

14.1 Programming the system, and development tools

14.1.3 Other programming techniques

Your application needs to address major differences in hardware capabilities, colour versus monochrome screens, for example, although the code handling these differences can be isolated to one part of the program. It also needs to take account of interactions with the window manager, and that it must share resources (colours, memory, etc.) with other clients. Applications should be user-customizable so they can be used in different countries and in different environments.

Taking account of different hardware capabilities

While **X** is almost completely hardware independent, there are some fundamental hardware characteristics that the application or the toolkit it uses must take account of. For example, different screens have different sizes, you can't display colour on a monochrome screen, and the user can't press a middle button on a two-button mouse.

Even so, the design of the **X** system simplifies your work. All **X** servers have a large core of common functionality, and differ only in the few areas relating to hardware capability. As a result, programs don't need multiple control paths (Figure A) with frequent checks to see if some particular facility is available on this implementation. Such branching program structures are common with systems like GKS, for example, which allow many aspects of the implementation to be optional. But with **X**, you can normally isolate the specific programming required for the few areas of difference to the setup or initialization part of the application, and thereafter use a single control-path (Figure B).[1] And as we mentioned in Module 7.1, by using the Toolkit, most applications programmers can avoid having to learn much about the low-level Xlib programming, and leave the handling of different server capabilities (such as colour versus monochrome) to the Toolkit internals.

Interactions with window manager and other applications

As we saw in Module 9.5, when writing an **X** application you have to consider its interaction with the window manager. You can't assume that you will have a particular window manager, nor that your application's window is a particular size. You must be prepared to operate in the environment that the window manager gives your application. You must also be aware that there are likely to be other clients running on the same display, and that to some extent these will be competing for server resources, such as colours in the colormap, server memory for fonts, etc. It is good practice to free resources after use when you don't need them any more.

---

[1] In many cases, what is happening internally is that Xlib is finding out about the server's capabilities, and is setting up internal parameters accordingly; later, when other Xlib functions come to be called, they will operate within these constraints determined during initialization. So within Xlib different control-paths may be used, but this is transparent to the applications programmer.

Making your application customizable

Module 12.1 showed how applications employing Xlib's resources mechanism are easier to use and to integrate into an overall system, because they can be customized. You too should follow the conventional wisdom, and ensure that your applications are user-customizable. When you are writing an application, remember that you can't really be sure where that application may eventually be used, and the users may speak a different language and be working in a very different environment.

In almost any application area, programming for portability and machine independence is good discipline even if, to the best of your current knowledge, the software will will only ever be run on the one platform. Similarly when you are writing programs, if you keep in mind that your software may need to be heavily customized later on in ways that you can't easily foresee, you can anticipate problems and avoid pitfalls and bad design which would limit the usefulness of your software.

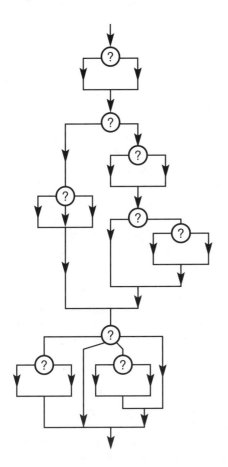

Figure A.   Optional functionality in a system can lead to complex, branching, control paths in applications.

Figure B.   X applications have predominantly a straight, unbranched, control path.

14.2   User interface management systems and other development tools

'User interface management systems' and 'interface design tools' let you develop the user interface of your program interactively by manipulating objects on screen rather than specifying them by writing lines of code. They let you build prototype applications quickly and easily. Other development systems use interpreted languages to facilitate rapid development.

Even though toolkits simplify **X** programming a lot and reduce the amount of code required, writing **X** applications in the conventional way is still complex, lengthy, and error-prone. This is partly because there is a lot of detail to be handled, partly because some aspects of **X** programming are genuinely tricky, but mostly because it is so long-winded: as we saw in Module 5.2.2, even a tiny **X** program can take hundreds of lines of code. Another factor is that you are designing something which is essentially visual — the graphical user interface — using the verbal and procedural methods of a programming language.

Interface design tools (IDTs) or **layout editors** are a way of simplifying **X** programming. They allow you to build the layout part of the application graphically and interactively. You no longer write some code to create an 'XYZ' widget, and define its colour and text characteristics, and position. Instead, you drag into a work area an icon representing the type of widget you want, position it where you want it, type directly into the label the text that it is to contain, etc. (Figure A). You can set other more complex characteristics with interactive dialogs — still without programming. Module 7.1 illustrated an idealized view of what building an interface ought to be like! An interesting development would be to combine the interactive layout approach with a virtual reality system so that, with a data glove and a video headset, you could open a toolbox of widgets with your hand, pick up in your fingers the widgets you want, and place them directly on your workplace. You could write the text labels in with your virtual pen, and paint the widgets with spray-cans!

Some systems let you develop the interface graphically, but when you are finished they generate lines of C or some other language from the graphical definition, which you then incorporate in the program. The problem with this is that once you've finished the program, if you want to alter the interface you have to go back, change the graphical representation, and regenerate the C code: any manual changes you have made to the original generated code are lost and have to be re-incorporated.

User interface management systems (UIMSs) are a further extension of layout editors, allowing you to specify not just the static layout and appearance of the interface, but also its dynamics or behaviour as well. For example, you can create and destroy components, change the contents of labels and buttons, manage menus and pop them up and down as appropriate, resize windows, and similar functions which are beyond the capabilities of a layout editor. Typically you do this using an in-built interpreted language specially designed for **X** programming, making specification of callbacks and other aspects of user interface coding very easy. These systems are usually well integrated, and you make changes to a program in just the same way as you developed it: the graphical representation you work with and the specification language *is* the source-code of the program, so there is no separate, previously generated code, which can get out of step with the graphical representation. Some UIMSs even include C-language interpreters, so you can interactively run your (half-built) application and check that what you've done so far is correct.

UIMSs are an area of **X** where major developments are occurring; there are already dozens of different systems available from commercial and academic sources, and more and more sophisticated systems are becoming available.

The Motif user interface language, UIL (Module 7.5.1), addresses some of the same problems as UIMSs, but it is still a procedural method, and only specifies the static layouts of the widgets and their characteristics. It doesn't let you change things graphically or interactively, nor does it have any programming facilities for specifying the dynamics of the user interface — how windows change in response to user actions, and how the different parts of the application relate to and invoke others.

Other development systems

New types of development system are also starting to emerge from the research community. Some systems of note are Xtent from AT&T, WINTERP (a widget interpreter) from Hewlett-Packard Labs, and Tcl from Berkeley. While they differ a lot in their style of use, all of these systems generally offer very rapid prototype development via an interpreted language. Some are based on Lisp, others on an extension the standard **X** notation used in defaults files. These tools are a good indicator of what to expect from commercial systems in the near future: a very productive environment, with very high-level and expressive programming facilities.

Another example of this type of system is WKSH from UNIX System Laboratories. This is a windowing version of the Korn shell; it is a shell (command-line interpreter) with enhancements that allow the programmer to create and handle Motif or OPEN LOOK widgets. Thus it is possible to develop windowed applications by writing shell scripts (command procedures) instead of C or other compiled code.

Figure A. With a UIMS you build the user interface interactively.

14.3   Migrating old applications to X — enhanced terminal emulators

---

Extended and programmable terminal emulators can be customized and configured for particular character-based applications, allowing a full graphical X user interface to be added as a front end, without changing the application at all.

Most existing programs have not been written to use **X**, because it is only a relatively new system. We already saw in Module 10.3 that terminal emulators allow you to use character-based applications within **X**. There are now enhanced systems available which, though they are still essentially terminal emulators, go far beyond straightforward mimicking of a character terminal, and allow you to add an **X** front-end to a character-based application without changing it at all. (These systems have sometimes been called 'frontware'.)

The simplest systems provide a terminal emulator window, but with an attached control panel containing pushbuttons. You can configure (with a script file) what each button does — typically enter text into the window as though it were typed from the keyboard, to run commands or to select some function in an application.

The more advanced systems are fully programmable, and can be used to provide much more sophisticated front-ends. The programmer can specify that when the terminal emulator receives a particular stream of characters from the application, instead of just displaying them at the appropriate position on the **X** window, the emulator is to perform other more complex actions, which are programmed in the script language. The programmer can use all **X**'s facilities to improve the user interface. For example, the front-end can make use of components such as scrollbars, pushbuttons, dialogs, etc. With sufficient programming, the old character-based interface can be completely hidden, and what the user gets is a full-function graphical interface.

As a simple example, consider a character-based application which always prints its cryptic, computer-oriented, error messages on line 24 of the screen — messages like ERR-72 or ERR-53, as shown in Figure A. We program the emulator to recognize when the characters output by the application would cause the string ERR- to be printed at the beginning of line 24. However, instead of printing them, we now extract the characters following the ERR- prefix, giving us the error number. Then in our emulator script we translate this number into the corresponding English-language message, and display it as an **X** dialog (Figure B). Of course, the application could be improved further by providing much more in the front-end than just error handling, as we describe in the next module.

The example above transforms characters coming *from* the application into an enhanced action on the user interface (**X**) side. We can also do the reverse: add extra components into the user interface on the **X** side, and transform their activity into characters to be sent *to* the application. For example, to provide a button to exit the application, we create a pushbutton in the script, and program it to input the characters QUIT<*return*> when it is pressed. Or consider incorporating a scrollbar into an enhanced version of a text editor: this is programmed so that when the scrollbar is moved, its callback inputs to the editor, as text, the commands necessary to scroll forward or back the appropriate number of lines.

A big advantage of these systems is that the original application hasn't been changed at all; it doesn't matter what language it was written in, and you don't even need the source code. You can enhance applications for which you have lost the source code (your 20-year-old invoicing program in Cobol, perhaps) or never had it (a commercial database system, or a standard utility program provided with your operating system). And because you're not changing the application, you are certain it will continue to work correctly, so you can use this technique on applications which are so old that nobody knows how to maintain them, but which are still crucial to your organization. The commercial **X** versions of a well-known integrated office-automation system and of a leading spreadsheet package use **Alex**, which is a system of this type.

In the next module we look in more detail at how these systems work, and how you can use them to add improved **X** user interfaces even to applications running on machines that don't support **X**.

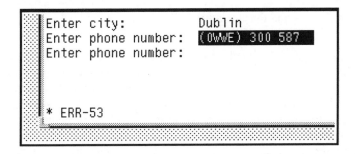

Figure A.   Cryptic textual error message from a character-based application.

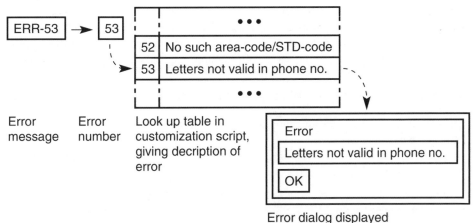

Figure B.   The same error message transformed by an enhanced terminal emulator.

14.3   Migrating old applications to X — enhanced terminal emulators

14.3.1   How enhanced terminal emulators work

Enhanced terminal emulators don't contain hard-coded rules specifying rigidly how characters from the application it is running are to be displayed on the emulator's window. Instead, they allow the programmer to write a customization program or script which creates a user interface in the emulator's X window, and specifies how this interface and the application interact.

With a physical terminal there is a fixed correspondence between characters the application sends to the terminal and what appears on the screen; this is determined by the firmware in the terminal. With a normal terminal emulator there is a similar relationship between characters sent and what appears in the emulator's **X** window, determined by the type of emulation — for example, VT100 or Tek 4014 — which is hard-coded into the emulator program (Figure A). However, with the new tools this mapping is no longer fixed; it is programmable in a high-level language so you can tailor the emulator for a particular application by writing a customization script. So the user gets an enhanced **X** interface (provided within the emulator) while leaving the original application unaltered (Figure B).

In the simplest case the interface in the emulator's window will look very like the screen of the character-based terminal. More sophisticated customizations will provide a highly graphical interface which hides most of the complexity, and perhaps awkwardness, of the original application. For example, the character-based application may require the user to type in a particular code in some field, obliging the user to remember the type of code and which particular one to use. The **X** front-end could easily alter this, so that a menu or dialog listing the valid codes is presented instead, and the user just has to select one with the mouse-pointer.

A different customization script is required for each application customized, although the main terminal emulator program remains the same in each case. For commercial applications built using systems like these, such as the spreadsheet mentioned in the previous module, the total product shipped consists of the emulator itself, the standard application, and the customization script. For major applications, the customization process is quite lengthy and involves a lot of programming in the customization language.

Migrating applications on platforms that do not support X

Module 10.3.1 showed how an emulator need not run on the same machine as the application: they can be connected via a network, and the same is true here. Figure C shows an elderly Cobol application running on an elderly IBM mainframe, customized using an emulator executing on a UNIX workstation, with the **X** server running elsewhere.

In this way an **X** front-end can even be added to an application continuing to run on a platform which does not itself support **X**. The only requirement is that the emulator and the application be able to communicate over the network; in practice this means that the 'old' machine must at least support networking software and some form of remote execution, such as telnet for a TCP/IP network.

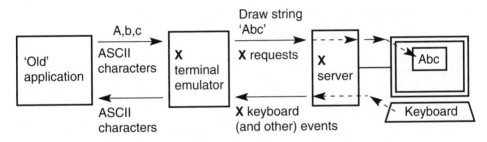

Figure A.   Output on the X screen in a standard terminal emulator is determined by the
type of physical terminal emulated.

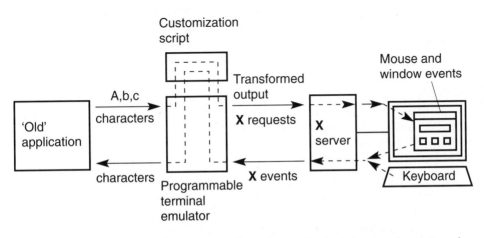

Figure B.   In a programmable terminal emulator, the application's input and output can be
manipulated by a customization script.

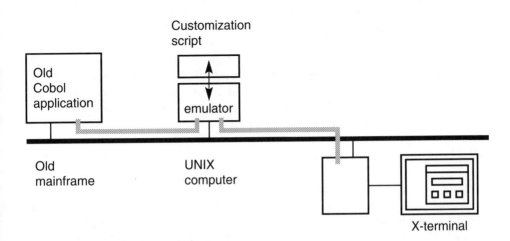

Figure C.   The 'old application', the terminal emulator, and the X server can all be
executing on different computers.

14.4   Porting from other window systems, and multiple-platform applications

Specially developed toolkits simplify porting applications written for other window systems to run under **X**. Development systems are available which let you write a single source program that you can then compile and link on different target platforms, such as Microsoft Windows and the Macintosh, to give you the same application on several platforms, each with the native look and feel of its particular platform.

Terminal emulators let you use character-based applications under **X**, but they don't let you use applications that were written for other window systems. If the particular window system is the native one for your workstation or PC, there may be an **X** server that runs on that window system, and that will let you run both **X** and native window applications together on your screen. Otherwise, you must get the source code of the application, and port it to **X**.

Converting an application manually can be very difficult: the functions provided by the other window system, and the style of programming it requires, may be very different from **X**'s. To reduce the amount of work required, some vendors have provided special migration toolkits.

- Sun produced the Xview toolkit to simplify converting SunView applications to **X**. This has been designed so that with the minimum of modification an Xview source program can be recompiled and relinked with the Xview and **X** libraries instead of the old SunView ones. The structure of the source program is the same as before, and converting a program takes a fraction of the time that would be necessary for a re-write. Xview is not a standard toolkit (that is, not Intrinsics-based) because it has to follow the program structure imposed by SunView and cannot use the event loop and despatch architecture of the standard **X** Toolkit.

- A toolkit has recently been announced which allows you to port Microsoft Windows programs to Motif and UNIX. On your UNIX system you compile your Microsoft Windows source using this special toolkit, and the result is a UNIX Motif application. (There are also courses available on how to port Microsoft Windows applications to Motif without special toolkits.)

GUI-independent toolkits

Special toolkits for converting from another window system to **X** are not common. However as we mentioned in Module 7.6, there are several GUI-independent toolkits available, which allow you to write a single application suitable for multiple platforms. They support not just different machine-types, but also different combinations of GUI and operating system. Rather than using a portable window system such as **X**, these systems aim to let you write an application that is portable across window systems.

Typically these systems allow the same source program to be used for **X** (usually Motif under several variants of UNIX and perhaps VMS, and occasionally OPEN LOOK under UNIX), Microsoft Windows, the Macintosh, and maybe Presentation Manager. Instead of writing your program to use the specific components, characteristics and features of one GUI, you program in terms of generic objects and functions. For example, you don't use a Motif scrollbar and Motif-specific features for controlling scrolling. Instead, you work with a more abstract scrollbar and scrollbar functions, which at a lower level inside the toolkit map onto the particular functionality provided by each GUI's scrollbar. In each case the resulting application is true to the style of its target system. (So the version of the application generated for the Macintosh has the standard Macintosh look and feel, and is quite different from the version of the same program generated for a VMS Motif system, although overall they offer similar functionality.)

These systems achieve portability by providing a 'virtual interface' to the graphics and user interface facilities, that is, by abstracting the basic functions and objects required, and providing them at a high level in a platform-independent way. Underneath, a lower-level library on the particular platform maps these high-level abstractions onto the specific mechanisms provided by this system, as shown in Figure A. (Note that for the **X** versions of the application produced this way, it is the look and feel we are most interested in, not the implementation. So, the blocks labelled 'Motif' on the VMS and UNIX systems in the diagram are not necessarily standard, Intrinsics-based, Motif toolkits; how the look and feel is implemented internally is the decision of the developer of the GUI-independent toolkit.)

These systems are useful where the same application has to be made available on many platforms, and where you can't assume that **X** is available, or where users may want not to use **X** — for example, if the application you are writing is targeted for standalone PCs and Macintoshes.

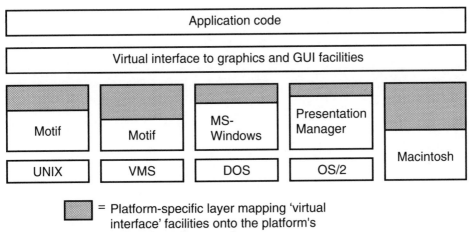

Figure A.   The architecture of a GUI-independent programming system.

14.5   User interface design, and programming

User interface design is a specialist discipline that has very little to do with programming. It should be carried out by specialist user interface designers and not by programmers.

User interface design is a discipline in its own right. It demands its own particular set of skills and experience, and involves a very different approach to that required for programming. For example, one of the most useful approaches in developing a user interface is to produce an initial version quickly, test it on users to find out what is wrong, and iterate like this more or less by trial and error until a representative group of users find the interface satisfactory. If you handled software system design in the same way (as we did in the good old days!) you would end up with a flawed and unmaintainable system (as we did in the good old days!)

Good user interface design requires specialists, usually with graphic design or psychology training, and the interface has to be tested on real end-users. Often, some of the most serious flaws in a program's usability are in completely unexpected areas, and once identified may require very little programming effort to rectify. It is amost impossible to find these problems without end-user testing.

Increasingly, major software project teams now include a 'human factors' or 'human-computer interface' (HCI) member. Unfortunately, many software engineers don't accept the rationale for this, believing that if it involves programming they can do it as well as or better than anyone else. This may explain why many software products are almost unusable.

Summary

This chapter has outlined the factors you have to bear in mind when developing **X** programs. First we looked at the basic components that are required on a development system, and the mechanics of compiling an **X** application. We saw that writing an event-driven application requires its own style of programming, and constraining the user so that data is entered for a particular field requires special handling: for example, using modal dialogs. We moved on to development tools, and looked at user interface management systems for developing new programs, special toolkits and programmable terminal emulators for migrating existing programs to **X**, and systems to let you write a single program which can be built for many different platforms. Finally, we looked at the development of the human aspect of the user interface, and suggested that this should not be left to programmers at all.

Chapter

15 Epilogue

15.1 The MIT **X** Consortium

15.2 The **X** standards

15.3 Sources of further information and assistance

Introduction

In this epilogue we finish by looking at factors that affect the future viability of **X** — how you can be confident that **X** will continue to be developed and enhanced, without allowing incompatible and divergent versions to proliferate, how you can get more information to help you use **X** to your best advantage, and how the future of **X** might develop.

15.1   The MIT X Consortium

The MIT X Consortium is a self-financing 'vendor-neutral' body, which promotes the development of X. It administers the current X standards, and plays a large part in enhancing and developing the core system.

Initially **X** was developed at MIT, jointly by the Laboratory for Computer Science and Project Athena for their own purposes. Other organizations started to adopt it and when it became clear, at the beginning of 1988, that **X** was going to have a significant role in the commercial computer industry, the **X** Consortium was founded. Its aims are:

- to promote the further development of **X**,

- to promote cooperation in creating standard interfaces for all layers of **X**,

- to provide coordinated technical and administrative leadership in these efforts, in a way that is vendor-neutral.

Another way of looking at it is that the Consortium is the keeper of the standards, but unlike most formal standards bodies, it is also a driving force pushing **X** forward. It needed to be formed to reassure commercial vendors in the early days that **X** would have a continuing and standardized future. MIT was the natural choice for leading such a body, because that is where **X** began, it is a neutral third party as far as vendors are concerned, and a single system architect was necessary to avoid design by committee.

The Consortium is financially self-supporting. Any organization can join. Large organizations become 'members', small organizations can become 'affiliates' (which is much cheaper but carries the same benefits).

The Consortium carries out its work mostly by electronic mail, with occasional meetings, followed by public reviews (and revision if necessary) of the resulting work.

The Consortium defines standards for **X**, and also produces sample releases of **X** software. (By 'sample' we mean 'not reference': if the software doesn't behave according to the standards or protocol specifications, then you assume it is the software that is wrong, not the specification.) The best known software is of course the set of full releases of **X**, the most recent being Release 5. The Consortium also funds specific developments, such as the sample implementation of PEX (the Phigs extension), and the **X** testing suite.

The Consortium is also involved in the following activities, some of which have their own working groups of Consortium members:

- Low Bandwidth **X** (LBX) — mechanisms to allow **X** to be be used over low bandwidth connections such as serial lines.

- Multi-threaded server and Xlib, so that **X** Protocol requests which take a long time to execute (such as some PEX 3-D graphics) don't lock up the server completely and stop the user interacting with other applications.

Multi-threading will also let servers take advantage of the multi-processor hardware that is coming into more widespread use.

- The **X** Test Suite (see Module 13.4).

- Revising the PEX protocol, both to accommodate changes necessary to match the final ISO standard of Phigs Plus, and to overcome some problems in the existing implementation.

- Extensions for multi-buffering, and to allow very large requests, which are necessary for PEX and for handling large images.

- Synchronization extension, to allow several streams of **X** activity to be synchronized with each other, and to allow **X** streams to be synchronized with non-**X** activities, such as audio or video.

- Image extension, to support fax group-3, fax group-4, and JPEG compressed images, and to provide image enhancement, geometric transformations and image-drawing operations such as dithering.

- Improved typographic support, to allow kerning, scaling and rotation of characters, and other features such as vertical writing (required by Chinese text, for example).

- Standards and protocols for internationalization, so that new input methods can be added more easily in a way that is not specific to the vendors' implementation of Xlib, and to support bi-directional writing (required by text containing both Arabic and English, for example).

- Designing a toolkit for C++.

- Extensions to the ICCCM, covering among other topics improvements in session management, the Selections Service and handling colormaps. Drag and drop is also being worked on, so that it will operate consistently across different vendors' GUIs — for example, allowing you to drag a Motif item and drop it into an OPEN LOOK application.

In the next module we look at how the Consortium and other bodies define **X** standards.

15.2 The X standards

The current **X** standards are administered by the **X** Consortium. Other organizations such as ANSI and IEEE are actively drawing up standards for various components of the **X** system. Major bodies such as the USA's NIST and the Commission of the European Community have included **X** in their development standards.

X Consortium standards

The major standards defined by the **X** Consortium are:

- The **X** Protocol itself.

- The programming interfaces and 'rules': the basic **X** library Xlib, the Toolkit Intrinsics, and the *Inter-Client Communication Conventions Manual* (IC-CCM).

- The Display Manager protocol, XDMCP.

- Font-related standards: the XLFD naming system, the BDF portable distribution format, and the font server protocol.

- Extensions: the Input Extension and its programming interface, and the Shape Extension for non-rectangular windows. Forthcoming standards will include the following extensions too:

    - PEX
    - Double-buffering, multi-buffering and stereo.

Other standards bodies

The formal standards bodies are developing **X** standards. The ANSI task group X3H3 is working on a standard, *The X Window Data Stream Definition*, that is, the **X** Protocol, including how it should operate over OSI networks. The IEEE P1201.1 group is working on standards for the user interface (which are not specific to **X**, although the group did start out aiming to standardize on an **X** toolkit).

Other large influential bodies have adopted **X** and related technologies. Examples are the European Commission which has specified **X** and Motif as standards for its own use, and the USA's NIST/FIPS which has specified **X** as a standard for US Government systems.

The standards for the look and feels remain with their developers — the Open Software Foundation for Motif, and UNIX System Laboratories (USL) for OPEN LOOK.

15.3   Sources of further information and assistance

Hundreds of articles and many books have been written about **X**. Product catalogues, user groups, consultancy houses and training companies are proliferat-
ing. Much advice and free software is available on the public networks.

As **X** has become increasingly important commercially, we have seen a corresponding
increase in the amount of information and literature relating to it. All the major **market research companies** have produced reports on it, and there is even one research
company specializing exclusively in **X**.

User Groups

On the non-commercial side, there are now many user groups addressing the needs of
the **X** community throughout the world. Many of these serve a local area, while other
cover a whole country or an even wider area. Unfortunately, the contacts for the groups
change frequently, and published lists tend to get out of date very quickly. So, if you
want to find a group near you, the best thing to do is get in touch with the European
group, who may be able to give you up-to-date details of other groups:

> **European X Users' Group (EXUG).** The Group holds a major technical
> conference annually, as well as smaller local meetings. It publishes quarterly
> newsletters, and distributes a hard-copy version of the list of 'Frequently
> Answered Questions' about **X** (FAQ) which is widely circulated on the
> electronic mail networks,[1] and is compiling a catalogue of publicly available
> **X** software. The Group's contact address is:

> The Secretary
> European X Users Group
> PO Box 458
> Cambridge CB4 4AA
> England

> phone: +44 223 426 534
> fax: +44 223 420 251

> *email address:* P.Whitehead@Imperial.ac.uk

Conferences

Conferences covering both commercial and technical issues, and vendor exhibitions of
products and services, are now held regularly throughout the world. The **X** Consortium
itself hosts the **X** Technical Conference every January in Boston, USA. The printed
proceedings of these conferences provide timely information on current trends in **X**.

---

[1] If you have difficulty getting a copy, contact the EXUG, or write or e-mail the author of this book at
the address given in the Preface.

Other information

The MIT **X** Consortium maintains a **register of consultants and trainers** in **X**. It also provides two **electronic mail services**. The first is a bulletin board or electronic mailing list for discussion of **X** topics, which anyone can participate in (and which is also available on the Usenet 'network news' group `comp.windows.x`). To join, send an e-mail message to:

    xpert-request@expo.lcs.mit.edu

The second service is an information repository of programs, documentation, etc., which you can request directly using e-mail. To find out more, send an e-mail message, with the single word 'help' as the subject, or as the only word of the first and only line of the message, to:

    xstuff@expo.lcs.mit.edu

There are many other publicly accessible **archives of software and information** and **discussion groups** on the public networks. These often include new user-contributed software, and are a source of very useful tools. Unfortunately there are so many and they change so frequently that we can't give detailed information here; try asking your organization's network or system manager, or your local user group, or a network provider in your country. (Most of these facilities are supported by research, academic, or computer science organizations, and so are most easily accessed on TCP/IP 'Internet' networks and UUCP e-mail networks. So providers of this type of network are the most likely to be able to help you.)

Software and hardware vendors have a lot of material of more or less usefulness regarding **X**. One of the more interesting is a **catalogue of X software** available from NCD, the X-terminal manufacturer.

Many books and articles have been written about **X**. There are also two regular (monthly/quarterly) publications dedicated to **X** (*The X Resource*, and *The X Journal*) as well as good coverage in many specialist computing publications, especially those dealing with UNIX and open systems (and *Unix World* in particular).

How to obtain X and its documentation

Most workstation vendors already provide **X** for their systems, although sometimes as a chargeable extra option. The many software and consulting companies concentrating on **X** also provide competitive **X** systems which may address any special needs you have, as well as providing **X** as an add-on for systems such as PCs.

Many of these third-party companies can also provide copies of the source code of the MIT Release, as well as the MIT documentation (which provides a complete, if very technical, description of the system). They also offer toolkits such as Motif and OPEN LOOK for systems that don't include them as standard.

Summary

In the three Parts of this book you have seen all the important aspects of the **X** system:

- In the first Part (**X** *in a Nutshell*) you saw briefly how **X** worked, and how it could help you build more flexible and integrated systems, to make your organization more effective.

- The second Part (*How* **X** *Works, in Detail*) covered the details of **X**'s operation, including some of the more complex internal aspects necessary for an understanding of the system and how it can be applied. It described the functions and operation of the server itself, the network link together with the events and requests transmitted over it. You saw the role of the client programs, how they get the look and feel from toolkits, and how the window manager contributes it own look and feel.

- This final Part (*Using the System*) of the book has concentrated on practical matters — how to get started with the system, what's involved in making it available to your users and customizing it for them, how you write **X** programs, and how to go about getting the best performance out of your system. We finished off with a very brief outline of where you can go for further information and assistance.

X is developing on many different fronts: new applications, new development tools, and new user interface systems are constantly emerging. In parallel, existing aspects of the system are being officially standardized so they can form a solid basis for future developments. **X**'s usefulness and power is being enhanced still further by advances in hardware and networking technology, and soon we'll be seeing **X** systems integrated with sound and multimedia facilities, taking advantage of video and synchronization extensions. **X** is continually being applied to new application areas, from medical imaging to hypertext to financial dealing, and even to mission-critical tasks with real-time requirements such as air-traffic control. On the development side, a vast amount of effort is being devoted to making **X** programs easier to produce, we hope to the extent that people who are not computer specialists will be able to build and control useful tools for themselves.

X is a dynamic and rapidly expanding area — we hope you find it as productive and exciting as we have!

Index

In this index, page numbers shown in **bold** type indicate a definition. Entries typically point to the two-page module dealing with a topic, not necessarily to the specific page within that module.

16-bit font, 72, 142
2-D graphics, 17, 68, 88
24-bit colour, 84, 86
3-D graphics, 17, 68, 94, 338
386 PC, 44
4-bit colour, 86
486 PC, 44
7-bit characters, 246
8-bit characters, 246
8-bit colour, 84, 86
8-bit font, 72, 142

A key, 108
accelerators, **158**
access permissions, 270
    .Xauthority file, 270
    administration, 279
    none for selections, 224
    window, 268
accounts package, 28
action
    arm, 294
    move-to-next-message, 294
    notify, 292, 294
    send-this-message, 294
    set, 292, 294
    unset, 292, 294
action procedures, **292**
    user-defined, 294
    widget-defined, 294
actions, **292**, 294, 298
    callbacks and, 294
    translations and, 294
Activate callback, 180
activate pushbutton when released, 292
Ada language, 158, 159
Adobe, 19, 95
advanced inter-client communication, 216
advantages of
    remote execution, 238
    terminal emulators, 242

X, *see* benefits
    xdm, 258
air-traffic control, 344
Alex X program, 329
Alt key, 200, 205
Alt modifier key, 105–107, 112, 264
alternate input sources, **184**
Amiga, 34, 58
ANSI, 138, 139, 340
    standards, 340
ANSI C language, 141
API, *see* application programming interface
Apollo, 38
Apple, 19, 154
Apple Macintosh, *see* Macintosh
AppleTalk, 116, 250
application, *see also* client
    character-based, migrating, 32, *see also* terminal emulator
    class name, 288
    customization, 282–296
    data-driven, **130**
    event-driven, **130**, 322
    independent of window manager, 202
    integration of, 26–37
    multiple, 24
    non-windowed, *see* character-based applications
    other window systems, for, 34
    personal, 41
    profiling, 314
    requirements, 46
    running locally, *see* local execution
    running remotely, *see* remote execution
application class-name
    XClock, 288
    Xedit, 288
    XFontsel, 288
application interface, **14**, **202**
    separate from management, 202

application modal dialog, **323**
application performance, *see* client performance
application programming interface, 38, 166
application window, **64**
application-defaults file, 279, **290**, 292
appres X program, 296
Arabic, 339
arc drawing requests, 68
architecture of
    programs, 322
    server, 58
    server extension, 96
    widgets, 168
    X, client/server, 4
arm action, 294
ASCII, 22, 32, 56, 72, 107–110, 132, 138, 141,
    142, 178, 220, 221, 264, 290
    character encoding, 72
    terminals, limitations of, 22
ASCII character handling in terminal emulator,
    246
ASCII representation of pictures, 88
aspect ratio requested, window, 206
Aster*x commercial **X** application, 146
asynchronous operation of events, 104
asynchronous request transmission, 102, **116**
    contrasted with synchronous, 102
    contrasted with system calls, 102
Asynchronous Transfer Mode, *see* ATM
AT&T, 10, 12, 156, 327
Atari, 34, 58
Athena, 156, 169, 182, 288, 292, 294, 296
    pushbutton, 292
ATM network connection, 305
atobm X program, 88
attribute, class name, 288
attribute, resource, **284**
authenticate, **272**
authentication system, *see* Kerberos
authenticator, Kerberos, 276
authenticators, **276**
authorization scheme, Magic Cookie, 269, 270
AUTOEXEC.BAT file, 256
    starting the system from, 256

background resource, 287
backing store, 301, **302**, 303, 308
    performance, 302, 308
backward compatibility, 122
bandwidth, network, 102, **119**, **304**
    versus latency, 119, 304
bandwidth-on-demand network connection, 305
base system, **54**
bc, 123
BDF font format, **72**, 340

benchmarks, 301, 312–315, *see also* performance,
    see also bandwidth
    commercial, 312
benefits for
    directors, CIO, 48
    hardware developers, 48
    management users, 48
    professional users, 48
    sales and marketing, 48
    software developers, 48
    support staff, 48
    system manager, 48
    users, 48
benefits of
    X, 22–49
    freedom of choice, 46
    GUI, 22, 38
    scalability, 44
    upgradability, 46
    window systems, 22
    X-terminal, 36
benefits, financial, of **X**, 44–47
Berkeley, 327
Berkeley UNIX, *see* BSD UNIX
–**bg** flag, 291
bitmap, **88**, *see also* pixmap
    external representation of, 88
    file format, 88
    fonts stored as, 72
    mask for a, **92**
Bitmap Distribution Format, *see* BDF
bitmap fonts, disadvantages, 74
bitmap X program, 88, 147
Bitstream, 73
block, requests do not, *see* requests, asynchronous
    transmission
Bold, Times, font name, 266
Boolean values, 290
branch and head offices, integration, 30
BSD UNIX, 240
bug compatibility mode, 264
button, 10, 174
    insert, 114
    Save, 289
    Select, 224
button grabs, 204
ButtonPress event, 106, 160, 175, 182
ButtonRelease event, 106, 182
buttons widget, 286
byte-ordering, 266

.c file, 188
C key, 107
C language, 11, 88, 120, 138, 139, 158, 166,
    176, 188, 190, 216, 326, 327
    ANSI, 141

C++ language, 176, 190, 339
CAD, 41, 46, 90, 144, 159
CAE, 46, 144, 159
callback, **182**, 180–185, 190, 192, 292, 294, 298
    Activate, 180
    modifyVerify, 180
    notify, 182
    valueChanged, 180
    actions and, 294
    defined by widget, 180
    example of, 182
    file input, 184
    function of, 180
    long, 322
    timer, 184
    translations and, 294
    work procedure, 184
callback function, 185, 290, 294, 322, *see also*
    callback procedure
callback procedure, **180**, 182, 183, 185, 189
    registration of, **180**
CapsLock modifier key, 112, 264
car, look and feel of, 150
cat UNIX program, 228, 242
catalogues, font server, **75**
cc UNIX program, 32
cc:Mail commercial **X** application, 146
centralizing effect of **X**, 40
Cerberus, 272
changing window manager in mid-session, 14
character
    7-bit, 246
    8-bit, 246
    Delete, 246
    newline, 248
character encoding
    in a font, **72**, 141, **142**
    multibyte, 141
    wide, 141
character sets, 142
character underlining, terminal emulator, 248
character-based applications, *see also* terminal
    emulator
    migrating, 32
    integration, 242–248
character-based and X-terminal, compared, 60
child widget, **168**
    managed by composite, 170
child window, **64**
Chinese, 74, 339
chooser, XDMCP, 263
chords, 105, **107**, 112
CIE, 80
CIE L*a*b*, 80
CIE L*u*v*, 80

CIE uvY, 80
CIE xyY, 80
CIE XYZ, 80
CIO, benefits for, 48
class hierarchy, *see* class tree
class name
    application, 288
    attribute, 288
    resource, 288
    widget, *see* widget class
class tree, 176
    gadget, 177
    widget, 296
class, object, **176**
click to type focus policy, **194**
client, **4**, 126–147, *see also* application
    as application program, 4
    communication, *see* inter-client communi-
        cation
    communication with window manager, 206
    connected to multiple servers, 5, 178
    contains application code, 4
    contents of, 128–137
    determines look and feel, 154
    device independence, 16
    effect of colour on, 70
    effect of screen resolution on, 70
    event driven, 130
    examples of, 144–147
    fighting with window manager, 206
    handling two-button mouse, 70
    hardware dependence, limited, 70
    hardware independence, 70
    initial, *see* starting the system
    input method in, 110, 140
    installing, 279
    libraries contained in, 128
    local, on X-terminals, 62
    performance, 308–310
    redraws window, 56
    role of, 126
    sending events between, 218
    separation of server and, 4
    server extension, effect of, 96
    speeding up, 126
    user interface, contains, 56
    window management, performs, 56
client/server architecture of **X**, 4
client/server communication, 100–123
ClientMessage
    WM_DELETE_WINDOW, 206, 207
    WM_SAVE_YOURSELF, 207, 226, 261
ClientMessage event, 207, 218
clipboard, Motif, 186
CLIPBOARD selection name, 220, 224

clipping a window, **66**
clipping region, **88**
closing down the system, 260
    mwm, 260
    xterm, 260
Cobol language, 330
conformance to standards, 122
colormap, **54**, **84**–87, 90, 161, 290, 339
    determines colours visible, 84
    hardware, 86
    installing a, **86**
    manager by window manager, 194
    manipulation, in applications, 84
    pixel value in, 84
    software, 86
    window manager using slots, 86
colour, 78–87
    24-bit, 84, 86
    4-bit, 86
    8-bit, 84, 86
    device independence, 80–82
    effect on client of, 70
    handling many, 86
    requests, 68
    'technicolor' effect, 86
    versus monochrome, 78
colour capabilities, server, 78
colour database, 78
colour resource value, 290
colour specifications
    device independent, *see* Xcms
    internal format, 78
    RGB, 78
colour specifications, **rgb:** prefix in, 78
command procedures, 327
Command widget class, 288
command-line, 78, 126, 160, 178, 240, 242, 291
    flags, 291
    interpreter, 327
commercial benchmarks, 312
commercial **X** application
    Aster*x, 146
    cc:Mail, 146
    FrameMaker, 146
    InterLeaf, 146
    Lotus 1-2-3, 146
    Wingz, 146
    WordPerfect, 146
Commission Internationale de l'Eclairage, 80
comp.windows.x, 343
compatibility between releases, 122
compatibility mode, bug, 264
compatibility, backward, 122
compatibility, upward, 143
compiler, UIL, 188

compiling programs, 320
complex controls hidden on
    televisions, 23
    video cassette recorders, 23
components of server, 58
compose key, **110**
    input method, 140
composite widget, **168** , 170
    keyboard handling, 170
    layout manager, 170
    managing child widgets, 170
Composite widget class, 176, 177
computer aided design, *see* CAD
computer aided engineering, *see* CAE
configuration management, programs, 320
configuration redirection, window manager, 204
conflicting resource specifications, 289
console type, *see* display type
Consortium, *see* **X** Consortium
construction kit for toolkit, Intrinsics, 164
container widget, *see* composite widget
contents of
    ICCCM, 226
    MIT release, 236
contents of events, 106
contrib distribution, 73, 82, 91, 122, 146, 279,
    318
    MIT-developed programs moved to, 122
control character, keysym interpreted as, 108
Control key, 107–109, 205
Control modifier key, 105–108, 112, 264
converter functions, resource, 290, 291
converting resource value, 290
converting selection data, 220
coordinate system, **X**, 68
core distribution, 122
    contents of, 236
Core widget class, 177
corporate computing, integration, 30, 40
cpicker **X** program, 84
CPU power required for X-terminal, 36
CPU, performance, 310
Cray, 11
ctl-alt-Delete key, 107
ctl-C key, 107
ctl-D key, 260
ctl-F key, 109
ctl-S key, 158
Ctrl, *see* **Control**
currency format, internationalized, 138
curses, 136
cursor, **92**
    bitmap, is a, 92
    hot spot, **92**
    user-defined, 92

cursor addressing, terminal emulator, 248
cursor font, 92
customization
    applications, 282–296
    font directory, 264
    problems, 282
    programming for, 325
    requirements, 282
    root window, 264
    server, 264
cut buffers, **214**, 221
    selections, differences, 220
    superseded by selections, 214
cut-and-paste, **24**, 117, 126, 161, 178, 186, 214,
    216, 220, 242
    as inter-client communication, 210
    other window systems, to/from, 34
    properties used for, 214
    terminal emulator, 242
CUT_BUFFER property, 216, 225
CUT_BUFFER0 property, 214
cutting, *see* cut-and-paste
Cyrillic alphabets, 140

daemon, 278
dark-adaptation, 283
data and applications, integration, 30
Data Encryption Standard, *see* DES
data transfer using selections, 222
data-driven applications, **130**
database, 28, 329
database application, integration, 26
database, RGB, *see* colour database
datatypes of properties, 216
dc UNIX program, 23, 152
DEC, v, 10, 12, 19, 42, 94, 112, 156, 158, 242,
    248
decisions
    hardware choice, 42
    software choice, 42
DECnet, 6, 116, 117
decorations added by window manager, **200**
DECwindows, 19
DECwindows, and Motif, 156
defaults file, 178, 218, **284**, 285, 290, 327, *see
    also* resources file
delayed data conversion, selection, 220
Delete character, 246
departmental computing, integration, 30, 40
depth
    of pixmap, **90**
    of screen, **84**
DES, 268, 270
    encryption, 268
    password, 268

design principles of **X**, 8, 55, 143, 203, *see also*
    mechanism as opposed to policy
design principles, server, 54
desk accessories, 144, 146
desk top publishing, *see* DTP
desktop manager, **228**
desktop, virtual, **59**, 196
detecting changes in a property, 216
device calibration for Xcms, 82
device characterization for Xcms, 82
device drivers in server, 4, 70
device independence, 6
    client, 16
    colour, 80–82
    colour specifications, *see* Xcms
    server, 16
Dhrystones, 312
dialog, **22**, 185, 328, 330
    application modal, **323**
    modal, **323**
    modeless, **323**
    system modal, **323**
Digital Equipment Corp., *see* DEC
DIR VMS command, 228, 242
direct manipulation, **22**
DirectColor, 84
directors, CIO, benefits for, 48
directory, font, 76
    customizing, 264
disadvantages of gadgets, 174
discarding unwanted events, 104
display, **4**
display control program, server, 4
DISPLAY environment variable, 240
–display flag, for remote execution, 240
Display Manager Protocol, *see* XDMCP
Display PostScript, **95**
    as example of server extension, 95
display type, 26, 34, 70, 78, 82, 136, 318
distribution, *see* **contrib** distribution, *see* **core**
    distribution
dog, three-headed, 272
DOS, 18, 19, 26, 28, 32–34, 42, 44, 58, 70, 147,
    150, 153, 156, 250, 300, *see also* PC
DOS PCs, emulators for, 32, 250
DOS Windows, *see* Microsoft Windows
double encryption, 274
DPS, *see* Display PostScript
drag, 106, **228**
drag and drop, **156**, 186, 227, 228, 339
drawable, **68**
    pixmap, 90
drivers, *see* device drivers
dropping, **228**
DTP, 19, 43, 46, 144, 160, 185, 220, 228

dynamic memory requirement of X-terminal, 60
dynamic operation of selection, 222

e-mail, *see* electronic mail
ease of use of graphical programs, 22
EBCDIC, 22, 56, 107, 109, 141, 264
    terminals, limitations of, 22
editor, multimedia, 114
editor, resource, 296
editres **X** program, 185, 210, 218, 296
EDT VMS command, 32
EGA, 70
eight-bit, *see* 8-bit
electronic mail, 184, 228, 236, 252, 294, 295,
    343
emacs UNIX program, vii, 32, 146
emulation of three-button mouse, 70
emulation of other look and feel, 154
emulator
    DOS, 250
    PC, software, 32, 250
emulator, terminal, *see* terminal emulator
encapsulation of data, procedures in object, **168**
encoding
    ASCII character, 72
    of characters in a font, **72**, 141, **142**
    of requests and events, **120**
encryption, 272–277
    DES, 268
    double, 274
Enter event, 106, 175 , 182, 292
    used in menus, 106
Enter key, 182
EnterNotify event, *see* **Enter** event
environment variable, 139
    DISPLAY, 240
    PATH, 279
    XAPPLRESDIR, 285
    XFILESEARCHPATH, 285
    XUSERFILESEARCHPATH, 285
    administration, 279
ERR-53, ERR-72, 328
Escape key, 108
escape sequence
    request, similar to, 60
    terminal emulator, 248
/etc/ethers file, 278
Ethernet, 6, 116–118, 235, 305, 306
European Commission standards, 340
European languages, 142
event
    ButtonPress, 106, 160, 175, 182
    ButtonRelease, 106, 182
    ClientMessage, 207, 218
    Enter, 106, 175, 182, 292
    Expose, **56**, 106, 292

    KeyPress, 105–107, 218
    KeyRelease, 105, 107
    Leave, 106, 175, 182, 292
    MotionNotify, 105, 106, 175
    PointerMotion, 105
    PropertyNotify, 216
event handling
    performance, 308
    toolkit, 180–185
event-driven applications, **130**, 322
event-driven programming, 322
event-loop, 185, 322
events, **4**, 104–110
    asynchronous operation of, 104
    contents of, 106
    discarding unwanted, 104
    encoding of, **120**
    function of, 104
    intercepting, 112–115
    keyboard input, 106
    keyboard, interpretation, 106–110
    mechanism, 104
    modifier keys in, 106
    recording, 112
    replaying, 112, 314
    selecting for, **105**
    sending between clients, 218
example of remote execution, 238
example of callback, 182
example of selection, 220
Exit window manager function, 198
Expose event, **56**, 106, 292
    client redraws window, 56
    handled by toolkit, 160, 180
    pixmap used for redraw, 90
Extended Portable Bitmap Toolkit, vii
extensions mechanism, **17**, 120
extensions to **X**, *see* server extension
external representation of bitmap, 88
extra facilities, X-terminal, 62
extras in server, 58

F31 key, 108
f77 UNIX program, 32
False, 185
FDDI, 116, 305
–**fg** flag, 291
file
    *.h, 318
    .login, 279
    .profile, 279
    .rhosts, 279
    .uid, 188
    .uil, 188
    .Xauthority, 270
    .Xresources, 260

.xsession, 260
/etc/ethers, 278
AUTOEXEC.BAT, 256
hosts.equiv, 279
my_startx, 256
myresf, 214
defaults, *see* defaults file
resources, *see* resources file
file access permissions, 270
.Xauthority, 270
file descriptor, 184
file input callback, 184
file manager, 156, 228
File menu, 152, 180
file-server, 62, 273, 276
financial benefits of **X**, 44–47
financial dealing, 344
financial system, integration with, 26
FIPS standards, 340
fixed width font, 72
flags, command-line, 291
floating licence, **43**
–fn flag, 291
focus control, ICCCM rules, 226
focus policy
 click to type, **194**
 controlled by window manager, 194
 pointer-driven, **195**
focus, keyboard, **194**
font, 72–77
 cursor, 92
 16-bit, 72, 142
 8-bit, 72, 142
 administration, 266
 bitmaps, stored as, 72
 catalogues, 75
 directory, 76
 directory listing, 266
 directory, customizing, 264
 encoding of characters in, **72**, 141, **142**
 fixed width, 72
 freeing a, **77**
 ligatures in, 142
 loading a, **76**
 management requests, 68
 naming scheme, *see* XLFD
 outline, *see* scalable font
 PostScript, scalable, 72
 proportional, 72
 rotated, 72
 scalable, 72, 74, 267
 Speedo, scalable, 72
 storage required for, 74
 stored in server, not client, 72
 support for many, 72

text drawing requests, 68, 76
 variable width, 72
 wildcards in name, 72
font encoding
 iso8859-1, 72, 142
 ksc5601.1987-0, 76
 Latin-1, 142
font format
 BDF, 72, 266, 340
 PCF, **72**, **266**
 SNF, **72**, 266
 implementing new, 74
font information, querying for, **76**
font name, wildcard in, 266
font name resource value, 290
font path, **77**
font server, **74**, 120, 121, 123
 chaining, 74
 protocol, 340
font, Times Bold, name, 266
fontset, **142**
fontset, internationalization, **142**
Ford, 150
foreground resource, 284, 288
format of selection, 224
format, font, *see* font format
FORTRAN VMS command, 32
frame relay network connection, 305
FrameMaker commercial **X** application, vii, 146
free software, 169, 252
Free Software Foundation, vii
freedom of choice, benefits of, 46
freedom of choice in hardware and software, 42
freeing a font, **77**
front-end, 184, 244, 328, 330
frontware, 328
ftp UNIX program, 252
ftpd UNIX program, 278
function of callback, 180
function, callback, 184, 185, 290, 294, 322
functions provided by
 Xlib, 132–134
 Intrinsics, 178
 toolkit, 136, 160
 window manager, 194–196

gadget, 308
 class tree, 177
 disadvantages, 174
 Motif, 174
 performance, 174
 pushbutton, 175
 replacement for widget, 174
 window tree, 174
GC, *see* graphics context
-geometry flag, 260

geometry specification, **132**, 290
getting started
    using remote execution, 235
    with **X**, 234–237
getting **X** software, 252
GIFF format pictures, 90
GKS, 128, 320, 324
GNU, vii
goto-end-of-file, 185
grabs, **204**
graphical programs, ease of use of, 22
graphical user interface, *see* GUI
graphics context, **54**, **68**, 69, 76, 142, 161
    text drawing, used in, 76
    use of, 68
graphics hardware limiting performance, 118
graphics requests
    output, 68
    processing, 68
    text, 76
    types, 68
green, 284
groups, window, 196, 226
GUI, benefits of, 22, 38
GUI wars, 154
GUI-independent programming, 332
GUI-independent toolkit, 190
gwm window manager, 196

*****.h file, 318
hardware colormap, 86
hardware dependence
    client, limited, 70
    programming, 324
    server, isolated in, 70
hardware developers, benefits for, 48
hardware independence, client, 70
hardware limiting performance, 118
HCI, 334
head and branch offices, integration, 30
header files required, programming, 318
'Hello world' program, 133, 134, 137
heterogeneous computing environment, 16, 26
Hewlett-Packard, 10–12, 19, 39, 49, 94, 156, 327
hiding network architecture, 28
hierarchy, *see also* tree
    class, 176
    resource names, 286
    widget, 168
    widget, UIL, 188
    window, **64**
hooks, security, 268
horizontal text, 72
host-based security, 268, *see also* **xhost**
hosts.equiv file, 279

hot spot, cursor, **92**
hour-glass, 308
human factors, 334
human-computer interface, 334
hypertext, 344

i18n, 139, *see also* internationalization
IBM, v, 12, 26, 28, 32, 39, 42, 43, 109, 156, 330
–**ic** flag, 291
ICCCM, 206, 210–230, 261, 339, 340
    contents of, 226
    focus control, 226
    property rules, 226
    window grouping, 226
    window manager rules, 226
icon box, **194**, 200
iconic resource, 291
icons implemented by window manager, 194
ideographic oriental language, **140**
IDTs, 326
IEEE, 340
    standards, 340
images, 88–92
imake X program, vii, 320
implementation of
    PC **X** servers, 60
    server, 58–63
    server, third-party vendor, 58
    X-terminal, 60
incompatibility
    between releases, 122
    between toolkits, 122
    caused by server extension, 122
initial client, starting the system, 258–260
initial ticket, Kerberos, **274**, 276, 277
input method, 109, **110**, 120, 124, 126, 140, 141, 225, 339
    client, in, 110, 140
    compose key, **110**, 140
    internationalization, for, 140
    server, separate, 110, 140
input processing in server, 54
input server, **110**, **140**
    pre-editing, 140
Input server extension, 184
insert button, 114
installing
    X, 252
    client, 279
    server, 278
installing a colormap, **86**
INTEGER property type, 216
integration
    applications, 26–37
    branch and head offices, 30

character-based applications, 32, 242–248
corporate computing, 30, 40
data and applications, 30
database application, 26
departmental computing, 30, 40
financial system, 26
head and branch offices, 30
isolated offices, 30
local and remote applications, 28–30
mainframe, with, 26
other window system applications, 34
personal computing, 40
remote and local applications, 28–30
technical barriers to, 42
with Macintosh, 250
with Microsoft Windows, 250
with other window systems, 26, 250, *see also* terminal emulator
workgroup computing, 30, 40
Intel, 32
Inter Client Communication Conventions Manual, *see* ICCCM
inter-client communication, 210–229
advanced, 216
cut-and-paste, 210
properties, 212
requirements, 210
server implements, 210
talk program, 210
inter-process communciation (IPC), 116, 132
intercepting events and requests, 112–115
XTrap, 112
interface design tools, **326**
interface development systems, 189
InterLeaf commercial **X** application, 146
internationalization, 110, 120, 121, **139**, 138–143, *see also* localization, *see also* locale
16-bit font, 142
8-bit font, 142
fontset, **142**
input methods used, 140
multilingual, difference, 139
requirements, 138
internationalized
currency format, 138
menu, 138
number format, 138
text input, 138, 140
text printing, 138, 142
Internet, 343
interpretation of keysym as
control character, 108
lowercase, 108
uppercase, 108

interpreter, command-line, 327
interrupts, 104
Interviews toolkit, 190
Intrinsics, toolkit, **164**–192, 290, 332, 333, 340
as construction kit, 164
functions provided by, 178
resource handling, 281–298
utility functions, 178
widget handling, 176–179
inverse video, terminal emulator, 248
IPC, *see* inter-process communication
ISDN, 30, 116
ISO, 72
font encoding, 72
seven-layer reference model, 128
iso8859-1 font encoding, 72, 142
isolated offices, integration, 30
IST, vii

Japanese keyboard input, 108

kana, 142
Kanji, 109
Kerberos, 269, 272–277, 279, 281
authenticator, 276
how it works, 274
how it works, detailed, 276
initial ticket, **274**, 276, 277
password used in, 270–277
session key, **276**
Ticket Granting Service, **276**, 277
timestamps in, 276
key
Alt, 200, 205
Control, 107–109, 205
ctl-alt-Delete, 107
Enter, 182
Escape, 108
F31, 108
Left, 108
Meta, 196
Return, 292
Right, 108
Shift, 109, 205
Space, 182
compose, **110**
modifier, 112
key grabs, 204
keyboard
re-configuring, 264, 292–295
type, 108
keyboard focus, **194**
keyboard handling
composite widget, 170
terminal emulator, 246
keyboard input

events, 106
interpretation, 106–110
Japanese, 108
keyboard mapping, *see* keyboard re-configuring
keycode, **107**, 108, 264
keysym, mapping to, 108
KeyPress event, 105–107, 218
KeyRelease event, 105, 107
keysym, **108**, 264
case of, 108
keycode, mapping to, 108
Korean graphic character set, 76
Korn shell, 327
windowing, 327
ksc5601.1987-0 font encoding, 76

LAN, *see* local area network
language
Ada, 158, 159
ANSI C, 141
C, 11, 88, 120, 138, 139, 158, 166, 176,
188, 190, 216, 326, 327
C++, 176, 190, 339
Cobol, 330
Lisp, 158, 159, 190, 196, 327
object-oriented, 176, 190
PostScript, 19, 59, 69, 73, 95, 96
language binding, protocol, 132
large data-transfer using selection, 224
latency, network, **119**, **304**
LaTeX UNIX program, vii, viii
Latin-1 font encoding, 142
lawsuits, look and feel, 150
layout editors, **326**
layout manager
LBX, *see* Low Bandwidth X
leaf in tree, primitive widget as, 168
Leave event, 106, 175, 182, 292
used in menus, 106
LeaveNotify event, *see* Leave event
Left key, 108
left-to-right text, 72
libraries contained in client, 128
libraries required, programming, 318
library, *see* Xlib, *see* toolkit
licence
administration, 279
costs, and X, 42
floating, **43**
ligatures in font, 142
limitations of ASCII terminals, 22
limitations of EBCDIC terminals, 22
line drawing requests, 68
Lisp language, 158, 159, 190, 196, 327
listres X program, 296
loading a font, **76**

loading on network connection, 118
local area network, 28, 30
local clients on X-terminals, 62
local connections, 116
local execution, 6, *see also* remote execution
applications on X-terminals, 62
performance, 306
performance optimization, 300
remote, compared with, 306
local telnet on X-terminals, 62
local terminal emulator on X-terminals, 62
local window manager on X-terminals, 62
locale, **139**, *see also* internationalization
localization, **139**, *see also* internationalization
localized
labels, 143
messages, 143
text printing, 143
locally, running applications, *see* local execution
.login file, 279
login window, xdm, 258
long callback, 322
look and feel, **10**, **38**, 150–162, 190
car, 150
client determines, 154
different implementations of same, 190
emulation of other, 154
implemented by toolkit, 158
keyboard, 150
lawsuits, 150
many supported, 154
Motif, OPEN LOOK compared, 156
Motif, standard, 156
OLIT and Xt+, 164
OPEN LOOK, 186
OPEN LOOK and Motif combined, 187
OPEN LOOK, standard, 156
requirements, 152
standard, 156
widget, 164
window manager, 200–203
Xt+ and OLIT, 164
Lotus 1-2-3 commercial X application, 146
low bandwidth network connection, 118, 307,
338
Low Bandwidth X, **307**, 338
lowercase, keysym interpreted as, 108
lpr UNIX program, 32
ls UNIX program, 228, 242

Macintosh, 19, 26, 34, 38, 42, 43, 49, 71, 154,
186, 190, 202, 228, 229, 250, 332, 333
compared with X, 19
hijacking, for X, 34
integration with, 250
Magic Cookie authorization scheme, 269, 270

.Xauthority file, 270
mail, *see* electronic mail
mainframe, 28
  integration with, 26
major opcode of server extension, **96**
make UNIX program, vii, 320
Makeindex UNIX program, vii
management interface, **14**, **202**, *see also* window
    manager
  separate from application, 202
management users, benefits for, 48
manager, desktop, **228**
manual disabilities, 112
manualPage widget, 292
mapping a window, **64**
mars host name, 238
Mary, security example, 274
mask for a bitmap, **92**
Massachusetts Institute of Technology, *see* MIT
maximum size requested, window, 206
mechanism as opposed to policy, 8, 17, 164, 198,
    203, 226, *see also* design principles of
    X
medical imaging, 344
memory
  allocation, and performance, 309
  performance impact, 301, 302, 310
  pixmap requirements, 90
  shared, 302
  virtual, 301
menu, 22, 128, 202
  File, 152, 180
  internationalized, 138
  pop-up, 185
  pull-down, 180, 183, 186
  subwindows in, 64
menu button, 288
menu selection
  paste, 210
  Open, 152
  Save, 180
merging single requests into poly, 132
Meta key, 196
Microsoft Windows, v, 12, 15, 19, 26, 33, 34,
    38, 153, 154, 156, 186, 190, 250, 332,
    333
  compared with **X**, 18
  hijacking, for **X**, 34
  integration with, 250
  Motif similar to, 14, 152, 156, 200
  TCP/IP for, 19
  toolkit for porting, 190
  using telnet with, 19
migrating character-based applications, 32
minimum size requested, window, 206

minor opcode of server extension, **96**
MIT, v, vii, 16, 17, 58, 74, 78, 82, 88, 94, 96,
    97, 120–123, 156, 159, 166, 169, 176,
    184, 210, 212, 214, 218, 224, 236,
    242, 252, 260, 263, 264, 266, 268,
    270, 272, 279, 285, 286, 292, 296,
    305, 312–315, 318, 320, 338, 343, *see*
    also **X** Consortium
  contrib distribution from, 73, 82, 91, 122,
    146, 279, 318
  core distribution from, 122
MIT release, contents of, 236
MIT test suite, 313
MIT **X** Consortium, *see* **X** Consortium
MIT's Release of **X**, 95, 112, 114, 122, 224, 235,
    252, 266, 270, 272, 300, 320, 343
MIT-developed programs moved to **contrib** dis-
    tribution, 122
MIT-MAGIC-COOKIE-1, 268
MIT-SHM server extension, 94, 300
MIT-SUNDRY-NONSTANDARD server exten-
    sion, 264
mnemonics, **158**
modal
  application, *see* application modal
  system, *see* system modal
modal dialog, **323**
modeless dialog, **323**
modifier key, **106**, 112
  Alt, 105–107, 112, 264
  CapsLock, 112, 264
  Control, 112
  Ctrl, 105–108, 264
  Shift, 105–108, 264
  events, in, 106
modifyVerify callback, 180
monochrome, 136, 324
  versus colour, 70, 78
MooLIT toolkit, 187, 202
more UNIX program, 228
Motif, vi, vii, 10, 12, 15, 21, 38, 152–154, 156,
    158, 162, 164, 169, 170, 172, 174,
    176, 177, 180, 187, 188, 190, 191,
    193, 200, 202, 224, 238, 250, 260,
    294, 323, 327, 332, 333, 339, 340, 343
  clipboard, 186
  DECwindows, 156
  gadget, 174
  illustration, 12
  look and feel standard, 156
  Microsoft Windows similar to, 14 , 152,
    156, 200
  OPEN LOOK, combined toolkit, 187
  OPEN LOOK, compared, 156
  Presentation Manager similar to, 14, 152,

156, 200
pushbutton, 294
selection box, 170
toolkit implementation, 186
UIL, 188
Motif Resource Manager, 188
Motif Window Manager, *see* mwm
MotionNotify event, 105, 106, 175
mouse, two-button versus three, 70
move-to-next-message action, 294
MRM, *see* Motif Resource Manager
MS-DOS, *see* DOS
MS-Windows, *see* Microsoft Windows
multi-threaded server, 338
multi-threaded Xlib, 338
multi-threading, 322
multibyte character encoding, 141
multilingual, internationalization is not, 139
multimedia editor, 114
multimedia with Virtual Screen, 114
multiple applications, 24
multiple clients supported by server, 4
multiple servers used by one client, 4
multiple screens, 64
multitasking, 24
MVS, 42
mwm window manager, 202, 238, 260
    closing down the system, 260
my_startx file, 256
myresf file, 214

−name flag, 289
name of server extension, 96
naming of fonts, *see* XLFD
NCD, 343
network
    bandwidth, 102, **119**, 304
    latency, **119**, 304
    performance, 304–307
    performance figures, 118, 304
    performance, limits, 118
network architecture, hiding, 28
network connection
    Xlib's role, 132
    ATM, 305
    bandwidth, **119**, 304
    bandwidth-on-demand, 305
    frame relay, 305
    latency, **119**, 304
    loading on, 118
    low bandwidth, 118, 307, 338, *see also*
        Low Bandwidth X
    phone lines, 118
    physical, 116
    record-oriented, 116
    reliable stream, **102**

remote, 116
RS-232, 307
stream, 116
types supported, 6, 116
Network extensible Window System, *see* NeWS
Network File System, *see* NFS
network independence, **6**, 16, **116**
network loading
    diskless workstation, 36
    figures, 118, 304
    gadgets, 174
    X-terminal, 36
network transparency, **6**, 16
Neuron Data toolkit, 190
newline character, 248
NeWS, 19
    compared with **X**, 19
    PostScript used by, 19
NeXT, 26, 34, 250
NFS, 234, 238, 270, 278, 279
    use in X-terminal, 60
NIST standards, 340
non Intrinsics-based toolkits, 186, 190
non-windowed applications, *see* character-based
        applications
notify action, 292, 294
notify callback, 182
Novell, 250
number format, internationalized, 138
numeric keypad, 108

object
    widgets as, **168**
    class, **176**
    encapsulation of data and procedures in, **168**
    window, 177
object-oriented
    language, 176, 190
    programming, **168**, **176**
    programming, widgets, 176
    toolkit, 10
obtaining **X** software, 252
oclock **X** program, 146
Off, 290
off the spot pre-editing, 140
off-screen images, performance, 308
offices, computer integration, 30
OI toolkit, 190, 191, 202
old applications, *see* character-based applications
OLIT toolkit, 164, 186
    implementation, 186
    OPEN LOOK look and feel, 186
    Xt+, Xview, same look and feel, 164
olwm window manager, 238
On, 290
on the spot pre-editing, 140

opcode
    major, of server extension, **96**
    minor, of server extension, **96**
Open File, 102
Open Interface toolkit, 190
OPEN LOOK, vi, vii, 10, 12, 21, 38, 153, 156,
    162–164, 169, 186–188, 190, 191, 193,
    200, 202, 203, 212, 224, 327, 333,
    339, 340, 343
    illustration, 12
    look and feel, 186
    look and feel standard, 156
    Motif, combined toolkit, 187
    Motif, compared, 156
    push pin, 156, 200
    toolkit implementation, 186
OPEN LOOK Intrinsics Toolkit, *see* OLIT toolkit
OPEN LOOK Window Manager, *see* olwm
Open menu selection, 152
Open Software Foundation, *see* OSF
open systems, 43, 343
OpenWindows, vii, 12, 19
    compared with **X**, 19
operating system
    Xlib analogy, 132, 158, 166
    independence, desktop manager, 228
    support for **X**, 26
    synchronous system calls, 102
    system administration, 36
OSF, 12, 156, 186, 313, 340
OSF/Motif, *see* Motif
OSI, 6, 38, 116–118, 340
other window systems
    compared with **X**, 18
    cut-and-paste to/from, 34
    hijacking, for **X**, 34
    integration with, 26, 250
    porting from, 332
    W, 102
outline font, *see* scalable font
output graphics requests, 68
output handling, terminal emulator, 248
output processing in server, 54, 64–69
output, text, *see* text printing
over the spot pre-editing, 140
overlapping windows, 24
ownership, selection, **220**

P1201.1, 340
paging, 36
palette, **84**
paned widget, 286
password, 240, 268
    used in Kerberos, 270–277
    DES, 268
paste menu selection, 210

pasting, *see* cut-and-paste
PATH environment variable, 279
pbmplus, vii
PC, v, 16, 18, 19, 26, 28, 32–34, 42, 44, 47, 49,
    58, 60, 63, 70, 74, 86, 107, 109, 145,
    147, 150, 160, 190, 250, 256, 258,
    264, 281, 332, 333, 343
    X servers for, 34, 42, 44, 58, 60, 62, 63,
    256, 258, 262, 300, 310
    386, 44
    486, 44
    DOS, emulators for, 32
    emulator, software, 250
PCF font format, **72**, **266**
performance, 300–315
    X Toolkit, effect of, 309
    Xlib special features, 132
    asynchronous network, 304
    backing store, 302, 308
    bandwidth, effect of, 119, 304
    client, 308–310
    CPU, 310
    event handling, 308
    gadgets, effect on, 174
    graphics hardware, 300
    intercepting events and requests, 112
    latency, effect of, 119, 304
    limited by hardware, 118
    local execution, 306
    local execution optimization, 300
    memory allocation, 309
    memory, impact on, 301, 302, 310
    network, 118, 304–307
    network loading figures, 118, 304
    off-screen images, 308
    platform optimization, 300
    remote execution, 306
    response time, 306
    round-trip, effect on, 103
    round-trips, minimizing, 308
    save-unders, 302, 308
    server, 300–303
    shared libaries, 310
    shared memory, 302
    X-terminal, 62
personal applications, 41
personal computers, 58, *see* Macintosh, *see* PC,
    see Amiga, *see* Atari
personal computers, server for, 58
personal computing, integration, 40
PEX server extension, 68, 95, 338–340
Phigs, 68, 95, 338, 339
Phigs extension to **X**, *see* PEX
phone lines, network connection, 118
pictures, 88–92

ASCII representation of, 88
bitmaps, 88
cursor, 92
GIFF format, 90
pixmaps, 90
raster file, 90
TIFF format, 90
pink, 289
pixel oriented, **X**, 160
pixel value in colormap, 84
pixel-based drawing, 68
pixmap, **54**, **68**, **90**, 290, 301, *see also* bitmap
    as drawable, 90
    depth of, **90**
    in expose-event handling, 90, 308
    memory requirements, 90
    stored in server, 90
    used for tiling, **90**
platform-independent programming, 332
plug-in-card server, 58
point-to-point protocol, 30, 116
pointer, **92**
pointer-driven focus policy, **195**
PointerMotion event, 105
policy, mechanism as opposed to, *see* mechanism as opposed to policy
poly, merging single requests into, 132
polygon drawing requests, 68
pop-up menu, 185, *see also* menu
    window manager, 196
portability of server, 70
portability limitations, 105, 107
Portable Compiled Format, *see* PCF
PostScript, 19, 59, 69, 73, 95, 96
    Display, *see* Display PostScript
    scalable font, 72
    Type 1 font, 73
    used by NeWS, 19
PPP, 30, 116
pre-editing, input server, 140
Presentation Manager, 12, 15, 38, 153, 154, 156, 190, 200, 333
    Motif similar to, 14, 152, 156, 200
price/performance, 44
PRIMARY selection name, 220, 222
primitive widget, **168** , 172
    as leaf in tree, 168
    illustrated, 172
Primitive widget class, 177
PRINT VMS command, 32
procedure, callback, 180, 182, 183, 185, 189
professional users, benefits for, 48
.**profile** file, 279
profiling, application, 314
program generators, 189

program, 'Hello world', 133, 134, 137
programmable terminal emulator, 328–330
programmable window manager, 196
programming, 318–334
    Xlib, 166, 179
    customizability, 325
    event-driven, 322
    GUI-independent, 332
    hardware dependence, 324
    header files, 318
    input, 323
    libaries, 318
    object-oriented, **168**, **176**
    other window system programs, 332
    platform-independent, 332
    requirements, 318
    sample programs, 134–137
    shared libaries, 318
    techniques, 322–325
    toolkit, 166, 179
    toolkit use intended, 158
    toolkit versus **Xlib**, 166, 179
    UIMSs, 326
    user interface, 334
    window manager interface, 324
programs
    architecture of, 322
    compiling, 320
    configuration management, 320
progressive disclosure, 23
Project Athena, 272, 338
property, 54, **100**, 103, 104, **206**, 207, 211–216, 220, 222, 224, 226, 230, 231
    CUT_BUFFER, 216, 225
    RESOURCE_MANAGER, 214, 285
    WM_CLASS, 212, 288
    WM_COMMAND, 207, 261
    WM_HINTS, 226
    WM_ICON_NAME, 226
    WM_INFORMATION, 226
    WM_NAME, 212
    WM_PROTOCOLS, 206, 207, 218, 226
    XDCCC_LINEAR_RGB_CORRECTION, 82
    XDCCC_LINEAR_RGB_MATRICES, 82
    cut-and-paste, used for, 214
    detecting changes in, 216
    how it works, 206
    ICCCM rules, 226
    inter-client communication, 212
    per window, 212
    reading/writing, 212
    round-trip required, 212
    stored on root window, 214
    storing system-wide resources, 214
    typing of, 216

used by window manager, 206
used by **xrdb**, 214
user-defined types, 216
versus file, for resources, 214
Xcms, use in, 82
property type
    INTEGER, 216
    STRING, 216
    WINDOW, 216
    WM_HINTS, 216
    WM_SIZE_HINTS, 216
PropertyNotify event, 216
proportional font, 72
proprietary, **X** is not, 16
protection, window, *see* window security
protocol, *see also* XDMCP, *see also* font server
        protocol, *see also* **X** Protocol
    language binding, 132
    reliable stream, **116**
protocol analyser, 314
protocol, font server, 340
pseudo-terminal, **246**
PseudoColor, 84
pull-down menu, 180, 183, 186, *see also* menu
push pin
    added by window manager, 200
    OPEN LOOK, 156, 200
pushbutton, 10, 96, 112, 128, 175, 180, 182,
        288, 289, 292, 294, 314, 328
    Athena, 292
    activate, when released, 292
    gadget, 175
    Motif, 294
    reset, when released, 182
    set, when pressed, 182, 292
pwd UNIX program, 242

querying for font information, **76**
Quit window manager function, 198

radio button widget, 170
rarpd UNIX program, 278
raster file pictures, 90
reading alternate input sources, 184
real-time **X**, requirements for, 344
record-oriented network connection, 116
recording events and requests, 112
rectangle drawing requests, 68
rectangular objects, 177
RectObj widget class, 177
redraw, window, client performs, 56
reference implementation, 58, **338**, *see also* sample implementation
        ple implementation
regions, **132**
registration
    alternate input sources, **184**

callback procedure, **180**
timer, **184**
work procedure, **185**
release number, **X**, **121**
releases, **121**
    compatibility between, 122
    incompatibility between, 122
reliable stream
    network connection, **102**
    protocol, **116**
remote execution, 6, 116, 330
    −display flag, 240
    rexec used for, 240
    rsh used for, 240
    setenv used for, 240
    telnet used for, 240
    advantages of, 238
    commands used for, 240
    example of, 238
    getting started with, 235
    local, compared with, 306
    performance, 306
    problems, 306
    security threat, 240
    terminal emulator, 244
    using, 238–240
    window manager, 198
remote login compared with **X**, 18
remote network connection, 116
remotely, running applications, *see* remote execution
        cution
reparenting window by window manager, **205**
replaying
    events, 112, 314
    messages, security threat, 272, 276
    requests, 112
    sessions, 314
replies to requests, 102, **103**, 212
requests, **4**, 100–103, *see also* graphics requests
    asynchronous transmission, **102**, **116**
    block, do not, *see* asynchronous transmission
        sion
    constructed by Xlib, 100
    contents of line drawing, 68
    encoding of, **120**
    escape sequence, similarity, 60
    function of, 100
    high-level, are, 100
    intercepting, 112–115
    merging single into poly, 132
    network load of, 100
    recording, 112
    replaying, 112
    replies to, 102, **103**, 212
    round-trip, requiring, 103

synchronous transmission, 103
translated into hardware commands, 70
types, 100
requirements
inter-client communication, 210
to get started, 234
window manager, 194
reset pushbutton when released, 182
resizing, widget, 170
resolution independence in toolkit, 160
resource, **284**–296
Xlib, implemented by, 284
Xlib, using with, 284
background, 287
foreground, 284, 288
iconic, 291
attribute, **284**
class name, 288
command-line, on, 291
conflicts, resolving, 289
converter functions, 290, 291
editor, 296
names, 284–289
semantics, 290
system-wide, stored in property, 214
Toolkit, used by, 290
tools, 296
use recommended, 325
viewer, 296
where specified, 285
widget, related, 284
wildcards, 288
resource converters, **290**
Resource Database, **284**, 285, 289
resource file, 279, **284**, 285, 288, 290, *see also*
defaults file
Resource Manager, **284**–296
resource names
hierarchy, 286
tree, 286
resource specifications
conflicting, 289
sub-name in, 286–288
wildcards in, **288**
resource value, 284
converting, 290
translation table, 292
types, 290
using returned, 285
RESOURCE_MANAGER property, 214, 285
resources, computer, use of, 24
response time, 306
Return key, 292
reusability of widgets, 176
reverse video, *see* inverse video

rexec used for remote execution, 240
RGB colour specifications, 78
disadvantages of, 78, 80
RGB colour value, 78, 80–82, 84, 86, 87, 290
RGB database, *see* colour database
rgb: prefix in colour specifications, 78
.rhosts file, 279
Right key, 108
RISC, 145
rlogin UNIX program, 18, 268
role of
client, 126
server, 54–57
session manager, 261
toolkit, 136, 158
widget sets, 169
window manager, 194–196
ROM, 55
Roman-language, 74, 76
root, 272, 279
root window, **64**, 66, 82, 114, 205, 214, 285
customization, 264
property stored on, 214
virtual, **59**, 64
rotate text, 72
round-trips, 62, **102**, 103, 119, 212, 304, 307–
309
effect on performance, 103
minimizing, for performance, 308
minmized by **X** Toolkit, 309
requests requiring, 103
when reading/writing property, 212
RS-232 network connection, 307
rsh UNIX program, 235, 240, 256, 258, 268
starting the system, 256
used for remote execution, 240
rubber-banding, 56, 62, 105
running applications
locally, *see* local execution
remotely, *see* remote execution

s++, 141
sales and marketing, benefits for, 48
sample implementation, 58, 120, 156, **338**, *see
also* reference implementation
sample program
Xlib, 134
toolkit, 136
save, 158, 182
Save button, 289
Save menu selection, 180
save widget, 287
save-unders, **302**, 303, 308
performance, 302, 308
save_myfile(), 182
scalability, benefits of, 44

scalable font, 72, 267
    PostScript, 72
    Speedo, 72
sccs UNIX program, vii
screen, **64**
    colour profile, 82
    depth of, **84**
    server supports multiple, 64
    virtual, **58**, **64**
screen resolution, effect on client of, 70
screen saver, **264**
script file
    starting the system, 256–260
    startup, server settings, 264
scrollbar, 10, 22, 39, 84, 126, 128, 150, 152,
        154, 160, 164, 169, 170, 172, 180,
        187, 188, 200, 202, 294, 314, 328, 333
search widget, 289
seat, **4**
SECONDARY selection name, 220
security, 268–277
    authentication, 272
    encryption, 272–277
    hooks, 268
    host-based, 268, *see also* **xhost**
    Magic Cookie authorization, 270
    per window, 268
    remote execution, 240
    restricting access, 268
    snoopers, 268, 270, 272
security threat
    remote execution, 240
    replaying messages, 272, 276
    sending events between clients, 218
Select button, 224
selecting for events, **105**
selection, *see also* Selections Service
    advantages, 224
    clipboard application, 224
    cut buffers superseded by, 214
    cut buffers, differences, 220
    data transfer mechanism, 222
    delayed data conversion, 220
    dynamic operation of, 222
    example of, 220
    format of, 224
    input methods, use for, 224
    large data-transfer using, 224
    no data stored in, 220
    ownership, **220**
    requesting list of formats, 224
    unrestricted access, 224
selection box, Motif, 170
selection name
    CLIPBOARD, 220, 224

    PRIMARY, 220, 222
    SECONDARY, 220
    user-defined, 224
Selections Service, 126, 178, 214, 219–226, 230,
        339
    sending events between clients, 220
send-this-message action, 294
sending events between clients, 218
    ClientMessage events, 218
    talk program, 218
    by window manager, 218
    for testing, 218
    security threat, 218
    Selections Service, 220
sending requests asynchronously, **102**
senior management, 45
separation of client and server, 4
serial line Internet Protocol, 30, 116
serial lines, 6, 62
server, **4**, 54–97
    architecture of, 58
    colour capabilities, 78
    components of, 58
    controls the display, 4
    customization, 264
    design principles, 54
    device drivers in, 4, 70
    device independence, 16
    extras in, 58
    hardware dependence isolated in, 70
    implementation of, 58–63
    input processing in, 54
    inter-client communication, implements, 210
    keyboard mapping, 264
    likened to a terminal, 126
    multi-threaded, 338
    multiple clients supported by, 4
    many, used by one client, 5, 178
    optimization, 300
    output processing, 64–69
    output processing in, 54
    PCs, for, 34, 40, 42, 44, 58, 60, 62, 63,
        256, 258, 262, 300, 310
    performance, 300–303
    personal computers, for, 58
    plug-in-card, 58
    portability, 70
    role of, 54–57
    screens, multiple, 64
    separation of client and, 4
    settings in startup script, 264
    translating requests into hardware commands,
        70
    type, *see* display type
    user interface, does not contain, 56

window management, doesn't perform, 56
Xcms, not affected by, 80
server extension, 94–97
    Input, 184
    MIT-SHM, 94, 300
    MIT-SUNDRY-NONSTANDARD, 264
    PEX, 68, 95, 338–340
    Phigs, *see* PEX
    SHAPE, 94, 96, 123
    VEX, 95
    X3D-PEX, 95
    XTEST, 313
    XTrap, 112
    architecture, 16, 96
    Display PostScript as example of, 95
    listing supported, 96
    major opcode, **96**
    minor opcode, **96**
    name of, 96
    scope of, 94
Server Natural Format, *see* SNF
server, input method, 110, 140
session, **260**
    management, 260, 279, *see also* xdm
    replaying, 314
session key, Kerberos, **276**
session manager, **261**
    WM_COMMAND ClientMessage, 261
    WM_PROTOCOLS property, 261
    WM_SAVE_YOURSELF ClientMessage, 261
    role of, 261
set action, 292, 294
SET HOST VMS command, 18, 244
set pushbutton when pressed, 182, 292
setenv used for remote execution, 240
seven-layer reference model, ISO, 128
SHAPE server extension, 94, 96, 123
shared libraries, 122, 235
    performance, 310
    programming, 318
    version skew with, **319**
shared memory performance, 302
shell scripts, 327
Shift key, 109, 205
    interpretation, 108
Shift modifier key, 105–108, 264
short-cut keys, *see* accelerators
SHOW DEF VMS command, 242
showrgb X program, 78
simulation, 41
sixteen-bit, *see* 16-bit
SLIP, 30, 116
SNF font format, **72**, 266
snoopers, 270, 272
    network, 268, 272

software colormap, 86
software developers, benefits for, 48
Solbourne, 190
SONET, 305
Space key, 182
SPARCstation, vii
special purpose toolkit, 190
speeding up a client, 126
Speedo scalable font, 72
spreadsheet, 28, 45, 138, 210, 220, 222, 228
SQL database client compared with **X**, 18
standard graphical user interface, 10
standard look and feel, 156
standards
    X Consortium, 340
    ANSI, 340
    European Commission, 340
    FIPS, 340
    IEEE, 340
    NIST, 340
standards, conformance to, 122
starting a different window manager, 198
starting the system, 256–263
    rsh, 256
    telnet, 256
    xdm, 258–263
    xinit, 256
    from AUTOEXEC.BAT, 256
    initial client, 258–260
    script file, 256–260
    X-terminal, 256
StaticColor, 84
StaticGray, 84
stdio, 136, 158
storage required for font, 74
stream network connection, 116
STRING property type, 216
string resource value, 290
sub-name in resource specifications, 286–288
sub-windows, **64**
subclass, **176**
subclassing, widget, **168**, 176
subwindows in menu, 64
Sun Microsystems, vii, viii, 10, 12, 19, 26, 33,
        156, 158, 186, 268, 300, 332
Sun workstations compared with **X**, 19
SunOS, vii
SunView, 19, 34, 38, 186, 250, 332
    compared with **X**, 19
    toolkit for porting, 190
superclass, **176**
supercomputers, 26
support staff, benefits for, 48
swapping, 36
Synchronous Optical Network, 305

synchronous request transmission, 103
system, 279
system administration, 256–279
    fonts, 266
    operating system, 36
    security, 268–277
    starting the system, 256–263
    summary, 278
    workstation, complexity of, 36
    X-terminal, 36, 62
system manager, benefits for, 48
system modal dialog, **323**
System V UNIX, 240

talk program, 218
task management with **Virtual Screen**, 114
Tcl **X** program, 327
TCP/IP, 6, 18, 19, 34, 38, 116, 117, 235, 240,
    250, 330, 343
    for Microsoft Windows, 19
technical barriers to integration, 42
technical support, benefits for, 48
technicolor colour flashing, 86
techniques, programming, 322–325
TekHVC, 80
Tektronix 4014, 242
    terminal emulator, 330
Teletype terminal, 32
televisions, complex controls hidden on, 23
telnet, 18, 19, 235, 240, 244, 256, 268, 330
    compared with **X**, 18
    local, on X-terminals, 62
    starting the system, 256
    used for remote execution, 240
    using, with Microsoft Windows, 19
terminal, *see also* VT100, *see also* VT102, *see*
        also character-based
    X, *see* X-terminal
    Teletype, 32
    Wyse, 32
terminal emulator, 27, 32, **242**–248
    advantages of, 242
    ASCII character handling, 246
    character underlining, 248
    cursor addressing, 248
    cut-and-paste, 242
    escape sequence, 248
    for character-based applications, 242
    front-end with, 328
    how it works, 246, 330
    inverse video, 248
    keyboard handling, 246
    local, on X-terminals, 62
    multiple sessions, 242
    on different machine, 244
    output handling, 248

programmable, 328–330
pseudo-terminal used by, 246
remote execution, 244
Tektronix 4014, 330
VT100, 330
Test Environment Toolkit, 313
test suite, MIT, 313
testing
    by sending events between clients, 218
    MIT test suite, 313
text, *see also* font
    horizontal, 72
    left-to-right, 72
    rotated, 72
text drawing
    GC used in, 76
text editor, 286
text input, internationalized, 138, 140
text printing, internationalized, 138, 142
tftpd UNIX program, 278
TGS, *see* Ticket Granting Service
third-party authentication, 272
third-party vendor, 252
    implementation of server, 58
three dimensional, *see* 3-D
three-button mouse emulation, 70
three-headed dog, 272
ticket, **273**
Ticket Granting Service, Kerberos, **276**, 277
TIFF format pictures, 90
tiling window manager, **194**
tiling, pixmap used for, **90**
time-sharing, 37
timer callback, 184
Times Bold font name, 266
timestamps in Kerberos, 276
title-bar, 200, 206
    added by window manager, **200**
token ring, 6, 116, 118
toolkit, 10, **136**, 150–161, 164–191
    Expose event handled by, 160, 180
    Interviews, 190
    MooLIT, 187, 202
    OI, 190, 191, 202
    Xlib, doesn't duplicate, 166
    Xt+ and OLIT, 164
    Xview, 186, 190
    Xview, implementation, 186
    development systems, 327
    event handling, 180–185
    functions provided by, 136, 160
    GUI-independent, 190
    implements look and feel, 158
    input handling, 160
    Microsoft Windows, for porting, 190

Motif, implementation, 186
Neuron Data, 190
non Intrinsics-based, 186, 190
object-oriented, 10
OLIT, 164, 186
OLIT and Xt+, 164
OLIT, implementation, 186
Open Interface, 190
programming, versus Xlib, 166
reasons for, 128, 136
resolution independence in, 160
role of, 136, 158
sample program, 136
special purpose, 190
SunView, for porting, 190
user interface, **158**
user interface implemented by, 10
widget defined by, 164
XVT, 190
toolkit Intrinsics, 164–191
toolkit programming, 166, 179
versus Xlib, 179
toolkits, incompatibility between, 122
tools for resources handling, 296
top-level window, **64**
TPU VMS command, 32, 242
translation table, 109, **180**, **292**–295, 298
actions and, 294
callbacks and, 294
translations, *see* translation table
tree, *see also* hierarchy
class, 176
resource names, 286
widget, 168, 286, 296
widget class, 296
window, **64**, 174, 205
True, 185
TrueColor, 84
twm window manager, 194, 218, 260
two dimensional, *see* 2-D
two-button mouse, 70
Type 1 font, PostScript, 73
TYPE VMS command, 228, 242
type, console, *see* display type
TYPE/PAGE VMS command, 228

.uid file, 188
UIL, **188**, 189, 327
compiler, 188
.uil file, 188
UIMSs, vii, 145, 147, **326**, 327
unique features of X, 16
UNIX, 23, 26, 32, 39, 43, 49, 58, 152, 154,
184, 186, 190, 234, 240, 242, 250,
252, 272, 320, 330, 332, 343
Berkeley, *see* BSD UNIX

BSD, 240
System V, 240
UNIX International, 313
UNIX System Laboratories, 12, 187, 327, 340
unmapping a window, **64**
unset action, 292, 294
upgradability, benefits of, 46
upgrading of X-terminal, 36
uppercase, keysym interpreted as, 108
upward compatibility, 143
Usenet, 343
user groups, 252, 342
user interface, *see also* look and feel
application interface, **14**, 149-162
client contains, 8, 56
implemented by toolkit, 10
implemented by Xlib, 10
management interface, **14**, 200–203
not in server, 8, 56
of other window systems, 8
standard graphical, 10
two component parts, 14
uniform across different platforms, 11, 38,
158
User Interface Language, *see* UIL
User interface management systems, *see* UIMSs
user interface programming, 334
user interface toolkit, **158**
user productivity, 44
user's agent, window manager is, 194
user-contributed software, *see* **contrib**
user-defined
action procedures, 294
cursor, 92
property types, 216
selection name, 224
widget, 168, 176
user-name, 274, 276
users
benefits for, 48
defined, 42
management, benefits for, 48
professional, benefits for, 48
requirements, 46
using remote execution, 238–240
using X, 234–252
utility functions, Intrinsics, toolkit, 178
UUCP, 343

valueChanged callback, 180
values
Boolean, 290
resource, *see* resource value
Resource Database, in, 284
variable width font, 72
VAX, 11, 19, 28, 33, 39, 43, 49, 117, 158

VAX VMS, *see* VMS
VCRs, *see* video cassette recorders
vendor exhibitions, 342
vendor, third-party, 252
version number, **X**, **120**
version skew with shared libraries, **319**
VEX server extension, 95
VGA, 70, 86
vi UNIX program, 32, 242
video cassette recorders, 23
viewer, resource, 296
viewres **X** program, 296
virtual
    desktop, **59**, 196
    desktop, in window manager, 196
    memory, 301
    root window, **59**, 64
    screen, **58**, **64**
virtual reality, 326
Virtual Screen X program, 114, 115, 125
    multimedia with, 114
    task management with, 114
visibility, *see* window, mapping, *see* window,
    clipping, *see* window, unmapping
visual, **84**
visual appearance of window manager, 200–203
visual class, **84**
VMS, 11, 18, 19, 26, 28, 32, 38, 42, 49, 117,
    190, 234, 333
Volkswagen, 150
VT100, 16
VT100 terminal emulator, 330
vt100 widget, 286
VT102, 242, 248
VT220, 16, 32, 54, 301

W window system, 102
WAN, *see* wide area network
Whetstones, 312
wide area network, 27, 30
wide character encoding, 141
widget, **164**, 168–175
    buttons, 286
    manualPage, 292
    paned, 286
    save, 287
    search, 289
    vt100, 286
    xedit, 286
    action procedures defined, 294
    architecture of, 168
    as objects, **168**
    callback defined by, 180
    callback example, 182
    child, **168**
    child, managed by composite, 170

class name, 288, 289
compared with gadget, 174
composite, 170
container, *see* composite widget
defined by toolkit, 164
gadget replacement for, 174
hierarchy, 168
hierarchy, UIL, 188
keyboard handling, 170
layout manager, 170
look and feel, 164
object-oriented programming, 176
primitive, 172
primitive, illustrated, 172
radio buttons, 170
resizing, 170
resources, 284
reusability of, 176
sets, *see* widget sets
subclassing, 168, 176
tree, 168, 286, 296
user-defined, 168, 176
window tree, 174
widget class, 288, 289
    Command, 288
    Composite, 176, 177
    Core, 177
    Primitive, 177
    RectObj, 177
    WindowObj, 177
    XmPrimitive, 177
    tree, 296
widget class name, *see* widget class
widget sets
    combining, 169
    role of, 169
widget type
    composite, **168**
    primitive, **168**
wildcards in
    font name, 72, 266
    resource specifications, **288**
window
    access permissions, 268
    application, **64**
    aspect ratio requested, 206
    child, **64**
    clipping, **66**
    configuration, by window manager, 204
    groups, 196, 226
    groups, ICCCM, 226
    hierarchy, **64**
    management, client performs, 56
    management, server doesn't perform, 56
    mapping, **64**

maximum size requested, 206
minimum size requested, 206
overlapping, 24
protection, *see* window security
redraw, client performs, 56
reparenting by window manager, **205**
root, virtual, **59**
security, 268
top-level, **64**
tree, **64**, 174, 205
tree, gadget menu, 174
tree, widget menu, 174
unmapping, **64**
virtual root, **59**
zooming, client performs, 56
window manager, **14**, **194**–207, *see also* management interface
    gwm, 196
    mwm, 202, 238, 260
    olwm, 238
    twm, 194, 218, 260
    applications independent of, 202
    changing, in mid-session, 14
    client fighting with, 206
    client, is a, 198
    colormap handling, 194
    colormap slots used, 86
    communication with client, 206
    configuration redirection by, 204
    decorations added by, **200**
    focus control, 194
    functions provided by, 194–196
    grouping windows, 196
    how it works, 204–207
    ICCCM rules, 226
    icons, implements, 194
    interface, programming, 324
    local, on X-terminals, 62
    look and feel, 200–203
    look and feel, source of, 202
    not part of the server, 14, 198, 204
    not essential, 198
    pop-up menus, 196
    programmable, 196
    properties, 206
    push pin added by, **200**
    remote execution, 198
    reparenting window by, **205**
    requirements, 194
    role of, 194–196
    sending events to client, 218
    starting a different, 198
    tiling, **194**
    title-bar added by, **200**
    user's agent, is, 194
    using, 198
    virutal desktop, 196
    visual appearance of, 200–203
    window configuration, 204
window manager function
    Exit, 198
    Quit, 198
window object, 177
WINDOW property type, 216
window systems, benefits of, 22
windowing Korn shell, 327
WindowObj widget class, 177
windows as building blocks, 64
Wingz commercial **X** application, 146
WINTERP **X** program, 327
WM_CLASS property, 212, 288
WM_COMMAND property, 207, 261
WM_DELETE_WINDOW ClientMessage, 206, 207
WM_HINTS property, 226
WM_HINTS property type, 216
WM_ICON_NAME property, 226
WM_INFORMATION property, 226
WM_NAME property, 212
WM_PROTOCOLS property, 206, 207, 218, 226
    session manager, 261
WM_SAVE_YOURSELF ClientMessage, 207, 226, 261
    session manager, 261
WM_SIZE_HINTS property type, 216
word processing, 42, 46, 114, 138, 144, 216, 228, 323
WordPerfect commercial **X** application, 146
work procedure, **185**, 322
    callback, 184
    registration of, **185**
workgroup computing, integration, 30, 40
workproc, *see* work procedure
workstation
    disadvantages of, 36
    diskless, network loading, 36
    compared with X-terminal, 36
Wyse terminal, 32

X
    benefits of, 22–49
    centralizing effect of, 40
    client/server architecture of, 4
    compared with other window systems, 18
    coordinate system, 68
    financial benefits of, 44–47
    installing, 252
    licence costs, and, 42
    pixel oriented, 160
    predecessor, W, 102
    real-time, requirements for, 344

release number, **121**
version number, **120**
X Colour Management System, *see* Xcms
X Consortium, v, 58, 62, 63, 91, 141, 164, 252, 270, 304, 307, 313, 322, 338–340, 342, 343
  activities, 338
X Display Manager Protocol, *see* XDMCP
X Imaging Extension, 91
X Logical Font Description, *see* XLFD**X** Protocol, 58, 114, **120**, 121, 123, 124, 143, 256, 263, 268, 313, 338, 340
X server, *see* server
X station, **34**
X Technical Conference, 342
X Toolkit, 163–192, 193, 281–298, 308, 309, 320, 322, 324, 332, 340
  performance, 309
  resource handling, 281–298
  round-trips minmized, 309
X, design principles of, 8, 55, 143, 203, *see also* mechanism as opposed to policy
X-coordinate, 248
X-terminal, 27, 34, 36, 37, 40, 42, 49, 55, 58–63, 73–75, 99, 118, 121, 122, 127, 198, 235, 238, 256, 258, 262, 278, 279, 281, 301, 304, 310, 343
  benefits of, 36
  character-based terminal, differences, 60
  character-based terminal, similarities, 60
  compared with workstation, 36
  components, 36
  CPU power required for, 36
  dynamic memory requirement of, 60
  extra facilities, 62
  implementation of, 60
  local clients on, 62
  local terminal emulator on, 62
  local window manager on, 62
  local **telnet** on, 62
  NFS use, 60
  performance, 62
  starting the system, 256
  system administration, 62
  upgrading of, 36
  xdm controlling, 260
X.25, 6, 116, 117, 304
X/Open, 313
X11, v, 120, *see also* **X**
x11perf **X** program, 312, 313
x11perfcomp **X** program, 313
X12 unlikely, 120
X3D-PEX server extension, 95
X3H3, 340
XAPPLRESDIR environment variable, 285

xauth **X** program, 270
.Xauthority file, 270
xbench **X** program, 312
xbiff **X** program, 146
xcalc **X** program, 146, 152
xcalendar **X** program, 146
XChangeProperty() Xlib function, 212
xclipboard **X** program, 224
XClock application class-name, 288
xclock **X** program, 107, 146, 288, 314
Xcms, **80**–82, 86, 120
  client only affected, 80
  device calibration for, 82
  device characterization for, 82
  properties used by, 82
  RGB, mapping to, 80
xcmsdb **X** program, 82
xconsole **X** program, 184
xcrtca **X** program, 82
XDCCC_LINEAR_RGB_CORRECTION property, 82
XDCCC_LINEAR_RGB_MATRICES property, 82
XDesigner, vii
xdm **X** program, 62, 120, 147, 256, 258, 260, 262, 263, 265, 270, 279–281, *see also* XDMCP
  advantages of, 258
  for X-terminals, 260
  login window, 258
  starting the system, 258–263
XDMCP, 62, 120, 121, 123, 147, 258, **262**, 263, 279, 280, 340, *see also* xdm
  how it works, 262
  chooser, 263
xdpyinfo **X** program, 97
XDrawLine() Xlib function, 248
XDrawString() Xlib function, 76, 133, 248
XDrawText() Xlib function, 76
Xedit application class-name, 288
xedit widget, 286
xedit **X** program, 146, 236, 240, 286, 288, 289
Xerox, 12, 156
xeyes **X** program, 88
xfd **X** program, 92, 147
XFILESEARCHPATH environment variable, 285
XFontsel application class-name, 288
xfontsel **X** program, 224, 288
XGetProperty() Xlib function, 212
xghost **X** program, 314
XGL, 300
xhost **X** program, 268, 279
Xi18n, 139, *see also* internationalization
xinit **X** program, 256, 258
xkill **X** program, 147

XLFD, **72**, 76, 123, 142, 266, 267, 340
Xlib, **10**, 81, 88, 96, 100, 102, 108, **120**, 126,
 128, 132–134, 136, 137, 140–142, 145,
 148, 149, 158, 160, 164, 166, 179,
 180, 190, 193, 204, 212, 270, 282–
 287, 290, 298, 300, 309, 318, 320,
 324, 325, 338–340
  functions provided by, 132–134
  multi-threaded, 338
  operating system analogy, 132, 158, 166
  performance features, 132
  programming, 166, 179
  programming, versus toolkit, 166
  requests constructed by, 100
  resources, using, 284
  sample program, 134
  toolkit doesn't duplicate, 166
  user interface implemented by, 10
Xlib function
  XChangeProperty(), 212
  XDrawLine(), 248
  XDrawString(), 76, 133, 248
  XDrawText(), 76
  XGetProperty(), 212
  XOpenDisplay(), 133, 270
xloadimage **X** program, 91, 146
xlsfonts **X** program, 147
xmag **X** program, 185
xman **X** program, 292
xmh **X** program, 146
xmodmap **X** program, 109, 147, 264, 265
XmPrimitive widget class, 177
XOpenDisplay() Xlib function, 133, 270
xpert, viii, 343
xpr **X** program, 147
xprop **X** program, 212, 214, 288
xrdb
  properties used by, 214
xrdb **X** program, 214, 285
xrecorder **X** program, 314
.Xresources file, 260
−xrm flag, 291
xscope **X** program, 313, 314
.xsession file, 260
xset **X** program, 147, 264, 265
xsetroot **X** program, 265
Xstones, **312**
xstuff, 343
Xt, 159, 164, 166, 192, 193
Xt+, 164, 186, 191
  OLIT, **Xview**, same look and feel, 164
Xtent **X** program, 327
xterm
  closing down the system, 260
xterm **X** program, 214, 218, 234, 236, 238, 240,

 242, 248, 256, 258, 260, 283, 284,
 286, 291, 294
XTEST server extension, 313
XTrap server extension, 112
XUSERFILESEARCHPATH environment variable, 285
Xview toolkit, 186, 190, 191, 332
  not Intrinsics-based, 186
  OPEN LOOK look and feel, 186
XVT toolkit, 190
xwd **X** program, 147
xwud **X** program, 147, 305

Y-coordinate, 248

zooming, client performs, 56